ECONOMICS OF URBAN PROBLEMS

ECONOMICS OF URBAN PROBLEMS
An Introduction

SECOND EDITION

Arthur F. Schreiber

Georgia State University, Atlanta

Paul K. Gatons

United States Department of Housing
and Urban Development, Washington, D.C.

Richard B. Clemmer

United States Department of Housing
and Urban Development, Washington, D.C.

HOUGHTON MIFFLIN COMPANY   BOSTON
Atlanta   Dallas   Geneva, Illinois
Hopewell, New Jersey   Palo Alto   London

Printed in the U.S.A.
Library of Congress Catalog Card Number: 75-31004
ISBN: 0-395-20619-7

CONTENTS

Preface   xiii

1 / Introduction   **1**

2 / Land Use: The Location of Jobs   **7**
and People in Urban Areas

Definition of an Urban Area   *8*

Changing Technology and the Decentralization of
Jobs and People   *11*

The Rise and Decline of the Core-Dominated City:
The Impact of Changing Transportation
Technology   The Future of the Central Business
District   Decentralization Trends in Urban Areas

Current Land-Use Patterns in Urban Areas   *19*

An Example of Present Land-Use Patterns in Urban
Areas   Qualifications of the Land-Use Example

Urban Spatial Form and Urban Problems   *28*

3 / Economic Efficiency   **31**

The Efficient Allocation of Resources   *32*

The Efficiency Criterion   Costs and Benefits over
Time   Incorrect Resource Allocation Criteria

The Private Market System and Efficient Resource
Allocation   *45*

Market Prices and Maximization of Net Private
Benefits   Marginal Private Benefits and Costs:
Relationship to Market Demand and Supply

4 / Analysis of Urban Problems: 56
Efficiency and Equity

Private Market Failure: Inefficient Allocation of Resources   *57*

The Problem of Externalities   The Problem of Monopoly Power   The Problem of Imperfect Information

Income Distribution and the Efficient Allocation of Resources   *68*

An Example   Cash Versus In-Kind Income Redistribution

Equity in Government Programs   *72*
Horizontal and Vertical Equity   The Benefit Principle   The Ability-to-Pay Principle

Equity Versus Efficiency: A Concluding Note   *78*

Benefit-Cost Analysis   *78*

The Basic Procedure   Definition and Calculation of Present Value   An Example   Problems in Benefit-Cost Analysis

5 / Poverty: The Problem   89
and the Long-Run Approach

Money Income: A Measure of Poverty   *90*

Money Income as a Measure of Standard of Living   Determination of the Poverty Cutoff   Official Poverty Statistics

Scope of United States Poverty   *95*

Causes of Poverty   *99*

Inadequate Human Capital   Discrimination Other Causes of Poverty

Long-Run Approaches to Reduce Poverty   *101*

Increasing the Stock of Human Capital   Family Planning and Child Care   Combating Discrimination

6 / Poverty: The Short-Run Approach 113

Cash Versus In-Kind Transfers *114*

The Negative Income Tax: Basic Features *116*

The Hours-Wages Form of Negative Income Tax *120*

Current Short-Run Poverty Programs *122*

Welfare Programs   Social Security   In-Kind
Redistribution Programs

Maintaining a Tight Labor Market *132*

7 / Urban Housing Problems 136

Measuring Housing Consumption *137*

The U.S. Census Measure of Housing
Consumption   A Conceptual Measure of Housing
Consumption

The Housing Problem: Equity Versus Efficiency *141*

The Operation of the Private Housing
Market   Inadequate Housing Consumption: Equity
Versus Efficiency

Barriers to Efficient Allocation of Resources in the
Housing Market and Some Potential Solutions *144*

Externalities and Housing Maintenance and
Improvement   Housing Finance Costs   Property
Taxes   Zoning   Building Codes and Housing
Construction Practices   Housing Codes   Racial
Discrimination   Eliminating Market Failure and
Reducing Housing Costs: Concluding Note

8 / Analysis of Housing Programs 167

The Basic United States Housing Policy *168*

The Turnover Process: Construction Standards and
Subsidies   Income Tax Subsidies to
Homeowners   The Turnover Process and Its
Relationship to Housing Segregation and Poverty in
Urban Areas   Income Taxation of Rental Property
and Slums

Other Housing Programs *177*

Urban Renewal   Public Housing and Other
Low-Income Housing Subsidy Programs   The
Housing and Community Development Act of
1974   An Alternative to Existing Low-Income
Housing Subsidies: Housing Vouchers
A Concluding Note

9 / Urban Transportation: 192
The Short Run

An Overview of Transportation in Urban Areas *193*

Public Transit   Auto Transportation

The Short-Run Problem: Inefficient Use of Existing Transportation Facilities *196*

The Congestion Problem   The Efficient Level of
Congestion

Achieving Short-Run Efficiency: Rationing Use of Existing Transportation Facilities *203*

Rationing by Prices   Other Forms of Rationing
Potential Long-Run Effects of Short-Run Policy
Efficient Pricing of Other Modes of Transportation

10 / Urban Transportation: 217
The Long Run

Estimating the Benefits of Transportation Investments *218*

The Cost of Alternative Transportation Modes *221*

Rail Transit   Highways for the Use of Autos   Rapid
Bus Systems   Summary of Comparative Costs

Transportation Subsidies *230*

Efficiency Aspects   Equity: Distribution of Costs and
Benefits from Transportation Investments

The Low-Income Transportation Problem *236*

A Proposal for Public Transit in Urban Areas *239*

11 / The Urban Pollution Problem
243

Pollution: Definition and the Problem 244

Definition of Pollution   The Efficient Level of
Pollution

Pollution: Types, Sources, Trends, and Costs 247

Determinants of the Level of Pollution   Air
Pollution: Types and Effects   Air Pollution: Sources
and Levels   Water Pollutants   Other Pollutants

Pollution as an Urban Problem 255

Water Pollution   Air Pollution   Other Forms of
Pollution

Achieving Efficient Use of the Environment 258

The Efficient Level of Environmental Quality   Basic
Alternatives for Reducing Pollution Levels
Achieving a Given Level of Environmental Quality at
Lowest Cost

12 / Urban Pollution: Evaluation
of Alternative Policies
265

Rationing the Use of the Environment 266

Establishing the Standards   The Least-Cost Form of
Rationing: A Numerical Example   Achieving the
Least-Cost Form of Rationing: Effluent Fees

Equity Aspects of Improved Environmental
Quality 277

Effects on Business and Labor   Effects on Households in Different Income Groups

An Evaluation of Major Existing Pollution Programs
and Alternatives 280

Water Pollution   Air Pollution   Automobile
Pollution Policy

Some Long-Run Implications of Rationing the Use
of the Environment 290

Standards of Living and Population   Urbanization
and Urban Form

13 / Crime   294

Crime as an Economic Problem *295*

Amount and Types of Crime   The Efficient Amount
of Crime: Social Benefits and Costs

Crime as an Urban Problem *302*

**Costs and Benefits of Crime from the Criminal's
Viewpoint** *303*

Economic Approaches to Crime Prevention *307*

Victims   The Criminal Justice System   Economic
Conditions

"Victimless Crimes" and Organized Crime *317*

Heroin Addiction and Drug-Related Crimes *320*

**Equity Aspects of Crime and Crime
Prevention** *323*

The Probability of Being a Victim   Types of Crime
and Punishment by Income Group

14 / The Urban Public Sector: Part One   329

**The Role of the Urban Public Sector in Achieving
Equity and Efficiency Objectives** *330*

Income Redistribution: A Role That Should Not Be
Performed by Urban Government   Resource
Allocation: A Role for the Urban Public Sector

**Criteria for Efficient Production of Local Public
Outputs** *335*

Registering and Satisfying Effective Demands of
Consumer-Voters   Criteria for Efficient Production
of Local Public Outputs

15 / The Urban Public Sector: Part Two   355

**Provision of Private-Benefit Outputs: The Role of
User Charges** *356*

An Example: The City Zoo   Marginal Cost Pricing:
A Dilemma

Provision of Mixed-Benefit Outputs: Elementary and Secondary Education *359*

Mixed-Benefit Outputs and Benefit Financing
Evaluation of Present Methods of Providing
Education   Possible Methods of Improving the
Provision of Education   Provision of Local Public
Outputs: Conclusion

Local Tax Revenue Sources *368*

The Property Tax   Alternatives to the Property Tax

The "Plight of the Central City": Equity Versus Efficiency *379*

16 / Benefits and Costs of Urbanization   381

The Benefits of Urban Economic Growth *382*

Demand Economies   Supply Economies
Interrelation of Demand and Supply Economies

Costs of Urbanization *389*

The Future of the Central City *390*

Future Public Policies and the Urban Area *393*

Democracy and the Private Market System *394*

Art Credits   397

Index   398

PREFACE

This is a book about the economics of important problems facing urban areas, whether or not these are purely urban problems or are problems that fit into a preconceived definition of urban economics. While this book touches on all the subject areas in the field of urban economics, the emphasis is on the economics of urban problems rather than on the location theory and urban growth content of this field. We believe that this emphasis provides the student who is not specializing in urban economics with the material most important and most relevant to gaining an economic perspective on the problems besetting urban areas.

This text is intended for use in an introductory course in urban problems at the undergraduate level and in graduate programs in urban affairs and public administration. While we have endeavored to make it accessible to the student with no previous courses in economics, the student with such courses, particularly the "micro" part of the principles of economics sequence, will find the material easier to understand. The concepts developed early in the book are fundamental, and are applied throughout the remainder of the book. Our goal has been to minimize discussion of theories that do not find application later in the book. Also, we have tried to achieve a consistent level of analytical sophistication throughout the book. Too many textbooks intersperse chapters that are needlessly difficult with chapters that are needlessly unanalytical. Throughout, we have attempted to relate real world considerations to proposed policies by pointing out the difficulties inherent in their implementation.

The first chapter discusses the subject matter of urban economics and the emphasis of this book, as well as provides an overview of the contents of the text. Chapters 2, 3, and 4 serve as the background for the discussion of specific urban problems found in the remainder of the text. Of particular importance is the distinction between the concepts of equity and efficiency, both for determining the causes of urban problems and evaluating potential solutions to these problems. The reader is encouraged to devote considerable time to understanding the theoretical framework of Chapters 3 and 4, since this will pay large dividends in later chapters. Chapters 5 through 15 deal with specific urban problems—poverty, housing, transportation, pollution, crime, and urban public finance—as well as their interrelationships. The last chapter of the book deals with the benefits and costs of urban growth. This topic is placed last because we believe the reader is then in a better position to gain a perspective on the advantages and disadvantages of urbanization. Review and discussion questions are included at the end of chapters.

The revised edition differs from the first edition in several ways. First, the length has been more than doubled, although the basic subject matter is the same. This results from more analysis of existing programs and the presentation of more background data. Also, some topics only briefly treated in the first edition deserved greater discussion. Further, almost the entire text has been rewritten and the exposition clarified at several points. The result is that the second edition is more of a self-contained text that does not require extensive supplementation with outside reading materials.

David Black of Duke University, E. J. Ford, Jr., of the University of South Florida, and George R. Meadows of the University of Wisconsin-Milwaukee reviewed the manuscript and made many valuable suggestions. Our appreciation is extended to users of the previous edition and to the many students we have taught and learned from over the years. They has provided valuable feedback regarding the strengths and weaknesses of the first edition; the improvements in this edition are largely attributable to them. Any errors remain the responsibility of the authors.

Arthur F. Schreiber
Paul K. Gatons
Richard B. Clemmer

ECONOMICS OF URBAN PROBLEMS

1/ Introduction

One of the most striking trends of modern economies during the past century has been the increasing concentration of people and economic activities on the landscape, usually referred to as the process of urbanization. Some 70 percent of the United States population now lives on about 2 percent of the total land area—the urban areas. In contrast, a century ago the United States was predominantly rural. Sometime between 1910 and 1920, urban population passed rural in total numbers and this trend continues.

While the population trend has been toward centralization (concentration of population in urban areas), most of the population growth in major urban areas in recent years has been in the suburbs—a trend toward decentralization within these urban areas. Both of these trends in the urbanization process have proceeded so rapidly that we have yet to make many major adjustments required by the process. Accordingly, many of the most pressing economic and social issues of the day, which affect the majority of the United States population, are related to living in urban areas.

There are advantages to be gained (increases in the standard of living) from concentrating economic activities in close proximity to each other, and the costs of moving goods and people around within urban areas are a major determinant of the land-use patterns in these areas. The present degree of urbanization and present land-use patterns are primarily the aggregate result of decisions made by producers and consumers in the private market. At the same time, this concentration of jobs and people in urban areas and their spatial arrangement within these areas have created many problems (such as traffic congestion and pollution), which exist primarily because markets are not very satisfactory in resolving them.

This book analyzes the economic problems stemming from urbanization and evaluates potential solutions to these problems. An understanding of the historical trends in the location of jobs and people and the underlying reasons for these trends (Chapter 2) is a necessary prerequisite to a discussion of urban problems, because many of the problems are caused by the spatial separation of jobs and people within urban areas. For example, it is difficult to discuss traffic congestion and potential solutions to that problem without an understanding of the spatial distribution of jobs and people within urban areas—the cause of the problem. No matter how large the urban area, if most people lived very close to their jobs, then urban transportation problems would be significantly reduced. However, for most people in urban areas the place of residence and place of employment are a considerable distance apart. Many people consider the only urban transportation problem worth discussing is traffic congestion associated with people commuting to jobs located in the central business district (CBD) of the urban area, and they presume that this will get much worse over time as the number of jobs in the CBD increases. But there may be forces at work that are more likely to decrease than to increase the number of jobs in the CBD during the rest of this century. The magnitude of the problem and potential solutions to it (should we spend billions on rail systems?) critically depend on these locational forces.

The market is the primary allocator of resources in our economy; yet, it may be incapable of resolving many of the problems resulting from urbanization. Two economic criteria underlie the analysis of all urban problems. The first criterion is efficiency, or optimal use of resources. Even in an affluent society, resources are always scarce relative to the wants of the members of that society. Given this scarcity, resources must be used in the most productive way if society wants to maximize the satisfaction it receives from the use of these resources. This is the basic efficiency concept, defined in a benefit/cost framework in Chapter 3 with a discussion of conditions under which the market can allocate resources so as to achieve efficiency. In many cases, the conditions necessary for the market to achieve efficiency do not exist (Chapter 4), and this situation is the source of many urban problems.

Society may consider some economic outcomes undesirable or "unfair." If these outcomes are not attributable to an inefficient use of society's scarce resources, then they are attributable to the distribution of income (purchasing power) among members of society. The term "equity" is used here to refer to the fairness of the distribution of income. Most urban problems arise because of either inefficiency or inequity. The treatment of urban problems in this book emphasizes the distinction between these two causes of urban problems, because it is critical to determine the cause of a problem in order to arrive at a rational solution. Many proposals for solving urban problems are couched in terms of equity when the real problem is a matter of resource misallocation (inefficiency).

After completing the development of a theoretical benefit/cost framework, Chapter 4 discusses the use of benefit/cost analysis as a tool in real-world analysis of resource allocation decisions. The authors' intent was to make the material in Chapters 3 and 4 comprehensible to students and general readers without a background in economics, but the reader with such a background will find his understanding broadened. The reader is encouraged to devote considerable time to understanding this economic framework, since its concepts are applied to various urban problems in all of the remaining chapters.

Poverty is not found only in urban areas; in fact, the proportion of the rural population in poverty is greater than the proportion in urban areas. However, poverty in urban areas seems to be interwoven with other economic problems that are primarily urban in nature—problems of housing, transportation, crime, and local government finance. A reduction in poverty in urban areas would have a large impact on such problems; therefore, the magnitude, causes, and potential solutions to poverty (Chapters 5 and 6) are discussed before other urban problems.

Defining "inadequate housing" is similar to defining poverty. Inadequate housing may be a symptom of poverty (low income) or may be due to inefficiencies in the housing market. Confusion over these two causes has led to many ill-conceived housing policies. Problems inherent in housing markets that lead to inefficiency must be analyzed in order to evaluate present and potential housing programs as solutions to the housing problem (Chapters 7 and 8).

Urban transportation and pollution problems and policies are grouped together in Chapters 9 through 12, because they have conceptual similarities that will become apparent to the reader as he covers this section of the book. It might be worth noting now that the similarities have nothing to do with the fact that transportation is a source of pollution (although this and other sources of pollution will be discussed). Some forms of pollution are primarily the result of urbanization; others may be lessened by urbanization. Peak-hour congestion is the urban transportation problem of concern to most people; however, the traditional solution of building more transportation facilities (expressways, rapid rail systems) is usually not the efficient solution to the congestion problem.

Crime has always existed in society whether it was urban or rural, but crime rates in urban areas are much higher than in rural areas and crime is a major concern to many urban residents. Economic reasons for higher urban crime rates and the economic motivation to engage in criminal activity differ significantly from the more traditional legal and moral approaches to crime. Reducing crime requires the use of society's scarce resources; therefore, the goal is to achieve the efficient level of crime and not to eliminate it (Chapter 13).

Because of the concentration of economic activity in urban areas, the provision of public services by local governments in urban areas is more complex and difficult than it is in a nonurban setting. For example, animal control (rounding up stray and rabid dogs, etc.) is a service that might not be provided at all by some local governments in rural areas, because the low population density and the small total population do not warrant it. However, in large urban areas animal control is essential because a large number of people are affected by failure to provide such a service. Chapter 14 develops economic criteria for the efficient use of resources in providing public services and analyzes alternative means of determining demands for, financing of, and production of public services. These criteria are applied in Chapter 15 to public services such as education and to

the property tax and alternative sources of local government revenues.

As mentioned earlier, the motivation for urbanization has been to
improve our standards of living. At the same time this concentration
of jobs and people has created many presently unresolved problems,
most of which are discussed in Chapters 1 to 15. Having gone through
the rest of the book, the reader should then be in a better position to
gain a perspective on the advantages and disadvantages of urbanization. Chapter 16 discusses some of the economic concepts that have
been developed to explain why people may be better off from high-
density living. It is left to the reader to weigh these benefits against the
costs of urbanization and to gain a perspective on the future course of
urbanization in the United States.

2 / Land Use: The Location of Jobs and People in Urban Areas

Such terms as "city" and "metropolis" are often used rather loosely. To avoid this, we shall define at the outset some of the terms used throughout this book. The location of economic activities within urban areas was relatively more concentrated in the past than it is today. Changes in transportation technology are used to explain why there was a concentration of economic activity in the core (center) of large urban areas in the past and why this concentration has been decreasing in this century and continues to do so today. Other factors are then introduced to explain the processes of decentralization of residential and employment locations in more recent times (suburbanization). The changing urban spatial form that results from these forces is related to many of the urban problems discussed in this book; an overview of these relationships concludes the chapter.

Definition of an Urban Area

At the broadest level, an urban area is an economic unit. In geographic terms, it could be defined as an area containing jobs and most of the people who work at those jobs. However, rural areas or farms might meet this definition, so that additional criteria are required for defining an urban area. The most common criterion and the one employed by the U.S. Bureau of the Census for compiling statistics on urbanization is the population size and density of a geographic area. The term "urban area" as used in this book refers to a central city and the surrounding commercial, industrial, and residential area that is economically interdependent with it. It is useful to compare this definition of an urban area with the following official census definitions:

A *city* is a political subdivision of a state, within a defined area, over which a municipal corporation has been established to provide local government functions and facilities.

A *central city* is a city of at least 50,000 population.

An *urban place* is any concentration of population (closely settled population), usually an incorporated village, town, or city of at least 2,500 population. The definition of an urban place is of little value in discussing urban areas; most of the United States population lives in urban places, and an urban area usually contains many urban places.

An *urbanized area* is the census definition which comes closest to coinciding with the definition of an urban area given above. It consists of a central city (or cities) and the surrounding closely settled territory. Thus, it is defined without regard to political boundaries (except that the entire central city is included) and represents both high population and high population density. In 1970, the census defined 248 urbanized areas in the United States, which contained approximately 118 million people, or about 58 percent of the population.

A *standard metropolitan statistical area (SMSA)* is a more inclusive geographic area than an urbanized area. An SMSA consists of a central city (or cities), the counties containing the central city (cities), and any contiguous counties that, according to certain criteria, are "socially and economically integrated with the central city." The criteria for including a contiguous county are the percentage of its labor force that is nonagricultural and the meeting of at least one of three other conditions relating to density of population, number of nonagricultural jobs, and number of nonagricultural employees living in the county. There is generally one urbanized area in each SMSA; however, since the SMSA is defined with respect to whole counties, it usually contains areas which are of relatively low population density and little interdependence with the central city. Since SMSAs are larger in area than urbanized areas, they have larger populations but lower densities of population. In 1970 about 139 million people, 69 percent of the United States total, lived in 243 SMSAs. These SMSAs contained about eleven times the land area of the 248 urbanized areas, and population densities were 360 per square mile in them versus 3,376 in urbanized areas.

In summary, the census definition of an urbanized area more closely fits the definition of urban area used in this book than does the SMSA definition; however, when one refers to employment, population, income, and other data on urbanization, the only data generally available are for SMSAs, not for urbanized areas. Thus, many of the data presented in this book are either for entire SMSAs or for the central city of the SMSA and the rest of the SMSA (the latter is sometimes referred to as "outside central city" or the "ring" of the SMSA). Other terms used in this book, in addition to urban area and central city, are "suburban" (the outlying portions of the urban area) and "central business district" (CBD). The central city is the same as in the census definitions of an urbanized area and SMSA—the principal city around which the urban area is formed. Suburban refers to that part of the urban area which is not in the central city. Central business district is not precisely defined by the census but here refers to the commercial center of a large city that is densely developed.

Figure 2-1 gives an indication of the relative geographic areas covered by these census definitions, using Atlanta as an example. In 1970, Atlanta was the twentieth largest SMSA in the United States; as seen in Figure 2-1, the SMSA was comprised of five counties totalling 1,727 square miles and a population of 1,390,164 (a population density of 805 per square mile). The urbanized area is less than one-fourth the area of the SMSA—435 square miles with a population of 1,172,778—with a population density of 2,696 per square mile. Atlan-

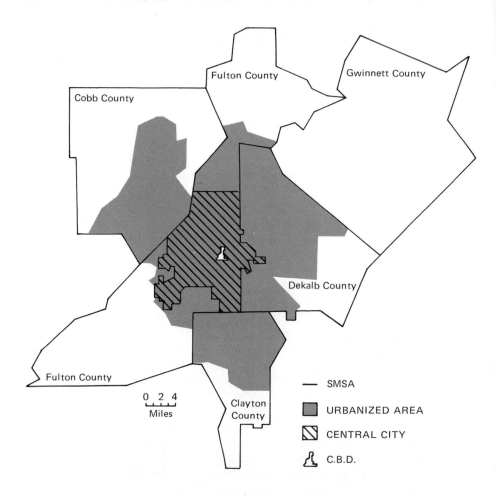

Figure 2-1: Atlanta Standard Metropolitan Statistical Area (SMSA), Urbanized Area, Central City, and Central Business District, 1970

SOURCE: Georgia State University, Department of Geography, Cartography Laboratory, 1973. Used with permission.

ta, the central city of the Atlanta SMSA, contained 131.5 square miles and a population of 497,024 (a population density of 3,783 per square mile).[1] The CBD is a very small portion of the total area of the central city, approximately 1 square mile.

Census data give an indication of the historical process of urbanization of the United States population. Using urban places as a definition of "urban," about 5 percent of the total population of 3.9 million was urban in 1790, the year of the first census. By 1970, over 70

[1]U.S. Bureau of the Census, *County and City Data Book, 1972,* Government Printing Office, Washington, 1973.

percent of the total population of 203.2 million was urban. In 1940, the first year the census data reflected the current definition of SMSA, 55 percent of the United States population lived in SMSAs. Thirty years later, this proportion had increased to 67 percent. A discussion of the basic economic reasons for urban growth is deferred until Chapter 16, which evaluates the advantages of concentrating jobs and people in urban areas relative to some of the disadvantages of urban growth. The remainder of this chapter discusses reasons for the changing location of jobs and people within urban areas—a consideration that is important in analyzing urban problems in the remainder of the book.

Changing Technology and the Decentralization of Jobs and People

Changes in transportation, production, and communications technology have resulted in changes in the relative attractiveness of central versus noncentral locations in urban areas for both business (jobs) and housing (people). To give a better understanding of the processes that influence the patterns of land use in urban areas today, it is useful to provide an explanation of why large core-dominated cities came into existence in the past.

The Rise and Decline of the Core-dominated City: The Impact of Changing Transportation Technology

Changing transportation technology was not the only force at work in the rise and decline of the core-dominated city;[2] it was probably the most important one and significant enough to provide a very useful explanation by itself. These technological changes are reflected in the cost relationships among three types of transportation activity: the movement of goods and raw materials *between* urban areas; the movement of goods and raw materials *within* urban areas; and the movement of people *within* urban areas (the journey-to-work trip between place of residence and place of employment).

In the latter part of the nineteenth century, most movement of goods and raw materials between urban areas took place by rail. Compared with the other existing alternatives, railroads were a relatively low-cost transportation mode. Manufacturing activities in urban areas (which then accounted for a much larger proportion of total business

---

[2]Much of the following discussion is based on analysis contained in Leon Moses and Harold Williamson, Jr., "The Location of Economic Activity in Cities," *American Economic Review* (May 1967), 211 - 221.

activity than in the present era of service-dominated business activity) required that the inputs used in production be brought to the manufacturing plants from outside the urban area and that most of the finished products be shipped to markets outside the urban area. In terms of loading and unloading trains going in and out of the city, lower costs could be achieved by having large freight terminals, perhaps only one in a city, rather than smaller terminals scattered throughout the city. For example, some freight customers might not need an entire car; significant cost savings would be realized if several smaller shipments headed for the same destination were loaded in the same car. Similar savings were realized with respect to assembling cars into a train. In other words, the more business concentrated at one freight terminal, the easier it was to assemble and match loads and cars into efficiently sized trains. Thus, the large central freight terminal became the focus for movement into and out of the urban area.

Given that intercity movement of freight revolved around the central freight terminal, the location of jobs relative to the freight terminal depended on which land-use pattern would result in the greatest profits. Goods and raw materials were moved between the freight terminal and manufacturers within the urban area by means of horse and wagon—a relatively expensive mode of transportation. To minimize these intracity transportation costs, manufacturers clustered around the central freight terminal. Residential areas then formed a dense ring outside this highly concentrated core of business activity. Before the use of the trolley in the middle of the nineteeth century, people had to live within walking distance of their place of work, so that high-density housing for low-income workers grew up around the factories. The advent of the trolley (at first horse-drawn but later electrified) greatly reduced the costs of intraurban movement of people and made it possible for residential areas to decentralize along trolley lines emanating from the core.

As illustrated by Figure 2-2, which shows the relationship of various costs to distance from the core, costs other than intracity transportation were lower as the distance from the core increased. The wage curve is horizontal (wages do not vary with distance) on the assumption that all employment was located at the core. While this was not completely true (e.g., employment at the neighborhood grocery), the concern here is with manufacturing employment, which depended on the movement of goods and raw materials between cities through the freight terminal located in the core. The horizontal wage curve means that no matter where an employee lived with respect to distance from the core, he would receive the same wage rate from being employed in manufacturing located at the core. However, the costs incurred by the employee for transportation to and from work increased as the distance of his residence from the core increased. These

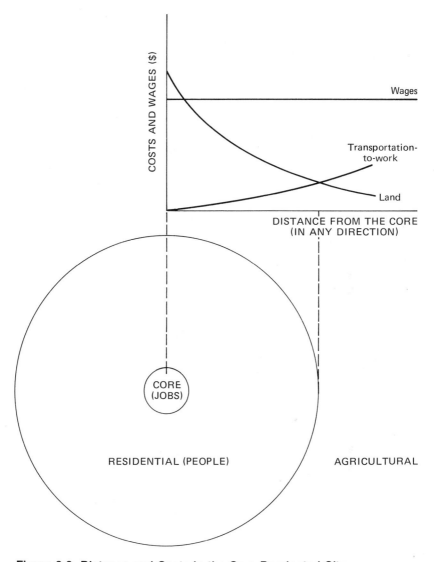

Figure 2-2: Distance and Costs in the Core-Dominated City

costs included not only trolley fare (which was likely to be a flat amount) but the value of time spent commuting. Thus, the transportation-to-work cost curve is upward-sloping as distance from the core increases, starting at zero at the core (there would be no commuting costs if a worker lived at his place of work).

If the wage was the same but transportation-to-work costs increased with distance from the core, there must have been a compensating savings in some other cost of residing further from the core; otherwise, the houses of workers would all have been closely clustered near the core. Of course, the offset is that the price of land (measured in price per square foot) decreased with distance from the core, for two basic reasons. First, manufacturing firms would pay more for land in or near the core because they saved on intracity horse-and-wagon transportation costs by being located closer to the central freight terminal. Second, workers would pay more for land for their housing closer to the core, because they incurred lower transportation-to-work costs. Therefore, the land-cost curve is downward-sloping as distance from the core increases. If land costs had not decreased to offset increased transportation costs at greater distances from the core, workers would have all tried to live very near the core in order to decrease their transportation costs. However, as this occurs, prices of land are bid up in locations near the core, and the pattern of land costs described above arises.

Given the cost relationships shown in Figure 2-2, if an employer located his plant away from the central freight terminal (outside the core), he would be able to hire workers for less than the wage rate shown in the figure, since they would be working closer to their homes and save commuting costs. Also, the employer would reduce the costs of land on which his plant was located, since land prices were cheaper away from the core. Despite these potential cost savings to the employer, the high costs of transporting goods and raw materials between the central freight terminal and his factory would still make it more profitable to locate near the terminal, in the core of the city. Thus, the barrier to decentralization of jobs in the latter part of the nineteenth century was the high cost of moving goods and raw materials within the urban area relative to the cost of moving people.

In the early part of the twentieth century, this barrier was broken by the introduction of the truck, which substantially reduced the relative cost of moving commodities within the urban area. It became economically feasible for employers to relocate their plants some distance from the central freight terminal because the savings in labor and land costs were now greater than the additional costs of moving goods to and from the central freight terminal, even though transportation distances were increased by moving away from the core. As a rough indication of the importance of the introduction of the truck, Moses and Williamson cite data for Chicago, where truck registrations increased from 800 in 1910 to 23,000 in 1920 while the number of horse-drawn vehicle registrations declined during the same decade from 58,000 to 31,000. Also, it appears at this time that the cost per ton-mile for trucks was about half that for horse and wagon and that the truck was approximately twice as fast.[3] Thus, the introduction of the truck significantly reduced the costs of intracity movement of goods relative to the cost of moving people, since trolley fares re-

[3]Moses and Williamson, "The Location of Economic Activity in Cities," p. 214.

mained at 5 cents throughout this period and, if anything, the value of time increased, tending to increase the cost of moving people.

While the introduction of the truck in the early part of the twentieth century permitted cheaper movement of goods within urban areas, most goods were still moved between urban areas by railroad during this period, and firms were still tied to the railroad's central freight terminal. However, the development of larger trucks and the public investment in highways, especially in the post - World War Two era, brought about cheaper movement of many goods and raw materials between cities via truck and broke the link of many manufacturers with the core freight terminal. During this same period, the labor force became more mobile. Improved streets and highways and extensive ownership of automobiles allowed firms to locate in areas with low population densities and draw upon a large geographic area for their labor supply. Without extensive automobile ownership, firms moving from the core would have been forced to locate in regions of high population density to insure a sufficient labor supply. This would have bid up the price of land in these densely populated areas and reduced the relative advantages of locating away from the core.

Changes in transportation technology help to explain the rise of the large core-dominated city and its decline in terms of accessibility to the core. The introduction of the truck meant that the core freight terminal was still accessible from greater distances with no greater transportation costs than had been incurred with horse and wagon. Changes in production and communications technology also contributed to the decline in the importance of the core for business locations. While the manufacturing plant located at the core was multistory (because of the high price of land in the core and because of nineteenth-century technology), production in one-story plants on a continuous-process (conveyor-line) basis eventually became a lower-cost technique. However, the implementation of such production technology had to await the ability to locate away from the core, on lower-priced land.

The movement of people within urban areas by trolley and other rail transit modes in the latter part of the nineteenth century contributed to the importance of a core location for many businesses besides manufacturing. Streetcar lines laid out like the spokes of a wheel were well designed for moving people from the outlying residential areas to core employment and shopping locations. Thus, before there was extensive auto ownership, many businesses, including the bookkeeping industries (banks, insurance companies, and similar office service operations), had to locate in the core in order to attract the large number of clerical employees they required. Central retailing locations predominated since the large downtown department store, located close to the center of the transportation hub, was near the large core work force and convenient for shoppers who came from outlying areas via trolley. Thus, the high-density core-dominated city existed because rail transportation was the cheapest means of moving both people and goods. Once the truck and later the car were introduced and changed relative transportation costs, the profitability in locating many business activities, in addition to manufacturing, at the core began to diminish.

The Future of the Central Business District

The intensively utilized center of the central city was referred to as the core in the preceding discussion. The commercial center of a large central city today is called the central business district (CBD), as defined earlier in the chapter. It is apparent that the economic activities conducted in the CBD today are significantly different from those found in the center in earlier times (especially manufacturing). The term CBD was not used to refer to the urban center of earlier times in order to restrict its use to the center of the modern large urban area.

Changes in production, transportation, and communications technology have resulted in the decentralization of jobs, and this trend is not likely to be upset in the near future. The large downtown department store is losing out to the suburban regional shopping center, which is more conveniently located for suburban residents. A central location for hotels and restaurants has also declined in importance with the advent of the automobile and airplane; the motel and restaurant at the airport or on the interstate highway bypassing the downtown area are more convenient than downtown facilities. The bookkeeping industries mentioned above, which historically located in the core to attract a large semiskilled clerical (and largely female) work force, have been transformed by the introduction of electronic data processing. With the smaller work force required to perform bookkeeping chores on a computer and the increase in auto ownership, a central location is no longer needed.

Most manufacturing has also left central locations (as discussed in considerable detail above). In a general sense, the technological revolution has resulted in the decreasing importance of a central location for most types of economic activity.[4] What is left for the CBD to do? Basically, it appears that the single most important remaining advantage to a central location is related to the need for face-to-face

---

[4]For a more detailed discussion of the impact of technology on central locations, see John Meyer, John Kain, and Martin Wohl, "Economic Change and the City: A Qualitative Evaluation and Some Hypotheses," in The Urban Transportation Problem, Harvard University Press, Cambridge, Mass., 1965. (Reprinted in Arthur F. Schreiber, Paul K. Gatons, and Richard B. Clemmer, eds., Economics of Urban Problems: Selected Readings, Houghton Mifflin, Boston, 1971, pp. 19 - 35.)

communications with customers or suppliers. Most of these are central office or executive functions, dealing with nonroutine business (high-level decisions on long-range matters, for example) and some of these decisions may have to be made quickly. In such instances, proximity of customers and suppliers of expert professional services may still be a necessity. This would include the executive suite of many business firms and would mean that some aspects of banking and insurance, law, government, advertising, publishing, and other supportive activities would be attracted to and remain in the CBD. However, these are only the nonroutine portion of all the business activities. For example, a bank may maintain a central location for its commercial loan and trust operations that require contact with business management, while practically all of the routine banking operations are decentralized to branch banks located throughout the urban area (subject to state banking laws, of course) and more convenient for the routine customer services—such as suburbanites depositing their paychecks at a drive-in window.

The above discussion implies that the only remaining important advantage of a CBD location is for the nonroutine management function of business and the related activities which it would attract (including some restaurants and hotels which serve an executive clientele). However, other activities may remain in a central location for noneconomic considerations, for example, many government activities. A state or local government complex may have been built up around a city hall or state capital building constructed many decades ago. Although this location may not be the most efficient today, the fact that the government does not have to respond to market forces may result in a continuation of high levels of routine government activity (such as record-keeping) in a central location while such functions have been decentralized by business firms. To the extent that the CBD is evolving into the above form, the composition of employment in the CBD is also dramatically changing. While in the old core-dominated city a large portion of the CBD labor force was unskilled and blue-collar, the CBD is increasingly becoming a location for high-paying technical and white-collar jobs. This trend has important implications for many urban problems discussed in this book.

Contrary to the opinions of many, employment does not appear to be growing in the CBD of most urban areas, and may indeed be declining. Although few data are available on CBD employment figures, fragmentary evidence on the number of people commuting into the CBD of several major urban areas indicates employment declines. Meyer, Kain, and Wohl reviewed CBD employment data for 13 SMSAs in the early 1960s. Among their findings: journey-to-work trips in the Philadelphia CBD declined from 260,000 in 1947 to

220,000 in 1960; approximate employment in the Chicago CBD in 1946 was 297,000 and declined to about 238,000 by 1961, a decrease of about 20 percent.[5]

However, these data are not recent and could possibly indicate an earlier phase of decentralization related to the outward movement of manufacturing. On the other hand, Atlanta has been one of the fastest growing urban areas in the country in the postwar period. Since it did not grow to prominence in the nineteenth century, its present growth pattern ought to be more illustrative of economic forces at work today, unlike the older cities who have a larger legacy of the past. Employment in the Atlanta SMSA grew from 419,300 in 1961 to 611,913 in 1970, a 46 percent increase, but CBD employment is estimated to have increased from 85,806 to 88,955 during the same period, an increase of only 3.7 percent. On the surface, this low employment growth in the Atlanta CBD appears difficult to reconcile with the tremendous boom in construction of new structures in the CBD during this time. The explanation seems to be the changing composition of CBD employment, from clerical to executive-technical, in this decade. Thus, the amount of office space per employee may have substantially increased while total employment remained relatively constant.

Many groups of people are concerned about the decline of the CBD relative to the urban area. Many city planners and other professionals appear to be working on the premise that the CBD is the "heart" of the organism (urban area) and that, if the heart is cut out or shrivels in size and importance, then the entire urban area will "die." In terms of economic reasoning, such analogies are devoid of logic. The more relevant question is whether apparently strong trends toward decentralization of jobs are the result of efficiency in the operation of the market system. In the absence of evidence to the contrary, attempts to counter these forces of decentralization in order to revive the CBD to its former position of dominance would involve huge amounts of resources with little apparent benefit to society.

Decentralization Trends in Urban Areas

While data on the declining importance of the CBD are difficult to obtain, census data seem to indicate that the post - World War Two trend is toward decentralization of jobs and people.

As of the 1970 census of population, 54 percent of the United States population living in SMSAs resided in the suburbs. If the total population is divided into central city, suburban, and rural, the largest group is now suburban. Table 2-1 presents some data indicating the trends in decentralization of population and economic activity in the nine largest SMSAs in the northern and eastern sections of the United

[5]Meyer, Kain, and Wohl, *The Urban Transportation Problem*, pp. 35 - 38.

States. Large SMSAs in other parts of the country (such as Los Angeles and Houston) were excluded because these urban areas grew to prominence in the twentieth century and were not large nineteenth-century core-dominated cities. The nine SMSAs in the table had a total population of about 40 million in 1970, or about 20 percent of the total United States population. Between 1950 and 1970 the central cities lost population while suburban population more than doubled.

Employment data for the central city and the rest of the SMSA over a twenty-year period (1947 or 1948 to 1967) are given in Table 2-1 for the four employment sectors for which the Bureau of the Census has collected such data. The nine central cities lost employment in three of these four categories and gained only in selected services, which includes hotels and motels, automobile repairs, miscellaneous business and personal services, motion pictures, and other amusement and recreational services. While the central cities have lost their dominant economic position (74 percent of total employment in these four sectors in 1948), in 1967 they still had a greater proportion of total SMSA employment in these four sectors (57 percent) than they had in population (46 percent in 1970). However, if 54 percent of the SMSA population is suburban, as well as 43 percent of the jobs in these four categories, this implies that many suburbanites work in the suburbs (unless there is very much commuting to the suburbs from the city, which does not appear to be the case). Thus, the terms commuter and suburbanite are not synonymous. The employment decentralization trends indicated in Table 2-1 are somewhat understated to the extent that central city boundaries expanded over the twenty-year period through annexation, thereby taking over some employment that had previously been suburban. On the other hand, the employment data probably overstate the rate of employment decentralization in that such important urban employment categories as government (including education) and nonprofit institutions are not included for lack of data. Some of the excluded services (insurance, financing, and real estate) are probably the most important categories of employment that require face-to-face contacts and hence a central location.

Current Land-Use Patterns in Urban Areas

In the preceding section, transportation technology and costs were the major factors used to explain why the core of the nineteenth-century city was so intensively utilized for the economic activities of the urban area. In recent years, many books and articles have been concerned with working out the interrelationships of variables such as land-value patterns, transportation costs, and the location of

POPULATION OR EMPLOYMENT	1947(8) OR 1950				1967 OR 1970				PERCENTAGE CHANGE, 1948 - 1967 OR 1950 - 1970	
	Central city		Suburban ring		Central city		Suburban ring		Central city	Suburban ring
	Amount	Percent	Amount	Percent	Amount	Percent	Amount	Percent		
POPULATION	19,169	64	10,630	36	18,296	46	21,243	54	−5	102
EMPLOYMENT										
Manufacturing	2,812	69	1,241	31	2,295	52	2,111	48	−18	70
Retailing	1,267	74	452	26	1,054	52	977	48	−17	116
Wholesaling	734	90	78	10	682	70	288	30	−7	269
Selected services	531	83	106	17	775	71	316	29	46	198
Total	5,344	74	1,877	26	4,807	57	3,692	43	−10	97

Table 2-1: Decentralization of Jobs and People in the Nine Largest SMSAs in the North and East, 1949 - 1970   The nine SMSAs, in descending population order, are: New York, Chicago, Philadelphia, Detroit, Washington, D.C., Boston, Pittsburgh, Baltimore, and Cleveland. Population and employment figures are in thousands.

SOURCES: Computed from data in U.S. Census of Population, 1950 and 1970; U.S. Census of Business, 1948 and 1967; and U.S. Census of Manufacturers, 1947 and 1967.

economic activity within urban areas today. The simplest models for urban areas are highly abstract and consider only the patterns of housing and transportation that evolve around a single point in two-dimensional space, where all employment is assumed to be located (i.e., the core of the city). Unfortunately, even with the simplest possible set of assumptions, the analysis becomes quite complex, and each refinement of assumptions magnifies the complexity.[6]

The key idea in these models is that there exists a relation between land values and travel cost. If there is a single employment center and if housing units each occupy the same amount of land, a commuter has the choice of living closer to his job and paying more for rent or living farther out and paying more for transportation and less for rent. If consumer tastes are homogeneous (everyone has the same taste for housing), then the market for housing will reach an equilibrium where people are indifferent between living closer in and farther out, since the total costs of rent plus transportation will be a constant. Were this not true, people could gain by moving in one direction or another; as this occurred, land prices would rise in the more desirable locations. Ultimately, equilibrium would be established in this case too. It is not within the scope of this book to work out the derivation of this result, but the key is the relation of land values and transportation costs. To get a flavor of how the model works, suppose equilibrium had been reached, and then transportation costs suddenly fell, owing to some sort of technical change (introduction of high-speed freeways, for example, has lowered the costs of transportation, particularly the time component). With the old system of rents, people will find they are better off by moving farther out, lowering their expenses for transportation plus rent. Eventually a new equilibrium will be established, in which rents near the center of the city will be lower than before. As a further illustration, suppose the costs of transportation were prohibitively high, except for walking. Everyone would have to live within walking distance of his place of work. A lowering of the costs of transportation would enable people to live at greater distances from the workplace.

Even with this highly simplified model of an urban area, we have a fair picture of the trend of land rents and transportation costs in the last few decades. Transportation costs have fallen; as a result, urban areas need not be so compact as before, and relative rents and land values in the center of the city have declined. This model is too simple to account for the observed ring of low-income people living close to the CBD, surrounded by a ring of higher-income people, and does not

---

[6]This literature is quite recent. See William Alonso, *Location and Land Use*, Harvard University Press, Cambridge, Mass., 1964, for essentially the first complete presentation of such a model, and Richard Muth, *Cities and Housing*, The University of Chicago Press, Chicago, 1969, for a refinement of the model, along with applications.

adequately take into account the outward movement of firms that has been observed in recent years (since all employment is assumed to be in the center of the city). The model does get across the idea of scarcity of land in urban areas. Were there no such scarcity, all economic activity could be located in the CBD (including housing on large lots).

An Example of Present Land-Use Patterns in Urban Areas

Analysis using rent gradients helps to explain how the market allocates land in various parts of the urban area to various uses, such as manufacturing, low-income housing, and high-income housing. In terms of Figure 2-2, the curve for land costs is a "rent gradient," since it shows the amount that some user of land (housing or business) would pay for a given quantity of land at a given distance from the core of the city. In the nineteenth-century core-dominated city business firms would bid highest for land located at or near the central freight terminal. Thus, the land-use pattern underlying this analysis was one of business, especially manufacturing, located in the core of the city and housing forming a ring around the core. In this section rent gradients will be used to provide a general explanation of present land-use patterns in urban areas.

Although it is a simplification, assume all land uses in an urban area can be divided into the following four categories: (A) CBD-oriented business activities; (B) suburban-oriented business activities; (C) lower-income housing; and (D) higher-income housing. The problem is the spatial arrangement of these four land-use categories within the urban area. The curves in Figure 2-3 labeled R_a, R_b, R_c, and R_d are usually called "bid-rent curves." They show the maximum amount that each type of land user would be willing to bid for a given quantity of land at each location (distance from the CBD in a typical direction). The heavy line is called a "rent gradient" and shows the combination of the various bid-rent curves according to which land use will pay the highest amount for land located at different distances from the center. As can be seen from the figure, CBD-oriented business will pay the most for land near the center of town, followed by lower-income housing, higher-income housing, suburban-oriented business activity, and more higher-income housing. The economic reasons for the assumed slope and height of the four rent-bid curves in Figure 2-3 that result in the rent gradient shown, as well as the spatial distribution of jobs and people on the urban landscape, are discussed next.

As stated earlier in the chapter, there are still a number of business activities that will maximize their profits with a central location. These tend to be central office functions—corporate headquarters, law and accounting firms, banking and other financial

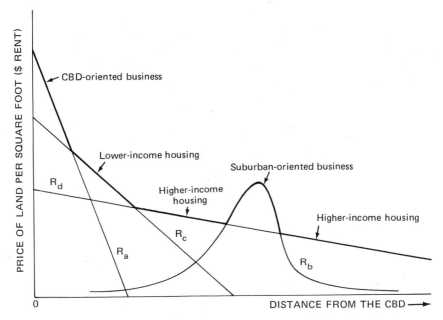

Figure 2-3: An Example of Urban Land-Use Patterns: A Rent Gradient

institutions—which require frequent face-to-face contact and must be located close together. The bid-rent curve R_a is the highest and most steeply sloped of the four curves. The closer such firms are to other similar firms, the lower the cost of each firm's transportation and personnel time expended in maintaining contacts with other firms. Also, accessibility of all people and business firms in the urban area who utilize such services is maximized by a location in the center of the urban area. Therefore, such firms are willing to bid the most for CBD locations since they have the greatest amounts of offsetting cost savings from being centrally located.

R_b represents the bid-rent curve for those business activities that no longer have a tie to the core of the urban area, because of changes in transportation, communication, and production technology. In the case of manufacturers who deal with goods and raw materials shipped between urban areas by truck, a central location would be undesirable because of high land costs and congested streets; there would be the additional problem of attracting workers to the plant site. The hump in R_b is assumed to be the location in the outlying area of perimeter transportation facilities, such as a belt expressway around the urban area. By locating near this perimeter road, many business activities have better access to both transportation of goods and raw materials and to people residing in suburban areas. Category B would also include suburban shopping centers and suburban office parks; their willingness to bid the highest for land located at the perimeter road would be related to the increased accessibility it provides for customers and employees residing in the suburban area. The highest bids would be found at intersections of radial roads (connecting with the CBD) and perimeter roads. Thus, the rent gradient would not be of the same height at every point, say ten miles, from the CBD. At favorable intersections the humps would be higher than those occurring along the perimeter highway at points between these favorable intersections.

R_c, the bid-rent curve for lower-income housing, is more steeply sloped than the bid-rent curve of higher-income housing, R_d. Thus, lower-income households reside on more expensive land (located closer to the CBD) than do higher-income households. This phenomenon of lower-income households living closer to the CBD holds almost without exception in large urban areas, paradoxical though it appears. However, the housing on the more expensive land is older and is built at a higher density than new housing, so that the amount of land used is much less per household. One explanation of the outward movement of higher-income people is the growth of the central city and the obsolescence of the housing stock associated with that growth. As the center of the urban area grows, residents of areas close to the center incur increased costs of congestion, pollution, and noise, and those who can afford it are motivated to move out to escape these costs. Also, the most central housing is the oldest and is the first to become obsolete, but since it still has some value, it is usually less expensive to build modern housing on outlying vacant land than to tear down the older housing and build new.

The most frequently cited economic explanation for why higher-income households live on the periphery of the urban area is that most households have strong preferences for space-consuming, low-density housing. However, such housing is expensive, and relatively high incomes are required to live in such a fashion. Even though the outlying land is relatively cheaper per square foot than closer-in land, the total amount paid for land may be quite high because lot sizes are large in low-density areas. Usually the only means of transportation in low-density residential areas is the automobile, and this sets a necessary condition of single or perhaps multiple car ownership, which lower-income people cannot afford. While the demand for low-density living may be strongly related to income, the offsetting factor is the longer journey-to-work trip, if the higher-income resident works in the CBD. For those higher-income residents who work in suburban job locations this is not a consideration (and, although the data are not available, it is probably true today that a majority of higher-income residents of urban areas have non-CBD jobs). For those higher-income residents who do commute long distances to work from outlying residential areas, the desire for low-density housing more than offsets the increase in commuting costs entailed by not living in a more central, higher-density, location.

From the perspective of lower-income households, lower-income people will bid more for land nearer the center of the urban area because they cannot afford the high commuting costs associated with automobile ownership and long commuting distances. The price of land per square foot is higher near the center of town but the amount of land used by lower-income households is less per household, since it is high-density living, usually in the form of apartment buildings or old houses converted to multiple-family occupancy. Transportation-to-work costs are reduced by reliance on public transportation (primarily buses), which provide better service in the higher-density areas near the center of the urban area.

Qualifications of the Land-Use Example

The analysis of the nineteenth-century core-dominated city implied that such a city was mononuclear—it had a single center and the rent gradient was downward-sloping in all directions from this center. The example in Figure 2-3 has a rent gradient which is not downward-sloping at all distances from the core (there is a hump for suburban business land uses). Many present-day large urban areas did not develop in the nineteenth century with a single, large, high-density core; for example, Los Angeles grew in the automobile era and does not fit the pattern of a mononuclear urban area. While technological change has resulted in many urban areas having several subcenters, Figure 2-3 still presents a relatively realistic portrayal of the general land-use patterns found in most urban areas today.

Figure 2-3 classified land use into only four categories; a more realistic portrayal would have many more categories for both various types of business activity and residential land use. Obviously, not all suburban business and residential land use would be spatially separated as in the figure. Some retailing would be found among residential areas (convenience stores, smaller shopping centers, and gasoline stations) and would be bidding land away from the residential uses implied in the figure. In fact, such types of retailing depend on being close to residential areas rather than other businesses. Thus, the desirability of location for any one land use depends on the use of surrounding land. In other words, all land uses are interdependent and it is somewhat simplistic to consider them one at a time. Ideally, all land uses should be considered simultaneously although this vastly complicates the analysis, and much work remains to be done on this subject.

Not all households in the same income class have the same preferences for housing, as implied in Figure 2-3. Some high-income households have relatively weak preferences for low-density housing and aversion to long periods of commuting. Such higher-income households may choose to reside in high-density luxury housing located close to the CBD. On the other hand, many low-income households may prefer to live in outlying parts of the urban area, and quite a few have always lived there. However, there are a number of barriers to a large-scale movement of low-income people into the suburbs. For one thing, zoning ordinances often require large lots and large dwellings to be built on them, effectively excluding the poor. Discrimination on the basis of race is also prevalent in the suburbs, and this is a further hindrance to outward movement of low-income people. These factors are discussed in more detail in Chapters 7 and 8.

The general notion behind the rent gradient derived from bid-rent curves is that the real estate market will allocate parcels of land to the highest bidder, the one who will receive the greatest excess of benefits over costs from the use of that piece of land. However, buildings constructed on a parcel of land may have a useful life of fifty years or more before demolition and replacement with a new structure become profitable. As technology has changed, making decentralization of many activities attractive, there has not been an immediate adjustment of structures, because of the long life of most buildings. If one studies the CBD of an urban area, one will usually find new office towers located next to old office buildings of three or four stories that were constructed several decades ago. Similar discrepancies may be found in almost any part of an urban area that has been in existence for a long time. The location of the worst housing in the urban area is usually due to its being also the oldest housing in the urban area, constructed in the era of the core-dominated city. This does not mean that the land uses in Figure 2-3 are worthless in explaining changing land patterns in urban areas over time or that the market is unresponsive to such changes. Rather, land occupied by older structures still returns a greater profit than tearing down the structures in order to build something else, and the market reflects this in the concentration of low-income housing in the older structures where apartment rents are relatively low even though land costs are very high. In this context, the housing market allocates old inner-city structures to their best use at present; at some time in the future, the continued deterioration of these structures will result in their demolition with the land devoted to another use.

Urban Spatial Form and Urban Problems

The changes in transportation, communications, and production technology discussed in this chapter have resulted in land use in the urban area becoming more homogeneous. While the only profitable use of outlying land in the nineteenth-century core-dominated city was for residential purposes (and then only land in proximity to trolley lines), land in the contemporary urban area can be used more or less interchangeably for various business and residential uses. The effect of technological change in time will be to make the rent gradient in Figure 2-3 increasingly flatter. The bid-rent curve for CBD locations is likely to become less steeply sloped as improved communications technology reduces the number of business activities that require face-to-face contacts, for example, when telephones containing television transmitters and receivers (picturephones) become available at lower cost and when documents can be better reproduced over data transmission lines. As a result, bidding for CBD locations should become less intense and the bid-rent curve should be less steeply sloped.

Evidence seems to indicate that the rent gradient is indeed already becoming less steeply sloped, reflecting the trend toward decentralization of employment and residences. This is looking at the rent gradient emanating from the CBD, however, and ignores the effect of secondary centers of economic activity. In a sense, each of these has a rent gradient that blends in with the rent gradient of the whole area. It is useful at this point to consider the rent gradient in three dimensions instead of two. A simple gradient showing rents declining as distance from the CBD increases looks like the roof of a circus tent when viewed in three dimensions. The height of the tent is equal to the rent at any point, the floor of the tent coincides with the urban area, and the center pole represents the CBD, with the highest rents. This was not too inaccurate a description of the nineteenth-century core-dominated city, but is less typical of modern cities or urban areas. Instead of having a single peak (the CBD), the modern urban area may have several peaks: the CBD, the airport, places where radial and perimeter interstate highways cross, and so forth. The CBD peak will probably always be the highest, though possibly not much higher than other peaks. There are always likely to be some highly specialized business activities serving the whole urban area who will prefer to locate in the CBD if land costs there are not much higher than elsewhere, since transportation costs will be minimized and accessibility maximized. Thus, the CBD will always have some locational advantage, although this advantage may continue to dissipate in time.

Many people tend to believe that suburbanization is an evil or undesirable event in the growth of urban areas. Such value judgments are reflected in the disdainful terms, "slurb" and "suburban sprawl," frequently applied to the land-use patterns that result from the decentralization of jobs and people in urban areas. However, the amount of land used for residential purposes per household in large urban areas is probably much less than is found in small towns and rural areas.

Therefore, as the population has migrated to the large urban areas, the amount of total land in the United States used for housing has probably decreased. Even though the critics may find suburban housing too low-density for their preferences, it is higher than would be found in the United States with a lesser degree of urbanization.

Nowadays, there is generally a significant spatial separation between people's jobs and residences. As previously discussed, the CBD is increasingly becoming an employment center for higher-income professional and technical personnel. To the extent that these employees reside in higher-income suburban residential areas, large spatial separations exist between them and their jobs. On the other hand, decentralization forces have resulted in the rapid dispersal of manufacturing jobs and many types of low-skill service jobs from the core of the central city. However, most of the lower-income households, who are equipped only for these low-skill jobs, reside in the older and cheaper housing of the central urban area. Since they often do not have access to transportation to new jobs opening up in suburban regions, they are trapped in poverty. Existing public transportation is not designed to move people efficiently from the central city to the periphery, having been designed for commuting into the CBD.

The separation of jobs and people caused by decentralization underlies many of the current urban problems to be discussed later in this book. The inaccessibility of many low-skilled jobs adds to poverty in central cities. At the same time, the residential location of many high-income jobholders who commute to CBD jobs creates transportation problems within the urban area. The large number of automobiles required for the movement of people residing in low-density suburban housing adds to the problems of environmental pollution. The concentration of low-income people in central cities contributes to the financial problems of these cities because such households not only contribute small amounts of taxes to the city, but they burden the city with additional expenses for schools, crime prevention, and many other services. This burden can become so heavy that upper-income residents migrate out of the city to escape the high taxes, adding to the city's financial woes.

The approach of this book is that not all forces of change, including decentralization, are necessarily bad, even though they may lead to many problems. Analysis will point out specific problems that could be solved by an application of economic principles; solving these problems would give us a better idea as to whether the process of decentralization is really the culprit. Until better evidence is presented, it appears that decentralization is a result of forces that can lead to higher standards of living for all urban residents, and to suppress it (were this possible) would not be in the best interests of society. As will be discussed in following chapters, the private market system (upon which our economy is based) can lead to very high levels of benefits to the members of society. When there is a good economic reason for intervening in the workings of the private market (and we shall point out many such instances), intervention can be justified. On the other hand, indiscriminately intervening in the market system can cause unexpected and undesirable results.

Suppose that the process of decentralization is taken as given, and the decentralization trend is projected ahead in time. One result to be expected is that the number of jobs in the CBD will continue to decline in relation to total urban area employment. The transportation problems will be very different from what exists presently, and plans that are based on a projected growth of CBD employment are likely to be far off the mark. Suppose a typical urban area believed that CBD employment was going to double in the next thirty years, and as a result built a rail rapid transit system to carry this expected number of people into the CBD. If, in fact, the decentralization continues (and there is no good reason to suppose that it will not), the number of jobs in the CBD may fall, and the urban area will be stuck with a transit system that is not needed. This is of course speculation, but, given the conclusions of this chapter, a situation that is not far-fetched.

REVIEW AND DISCUSSION QUESTIONS

1   Why is residential land usually cheaper per acre in the suburbs than in the central city?

2   In what way can it be argued that "the compact city of the late nineteenth and early twentieth century was the accidental result of a temporary lag in urban technology"?

3   Are there any factors involved in changing the location behavior of jobs and homes other than purely technological changes?

4   In the future, it is likely that the forces of centralization will tend to offset the forces of decentralization and the CBD (core) will rise to its prior position of prominence. Evaluate.

5   Think of a large SMSA with which you are familiar. Do the reasons for the rise and decline of the core-dominated nineteenth-century city apply to this SMSA? Why or why not? What evidence can you cite to support your conclusions? What is your prediction as to the form and size of this SMSA in thirty years?

6   Referring to the most recent *County and City Data Book* (a U.S. Bureau of the Census publication), determine the population and population density of the central city, urbanized area, and SMSA in which you live or the one closest to where you live.

7   Explain the apparent paradox of lower-income housing usually

being located in the urban area on land that is more expensive per acre than the land on which higher-income housing is located.

SUGGESTED READINGS

Kain, John. "The Distribution and Movement of Jobs and Industry." In *The Metropolitan Enigma,* edited by J. Q. Wilson, Garden City, N.Y.: Doubleday, Anchor Books, 1970.

Meyer, John, John Kain, and Martin Wohl. "Economic Change and the City: A Qualitative Evaluation and Some Hypotheses." In *The Urban Transportation Problem.* Cambridge, Mass.: Harvard University Press, 1965. (Reprinted in Arthur F. Schreiber, Paul K. Gatons, and Richard B. Clemmer, eds. *Economics of Urban Problems: Selected Readings.* Boston: Houghton Mifflin Company, 1971.)

Moses, Leon, and Harold Williamson, Jr. "The Location of Economic Activity in Cities." *American Economic Review* (May 1967), 211 - 220.

Vernon, Raymond. *Metropolis 1985.* Cambridge, Mass.: Harvard University Press, 1960.

Warner, Sam B., Jr. *Streetcar Suburbs.* Cambridge, Mass.: MIT - Harvard University Press, 1962.

3 / Economic Efficiency

One thing that is not in short supply is opinions regarding public issues. Nearly everyone has opinions on nearly every issue discussed in this book. Overwhelmingly, these opinions are based on equity considerations, while efficiency considerations are either not understood or simply ignored. For example, lower fares on transit systems are generally viewed from one of two perspectives—that they would be beneficial to the poor or that they would cost the taxpayer too much. These are matters having to do with "fairness" in the distribution of income and are thus equity issues, as will be made clear in the next chapter. The lower fares have many efficiency consequences, however. Underpricing of something can lead to overuse; on the other hand, perhaps current prices have led to underuse, so that lower fares might be more efficient. Another example would be higher gasoline prices during the "energy crisis" of early 1974. Almost all of the public discussion of gasoline prices centered around questions of equity, such as lower purchasing power of consumers and higher profits of oil companies. It was widely forgotten that, when prices were held at low levels, long lines at gasoline stations resulted, and that an immediate consequence of higher prices was shorter lines. The most important single concept in this book is the concept of efficiency. It will become apparent that evaluating issues solely on the basis of equity, and ignoring efficiency, can lead to severe errors in judgment.

The Efficient Allocation of Resources

If resources such as raw materials and manpower were unlimited, commodities (any good or service) could be produced in any variety and quantity, and people could obtain them for the asking. Stores could be established without checkout counters and people could choose whatever they desired, since everything would be free. However, resources are limited; therefore, society must somehow determine what goods and services are to be produced and in what quantities. If all available resources are employed (full employment), a decision to have more of one good or service requires a corresponding decision to have less of other goods or services. Even if we do not have full employment, the decision to have more of one commodity implies that we give up the *potential* of having other commodities.[1] In this section, a general criterion for allocating limited resources among alternative uses is developed.

[1]If wasteful production techniques are being used, the output could be increased by adopting better techniques. Inefficiency in housing production, though, does not imply that more housing should be produced but rather that more of *something* should be produced, since in effect this means there are more resources available.

Suppose society decides to produce more of a commodity and correspondingly less of other commodities. People will receive satisfaction from consuming more of the first commodity, and this extra satisfaction is termed the extra *social benefits* (the summation of the satisfaction received by individual members of society). However, producing more of one commodity implies producing less of others, or at least the potential of producing these other commodities, and this means that potential benefits are foregone. The additional benefits foregone by producing more of the first commodity are termed the additional *social costs*. It may seem strange, at first, to think of costs as foregone benefits, or as negative benefits, but this is exactly what they are. If you buy a magazine for $1, you may think of the cost to you as being $1, but consider the situation more closely and you will find that the true cost is equal to the benefits you could have obtained had you bought something else (a foregone opportunity). Buying the magazine might mean that you can no longer buy a sandwich, or something else. The foregone benefit is the true cost, often called the "opportunity cost."

Some measure of benefits or satisfaction is needed; rather than try to derive some abstract measure, they will be expressed in terms of dollars in this book. Above it was shown that the costs of a magazine were not really $1, but the benefits foregone. While the dollar is not itself the cost, it is a measure of the costs. If an individual is just willing to pay a dollar for an additional unit of a commodity, then the benefits of the additional unit are measured as $1. This example shows that people already consider costs in terms of dollars, and as long as it is kept in mind that the dollar cost is a measure of the true underlying opportunity cost (the foregone benefits), then the following discussion should be clear. The concepts of costs, benefits, and their measurement will be explained and further developed in the remainder of this chapter.

The Efficiency Criterion

Using the concept of social benefits introduced above, we can state the first and most general version of the efficiency criterion: *resources are efficiently allocated when the total amount of benefits received by members of society from the consumption of all commodities is maximized.* Thus, efficiency is concerned with the total amount of benefits (satisfaction) people in society receive from the use of their limited resources; later we shall see that equity is concerned with how the benefits are distributed among people. Careful analysis shows that over wide ranges of issues, equity and efficiency are not in conflict, but most people do not consider efficiency, instead basing their opinions solely on equity. If efficiency is ignored, then there will be a smaller "pie" of benefits to divide among the population. To take a simple example, suppose that in order to help the poor, bread were provided free to everyone and in any amount he wished. This would help the poor, of course, but it does not take too much imagination to see that people could substitute bread for other commodities, and bread might be used for animal feed, for example. One could counter that, of course, there would have to be restrictions, but these could be expensive to enforce and would negate much of the value of the program as a poverty-fighting device.

Grand total social benefits There are other ways of stating the efficiency criterion, and the following rather lengthy example will show that they are all equivalent. Suppose that only two commodities can be produced in an economy—ale and bread (goods A and B, respectively). The amount of bread that can be produced depends on the amount of ale produced, and vice versa. (We are assuming that resources are fully employed, so that to produce more bread, we must produce less ale.) The decision to produce more of one is identical to a decision to produce less of the other. This concept, very basic to economic analysis, is the concept of scarcity of resources referred to previously and is illustrated in Table 3-1, the *production possibilities schedule*.

In reality, society chooses a point on the production possibilities schedule, which simultaneously indicates an amount of bread and an amount of ale. Given the limited resources, if 4 gallons of ale are produced, only 5 loaves of bread can be produced. (The reader may be familiar with another type of production possibilities schedule used in wartime: guns versus butter, or more military goods means fewer civilian goods.) If we can attach benefits to the various amounts of ale and bread in the table, then we can determine the efficient point—the possible combination of commodities A and B on the schedule in Table 3-1 where the total amount of benefits is the greatest. Table 3-2 shows the values for the total social benefits (TSB) for ale (A) and bread (B).

Several things should be noted. The numbers chosen are deliber-

QUANTITY OF ALE (COMMODITY A) IN GALLONS	QUANTITY OF BREAD (COMMODITY B) IN LOAVES
0	15
1	14
2	12
3	9
4	5
5	0

Table 3-1: The Production Possibilities Schedule

COMMODITY A (ALE)		COMMODITY B (BREAD)	
Quantity in gallons(Q_A)	Total social benefits (TSB_A)	Quantity in loaves (Q_B)	Total social benefits (TSB_B)
0	$ 0	0	$ 0
1	100	1	15
2	160	2	29
3	190	3	42
4	210	4	54
5	220	5	65
		6	75
		7	84
		8	92
		9	99
		10	105
		11	110
		12	114
		13	117
		14	119
		15	120

Table 3-2: Total Social Benefits Received by Society from Various Quantities of A and B

ately small, to keep the example simple. An uneasy reader may choose to think of the units as millions of gallons and loaves, if he wishes, in order to represent an entire economy. Also, for each good, TSB increases rapidly at first and more slowly later. The first loaves of bread produce great benefits because they alleviate extreme hunger. Later loaves still yield additional benefits, lower in magnitude, although *total* social benefits continue to rise. If much larger quantities could be produced, TSB might fall, because if enough of almost anything is produced and consumed, it can detract from people's benefits. (Consider drinking a gallon of ale in thirty minutes, for example.) The point where TSB no longer increases as quantities increase is called the saturation point (rather appropriately in the case of ale).

Consider the definition of efficiency given earlier: the efficient allocation of resources is where the maximum amount of benefits obtains, given society's limited resources. These benefits come from consuming commodities A and B (ale and bread), so that, to have efficiency, we should maximize the sum of the TSB for ale and the TSB for bread, that is to say we should maximize the satisfaction received by members of society from the only two possible uses of its scarce resources. This sum will be called the grand total social benefit. Table 3-3 shows the relevant information. Columns 1 and 2 are identical to Table 3-1; column 3 is identical to the second column of

1	2	3		4		5
Q_A	Q_B	TSB_A	+	TSB_B	=	Grand total Grand total social benefit
0	15	$ 0		$120		$120
1	14	100		119		219
2	12	160		114		274
3	9	190		99		289
4	5	210		65		275
5	0	220		0		220

Table 3-3: Grand Total Social Benefits from Attainable Combinations of A and B

Table 3-2; column 4 is the TSB for B (bread) from Table 3-2 inverted to show the total social benefits corresponding to the production possibilities schedule quantities in column 2; the grand total social benefit (column 5) is simply the sum of columns 3 and 4. Notice that the grand total social benefit is equal to the sum of the total social benefits for A and B for each point on the production possibilities schedule. The reader can easily see that grand total social benefit is maximized if 3 gallons of ale and 9 loaves of bread are produced and consumed. Any other point on the production possibilities schedule yields a lower total level of benefits to the members of society from the use of its available resources.

Before proceeding, it should be noted that real-world societies produce more than two commodities, perhaps millions of them. This example is used because it is simpler to understand while still retaining the essence of the idea. An example with a few hundred commodities could be worked out, but doing so would require weeks, and would totally obscure the basic idea that, if more of one commodity is produced, less of others can be produced, and the idea that there is some mix of various commodities that maximizes the benefits to society.

Net social benefits   The above example showed the point of efficiency (3 gallons of ale and 9 loaves of bread) for a whole economy, considering both goods simultaneously. For a more useful efficiency concept, one that applies to a single commodity, the total social cost (TSC) for ale (A) will now be derived from Table 3-3. As previously discussed, cost is basically foregone benefit or opportunities. If more ale is produced and consumed, then less bread can be produced and consumed. The TSC for A is the amount of benefits foregone by producing A rather than B. Numerically, the amount of potential benefits we could get from producing as much bread as possible is

$120. If less bread is actually produced, an amount equal to the difference between $120 (the potential TSB) and the actual TSB for B is foregone. For example, suppose 2 gallons of ale are produced. This means that only 12 loaves of bread can be produced, and that the benefits from consuming bread (the TSB from 12 loaves of B) are $114. Thus, potential benefits of $6 are foregone (the maximum possible was $120, and $120 − $114 = $6). Similarly, if 3 gallons of ale are produced, only 9 loaves of bread can be provided, and the TSB of 9 loaves of bread is $99; thus, potential benefits of $21 ($120 − $99) are foregone, which is the opportunity cost (TSC) of the 3 gallons of ale. Column 3 of Table 3-4 shows these foregone benefits, which are defined as the total social cost for A (TSC$_A$). To recap, if we produce a certain amount of A, not as much B can be produced as could have been, and therefore the benefits from B are not as high as they could have been. This loss in potential benefits brought about because not as much B can be produced is called the total social cost for A.

We have seen that as we produce a certain amount of A, we generate both benefits and costs. It seems reasonable that to get the most out of consuming A, an amount should be produced where the largest difference between the TSB for A and the TSC for A is attained. This is much like a business firm trying to get the largest difference between its revenues and its costs (i.e., to maximize profits). Analogous to profit, net social benefit (NSB) is defined as the difference between TSB and TSC (TSB minus TSC). Thus, we have another way to state the efficiency concept: *resources are efficiently allocated to the production of a commodity when net social benefit (TSB minus TSC) is maximized.* The net social benefit for each possible quantity of A is shown in column 4 of Table 3-4 and is obtained by subtracting column 3 (TSC$_A$) from column 2 (TSB$_A$). The largest (maximum) net social benefit occurs when 3 gallons of A are produced. Note that this is, and must be, the same quantity we got when choosing where the grand total social benefit was maximized in Table 3-3.

1	2		3		4
Q_A	TSB$_A$	−	TSC$_A$	=	Net social benefits (NSB$_A$)
0	$ 0		$ 0		$ 0
1	100		1		99
2	160		6		154
3	190		21		169
4	210		55		155
5	220		120		100

Table 3-4: The Net Social Benefits of Various Quantities of A

1	2	3	4
Q_A	MSB_A	MSC_A	$MSB_A - MSC_A$
0	$—	$—	$—
1	100	1	99
2	60	5	55
3	30	15	15
4	20	34	-14
5	10	65	-55

Table 3-5: Marginal Social Benefit and Marginal Social Cost of Various Quantities of A There is no MSB and MSC for zero gallons, although TSC and TSB exist and are equal to zero, at zero units of production. Marginal social benefit is the additional benefit derived by producing the last (marginal) gallon. In order to apply this to the zero unit, we would need to go from minus one gallon to zero gallons. Since negative production is not possible, MSB and MSC are not defined at zero gallons of output.

Marginal social benefit and marginal social cost   Net social benefit is a concept that will be referred to in later chapters. Even more useful is another way of stating the efficiency concept, which is concerned with marginal social benefit and marginal social cost. Marginal means additional; thus, marginal social cost (MSC) is the additional social cost (i.e., increase in TSC) brought about by producing one more unit of something. In column 3 of Table 3-4, if we produce the fourth gallon of ale, TSC increases from $21 to $55, a difference of $34. Therefore, the MSC of the fourth unit of A (MSC_A) is $34, as shown in column 3 of Table 3-5. Similarly, marginal social benefit (MSB) is defined as the additional benefit derived (increase in TSB) if we produce one more unit of a commodity. In column 2 of Table 3-4, as the fourth gallon of A is produced, TSB increases from $190 to $210; thus, the MSB of the fourth gallon of A (MSB_A) is $20 ($210 − $190), as shown in column 2 of Table 3-5.

Consider the decision to produce an additional gallon of A. If this extra gallon adds more to benefits than it adds to costs, then it should be produced. This same thinking should apply to each gallon produced, so start with the first. If it is produced, benefits go up by $100 ($MSB_A$ = $100), as shown in column 2 of Table 3-5. Costs increase by $1 ($MSC_A$ = $1). Therefore, there will be a net gain of $99 if the first gallon is produced (column 4). (Checking Table 3-4, one can see that NSB also increases by $99.) The second gallon of A yields $60 in additional benefits and incurs $5 in additional costs, for a net gain of $55. From Table 3-4, one can see that the NSB of 2 gallons of A is $154, an increase of $55 over the NSB of 1 gallon. Thus, column 4 of Table 3-5 indicates the amount by which each additional gallon of A changes the net social benefits: the change is positive if MSB_A is greater than MSC_A and is negative if MSB_A is less than MSC_A. A unit of anything should be produced if MSB exceeds MSC, and this holds until 3 gallons of A are produced. If the fourth gallon of A is produced, MSC_A exceeds MSB_A; to get \$20 in additional benefits, \$34 in costs are incurred, decreasing NSB by \$14 from \$169 to \$155. Thus, our efficiency concept can be restated as follows: *resources are efficiently allocated to the production of a commodity if, for the last unit produced (gallons of A in this case), MSB is not less than MSC and, for an additional unit, MSC exceeds MSB*. And, of course, this is the quantity at which NSB is maximized, as shown by the two previous approaches to the efficiency concept.

If we were considering cases where quantities could be varied in smaller amounts rather than the large discrete jumps in this example, we could say that we have efficiency when MSB = MSC. In this rather lumpy example, MSB never exactly equals MSC, unless we can produce fractional units of A and B. If this were possible, then we could find the point where MSB = MSC. Figure 3-1 shows TSB, TSC, MSB, and MSC for A graphically, and Figure 3-2 shows a case where infinitely small variations in quantity are possible. In both cases, the efficient quantities indicated by TSB and TSC (which maximize net social benefits) are the same as when MSC and MSB (MSC = MSB) are used. Note that the TSB curve in both of these figures increases at a decreasing rate, which reflects the previous discussion that the more society consumes of a commodity, the smaller will be the addition to total social benefits from each successive unit, and, of course, this is reflected in the downward slope of the MSB curve. Similarly, the TSC curve increases at an increasing rate and the MSC curve is upward-sloping, reflecting the fact that social costs are benefits foregone through having less of other commodities. As each additional unit of a commodity is obtained, increasingly valuable units of other commodities must be given up.

A concluding note   We have seen that there are three equivalent ways of stating the efficiency concept. The efficient quantity of a commodity is the quantity where: (1) grand total social benefit is maximized, (2) net social benefit is maximized, and (3) marginal social benefit = marginal social cost. It will be shown that the third version is of more practical significance than the other two, but, in order that the reader might understand the underlying nature of efficiency, these other concepts were introduced. One reason why MSB = MSC is more useful is that it is easier visually to see where these curves cross than to try to determine the point where the TSB and TSC curves are farthest apart. More importantly, if we know only small portions of the MSB and MSC curves, we may still be able to make statements regarding efficiency; but, to find TSB, we need to know, in effect, all previous MSBs. The MSB of the first unit may be astronomical in

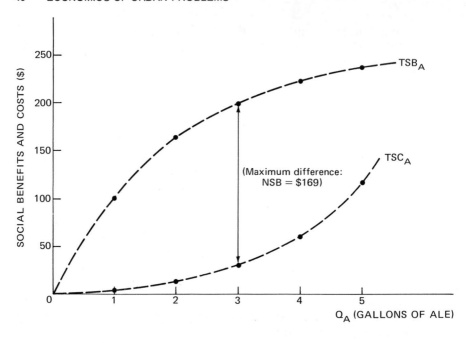

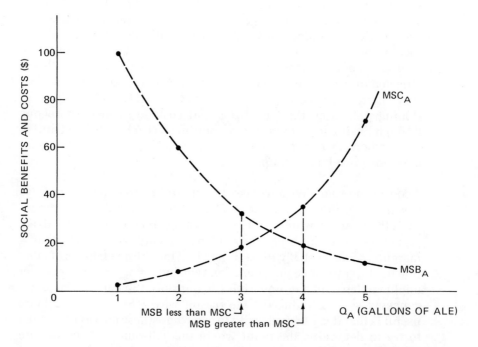

Figure 3-1: TSB, TSC, MSB, and MSC for Commodity A, Graphically Plotted

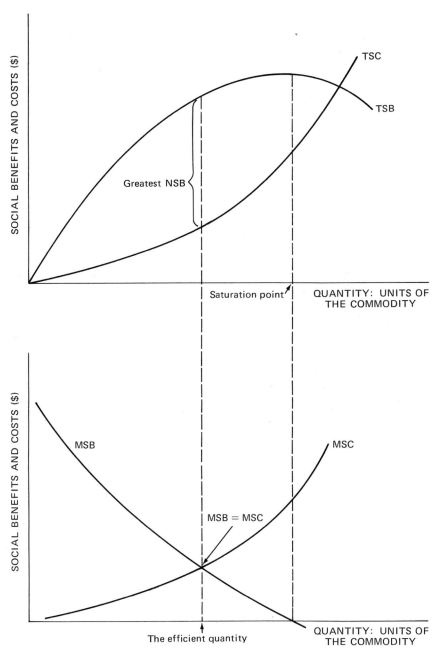

Figure 3-2: TSB, TSC, MSB, and MSC for a Commodity When Infinitely Small Variations in Quantity Are Possible

value. If people in a country are well fed, there is no easy way to determine the value the country would place on the first hundred loaves of bread produced. It is possible to measure with much greater accuracy MSB at current consumption levels, and this might be all the information needed. But, to measure the TSB for bread, we would need to compute the MSB of the first and *all* successive loaves of bread.

As an exercise, the reader might want to compute TSC, MSB, MSC, and NSB for commodity B. This involves interpolation, but will show that efficiency for B requires production of 9 units—the same quantity as indicated by the grand total social benefit approach to the efficiency concept above. It should be noted that total and marginal concepts are closely interrelated. If one knows the TSB, for example, the MSB can be derived as above by finding the increase in TSB when production is increased a unit at a time. This is another way of saying that marginal social benefit is equal to the rate of increase in total social benefit. Further, total social benefit can be thought of as the cumulative total of all previous marginal social benefits. For example, the MSBs for the first 3 units of A are $100, $60, and $30, the cumulative total of which is $190, and this equals the total social benefit of 3 units of A. Total and marginal costs are related in a similar way, as the reader can verify by an example like the one just given.

Finally, it is admitted that these concepts were derived from a rather simplified example, which was chosen to facilitate exposition. A more complicated model would yield similar results. Total social costs for a commodity would be not the loss in benefits for another single commodity, but rather the loss of benefits from all the myriad of other commodities that could have been produced with the resources used, or more correctly, the value that the resources could have produced in the best alternative use or uses. The commodities used in the example were arbitrary, and one could easily substitute education, steel, transportation, or football games. The important point is that for every commodity, there exists an efficient quantity. It is a major task of the remainder of the book to point out reasons why this quantity may not be attained (with a resulting urban problem) and to show how the economy might move toward the efficient quantity (correcting the problem).

Costs and Benefits over Time

In the case of most commodities, the costs of production and the benefits from consumption will not occur at the same point in time. If it takes two years to build a new elementary school, the costs of construction are incurred during years 1 and 2, but the benefits from the school are not received until the building is completed and in operation. Thus, the benefits start in year 3 and may be received each year for the next fifty or more years, depending on when the building is demolished or abandoned. Each commodity or possible use of resources has a different time stream of benefits and costs associated with it, and the costs and benefits of producing and consuming one commodity cannot be compared at the time of making a resource allocation decision with another commodity merely by adding up the total of costs and benefits without regard to the year in which they occur. Such comparisons of costs and benefits would not result in the efficient allocation of resources because both individuals and the community as a whole prefer benefits received today to the same amount of benefits received tomorrow: in other words, present consumption is preferred to future consumption. Alleviating poverty ten years from now is not the same thing as alleviating it this year. As another illustration, a person with $100 in his pocket would usually rather spend it today than to save it, unless he is compensated for putting off his consumption to a later date. If he is willing to sacrifice $100 today to receive $106 a year from now, then he can put his money in a bank that pays interest at 6 percent per year. Thus, the present value of $106 received a year from now is $100; the $106 is discounted to a present value of $100. In this example, the rate of discount of future benefits (or costs) is 6 percent. (Note that the term discount rate is also used to refer to discounts on loans by banks. These two meanings should not be confused.) The present value of all costs and benefits associated with the production and consumption of a commodity must be obtained to adjust for the time at which they will occur in order to make them comparable for efficiently allocating resources among alternative uses at the time such a decision is made.

It is assumed in the examples and graphs in this book that all costs and benefits have been discounted to their present values at a discount rate that reflects society's relative preferences for present versus future benefits. The computational procedure for determining present values, and problems with selection of a discount rate, will be discussed in Chapter 4, in the section on benefit-cost analysis. The important idea to keep in mind now is that the only way to properly compare benefits and costs that occur at different points in time is to compute their present values. To state that $200 in ten years is worth more than $100 today is meaningless unless the present value of the $200 is computed. If the present value of the $200 in ten years is greater than $100 (the present value of an amount at present, i.e., now, is just its value), then the above statement is correct and meaningful. Otherwise, it is not.

Incorrect Resource Allocation Criteria

The efficient quantity has been defined as that quantity at which net social benefits are maximized, or MSB = MSC. Other criteria are commonly used in popular discussions of urban problems. Thus, it is worthwhile to examine the community's satisfaction if criteria other than MSB = MSC are followed. The most important example of such an incorrect criterion would be the maximization of total social benefits for a commodity. If the total social benefits for commodity B in the previous example were maximized, only B would be produced. The TSB for B would be $120, but, since no resources would be left to produce A, the TSB for A would be zero, and the grand total social benefit would be $120—considerably short of the maximum possible of $289 shown in Table 3-3. The society could live by bread alone, but it would be inefficient.

This maximization of TSB may seem to be a straw man argument, but whenever costs are not considered, then implicitly the suggestion is for maximizing TSB. Yet, it is the loss of other benefits that it is crucial to account for. If someone states that society needs some amount of police protection, or education, or transportation, it is generally true that costs are not being considered. Pollution could very easily be eliminated, given the resources of the United States economy, but this would involve losses of benefits elsewhere. As will be shown in Chapters 11 and 12, it generally is not efficient to eliminate pollution completely, because of the tremendous loss of benefits for commodities whose production has the undesirable side effect of pollution. It is a serious error to focus on benefits to the exclusion of costs, or vice versa. Only if resources were unlimited could this approach be taken.

It is useful to consider MSB and MSC as we move toward a position of maximizing TSB for commodity A. Table 3-5 showed that the efficient quantity of A is 3 units. If we produce more, the fourth unit adds $20 to benefits, but costs (a loss of potential benefits elsewhere) $34. Adding the fifth unit of A in order to get the maximum TSB for A means that $10 in benefits are generated, but $65 of extra costs are incurred (benefits foregone from less of B are the opportunity cost of A).

Another example of inefficient resource allocation criteria is the failure to consider allocation at the margin. We should produce a commodity to the point where MSB = MSC. If spending an extra dollar means getting at least a dollar in benefits, this is an efficient decision at the margin. Suppose the government has already spent billions of dollars on the development of some program, and it appears that spending $100 million more might possibly pay off, but only $50 million in benefits would be generated. The extra spending should be considered separately from the original expense (it should be considered at the margin). The original spending can be considered a "sunk cost" (irretrievable), and if we evaluate things at the margin, sunk costs should be ignored. To argue for continuing to spend on a project because a large amount has already been spent is to argue for inefficiency. In the above example, you have already lost $x billion. Continuing the project will lose $50 million more ($50 million minus $100 million). This idea has implications for everyday personal decisions. Some students argue that, since they have already paid $x tuition for a course, they must attend every class. At the time the decision to pay for the class is made, the anticipated benefits should outweigh the tuition and other costs if an efficient decision has been made. For a particular class meeting, if the benefits of that meeting are outweighed by the costs, then the student achieves efficiency by not attending.

Another aspect of ignoring decisions at the margin is illustrated by systems of pricing various goods and services that are produced by the government and sold to the public. During a time when buses are not full, the marginal costs of an additional passenger are exceedingly low, compared with the fares charged. It may be inefficient to charge an amount that will make a profit for the transit authority, since marginal social costs may not equal marginal social benefits. If the fare is 50¢, the MSB is 25¢, and the MSC is 10¢, the fare may make a potential rider choose not to make the trip, even though it would be efficient. This marginal benefit/marginal cost kind of thinking has also led private businesses to charge lower rates in off-peak times, when additional users do not put a strain on the capacity of the facilities. Such reasoning could be applied to a much greater extent in the governmental sector, and it would lead to greater efficiency. Several such applications are discussed in subsequent chapters.

The Private Market System and Efficient Resource Allocation

In the United States and other western countries, heavy reliance is placed on the decentralized market system to make resource allocation decisions. Individuals receive income (purchasing power) through employment of their resources, and the way this income is spent determines what will be produced. Individuals base their consumption decisions on the benefits they receive from consuming commodities and the costs of these commodities as determined by the market price—the price the consumer has to pay to obtain the commodity. The benefits from consumption that accrue to the consumer are called private benefits, and the costs paid by him are called private costs. Similarly, producers make production decisions on the basis of the benefits they receive (the revenues received from selling the output) and the costs they incur in producing the output.

Just as society achieves efficient allocation of resources (maximizes its satisfaction) by maximizing net social benefits, the individual consumer maximizes his position (satisfaction) by maximizing net private benefits (private benefits minus private costs) and the producer achieves his optimal position by maximizing profits (revenues received minus costs incurred). Since a society is made up of many producers and consumers, one might guess that, if everyone maximizes his net private benefits, the net social benefits will be maximized also. In many cases, this is true, but, if it is not true, then some measure of the total amount of net benefits received by the direct consumers of a commodity is needed. This measure will be referred to as net private benefits, and the context should indicate whether an individual or society is meant, although it will usually refer to the whole society. Marginal private benefits (MPB) and marginal private costs (MPC) are defined as the benefits received and the costs incurred by the producer or consumer, that is, the costs or benefits to the party actually undertaking the production or consumption activity. Note that benefits or costs received by third parties are not included. If Jones kills all of his crabgrass, then his neighbors will receive benefits, but these are not private benefits. Only the immediate producer or consumer (in this case, Jones, the person undertaking the activity) receives private benefits. Similarly, if Jones keeps a coyote that howls at the moon, the costs imposed on his neighbors are not private costs (because they do not accrue to Jones), although we shall see that they are a part of social costs.

Market Prices and Maximization of Net Private Benefits

In order to facilitate understanding of the concepts just introduced, and to show what quantity would be produced in a private market system, an example will be developed. For simplicity, assume society is composed of only three individuals: A, B, and C. Table 3-6 shows the marginal benefits received by each of these three individuals from various quantities of some commodity X. Note that, for each individual, the marginal private benefit (MPB) of an additional unit of X becomes smaller as the quantity of X increases. As an example of this relationship between MPB and quantity, consider automobile ownership. The first auto one owns enables him to get to work and shopping, and probably adds to his private benefits more than the second auto. Adding a third auto may generate some additional benefits, but they are likely to be less than for the second car. Thus marginal private benefit falls as quantities go up. This same pattern applies to all other commodities with minor exceptions that apply to part of the MPB schedule (e.g., the second car might prevent family fights and add more to benefits than the first). For a commodity such as education, learning to read and write is an enormous benefit, and the first units of education have high marginal benefits. Successive education is valuable, but confers lower marginal benefits than the first units.

Suppose that the market price of the item in question (commodity X) is $3.95. An individual will want to purchase additional amounts of a commodity whenever the extra benefit to him (MPB) is greater than the cost to him (MPC), which turns out to be equal to the market price. The price of an item is a measure of the true cost to the individual, because in buying this item, he gives up the option of buying something else. If each dollar is spent so that the maximum benefits are generated by this action, the consumer is implicitly comparing potential benefits and spending his income, which is limited, in such a way as to maximize his net private benefits. By an argument similar to that in the previous section—net social benefits should be maximized at that quantity at which MSB = MSC— one can see that equating MPC and MPB results in maximized net private benefits. With the market price of $3.95, individual A would choose to buy 4 units of X, B would buy 2 units, and C would buy 4 units. Buying more than these quantities means that the extra benefit generated is less than the extra cost, and buying less means that more net private benefits can be attained, since the marginal private benefit exceeds marginal private cost. As simple addition shows, at a price of $3.95, the total quantity that will be bought when all three individuals maximize their net private benefits is 10 (4 + 2 + 4). At other market prices, A, B, and C would maximize net private benefits by buying other quantities.

Table 3-7 shows the aggregate marginal private benefit schedule for this three-consumer society. This is derived by looking at the maximum benefit obtained by one of the individuals (A, B, or C) through consumption of an additional unit. If only one unit of commodity X were produced, individual A would receive the maximum benefit ($10) from consuming it. Note further that if the market price were set

UNITS OF COMMODITY X	MPB$_A$	MPB$_B$	MPB$_C$
1	$10	$8	$7
2	8	4	6
3	6	0	5
4	4		4
5	2		3
6	0		2
7			1
8			0

Table 3-6: Marginal Private Benefits Received by Consumers of a Commodity

between $8 and $10, only A would buy the first unit. As seen in Table 3-6, the second unit would result in benefits of $8 if consumed by either A or B, so the marginal private benefit (MPB) of the second unit is $8 and the same is true for the third. The highest benefit for the fourth unit obtains if it is consumed by C. If the price were set somewhere between $6 and $7, then A would choose to buy two units, and B and C would each buy one unit. By continuing the above process, one can obtain the rest of the numbers in the MPB schedule.[2] As discussed above, if the price were $3.95, a total of ten units would maximize net private benefits. This can be seen in Table 3-7 where the tenth unit is the last point at which MPB equals or exceeds $3.95.

While MPB decreases as quantities increase, MPC tends to rise as quantities increase. If more of a commodity is produced, costs of production tend to be higher because resources have to be taken away from other uses. The producer sees this as higher costs of his inputs. As more and more inputs are bid away from other uses, the MPB of those other commodities that could have been produced becomes greater and greater. This is one reason why MPC rises as quantities increase. Another reason is that, as the capacity of a production facility is approached, it becomes more and more costly to get additional production. MPC will not be derived in an example as was MPB, but it is useful to think of MPC as reflecting production costs, and MPB as reflecting the benefits received by consumers. It remains true that producers and consumers are facing the same market from different angles. The MPB from consumption becomes the potential revenue for the producer, and the MPC of production becomes the price facing the consumer.

In the private market system, the quantity produced tends to be the quantity where MPB = MPC. If MPB = marginal social benefit (MSB) *and* MPC = marginal social cost (MSC), then the quantity where MPB = MPC is the same as where MSB = MSC (the point of efficiency). Thus, under certain conditions, the private market system leads to efficiency. The next chapter will explore specific cases where the above equalities do not hold and the private market system does not lead to efficiency. These cases are termed private market failure— cases in which the market fails to achieve efficient allocation of resources.

---

[2]A problem alluded to before should be made clear, and this is the problem of using discrete examples. Suppose, in the above case, the price of the commodity is $10. If A buys it, he incurs costs of $10 and also gains benefits worth $10. The net increase in his benefits is zero, so he may as well not buy the first unit. If we could infinitely vary quantity and buy 0.98 units, then the problem would not arise. This is merely a detail, but it was mentioned because the reader may wonder why exact equality of MPB and MPC is not obtained. In a whole economy, the same problem exists, but it is trivial since, if 1,000,000 units yield the same net private benefits as 999,999 units, there is little error in saying MPC = MPB at 1,000,000 units.

UNITS OF COMMODITY X	MARGINAL PRIVATE BENEFIT FOR THE SOCIETY
1	$10
2	8
3	8
4	7
5	6
6	6
7	5
8	4
9	4
10	4
11	3
12	2
13	2
14	1
15	0

Table 3-7: Aggregate Marginal Private Benefits to Society

Marginal Private Benefits and Costs:
Relationship to Market Demand and Supply

Before examining private market failure, it is useful to note some very important attributes of marginal private benefit and marginal private cost. MPB is equivalent to the *demand* for a commodity, and MPC is equivalent to the *supply* of the commodity under most circumstances. *Demand for a commodity is the schedule of the quantities that will be bought at various prices during some time period.* Looking back to Table 3-7, recall that this schedule shows not only the marginal private benefits placed on consumption of the commodity, but also the maximum prices consumers would be willing to pay to get various quantities. The table could have been labeled the demand schedule for the commodity. The same reasons that led to the conclusion that MPB is decreasing as total quantities increase lead to the conclusion that the quantity demanded increases as price decreases. If the price to the consumer is lower, then there will be more units for which MPB exceeds price, and it is optimal to buy more. Figure 3-3 shows a typical demand curve (or MPB curve) with the characteristic of sloping downward to the right, consistent with the above discussion.

Supply of a commodity is the schedule of the quantities that would be put on the market at various prices during some time period. As mentioned above, supply is equivalent to MPC. An intuitive explanation of this is that, whenever the price is greater than the cost per unit, profit is made by the producer. To maximize profits, the producer

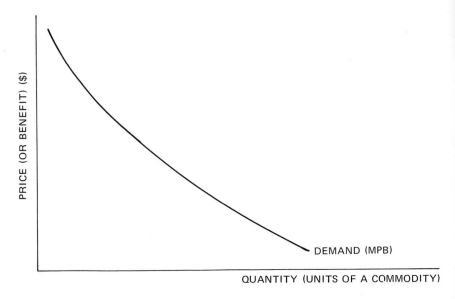

Figure 3-3: A Typical Demand (Marginal Private Benefit) Curve

should continue to produce until marginal costs are equal to the market price. To stop short of this quantity means that unexploited profits remain, and profits are not maximized. Generally, if prices are higher, it would be expected that producers would produce more of the commodity in order to get greater profits, and that new producers might want to get in on the production, leading to greater quantities being produced at higher prices. It has already been stated that, as production of a commodity increases, inputs worth more and more are drawn away from the production of other commodities, so MPC increases as quantities increase. Within the scope of this book, it is not possible to prove that MPC actually equals supply, but it is clear that: (1) the private market system tends to produce the quantity where MPC = MPB, and (2) the private market system tends to produce the amount where the quantity demanded equals the quantity supplied, as will be shown shortly. These observations, together with the fact that MPB equals demand, imply that MPC = supply. A supply curve that slopes upward in accordance with this conclusion is shown in Figure 3-4, along with the demand curve from Figure 3-3; both are shown as straight (instead of curved) lines for simplicity.

In Figure 3-4, demand and supply cross at a price of $1 and a quantity of 1,000; the quantity demanded equals the quantity supplied only if the price is $1 and the quantity produced at that price is 1,000. This quantity and price (equilibrium price) will tend to obtain in the private market, as the following discussion indicates.

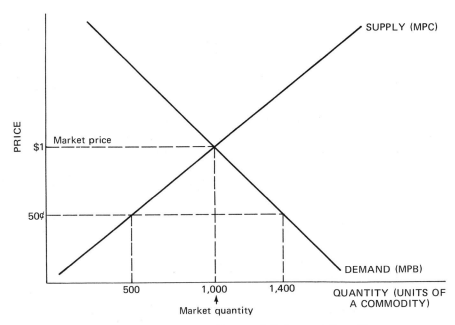

Figure 3-4: Market Supply and Demand, Price and Quantity

Suppose the price happened to be 50¢. At this price, the quantity demanded will be 1,400 units, but the quantity supplied will be only 500 units. Thus, at this price, there will be a shortage of the commodity (or excess demand) and an incentive for sellers to raise prices. As the price tends toward the equilibrium price of $1, the quantity people want to buy and the quantity that suppliers want to sell converge, eliminating the shortage.

In early 1974, gasoline was in a similar situation. The price needed to rise to clear the market, and indeed had risen somewhat, but government regulations prevented the equilibrium price from being established (the emotional term for charging the equilibrium price is "gouging"). The result of holding the price low was gasoline shortages; in fact, the lower the price, the greater the shortage. These shortages led to long lines at gasoline stations and attempts to allocate gasoline on some basis other than price (shortening hours of operation, selling only to old customers, and selling only to those willing to spend a long time in a line). Obviously, many would have rather paid $1 per gallon than wait in line to buy at 50¢. If it had been legal, stations could have had some pumps where you waited in line and others where the price was set to eliminate waiting. This might have eliminated objections that higher prices discriminate against the poor, since they would have had the option of waiting in line. In 1973, shortages were caused in red meats because prices could not rise to equilibrium levels, and suppliers could not make profits at the prices set. In general, if there is a shortage of anything in a private market system, it is because the price has not risen to the equilibrium level. This occurs over extended periods only if there is government intervention into the market.

On the other hand, if prices in a market are above the equilibrium price, they will tend to fall. Sellers are anxious to move their stocks of goods, and inventories will pile up until prices are lowered to the level that clears the market. Competition will tend to make individual sellers lower prices in order to sell more, and eventually the market equilibrium price will prevail. If raising prices is "gouging," then why cannot prices be raised to any level the seller wishes? The answer is that, in a competitive market, he would go out of business. If a gas station owner tried to sell gas for $50 per gallon, he would have few, if any, customers, and he would find that cutting prices down to market prices would increase his profits.

Prices were analyzed here as performing a resource allocation function, determining how much of a good or service would be produced and consumed. In the popular mind, they are viewed in a very different way. If gasoline prices increase, this is seen as a decrease in standard of living, and it may well be. The problem is that, if the market price is prevented from being realized, then the private market quantity, which maximizes net social benefits, will not be forthcoming either. In the recent past, government policies kept prices of agricultural commodities above market price, in order to augment farm incomes. The efficiency problems caused by this were many: prices were too high for food, which decreased consumption (as well as hurting the nonfarm poor), too many smaller farms were kept in operation for too long, and present efforts to expand food production in the face of greater demand were probably hampered.

No doubt demand and supply and the workings of the market are familiar to many readers. For these readers, the present section can be considered a review for the application of these concepts in later sections of this book. Other than the understanding that the equilibrium market price tends to prevail, the other important aspect of demand and supply has to do with adjustments when demand or supply shift. An increase in demand (which may be caused by increased population, increased incomes, or other factors) must mean that, at every price, people want to buy more. As Figure 3-5 shows graphically, the demand curve shifts to the right, from D_1 to D_2. The price (P_2) and quantity (Q_2) at the new equilibrium point are both greater than at the old equilibrium point $(P_1$ and $Q_1)$. Similarly, an increase in supply means that at each price, sellers will want to sell more. Graphically, the supply curve too shifts to the right from S_1 to S_2

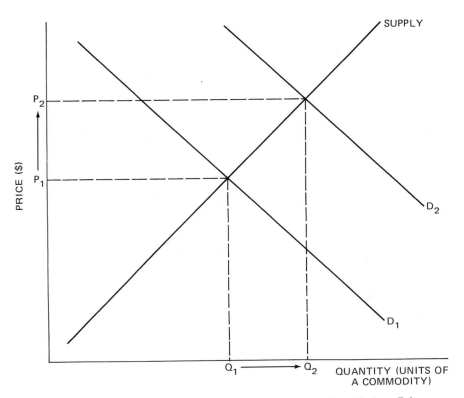

Figure 3-5: Shift in Demand and Resulting Market Equilibrium Price and Quantity

(Figure 3-6). In this case, the equilibrium quantity also increases from Q_1 to Q_2, but the equilibrium price falls from P_1 to P_2.

The main reason for discussing demand and supply here was to tie these concepts to MPB and MPC. Generally, demand is equal to MPB and supply is equal to MPC. An important exception occurs when the purchaser of something supplies part of the inputs himself. For example, the MPC of using a highway is not the price the use of the highway sells for, which may be zero, but rather the costs incurred by the driver for gas, oil, etc., and the value of his own time. Thus, market supply in the normal sense is not equal to MPC in this case, unless we think of the drivers as being the suppliers as well as the demanders.

It should be recognized that the analysis developed in this chapter applies not only to business firms and individuals in a private market system, but to a great extent to almost every decision-making individual or group. The manager of a collective farm in the Soviet Union considers costs and benefits, as do members of religious orders. In general, everyone is trying to maximize net benefits as he sees them, and this need not take place in a private market setting. Pollution will

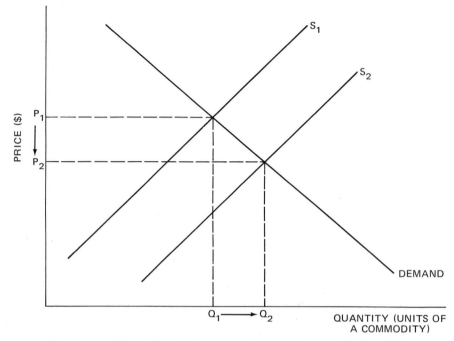

Figure 3-6: Shift in Supply and Resulting Market Equilibrium Price and Quantity

later be discussed as resulting from private market failure, but it also results from activities of governments, even in centrally planned economies, such as the Soviet Union.

Finally, it should be noted that costs may be incurred in order to buy something in the private market system. For example, one's own time is a scarce resource that has an opportunity cost associated with it, since there are only twenty-four hours in a day. Using one hour doing one thing means that hour is not available to do other things—a foregone benefit, which is the private cost of time. The purchase of an item may involve spending time and incurring travel costs in "shopping around," and these are costs in addition to the market price of the item. Time and other transaction costs may decrease the MPB as seen by the consumer and lead to a smaller quantity being sold, since demand is smaller. If transaction costs are sufficiently high, they may prevent a commodity from being supplied.

REVIEW AND DISCUSSION QUESTIONS

1 Assume that a city is considering using an existing public park as the site for a new municipal office building. Since the city already

owns the land, officials argue that there is no cost involved in using the land for the office building site. Are they correct?

2 Since the central city is the heart of the urban area, and since we have such a large investment there, we should spend whatever is necessary to insure that business firms return there, reversing their flight to the suburbs. Evaluate this statement.

3 What are the alternative ways of expressing the optimal level of production of a good or service? Why are they equivalent?

4 Why is the marginal social cost curve for a commodity upward-sloping? Why is the marginal social benefit curve for a commodity downward-sloping?

5 What is meant by the term "equilibrium price"? What meaning does the phrase "price is too high" or "price is too low" have in this context?

6 An investment of $100 that ultimately pays off $1,100 will increase your net private benefits. Evaluate this statement.

7 The price of sugar increased dramatically in late 1974, then decreased. Explain this in terms of supply and/or demand shifts. Analyze what would have happened if sugar prices had not been allowed to rise because of a price-control law.

8 If you knew the marginal social benefit schedule for a commodity, how would you calculate the total social benefit schedule?

4 / Analysis of Urban Problems: Efficiency and Equity

The previous chapter presented the basic concepts of efficiency and indicated how the private market system, under certain circumstances, leads to efficient allocation of resources. This chapter first considers some important conditions under which the market fails to achieve efficiency. Next, equity (income distribution) considerations, dealing with the distribution of social benefits among the members of society, and the relationship of income distribution to resource allocation are discussed. Finally, the chapter considers the practical implementation of some of these ideas through benefit-cost analysis.

Private Market Failure: Inefficient Allocation of Resources

In the preceding chapter, it was shown that the decentralized private market system achieves resource allocation through individual consumers maximizing net private benefits and producers maximizing profits, with market prices providing the signals to accomplish this. In this process, the market allocates resources so that the quantity of various commodities produced and consumed is the quantity at which MPB = MPC. If MPB = MSB and MPC = MSC, then the market-determined resource allocation is also the efficient allocation of resources. Thus, for the market to maximize net social benefits, all costs and benefits (that is, the social costs and benefits) associated with the production and consumption of the commodity must be reflected in the decisions made by individual producers and consumers in the market. There are some important and frequent situations where this does not hold true, which result in the market's failure to achieve efficiency. There are many potential causes of market failure; those discussed in this section are the most relevant to the subsequent analysis of urban problems.

The Problem of Externalities

One of the conditions for the efficient allocation of resources by the private market system is that marginal social benefits should equal marginal private benefits, the sum of marginal private benefits of all individuals in the community. When externalities exist, this does not hold true. An *externality* is defined as a cost or benefit in production or consumption that does not accrue to the producer or consumer of the commodity; it is an indirect cost or benefit. In other words, social benefits or costs from a production or consumption activity include something more than the costs or benefits accruing to the individual actually doing the consuming or the business firm doing the production. When externalities exist, social benefits or costs are no longer equal to the sum of private benefits or costs; instead, *social benefits* are equal to private benefits plus indirect benefits, and *social costs* are equal to private costs plus indirect costs. The difference between social and private costs or benefits is the indirect costs or benefits. Remember that private costs or benefits accrue to the actual producer or consumer of a commodity, while indirect costs or benefits (that is, externalities) accrue to someone else as a result of the production or consumption of the commodity.

In general, externalities exist when there is a divergence between social benefits and private benefits or between social costs and private costs. Consumption or production activities that result in indirect benefits (social benefits exceeding private benefits) are called *positive* externalities, and consumption or production activities that result in indirect costs (social costs exceeding private costs) are called *negative* externalities. The terms positive and negative stem from indirect benefits usually being considered a good (positive) attribute and indirect costs being considered a bad (negative) attribute.

Externalities cause problems in achieving efficient resource allocation because the private market system takes into account only private benefits and costs; net social benefits are not maximized, because indirect costs or benefits are excluded in making resource allocation decisions. Consumption decisions are assumed to be made by individuals on the basis of their own (private) benefits and costs.[1] Thus, demand in a market system reflects the consumer's net private benefits and ignores any indirect costs or benefits of consumption. The same is true of production decisions, so that supply in a market system does not reflect any indirect costs or benefits of production. Although externalities may exist in the consumption or production of almost any commodity, only those externalities that result in substantial indirect costs or benefits (and resulting substantial divergence from the efficient level of output) are of concern. For example, if Jones, your next-door neighbor, has a swimming pool installed in his back yard and the only externality is that the swimming pool makes you jealous because you cannot "keep up with the Joneses," the indirect cost would not be considered significant by most people. In fact, if the net private benefit to Jones were less than the indirect cost to you, then you could probably bribe Jones into not installing the

[1]This statement does not imply that individuals *never* take into consideration the effects of their actions on others. Many social norms have developed precisely to avoid externality problems. For example, because of these norms, most people would not force themselves to the front of a line of elderly ladies waiting to buy tickets to a wrestling match, even though private costs (excluding guilt) would be lower since time waiting in line would be saved.

pool. Otherwise, installing the pool is probably efficient in the sense in which we are using the term.[2] On the other hand, if the pool is operated in such a way as to be a safety hazard to neighborhood children, a significant externality may exist.

Positive or negative externalities often have widespread geographic effects for which the producer or consumer is not held accountable. Consumption or production in one geographic area may "spill out" benefits or costs into other areas, and these other areas, in turn, experience "spill ins" of benefits or costs. Spillovers frequently result from governmental decisions: a mosquito-control program in one area reduces mosquito bites to residents in another area; the traditionally low level of education in some parts of the South affects residents of other states through migration of poorly educated southern graduates to these states.

Positive externalities   The production or consumption of many commodities generates substantial indirect benefits. For example, fire protection for your neighbor's house reduces the chance that your house will catch fire. Improvement of your neighbor's property, in some cases, increases the value of your property.

Figure 4-1 portrays a situation in which a positive externality exists. The commodity in question is the number of people in a community vaccinated against polio (one vaccination per person). The vaccination of others reduces your exposure to disease and thus results in an indirect benefit. The marginal social benefit (MSB) and marginal social cost (MSC) curves for polio vaccinations are defined as before and are drawn as straight lines for simplicity. The positive externality is the indirect benefit to others from the vaccination of one individual, in other words, the divergence between private and social benefits. The vertical distance between the MPB and MSB curves represents the additional (marginal) indirect benefits received as a result of each vaccination. MSB would equal MPB at a quantity where (almost) everyone were vaccinated. As can be seen in Figure 4-1, the efficient number of vaccinations (the output where MSB = MSC) is 10,000. Thus, net social benefits are maximized at 10,000 vaccinations, but the private market system provides only 6,000—the quantity where MPB = MPC. (Remember that MPC can be thought of as supply and MPB as demand.) The equilibrium market price will be $7 and 6,000 units will be sold, since only at this price and quantity does the quantity people want to buy equal the quantity others want to sell.

Obviously, the existence of this positive externality results in the market-determined number of vaccinations being insufficient to maximize net social benefits. If these vaccinations were to be pro-

[2]See R. Coase, "The Problem of Social Cost," *Journal of Law and Economics* (1960).

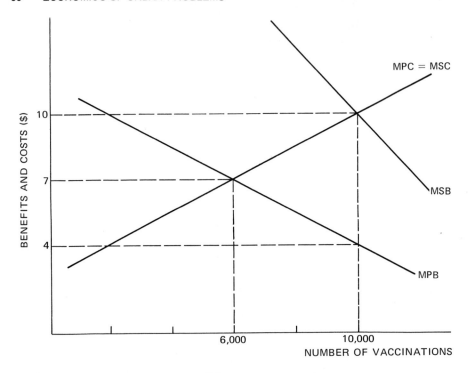

Figure 4-1: Positive Externalities

vided through the private market, the public sector could supplement or subsidize the private market in order to reach a quantity of 10,000. For example, the market price of a vaccination could be set at $4, with a subsidy of $6 per unit payable to either the producer or consumer of the vaccination. At this price, people would be willing to buy the efficient quantity. The subsidy could be financed through general taxation or some tax designed to place the burden on those receiving the indirect benefits, if this were feasible. Alternatively, vaccinations could be provided directly by the government, charging $4 and making up the difference out of tax revenues. If the price is set below $4, people will want to buy more than the efficient quantity, and this might not be any more efficient than the private market solution. If the price is set at $4, through either government provision or subsidy, then the costs borne by the consumers will have fallen to $4 from $7 and they will maximize their net private benefits at the efficient level of 10,000 rather than at the 6,000 that results when the market price is $7.

In general, if a positive externality results from production or consumption of a commodity, the amount of resources allocated to the production of the commodity by the private market will result in a smaller than efficient output. Stated briefly, positive externalities lead to underproduction (inefficiently low production).[3]

Public goods Suppose a commodity were produced that generated practically all indirect benefits. In that case, MPB might lie far below MSB (there would be a very large divergence between private and social benefits), and the private market system would obviously fail to provide efficient amounts. As an extreme case, one could consider a commodity that was almost a pure positive externality. Such a commodity is called a pure public good. It is difficult to discover clear-cut cases of pure public goods, but many commodities generating large indirect benefits (denoted public goods rather than *pure* public goods) are much like this extreme case; thus, it is useful to study the concept. The term "public good" is used because many commodities that generate indirect benefits are produced in the public sector (by the government) and also because these indirect benefits are received by the public as a group—they are collectively consumed. Collective consumption means that the same amount of a commodity is available to all members of a community, and consumption by one person does not reduce the amount of the commodity available to others. Each unit of the commodity is jointly consumed by many persons at the same time. One example of a public good is national defense. If it is provided, everyone derives the benefits of it, and benefits received by one person do not detract from the benefits received by others.

It is important to keep in mind that public goods are unlike private goods. Private goods such as an apple, can be simultaneously consumed by relatively few people, and each one's consumption reduces the amount left for others. A public good is like radio; if I turn on my receiver, no one else is affected with respect to his ability to listen to the same radio station on his receiver. One way to express the essence of public good is that, if you use it, you do not use it up in the sense that less is available for others. Once a public good is produced, the fact that the same quantity is available to all implies that an individual can use it without choosing to pay for it. Therefore, there is little incentive for an individual to voluntarily contribute toward the costs of provision, since he cannot be excluded from consumption whether he contributes or not. Even if you put a person in jail or otherwise try to physically prohibit his consumption, he cannot be excluded from receiving the benefits of a public good such as national defense. In the case of private goods (such as a candy bar), if you do not contribute by

[3]In the example just given, it may bother some readers that we assumed MPC = MSC (i.e., no indirect costs). This was done in order to isolate the effects of positive externalities, and a similar assumption will be made in the subsequent discussion of negative externalities. It is common in all sciences to make assumptions of this nature, at least implicitly. To estimate the effects of gravity, for example, one would want to rule out such things as high winds, effect of the medium through which the object was falling, and obstructions. This is all that is being done here.

paying the purchase price to the retailer, you do not get to consume the good. This characteristic difference between public and private goods is important in determining how you maximize your net private benefits and how society achieves efficiency.

To take a nonurban example, suppose that, if a flood control dam were built in a farming area, farmers would benefit to the extent that the dam would increase net social benefits. If the dam is to be paid for voluntarily, then many farmers will reason that: (1) their individual contributions will not determine whether or not the dam will be built, and (2) they will thus maximize net private benefits by not contributing to it, even though it will give them sizable benefits. A farmer could claim that he would receive no benefits from the dam (refuse to reveal his preferences), regardless of his true benefits, and yet not be excluded from the benefits when they occur. If many farmers felt the same way, the dam might not be built because not enough funds could be raised. Thus, an efficient project would not be undertaken. Often this problem is overcome by collective activity—voting that the dam be built and taxing everyone regardless of professed benefits. This is a major reason for governmental provision of public goods, or goods that generate substantial positive externalities. One might notice that the problem of revealing preferences is similar to the reason why many people do not vote in elections. One vote usually does not decide an election, but many people thinking in this way can lead to undesirable outcomes.

Ideally, to provide efficient quantities of public goods, one should determine the total of the individual benefits for each unit of the good and add these benefits together at each unit in order to arrive at MSB. If each person were to pay a price equal to his marginal private benefit, then the total of these prices would equal MSB; if the efficient quantity were attained, the total of the individual prices would also equal MSC, since MSB = MSC. This would involve charging different prices to different individuals on the basis of marginal benefits received, providing an incentive to conceal true preferences. If an individual received benefits from the first seven units of the public good produced and if the price were equal to marginal benefit, this would imply a zero price to him. In practice one might think of special assessments (e.g., taxes that depend on the number of feet of frontage of property owned) as crude attempts to exact prices according to marginal benefits, but these show the difficulties involved in actually determining the pricing of public-type goods.

If little or nothing of a public good is provided, some people may be induced to reveal some part of their preferences so that at least some amount will be forthcoming. This becomes a problem of individual strategy and the efficient output is unlikely to be obtained. For example, an AM radio station in an urban area, which played classical music, found that sponsors were unwilling to support it unless the format was changed to popular music. After a period of time, the station made a plea to listeners to contribute $12 per year to allow it to stay on the air as a classical station. It claimed to need 3,000 subscribers to cover operating losses, and it did temporarily induce enough people to contribute. After a few months, however, subscribers dwindled, and the station changed its format, abandoning classical music. While a radio station is a private good from the point of view of the station owners and sponsors, it is a public good from the listener's viewpoint. Many listeners probably felt that their failure to make individual contributions would not be the straw that would break the camel's back, and "knew" that they could continue to listen while paying nothing. Ultimately, enough thought this way to force the station to abandon its format.

In conclusion, the private market system cannot efficiently allocate resources to the provision of public goods. Market failure results because the private market system depends on preference revelation and there is little incentive to reveal preferences for public goods. Because of this, many commodities that generate substantial positive externalities, which are collectively consumed, are provided by the public sector with allocation decisions made through the political process. However, the political process has no proven mechanism to induce persons to reveal their true preferences for public goods. Thus, political decisions are imperfect with respect to efficient allocation of resources to such commodities. Benefit-cost analysis, discussed later in this chapter, is one attempt to improve the allocative efficiency of public decision-making.

Negative externalities   The production or consumption of many commodities generate substantial indirect costs. For example, if you are a nonsmoker, consumers of cigars may impose a negative externality on you, especially in a small, crowded room or automobile. Additional autos on the streets during rush hours increase your travel time. Additional steel production can lead to greater air pollution. These are a few examples of private consumption and production that decrease the level of satisfaction or benefits to others.

Figure 4-2 portrays a situation in which a negative externality, water pollution, exists. A chemical plant making fertilizer dumps its waste material into a river, imposing an expense on downstream users, say paper mills, who must purify the water before reuse. Because the private market system does not allocate the use of the river, the chemical company has avoided the expense of water purification by dumping waste into the river; thus, its private costs are less than the social costs, and a quantity of fertilizer greater than the efficient amount is produced. At the same time, the production costs of the paper mills are increased by the cost of water purification and an amount of paper below the efficient amount is produced because of

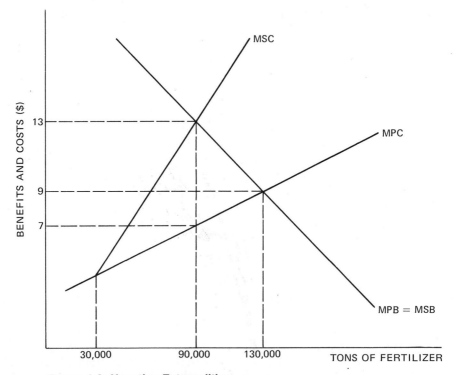

Figure 4-2: Negative Externalities

these extra costs. The water pollution caused by the chemical company may also reduce benefits received by individuals who use the river for recreational purposes, such as swimming and fishing, or increase the costs to municipalities who use the river for their water supply. The negative externality from pollution is the indirect cost— the divergence between private costs and social costs. The *vertical* distance between the MPC curve and the MCS curve in Figure 4-2 represents the additional (marginal) indirect costs resulting from each additional ton of fertilizer produced. Below a certain level of production (30,000 tons), there may be no indirect costs, if the water quality is not reduced enough to impose indirect costs on other users of the river. However, as production increases, the indirect costs or negative externalities grow rapidly. It is possible that production of even one ton could cause negative externalities, but even in this case, MSC and MPC would probably diverge as production increased (implying greater and greater marginal indirect costs).

As can be seen in Figure 4-2, the efficient number of tons of fertilizer (that output where MSB = MSC) is 90,000 tons. Thus, the production of 90,000 tons would maximize net social benefits, but the company will produce to the point where it maximizes profits (that output where MPB = MPC), or an output of 130,000 tons. It should be noted that at the efficient level of output there are still indirect costs, but the marginal benefits society places on additional production warrants incurring them. Thus, there exists an *efficient amount of negative externalities*. Further reduction from this level would lower net social benefits. A similar result held in the positive externality case. The mere existence of positive externalities does not imply that they should be maximized, but rather that they should be taken into account. By the same token, negative externalities should not always be eliminated, but rather reduced to the efficient level. A useful analogy would be the use of drugs to treat illness. The mere existence of side effects should not lead us to ban the drug (really all drugs) but rather to consider whether potential side effects are worth putting up with.

In general, if a negative externality results from the production or consumption of a commodity, the amount of resources allocated to the production of the commodity by the private market system will result in a level of production greater than the efficient level. Thus, some form of intervention into the private market system is required to achieve the efficient level of output. Later chapters will show in detail some ways of doing this; generally they amount to either prohibiting production beyond the efficient point or raising the private costs to the decision-maker so that he will voluntarily choose the efficient level of output. An example of the latter policy would be to impose a tax equal to the difference between MPC and MSC. Thus, the new MPC would coincide with MSC and the producer would then maximize net private benefits (profits) at the efficient level of production.

The Problem of Monopoly Power

In a well-functioning private market system, competition among large numbers of sellers leads to a uniform price over which individual sellers have no control. A competitor can sell all he wants at the market price (or below it if he chooses to be irrational), but finds that at higher prices he can sell nothing. Suppose a cattleman takes his stock to an auction and refuses to sell at less than $65 per hundredweight, while the market price of similar beef is $40. Clearly he would sell nothing, since buyers could easily buy from other sellers at $40. On the other hand, if there were only one seller (a monopolist), prices could be raised to $65 without a complete loss of sales. In general, smaller quantities would be sold at higher prices (the demand curve would not be vertical).

Technically, monopoly means one seller, but many firms who are not monopolists in this sense do have some degree of monopoly power, that is, they can sell successively smaller quantities at successively higher prices. Looked at from another angle, if a firm with monopoly power wants to sell more units, it must lower its price. This leads to a situation of inefficiency much like the case of a positive externality, as the following example illustrates. Suppose a firm is currently selling fifty units of a commodity at $4.95, and that, to sell the fifty-first unit, it must cut its price to $4.90. The firm will receive $4.90 additional revenue from the fifty-first unit, but this additional revenue will be partially offset by the lower price (5¢ lower) on the previously existing fifty units. Total revenue (price times quantity) will increase from $247.50 to $249.90, an increase of $2.40. Thus, the marginal private benefit (sometimes referred to as marginal revenue) to the monopolist is only $2.40, compared with a marginal social benefit of $4.90 (the marginal benefit to society is equal to the amount someone is willing to pay for the marginal unit). This is exactly parallel to the situation of a positive externality—MSB exceeds MPB. Therefore, monopoly (or monopoly power) is inefficient because it leads to a quantity less than that at which net social benefits are maximized. Monopolists are usually subject to criticism because they charge "high" prices in order to maximize their profits. Here, they are seen as being inefficient because they sell too little, and inefficiently small amounts of resources are allocated to the production of the monopolized commodities.

Monopoly provides a justification for public intervention in order to achieve the efficient level of output. Antitrust legislation (such as the Sherman and Clayton Acts) makes specified monopolistic practices illegal and is designed to promote a greater degree of competition. A monopoly situation may be justified, in cases such as water or sewer utilities, where the production costs from having duplicate water and sewer lines competing for customers in the same neighborhood would be higher than the production costs of having a single supplier of such services. In these cases of "natural monopoly," public intervention usually takes the form of regulation through such institutions as public service commissions, which are responsible for setting prices and otherwise regulating the monopoly.

The Problem of Imperfect Information

Individuals making decisions in the market, in their roles as producers or consumers, may not have full knowledge of the private benefits and costs involved in the choices made. In such cases, the maximization of *apparent* net private benefits results in quantities being produced or consumed which are not the same ones that would result from maximization of *actual* net private benefits. Thus, the market fails to achieve an efficient allocation of resources when information on the costs and benefits involved is highly imperfect, because the apparent costs and benefits are different from the actual costs and benefits; they could not equal the social benefits and costs even if no indirect costs or benefits existed. In other words, even if actual MPB = MSB and actual MPC = MSC, individual decision-makers are not maximizing net private benefits subject to the true MPBs and MPCs. As a result net social benefits are not maximized when imperfect information exists.

As an example of the problem of imperfect information, consider the maximization of net private benefits of a cigarette smoker shown in Figure 4-3. The MPC curve is the market price of cigarettes. The MPB (Apparent) curve, representing the apparent marginal private benefits of additional cigarettes smoked per day, is assumed to over-state the actual satisfaction received, because of the smoker's lack of knowledge as to some of the negative attributes of smoking cigarettes. Basing his decision on apparent benefits, the individual in Figure 4-3 maximizes net private benefits by smoking forty cigarettes per day. However, the actual benefits of cigarette smoking have been over-stated, because the smoker has not considered (that is, has no know-ledge of) the increased probability of incurring such respiratory dis-eases as lung cancer and emphysema, which result in decreased life expectancy, from smoking large amounts of cigarettes over a period of time. The MPB (Actual) curve in Figure 4-3, representing actual marginal private benefits, is assumed to represent the reduced pre-sent value of satisfaction received from smoking cigarettes due to

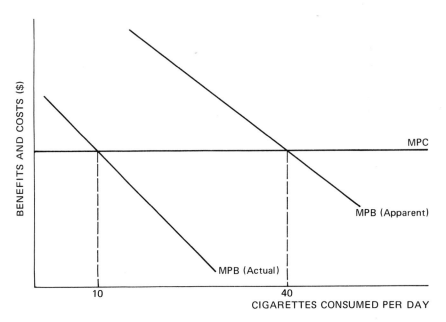

Figure 4-3: Maximization of Apparent Versus Actual Net Private Benefits

potential future impaired health. Basing his decision on actual benefits, the individual in Figure 4-3 would maximize net private benefits by smoking ten cigarettes per day.

In order to achieve efficiency in instances in which information on costs and benefits is imperfect, better information must be provided to decision-makers. For example, in recent years the federal government has assumed an active role in providing consumer information on various products (such as the relationship between cigarette smoking and health problems) and fraudulent business practices. The role of programs of this nature in remedying market failure attributable to imperfect information will be discussed at various points in the remainder of the book.

Income Distribution and the Efficient Allocation of Resources

The analysis in this chapter has so far considered inefficiencies in the allocation of resources. The distribution of income (purchasing power) among members of the community has been taken as given, and efficient allocation of resources in that situation was determined. However, this income distribution may not be acceptable—society may not consider it equitable or "fair" that some families do not have enough income to buy milk and bread for their children while others can afford to go skiing in Switzerland during the Christmas holidays.

A useful way of looking at the distribution of income among members of society is in terms of the percentage of total income received by various groups. Equality of income distribution relates to the percentage of total income received by the lowest x percent of households versus the percentage of total income received by the highest x percent of households. This has changed somewhat in recent years, as shown by Table 4-1, which indicates that the income of the lowest 20 percent (fifth) of families increased from 5.0 to 5.5 percent of total income between 1947 and 1970, while the proportion of total income received by the highest 5 percent of families decreased from 17.2 to 14.4 percent. Of course, this is a relative measure; the absolute average incomes (stated in 1971 purchasing-power dollars) received by families of different income ranks are also shown in Table 4-1 and they indicate that the real incomes (purchasing power) of families in all income ranks increased significantly between 1947 and 1970.

There is an infinite number of potential income distributions. Correspondingly, there is an infinite number of potential efficient allocations of resources, because there is one efficient allocation of resources for each possible distribution of income. Many of the possibilities can be ruled out as unlikely to be desired by society. For

INCOME RANK	SHARE OF TOTAL INCOME (PERCENT)		AVERAGE INCOME (1971 CONSTANT DOLLARS)	
	1947	1970	1947	1970
Lowest fifth	5.0	5.5	$ 1,616	$ 3,245
Second fifth	11.8	12.0	3,812	7,080
Middle fifth	17.0	17.4	5,491	10,266
Fourth fifth	23.1	23.5	7,462	13,864
Highest fifth	43.0	41.6	13,955	24,543
Top 5 percent	17.2	14.4	22,611	33,983

Table 4-1: Distribution of Family Incomes in the United States, 1947 and 1970
SOURCES: U.S. Bureau of the Census, *Current Population Reports,* Series P-60, No. 80, "Income in 1970 of Families and Persons in the United States," Government Printing Office, Washington, 1971, p. 28; Office of Management and Budget, *Social Indicators, 1973,* Government Printing Office, Washington, 1973, p. 179.

example, it is doubtful whether society could reach a consensus on relegating all present millionaires to poverty status while choosing from among the poor who should take the millionaires' places. Generally, society may wish to make incomes more evenly distributed, or eliminate poverty, or redistribute income to certain groups, or make the rich less rich; but this limits the number of potential income distributions and corresponding efficient allocations of resources we need consider. Once a particular income distribution prevails, then resources can be efficiently allocated. If society dislikes those results, then income can be redistributed and another efficient allocation determined. The main point is that efficiency need not be sacrificed because of equity considerations. Equity considerations should be used to determine the desired income distribution, and then efficiency considerations can receive attention.

An Example

A very simple example is provided to illustrate the relationship between income distribution and the resulting efficient allocation of resources. Assume that there are three individuals in society (A, B, and C), no externalities or other cases of market failure exist, only two commodities are produced and consumed—candy bars and whiskey—and the total community income is $382. The positions of the individual benefit (demand) curves for candy bars and whiskey are determined in part by individual tastes (preferences) and in part by the incomes of the individuals. If two individuals have identical preferences for whiskey and candy bars and identical incomes, both individuals' MPB curves for both whiskey and candy bars will be identical. Subject to the market price of the two goods, both would maximize net private benefits from consumption of identical amounts of whiskey and candy bars. Starting from this position, in general, stronger preferences for a good or higher income would shift the individual's MPB curve to the right, reflecting a greater demand for the commodity. Similarly, weaker preferences or a lower income would shift the individual's MPB curve to the left, reflecting a lower demand for the good. Each individual maximizes his net private benefits by purchasing some quantity of the two goods, given the market price of the goods and the individual's income and preferences (as reflected in the position of his individual benefit curves).

In the initial situation, assume that the $382 of community income is distributed as shown in Table 4-2 and that the marginal social cost of candy bars is 10¢ and the marginal social cost of whiskey is $5 per bottle, which are the respective market prices of the two goods. Given the distribution of income to each person, the three individuals maximize their net private benefits by purchasing and consuming the amounts of whiskey and candy bars indicated. With this distribution of income, the efficient allocation of resources results in the production and consumption of 70 candy bars and 75 bottles of whiskey.

Now suppose that the community, through the political process, decides that this distribution is "unfair" and redistributes income more equally, so that the resulting income distribution is that shown in Table 4-3. Individual C has the strongest preference for candy bars, since in the initial situation of Table 4-2 he had the lowest income but maximized his net private benefits by consuming more candy bars than either A or B. With the redistribution of income in Table 4-3, C's income has been substantially increased; thus, one would expect that his demand for candy bars would increase greatly and his demand for whiskey would increase slightly. On the other hand, individual A has strong preferences for whiskey, but his income has been substantially reduced; thus, a large decrease in demand for whiskey and a smaller decrease in demand for candy bars is expected. Assume that the MSC of candy bars is still 10¢ and the MSC of whiskey $5. Given the new

		NUMBER OF CANDY BARS		BOTTLES OF WHISKEY	
INDIVIDUAL	INCOME	Quantity	Total cost	Quantity	Total cost
A	$251	10	$1	50	$250
B	102	20	2	20	100
C	29	40	4	5	25
	382	70	7	75	375

Table 4-2: Initial Distribution of Income and Resulting Efficient Allocation of Resources

		NUMBER OF CANDY BARS		BOTTLES OF WHISKEY	
INDIVIDUAL	INCOME	Quantity	Total cost	Quantity	Total cost
A	$135.50	5	$ 0.50	27	$135
B	127.50	25	2.50	25	125
C	119.00	240	24.00	19	95
	382.00	270	27.00	71	355

Table 4-3: Redistribution of Income and Resulting Efficient Allocation of Resources

distribution of income, each individual maximizes his net private benefits by consuming the quantities indicated in Table 4-3. The efficient allocation of resources leads to the production of 270 candy bars and 71 bottles of whiskey. Thus, 75 bottles of whiskey and 70 candy bars is the efficient allocation of resources when income is distributed as in Table 4-2, while 71 bottles of whiskey and 270 candy bars is the efficient allocation of resources when income is distributed as in Table 4-3.

Cash Versus In-Kind Income Redistribution

Income can be redistributed in money or in kind (goods and services), although care needs to be exercised with in-kind programs. An in-kind program can have the same effect as a cash program, if the person is given goods he would already be buying. For example, suppose that, starting with the initial distribution of income in Table 4-2, individual C is given a bottle of whiskey. He will not, in general, buy the same quantities of whiskey and candy bars as before and consume the additional bottle. What will happen is that he will discover that he can have what he had before (five bottles) by buying only four bottles of whiskey, and, in addition, he has $5 more to spend. To insure that his consumption of whiskey increases to six bottles, we need to force him to consume six bottles, or prove that he is still buying five bottles, or sell him for $25 a voucher (coupon) that can be redeemed at a liquor store, good for six bottles of whiskey (that is, having a market value of $30). If this is not done, some of the increase in consumption will come in the form of candy bars. If the proper restrictions are put on distribution in kind, then society can increase a person's consumption of a particular good at lower cost by a distribution in kind rather than a cash grant (which will be spent in accordance with the consumer's demands and not necessarily all on the commodity desired by society). An additional problem with in-kind transfers is that the recipient has an incentive to sell the good received and convert it into cash. This may be one of the reasons why services are often provided rather than goods, since services cannot be resold. It is difficult to resell a medical examination, for example.

In-kind programs have also been objected to because they violate consumer sovereignty—the individual's freedom to maximize net private benefits subject to his income and preferences. It is generally true that an in-kind program (one designed not to be equivalent to a cash program) will provide the recipient with a lower level of benefits than an equivalent cash grant. Providing $20 worth of additional food to a family and requiring that pre-existing purchases of food not be cut would be an example of such a program. The family would derive benefits from the additional food, but might derive greater benefits from $20 worth of something else, perhaps badly needed dental care. The idea of consumer sovereignty is that the consumer is the best judge of his own benefits, so that a cash grant is preferable. If cash rather than food were given above, then the dental care could be purchased. It should be noted that many in-kind programs are designed precisely to violate consumer sovereignty, or to determine how the recipient should spend any aid received. It is felt by many people that providing cash to poor families will not necessarily help the children in those families (e.g., by buying more milk for them), but may go instead for liquor, presumably consumed by the parents.

If externalities are considered, then it may sometimes be efficient to violate consumer sovereignty. The consumption of certain items may generate positive externalities, and thus be underconsumed by the poor. An example is housing, which if consumed in small amounts may be unsightly to others and breed rats and disease. The consumption of food by others might not generate positive externalities but the consumption of additional housing might. Thus, the goal of a program might be not only to add to the well-being of the poor (an equity consideration) but to generate positive externalities to the nonpoor (an efficiency consideration), who are providing the funds for the transfer of income. Thus, "taxpayer sovereignty" often supersedes consumer sovereignty in the legislation of income redistribution programs.

Equity in Government Programs

Through taxation and expenditures, government programs play a major role in determining the distribution of income. Equity implies a "fair" distribution of income. Since ideas of what is fair vary among individuals, equity lies in the realm of subjective value judgments. A fair distribution of income, in turn, depends on a fair distribution of the costs and benefits among members of the community. The accepted standards of equity are determined by the community or its political representatives and obviously involve value judgments. In this context, one cannot "prove" that one distribution of income is "better" than another without interjecting personal value judgments.

Horizontal and Vertical Equity

There are two general standards that relate to equity: horizontal equity and vertical equity. In order to avoid confusion (and to follow the historical sequence of the ideas), these concepts will initially be defined as they apply to taxation and then extended to include the distribution of the benefits of government programs. A tax or other governmental levy achieves *horizontal equity* when those in the same position or circumstance pay the same amount of tax (equal treatment of equals). For *vertical equity*, taxes should differ as position or circumstance differs (unequal treatment of unequals). To make these equity concepts operational, position or circumstance (who is equal) must be defined. There are two ways of doing this, known as the *benefit* principle and the *ability-to-pay* principle. Under the benefit principle, those who receive equal benefits are defined as equals; thus, horizontal equity under the benefit principle requires that those receiving equal benefits pay the same tax. Agreement on who is equal under the ability-to-pay principle is more difficult, since a case may be made for many measures (such as income, consumption, wealth, etc.) and each contains elements that appeal to different values. The most often used measure of position is income, which will be used in the following discussion and the remainder of the book. Thus, as it is used here, the ability-to-pay principle could be termed the income principle, and horizontal equity requires those with the same income to pay the same tax.

Vertical equity under the benefit principle requires that those who receive greater benefits pay a greater amount of tax. Vertical equity under the ability-to-pay (income) principle requires that those with higher incomes pay higher taxes. Table 4-4 shows this simplified way of viewing the principles of equity in taxation, so the reader will have the basic concepts in mind. Later, these simple concepts will have to be modified to some extent, but for now they are adequate.

The Benefit Principle

The benefit principle states that individuals should pay for governmental goods and services in accordance with benefits received. If the commodity has the characteristics of a private good (such as candy bars), the same per unit price is charged to all, but the individual is free to select the quantity he wishes. Those who select the same amount (receive equal benefits) pay the same total and per unit amount, which achieves horizontal equity. If the commodity has characteristics of a public good, then the same quantity is available to all, but people derive different benefits from this quantity. Horizontal equity under the benefit principle is achieved in this case by having those individuals who derive equal marginal benefits pay equal amounts for provision of the public good; vertical equity is met if those receiving greater benefits pay greater amounts. In the case of a private good, vertical equity is met by those who consume more units of the commodity (receive greater benefits) paying more in total, although the per unit price is the same to all consumers. In the case of public goods, individuals receiving greater marginal benefits pay a greater amount for the quantity that is provided and equally available to all. Thus, the application of the benefit principle leads to an efficient allocation of resources in the government sector, because each individual is able to maximize net private benefits by paying for the efficient quantity (which maximizes net social benefits) on the basis of benefits received.

Market pricing as a means of cost sharing is identical with the benefit principle. Applying the benefit principle in the public sector to taxation is a form of pricing, so the effect tends toward the private market result—if there is no market failure, the benefit principle of taxation achieves the efficient level of output. However, there are serious problems involved in the pricing of some government goods and services. Consumers are unwilling and/or unable to reveal preferences when there is collective consumption, and those who do not use the service may still benefit without purchasing it. Moreover, the benefit principle cannot be applied to programs designed to redistribute income. For example, welfare recipients could not be taxed on the basis of benefits received, since they would be required to return their welfare checks to the government. The benefit principle is still useful in the case of "private" goods and services provided by the government. Charges can be, and sometimes are, levied for provision of water, sewage disposal, and garbage collection, and for the use of public facilities such as recreation areas. Such user charges could be greatly expanded in the public sector, thereby improving resource allocation. (This subject is treated in Chapter 15.)

	BENEFIT PRINCIPLE	ABILITY-TO-PAY PRINCIPLE
HORIZONTAL EQUITY	Those receiving the same benefits pay the same tax	Those with the same incomes pay the same tax
VERTICAL EQUITY	Those receiving greater benefits pay greater taxes	Those with higher incomes pay higher taxes

Table 4-4: Concepts of Equity in Taxation

The Ability-to-Pay Principle

At present, the benefit principle plays a minor role in taxation. The United States tax system is appreciably more influenced by the ability-to-pay principle. Although the benefit principle of taxation can be based on an economic criterion (efficiency in the allocation of resources), no such criterion can be applied to the ability-to-pay principle. Ability-to-pay taxation may be considered an attempt to redistribute income through the tax system and is based on value judgments rather than upon any economic criterion.[4]

As stated earlier, the ability-to-pay principle as used here could be termed the income principle. The determination of horizontal equity presents no problem if income can be accurately determined: those with equal incomes pay equal taxes. The tax rate structure that meets society's conception of vertical equity must somehow be determined through the political process and obviously involves value judgments. Stating that those with higher incomes should pay higher taxes does not settle the question of how *much* more. This is the problem of vertical equity under the ability-to-pay principle and relates to the tax structure.

Tax rate structure   Rate structure is defined here as the relationship between income and the tax paid. A structure is *proportional* if the same percentage of income is taken away at all levels of income. A *progressive* rate structure is one which taxes away an increasing percentage of income as income rises, and a *regressive* rate structure takes away a decreasing percentage of income as income rises.[5] In other words, a proportional tax leaves the income distribution unchanged (those receiving 10 percent of the income before the tax will also receive 10 percent of what is left after the tax), while a progressive tax reduces income inequality and a regressive tax increases income inequality. One useful measure of the degree of inequality in the income distribution is the proportion of total income received by various groups. For example, in Table 4-2, where there are only three members of society, the lowest one-third of all individuals grouped by income (individual C in this case) receives about 8 percent ($29/ $382) of the society's total income, while the highest one-third of all

---

[4]There is another view, that redistributing income is a kind of public good that people pay for through the tax system. For example, poverty alleviation could be considered to generate substantial positive externalities and might therefore be justified on efficiency grounds. Here, income redistribution will be considered as an equity policy, and not as a policy that moves the economy toward efficiency.

[5]The term "regressive" is used in a technical way here and should be thought of as a descriptive term devoid of emotional content. Any emotional connotations of the term should be set aside if they interfere with understanding its technical meaning.

individuals grouped by income (individual A) receives about 66 percent ($251/$382) of the society's total income. The income distribution in Table 4-3 is said to be more equal in this sense, since the group with the lowest one-third of income receives about 31 percent ($119/$382) of society's total income and the group with the highest one-third of income receives about 35 percent ($135.50/$382.00).

Table 4-5 shows three taxes: tax A is proportional, tax B regressive, and tax C progressive. Note that the type of tax is determined only by the percentage of income paid as tax, not by the total tax paid. With all three taxes, the total amount paid in taxes increases as income increases, but the characteristic that makes tax B regressive is that income increases faster than the tax, so the percentage paid as income increases falls even though the amount of tax increases.

The vertical equity standard requires society to decide how a taxpayer's ability to pay taxes changes with his income level. Society must determine not only whether the tax structure should be progressive or regressive, but also how progressive or how regressive. If the consensus of society is that the income distribution should be more equal, then regressive rate structures should be avoided, while progressive structures are encouraged. It must be emphasized that a statement that one rate structure is "better" than another is a value judgment. To say a regressive tax is inequitable is true only if society has decided that income inequality resulting from the operation of the private market system should be lessened. In other words, economists can objectively determine whether a given tax is regressive, but society or its representatives must subjectively decide whether that is good or bad. An individual can prefer progressive taxes because he prefers less inequality in income distribution, but this feeling is a value judgment on his part and should be recognized as such.

Tax incidence   An additional point on equity and the distribution of the tax burden should be made. This is the tax *incidence*, or who ultimately bears the burden of the tax. A tax may be levied on an individual or business firm, but the actual burden of the tax may be

	TAX A		TAX B		TAX C	
INCOME LEVEL	Amount	Percent of income	Amount	Percent of income	Amount	Percent of income
$ 1,000	$ 10	1	$10	1	$ 10	1
2,500	25	1	20	0.8	30	1.2
7,500	75	1	40	0.53	100	1.33
15,000	150	1	70	0.47	300	2

Table 4-5: Tax-Rate Structure: Taxes as a Percentage of Income

shifted or transferred. The final resting place of a tax is called its incidence. Since we are concerned with the burdens on various income groups, a table, such as Table 4-5, can be constructed to indicate amounts and percentages of income paid as tax in terms of ultimate incidence. If the numbers in Table 4-5 had indicated actual tax incidence, then the table could have been labeled as the incidence of taxes A, B, and C. The problem is that, if the government levies a tax on certain groups, these groups do not necessarily bear the burden of the tax, because of shifting. This can be forward shifting (a tax passed on to a consumer as a higher retail price) or backward shifting (offering lower wages to employees as a result of a tax). Thus, shifting can effect an entirely different distribution of the tax burden from that indicated by who pays the tax levies initially.

Application of equity concepts to distribution of benefits and net benefits   The concept of incidence can be applied to the distribution of benefits as well as costs (taxes). For example, the benefits of a government program can be classified according to the income groups receiving the benefits, to determine whether the benefit distribution is progressive, proportional, or regressive (vertical equity) and whether those in the same income group are receiving the same benefits (horizontal equity). This broadens the concepts of horizontal and vertical equity introduced earlier to include benefits as well as costs (taxes). In fact, benefits and taxes can be considered at the same time in analyzing the overall impact of a program on income distribution. Net benefits (benefits minus taxes) could be grouped according to income levels, and a program financed by a regressive tax might turn out to be highly progressive, if the benefits were distributed in an extremely progressive way. As an example, Table 4-6 uses the regressive tax shown in Table 4-5 and considers benefits received from a program financed by this tax. The overall impact of the program is progressive with respect to the income distribution. Also, if, in fact, each household with an income of $1,000 receives net benefits of $60

	BENEFITS		TAXES (COSTS)		NET BENEFITS	
INCOME LEVEL	Amount	Percent of income	Amount	Percent of income	Amount	Percent of income
$ 1,000	$70	7	$10	1	$60	6
2,500	40	1.6	20	0.8	20	0.8
7,500	20	0.27	40	0.53	−20	−0.27
15,000	10	0.07	70	0.47	−60	−0.4

Table 4-6: Incidence of Net Benefits of a Program

and the net benefits received by all households in any other income group are equal, then the program can be said to achieve horizontal equity—households with equal incomes receive equal net benefits.

Equity Versus Efficiency: A Concluding Note

Most urban problems arise because of either (1) cases of market failure that result in inefficient allocation of resources by the private market system, or (2) violations of the community's standards of equity. In the first case, the problems are due to efficiency considerations, and in the second case they are due to equity considerations. The remainder of this book analyzes specific urban problems with respect to equity and efficiency. It is critical that the reader be able to make the distinction between these two concepts. Many proposals for "solving" urban problems are couched in terms of equity considerations, when the actual problem is one of resource misallocation. It must be remembered that there is an efficient allocation of resources for every possible distribution of income among members of society. If efficiency is achieved and society does not like the outcome, then income should be redistributed and a new, but also efficient, allocation of resources attained. Many proposals which may achieve greater equity do so at the expense of efficiency, lowering the total amount of benefits available to apportion among the members of society. It is both possible and desirable to achieve goals of equity and efficiency simultaneously. We may observe billions of bottles of liquor being consumed while people are starving to death, and yet have efficient allocation of resources. This is an equity problem, not an efficiency problem, since there may be no market failure in the production of liquor. If income could be redistributed to the point where society felt equity was achieved, then resources could again be efficiently allocated; in this new allocation we would expect to find less whiskey and more bread being produced.

Benefit-Cost Analysis

Benefit-cost analysis (or cost-benefit analysis as it is sometimes called) is a tool for practical economic decision-making. It is a technique for evaluating the relative attractiveness of alternative uses of resources when resource allocation decisions must be made outside the market system. Since resources are limited, society must choose among various courses of action; therefore, alternatives always exist. For example, in the construction of a highway, an alternative which could be considered is nonconstruction, that is, the status quo. In practice, projects are usually evaluated in reference to the status quo, although this is not always made explicit. *All* alternatives should be considered, such as whether to build a two-, three-, or four-lane highway, or perhaps a limited-access facility. Benefit-cost analysis gives valuable assistance in making the choice.

In a broader perspective benefit-cost analysis can help determine how resources should be allocated among agencies of the government; and in its broadest perspective, it can help determine allocation of resources between the public and the private sectors. Benefit-cost analysis should be considered as a means of moving toward efficiency in the public sector. If a project is justified, this in effect means that MSB is greater than MSC, so that carrying out the project is a movement toward the efficient quantity of whatever the project is concerned with, say, education.

In its present state, benefit-cost analysis is not a totally refined tool that unerringly guarantees efficient outcomes whenever followed. Unfortunately, no rational alternative exists. Many governmental agencies make resource allocation decisions on the basis of intuition or on meaningless rules of thumb—such as increasing the budget for a certain program by 5 percent because it has always been increased by 5 percent in prior years. While benefit-cost analysis is not perfect, it does force decision-makers to use the best information available in making resource allocation decisions.

The Basic Procedure

Briefly, the application of the benefit-cost technique requires the analyst to complete the following procedure and deal with the problems involved in performing this procedure:

1 Costs and benefits of a particular project must be estimated in order to compare it with alternatives. This involves determining which costs and benefits are to be included and how they are to be measured. These costs and/or benefits occur in each year of the project's life; thus, the initial task is to calculate or estimate the costs and benefits for each year to obtain the estimate of net benefits (the difference between estimated benefits and estimated costs of the project) in each year.

2 As discussed in Chapter 3, benefits or costs occurring in the future are not equivalent to the same amount of benefits or costs occurring this year. A discount rate must be selected that reflects the community's relative evaluation of benefits or costs this year and benefits or costs in the future, so that all can be stated in comparable terms.

3 Once a rate of discount is selected, the present value of the net

benefits accruing over the life of the project can be calculated by the method given in the next section. If the present value is positive, compared with the alternative of the status quo, it deserves further consideration. The project that has the highest present value of all potential alternatives should be undertaken. Note that *all* particular alternatives within a program must be considered. For example, an alternative to a 50-foot dam is a 49-foot dam, and the one with the higher present value is the efficient dam to build. If a project has a positive present value, the total benefits exceed the total costs in present value terms (net social benefits are positive). If a project has the highest present value of all alternatives, then net social benefits will be maximized, and the project is the efficient allocation of resources. Marginal social costs and marginal social benefits are as close to being equal as possible. For example, if the present value of the 49-foot dam is greater than the present value of the 50-foot dam, the present value of the fiftieth foot is negative.

Definition and Calculation of Present Value

The definition and calucation of present value is illustrated in the following example. The important thing to keep in mind is that present value calculations are closely related to calculations of future value, that is, the value of an amount growing at some rate of compound interest.

If you put $100 in a bank at 5 percent, at the end of a year you will have $105, if interest is compounded annually. Thus, the future value of the $100 (the amount it is worth in one year) will be $105:

$$\$100(1 + 0.05) = \$105.$$

One hundred dollars at the present time is thus equivalent to $105 next year. If a person chooses not to put the money in the bank, he is in a way telling us that $100 now is equivalent to an amount next year that is at least $105 and maybe much more. Suppose we know that the individual is indifferent between $100 now and $110 next year. He would be willing to pay up to $100 for a note (IOU) worth $110 next year. Thus, the present value of the note worth $110 next year is $100. Paying $100 for a note worth $110 in a year is like putting money in the bank at 10 percent interest:

$$\$100(1 + 0.10) = \$110.$$

Suppose we know the amount to be received next year (the future value) and the rate of interest that reflects the way a person views the present versus the future (called the discount rate), and we want to compute the present value (PV). We know:

present value(1 + discount rate) = future value

or, dividing both sides of the equation by 1 + discount rate,

PV = future value/(1 + discount rate).

In the above example, using a future value of $110 and a discount rate of 10 percent, we have:

PV = $110/(1 + 0.10) = $100.

Thus, if we know the future value and the discount rate, the present value can easily be computed. Suppose now that the time period is two years rather than one year. In our example, $100 was equivalent to $110 in a year, which would be equivalent to something more in the second year. Let us calculate the future value of $110 in another year:

future value = $110(1 + 0.10) = $121

or

$110 = $100(1 + 0.10), so $121 = $100(1 + 0.10) (1 + 0.10) = $100(1.10)^2.

There is a formula for computing the future value. Following the steps above, if the discount rate (r) is known, and the future value is known, then the present value is:

$$PV = \text{future value}/(1 + r)^2$$

and for n years in the future the formula becomes:

$$PV = \text{amount in year } n/(1 + r)^n.$$

Present value can more generally be expressed as the sum of terms such as this, since the present values of the net benefits of a project need to be calculated for each year of the project and added together:

PV = amount in initial year + amount in first year/$(1 + r)$ + amount in second year/$(1 + r)^2$ + ... + amount in nth year/$(1 + r)^n$.

The initial year is from the start of the project to the end of the first year, and the amount in year n is the amount received during the year starting n years from now.

An Example

The following simplified example applies benefit-cost analysis to investment in college education. It illustrates the computation of present value and is presented from the viewpoint of private costs and benefits to the student rather than from society's point of view.

Suppose a nineteen-year old high school graduate is considering whether to go to college or pursue other alternatives. An important consideration is the money value of the investment in himself. In 1968, the average income of men with four or more years of college exceeded the average income of high-school graduates by somewhat more than $4,000 per year.[6] Since this figure includes holders of advanced degrees, assume that the average student could expect a return of about $3,000 per year after obtaining a bachelor's degree.

This education involves two types of private costs to the student: out-of-pocket costs and foregone earnings. Out-of-pocket costs might include tuition, books, and materials; in addition, there may be extra expenses for food, clothing, and other things. Ordinary living expenses are not included as a cost since the individual would incur them whether or not he was a student. In other words, the only costs and benefits to be included in evaluating the college education alternative are those additional costs and benefits that are incurred from undertaking the educational investment. Assume that extra out-of-pocket costs involved in going to college are $500 in tuition and $200 for other expenses. If the student attends school full-time, excluding the summer, he will forego earnings. If he could earn $6,000 per year working full-time and he earns only $1,500 while he is a student, his foregone earnings will be $4,500—the opportunity cost of time spent in school. Thus, as shown in Table 4-7, for four years (years 0 through 3) the student will incur additional costs of $5,200 per year ($500 + $200 + $4,500); however, he will be compensated with an additional income of $3,000 per year after graduation for each year (years 4 through 46) until he retires (assumed to be age 65).

To evaluate the attractiveness of this alternative, these benefits and costs must be converted into present values. Merely adding up the benefits and costs will yield a positive net benefit of $108,200, but this assumes that a dollar of benefits received forty-six years from now can be compared with a dollar of costs to be incurred today. Table 4-7 illustrates the process of computing the present value, assuming a 5 percent rate of discount. This would be the appropriate rate of discount if the student had a savings account yielding this rate, and his preferences for present versus future consumption were such that he preferred saving the costs of college education at 5 percent. The present value, at 5 percent, is about $25,000; thus, college education has higher net benefits to the student than getting a job after high school. If a discount rate of 10 percent more properly reflects his preferences for present versus future consumption, the present value of the college education is about $4,000, which still indicates a profitable investment compared with the alternative of getting a job after high school. If other opportunities (such as post-high school voca-

---

[6]U.S Bureau of the Census, *Statistical Abstract of the United States*, 94th Edition, Government Printing Office, Washington, 1973. Table 182, p. 119.

YEAR	ANNUAL PRIVATE BENEFIT (INCREASED) EARNINGS	PRIVATE COSTS				NET PRIVATE BENEFIT
		Tuition	Other out-of-pocket costs	Foregone earnings	Total	
0 (age 19)	0	$500	$200	$4,500	$5,200	−$5,200
1	0	500	200	4,500	5,200	− 5,200
2	0	500	200	4,500	5,200	− 5,200
3	0	500	200	4,500	5,200	− 5,200
4	$3,000	0	0	0	0	3,000
5	3,000	0	0	0	0	3,000
6 to 46 (age 65)	3,000	0	0	0	0	3,000

$$\text{Present value} = -\$5,200 + \frac{-\$5,200}{1.05} + \frac{-\$5,200}{(1.05)^2} + \frac{-\$5,200}{(1.05)^3} + \frac{\$3,000}{(1.05)^4} + \frac{\$3,000}{(1.05)^5} + \text{etc.}$$

$$= -\$5,200 + -\$4,952.38 + -\$4,716.55 + -\$4,491.96 + \$2,468.11 + \$2,350.58 + \text{etc.}$$

$$= \$24,793.95$$

Table 4-7: Present Value of College Education at Discount Rate of 5 Percent

tional training) are available, the present value of these alternatives should also be compared in order to decide upon that alternative which maximizes the individual's net private benefits.

Certainly there are private benefits to college education other than increased future earnings. The student may receive nonmonetary rewards in the form of enjoyment while at college, the possibility of a more enjoyable or higher-status job after graduation, and the acquisition of cultural tastes that add to future enjoyment of leisure activities. These nonmonetary private benefits need to be considered by the individual along with the earnings benefits in reaching an education decision.

Problems in Benefit-Cost Analysis

For many government goods and services, defining the unit of output is difficult, since there are many quantity and quality considerations involved. For example, what is the output unit of an elementary school? "Educated students" begs the question of what is an educated student, so this will not do. Satisfactory answers to such questions have not yet been given. Since defining and measuring output in such cases is difficult, it is a common practice to resort to comparisons of expenditures (usually on a per capita basis) as an indicator of differences in output of, say, education systems of different governmental jurisdictions. Measuring or comparing output on the basis of the expenditures made on inputs to the production process assumes that the output is directly proportional to the expenditure on inputs and that identical inputs will produce identical outputs. However, the type and amount of the various inputs used in various production processes called "education" can be very different. For example, consider two school systems with the same per student expenditure. One system may spend less on teachers (by having a higher student-teacher ratio or fewer teachers with master's degrees) but more on books, materials, and physical plant. Without a measure of the output resulting from these two different sets of production inputs, economic theory of production provides no reason for assuming that the outputs are identical merely because the amount spent per student is the same for the two school systems. Similarly, just because school systems A and B spend $700 and $600 per pupil per year, respectively, it does not follow that the output (benefits) of A are greater than those of B.

Certain methods exist for valuing the costs and benefits of a project once they are satisfactorily defined. Some benefits and costs are relatively easy to measure, since they involve the transfer of funds, that is, a price is charged. For example, tolls collected on a highway may measure the benefits, and expenditures for construction and maintenance of the highway may measure its costs. Some benefits can be estimated on the basis of what funds would change hands if the output of the project were sold rather than provided free of charge. In some cases, benefits can be estimated by reference to prices charged for similar services in the private market. For example, the benefits of a food distribution program could be measured by the market value of the food distributed.

Some benefits and costs of a project involve no transfer of funds and, therefore, no equivalent market transaction is available for reference, in which case, only crude estimates can be made. For example, aesthetic benefits from a project are usually not quantifiable. This points up an important limitation of benefit-cost analysis: it includes only quantifiable costs and benefits. It would be erroneous to conclude from this that nonquantifiable costs and benefits are unimportant. These must supplement the benefit-cost analysis, although, in many instances, the nonquantifiable aspects will be the same for the project and its alternatives, and, to the extent that this is true, they can be neglected.

Some benefits involve offsetting costs elsewhere in society. An example would be the construction of a new highway that renders an existing highway obsolete for purposes of interstate travel. One should not consider the benefits of new businesses that spring up along the new highway without simultaneously considering the businesses that die along the old route. New motels and restaurants may merely be replacing the old ones. Examples of this phenomenon can be observed in nearly every section of the country where a new interstate highway has been built. In the literature of benefit-cost analysis, these are called "pecuniary" or distributional benefits—they are counterbalanced by costs elsewhere in society and should not be considered in the analysis. Only true (real) benefits should be considered.

Project analysis is strongly influenced by the rate of discount used in computing the present value of net benefits.[7] The lower the discount rate, the higher will be the present value of all projects. However, when alternative projects have benefits accruing over substantially different time periods, the discount rate itself may determine which has the highest present value. Suppose that using a low rate of discount gives a project with a very long life a higher present value than an alternative. Using a higher discount rate could make the short-lived project have a higher present value. Thus, the discount rate may determine which alternative is more attractive (has the higher present value). For this reason, many benefit-cost analysts

---

[7]The selection of the appropriate rate of discount is the subject of considerable controversy. For an excellent discussion of this, see William J. Baumol, "On the Social Rate of Discount," *American Economic Review* (September 1968), 788 - 802.

compute present value using more than one discount rate to determine whether the choice of discount rate has a significant impact on which alternative has the highest present value.

Criteria other than selecting the alternative with the highest present value have sometimes been used in project analysis. The most frequently mentioned is one in which the analyst separately computes present values for the streams of benefits and costs and uses their ratio for comparing alternatives (the benefit-cost ratio). A benefit-cost ratio greater than one would correspond to a situation where the present value of the whole project was greater than zero. One difficulty with this approach is that small projects may seem a wiser allocation choice than larger projects with larger present values. For example, the present value of the benefits and costs of constructing a beaver dam across the Columbia River might have been $100 and $2, respectively—a benefit-cost ratio of 50. The respective benefits and costs of the Grand Coulee Dam might have been something like $100 million and $50 million—a benefit-cost ratio of 2. Thus, use of the benefit-cost ratio criterion would have led to the construction of the beaver dam. But the present value of the beaver dam is only $98, while the present value of the Grand Coulee Dam is $50,000,000. If the $50 million is the largest of all alternative dam projects, the construction of that dam comes closest to maximizing net social benefits.

Finally, it must regretfully be noted that benefit-cost analysis has sometimes been misused for political reasons. Grossly exaggerating benefits and underplaying costs is one way to make projects appear to be better than they are. Thus, benefit-cost analysis can become a glorified piece of propaganda that is used to sell a project to the skeptical. The formal process and an impressive-looking document replete with formulas and graphs may make a voter feel that a "scientific" appraisal has been made, when in fact the consulting firm conducting the benefit-cost analysis has been charged with the responsibility of making the project look good. Fortunately, benefit-cost analysis has progressed in that there seems to be an increasing uniformity of methods so that, at least in principle, the results could be checked by an outside party. This section has provided the reader with a guide to at least some of the more flagrant possible abuses, and hopefully will let benefit-cost analysis be viewed for what it is—an attempt to quantify as well as possible the benefits and costs of a project in order to provide a basis for rational comparisons and resource allocation decisions.

REVIEW AND DISCUSSION QUESTIONS

1 Describe how the "perfectly functioning" private market mechanism leads to an efficient allocation of resources. How do

externalities and pure public goods prevent the private market from achieving an efficient allocation of resources?

2 Evaluate the following statement by carefully distinguishing between the concepts of equity and efficiency: the present distribution of income among families in the United States is incompatible with an efficient allocation of resources.

3 Projects in the public sector should be undertaken on the basis of the highest benefit-cost ratio. Discuss.

4 Explain horizontal and vertical equity under the benefit principle and the ability-to-pay principle.

5 The story goes that the Dutch bought Manhattan from the Indians for trinkets worth $24, in the year 1625. If Manhattan is now worth $1 trillion, what was the present value of the $1 trillion (calculated in 1625)? In other words, how good a deal did the Dutch get? Use a 10 percent rate of discount. If the Indians had invested $24 in 1625 at 10 percent, what would it have been worth today? [Note: at 10 percent, money doubles about every 8 years.]

6 A regressive tax is one which increases as your income falls. Evaluate.

7 A thorough grasp of the definitions in this chapter is critical to the understanding of it and the remainder of the book. Define the following terms and try to give a real-world example of each that is not already in the book:

a. public good   b. positive externality
c. negative externality   d. regressive tax
e. horizontal equity

8 To what extent are the following public goods? Explain for each:

a. highways   b. golf courses
c. football games   d. the judicial system

9 Are regressive taxes inequitable?

10 The city of Altahama is considering building a new solid-waste-disposal plant to replace its existing facility. For simplicity, assume the structure will be useless after six years.

Cost of new facility: Land acquisition $50,000
                      Construction, first year   350,000
                      Construction, second year   100,000

Operating and maintenance costs:

Year	New plant	Old plant
Third	$100,000	$220,000
Fourth	105,000	240,000
Fifth	110,000	270,000
Sixth	115,000	300,000

In addition, the new plant is expected to reduce air pollution, with an annual benefit of $30,000 per year, but it will increase water pollution, at a cost of $3,000 per year.

a. Set up the present value problem using a discount rate of 10 percent.

b. Compute the present value.

c. Is the new plant an efficient use of resources?

5 / Poverty: The Problem and the Long-Run Approach

The American economy has suffered temporary setbacks, but the long-term trend has clearly been toward steadily increasing per capita incomes. Nevertheless, poverty remains, even though substantial efforts have been directed against the problem, such as the War on Poverty (the federal poverty legislation of the mid-1960s). Why is poverty an urban problem? One could argue that urban areas serve to reduce poverty, since rural areas have a higher percentage of their population in poverty than do urban areas. However, since an increasing percentage of the United States population lives in urban areas, about 58 percent of the poor (by official measurements) live in these areas. According to a recent report,[1] one out of twelve people living in urban areas is in poverty. In central cities, it is one in nine, and among blacks in central cities, it is one in four. Concentration of the poor in central cities seems to magnify the problems associated with poverty, and it is our opinion that poverty is the key to many other urban problems. One cannot fully discuss housing or crime without reference to poverty. If it were eliminated, many of these problems would be less severe. Thus, although poverty is not exclusively an urban problem, an understanding of poverty and its interrelations with other problems is important in analyzing problems facing urban areas today.

Money Income: A Measure of Poverty

A household's[2] standard of living is the quantity of goods and services—food, clothing, housing, medical treatment, etc.—consumed; thus, standard of living is a multidimensional concept. However, to get an overall picture of a household's standard of living, we need to add these things together, and this cannot be done without some common denominator. Therefore, we rely on a unidimensional concept, household money income, as an approximation of living standards. In this context, a household that does not have an income sufficient to buy an "adequate" standard of living is considered to be in poverty. We shall begin by discussing problems in translating money income into standard of living, then consider the problem of determining a poverty cutoff line (even with a perfect measure of standard of living), and finally consider official poverty statistics.

Some may object to lumping all aspects of poverty into a one-

[1]U.S. Department of Commerce, *Current Population Reports*, Series P-60, No. 88, Government Printing Office, Washington, June 1973.

[2]In this chapter, the "household" is generally the unit of poverty measurement; a household may be either an unrelated individual or a family.

dimensional concept, and indeed this is a simplification. A person could very well have income sufficient to buy adequate amounts of food, clothing, housing, and so forth, yet fall short in his consumption of some of these items. However, a multidimensional standard, one that sets a minimum consumption of each of these components of standard of living, is not perfect either. Suppose someone chooses to live in a flophouse, even though he is wealthy. Granted few such cases exist, but, if they do, then the minimum consumption standard would require that such people be considered poor. Someone who spends $1,000 a year for cigarettes and liquor might not have enough left over out of a limited budget for food and clothing. Should this person be considered poor, when a nonsmoker/drinker with the same money income is not? Similarly, official housing statistics show that a certain percentage of households with incomes in excess of $20,000 live in substandard housing, because their housing is considered crowded (having more than one person per room). A multidimensional poverty concept might include such households as in poverty, although they could easily afford standard housing.

Money Income as a Measure of Standard of Living

There are many difficulties in using money income levels to measure living standards. Sources of income data are generally restricted to measures of money income, but many factors can result in different standards of living for households with the same money income. To develop a poverty yardstick, we need to consider factors in addition to money income to discover which households are in equal circumstances with respect to standard of living (horizontal equity), and also to compare families with different standards of living (vertical equity). Some of the more important of these factors in addition to money income are as follows:

1   Income in kind (nonmoney income). A farm family with a money income of $4,000 may have a standard of living higher than the $4,000 would indicate, since it may be able to grow some of its own food and so receive income in kind. Thus, the real income of the family, including the value of home-grown food, is more than $4,000.

2   Size of family. A family of two with an income of $4,000 will, on the average, be much better off than a family of four with the same income.

3   Differences in location. The U.S. Bureau of Labor Statistics calculated that a retired couple living on an "intermediate budget" in 1971 would require $5,604 in Boston versus

$4,476 in Houston. The average cost outside of SMSAs was $4,136.[3]

4 Age structure of a family of given size. An elderly couple will generally have higher medical expenses than a young couple without children.

5 Differences in wealth. A family's wealth is simply its net worth: its assets minus its liabilities. If a family owns its home outright (there is no mortgage loan on the house), then it receives benefits from this ownership (a type of in-kind or nonmoney income) that amount to living there rent-free. The homeowner has to pay for upkeep and taxes, but a tenant of a similar house has to pay rent that not only covers these items but also includes a financial return to the landlord. Thus a single person with a cash income of $4,000 would have considerably more cash for purchases other than housing if he owned his own home.

This list of adjustments is not all-inclusive, but it does include probably the most important considerations that modify the use of money income as a measure of standard of living. Some of these adjustments have been incorporated into official poverty statistics but others have not.

There are two tacks that can be taken at this point. One can start with money income and then raise or lower it in accordance with factors such as those just mentioned, arriving at a family's *adjusted money income*. This concept will be used later to underscore the need to adjust money income to reflect standard of living. Another tack is to develop several categories and look at money incomes of those in a particular category, for example, families of four living in an urban area with a female family head. This is the approach taken in official measurements of poverty.

In terms of measuring poverty, neglect of the above considerations may result in inadequate accounting and classification for public policy purposes. For example, failure to take into account the value of home-grown food will result in a large proportion of farm families being classified as poor. Failure to take into account the nonmoney value of owner-occupied housing may result in a large proportion of elderly households being classified as poor, since many of the elderly own their own homes and have paid off most or all of the mortgage loan during their working years. The most important consideration is size of family. If no adjustment is made for family size, the number of children who are counted as poor will be understated. Before developing poverty programs, we need to know who the poor are.

---

[3]U.S. Bureau of the Census, *Statistical Abstract of the United States*, 1973, Government Printing Office, Washington, 1973, Table no. 581, p. 357.

Determination of the Poverty Cutoff

The discussion so far has been concerned with measuring standards of living. Even if this can be done without error, a very sticky problem remains, namely, what standard of living constitutes poverty? Or, in terms of the measure of standard of living used here, what amount of adjusted money income puts a household at the threshold of poverty? There is no good answer. Without an absolute definition of an "adequate" standard of living (the amount of money income required to purchase the "necessities" of life), the selection of a poverty cutoff line is highly arbitrary. As evidence of this, the U.S. Department of Commerce currently refers to the official poverty line as the "low income level" rather than its former term, "poverty threshold."

The poverty cutoff level must be expressed in money terms and is culturally determined—that is, determined by society through a process involving value judgments. A person may be "poor" in one society and not "poor" in another, even though his income is the same in both places, because standards vary. Also, the poverty standard in a given society may change over time. In the United States, by 1936 standards, very few people would be considered poor today. President Roosevelt's statement that a third of the nation was in poverty in 1936 implies a poverty cutoff line of about $2,000 per household in 1970 dollars. However, less than 5 percent of the 1970 population would fall below this cutoff level of income.[4] Conversely, applying current official poverty standards to the 1936 population, we would find a majority in poverty (about two-thirds of the population). Society's idea of what standard of living constitutes poverty rises as the overall level of affluence in the society rises. For example, a television set may be considered to be part of an adequate standard of living in an affluent society. Yet, twenty-five years ago, having orange juice for breakfast was a luxury in most households. The wealthier a society becomes, the more it feels it can provide its citizens. A poorhouse may have been all that earlier societies could provide for the poor; more affluent societies can and do provide considerably more, for example, maintaining a family in its own residence.

Once set, any poverty cutoff line becomes arbitrary, in that a family is either above or below the cutoff level. Thus, if the line were $4,000 for a household of given size and other characteristics, such a household with an income of $3,999.99 would be in poverty, while a family with an income of 1¢ more would not. To take account of this, the concept of the "poverty gap" has been introduced. This is the difference between the household's income and the poverty line, and is a measure of the intensity of poverty. The national aggregate poverty

---

[4]Bradley Schiller, *The Economics of Poverty and Discrimination*, Prentice-Hall, Englewood Cliffs, N.J. 1972, pp. 5-6.

gap according to official measurements was $12 billion in 1972 (in 1972 dollars).

Official Poverty Statistics

Official poverty measures take account of some of the problems above, but not others. The official method of calculating the poverty level for a household in a given category will first be sketched. Table 5-1 shows these levels for 1972, calculated as follows. The U.S. Department of Agriculture has compiled an "economy food plan," originally designed to meet the needs of families in temporary financial straits, which is essentially a grocery list of foods that offer some variety and provide a balanced diet at minimum cost. The cost of this for a family of a given size is calculated. Next, since, on the average, families seem to spend about one-third of their incomes on food (at least if their incomes are near poverty levels), the cost of the economy food plan is multiplied by three to give the "low income level" or poverty cutoff line. It is presumed that living on a farm gives one the opportunity to grow some of his own food, so an adjustment is made to account for this. (Table 5-1 shows lower cutoff levels for farm households of similar size.) It is easy to point out defects of the official measurements and this will be done subsequently; however, first, let us consider their merits. For one thing, compared with previous measurements, these are much more accurate. The War on Poverty originally used $3,000 per household, not adjusted for anything, not even family size. Second, these official measurements account for size and composition, sex and age of the family head, and farm or nonfarm residence. Third, the official cutoffs are periodically adjusted according to changes in the Consumer Price Index, so people will not be leaving poverty status because of inflation of prices, with no improvement in standard of living.

The drawbacks of the official measurements are serious. First, they are based on an absolute standard, and the only thing that can change the poverty cutoffs would be a movement of prices. We saw earlier that society's view of poverty can change as well, but no allowance is made for this. In a sense, this could be considered an advantage, since it is a standard against which progress can be measured. If poverty were to be defined as the lowest 20 percent of the income distribution, then obviously no progress could ever be made in alleviating it (20 percent of the population would *always* be in poverty). Second, several items are left out of the official poverty calculations, in particular, those discussed previously: differences in wealth and location. However, each new characteristic taken into consideration would double the size of Table 5-1 and increase the difficulty in calculating the poverty line. A major omission in calculating the official poverty

| | NONFARM | | FARM | |
SIZE OF FAMILY	Male head	Female head	Male head	Female head
UNRELATED INDIVIDUALS				
Under 65 years	$2,254	$2,085	$1,916	$1,772
65 years and over	2,025	2,000	1,722	1,698
FAMILIES				
2 persons (head under 65)	2,823	2,729	2,399	2,258
2 persons (head 65 or over)	2,532	2,516	2,154	2,141
3 persons	3,356	3,234	2,838	,2,702
4 persons	4,277	4,254	3,644	3,598
5 persons	5,048	4,994	4,301	4,355
6 persons	5,679	5,617	4,849	4,900
7 or more persons	7,000	6,841	5,963	5,771

Table 5-1: Official Poverty Cutoff Income Levels in 1972, by Size of Family and Sex of Head and by Farm or Nonfarm Residence. For unrelated individuals, sex of head of household simply refers to sex of individual.

SOURCE: U.S. Department of Commerce, *Current Population Reports,* Series P-60, No. 88, Government Printing Office, Washington, June 1973, Table 6, p. 8.

income level is the value of in-kind income redistribution to the poor. These nonmoney income transfers are not considered in determining a household's income for purposes of defining poverty status; however, federal outlays for food stamps exceed $2 billion per year, to give just one example. Certainly these in-kind transfer programs raise the standards of living of the poor, as do cash transfer payments, but this rise is not reflected in official measures. The $12 billion aggregate poverty gap in the United States in 1972 mentioned above would be less with the inclusion of in-kind transfers.

One possible way to define poverty is as the level of income at which families save nothing and start dipping into previous savings (decrease their net worth, or wealth) in order to maintain their standard of living. This level of income has been termed, rather picturesquely, the "wolf point"—when the wolf is at the door.[5] The wolf point was estimated as being $1,146 per person during the period 1947-1961, yielding an estimate somewhat above official poverty levels.

Scope of United States Poverty

In 1972, about 24 million Americans were below the official poverty cutoff level of income. Table 5-2 shows the trend since 1959, the first

[5]See Martin Bronfenbrenner, *Income Distribution Theory,* Aldine, Chicago, 1971, pp. 41 - 42.

YEAR	NUMBER IN POVERTY (THOUSANDS)
1959	39,490
1960	39,851
1961	39,628
1962	38,625
1963	36,436
1964	36,055
1965	33,185
1966	28,510
1967	27,769
1968	25,389
1969	24,147
1970	25,420
1971	25,559
1972	24,460

Table 5-2: United States Population Below the Official Poverty Cutoff Level by Year (1959 to 1972)

SOURCE: U.S. Department of Commerce, *Current Population Reports,* Series P-60, No. 88, Government Printing Office, Washington, June 1973.

year when the data were collected. The number of poor has declined, but has done so very little since 1968, partly as a result of attempts to deal with inflation, which are discussed in the next chapter. Since the total population has increased substantially, the percentage of Americans classified as poor has dropped markedly, falling from over 22 percent of the population in 1959 to under 12 percent by 1972.

An increasing proportion of the American poor live in SMSAs, since the economy has become increasingly urbanized. In 1972, about 58 percent of all poor families lived in SMSAs and over 60 percent of these lived in central cities. Table 5-3 shows the distribution of poor families and unrelated individuals with respect to race and residence in 1972. The table shows that a higher percentage of rural families are poor; however, since over two-thirds of the population lives in SMSAs, a majority of the poor are urban poor. Table 5-3 also indicates that a disproportionate number of blacks are poor. For example, only 5.6 percent of whites in SMSAs are below official poverty lines, while 25.7 percent of blacks are below the line. Although these statistics indicate a high incidence of poverty among blacks, other minority groups, such as Indians, Mexican-Americans, and Puerto Ricans, also have a high incidence of poverty among their members.

Another significant aspect is that more and more women are in poverty. The total number of persons in female-headed families and female unrelated individuals with incomes below the poverty cutoff level actually increased by over 1 million persons from 1959 to 1972, to a total of 11,587,000—almost half of the total poor. For male-

	WHITES		BLACKS	
	Number (thousands)	**Percent of group**	**Number (thousands)**	**Percent of group**
FAMILIES				
Residing in SMSAs	1,819	5.6	1,059	25.7
In central cities	901	7.2	892	27.3
Outside central cities	918	4.7	167	19.5
Residing outside SMSAs	1,622	10.0	471	41.0
UNRELATED INDIVIDUALS				
Residing in SMSAs	2,447	23.7	625	38.4
In central cities	1,429	24.7	498	37.4
Outside central cities	1,018	22.5	127	42.6
Residing outside SMSAs	1,488	35.5	244	61.3

Table 5-3: Families and Unrelated Individuals Below the Official Poverty Cutoff Level of Income, by Residence and Race (1972)
SOURCE: U.S. Department of Commerce, *Current Population Reports,* Series P-60, No. 88, Government Printing Office, Washington, June 1973.

headed families and male unrelated individuals, the corresponding number in 1972 was 12,873,000, having dropped by over 16 million since 1959. In percentage terms, 36 percent of all female-headed families were below the poverty line in 1972, compared with 7.4 percent of male-headed families. One reason for this divergence is discrimination in jobs and education. Another reason is the way the statistics are gathered. A female-headed family generally has no adult male present, while a male-headed family generally does have an adult female present. Thus, if there is only one parent at home, the difficulties in simultaneously working and raising children become important. This statistical aberration should not be overemphasized to the point where it is felt that female poverty poses no problem. The most difficult kind of poverty to eradicate appears to be that among female-headed families, whereas improved job opportunities have greatly reduced other kinds of poverty.

Age level is strongly related to poverty status, although poverty among the aged has dropped more rapidly in recent years than poverty in general, as Table 5-4 shows. Family size is also strongly related to poverty. Among families of three or four persons, 7.5 percent were below the poverty cutoff in 1972; with five persons, 8.6 percent; with

	PERCENT OF POPULATION BELOW POVERTY CUTOFF LINE			
	1966	**1968**	**1970**	**1972**
Total population	14.7	12.8	12.6	11.9
Population age 65 and over	28.5	25.0	24.6	18.6

Table 5-4: Proportion of Population, Total and Aged, Below the Poverty Cutoff Line (1966-1972)
SOURCE: U.S. Department of Commerce, *Current Population Reports,* Series P-60, No. 88, Government Printing Office, Washington, June 1973.

YEARS OF EDUCATION	PERCENTAGE OF FAMILIES BELOW POVERTY CUTOFF LEVEL OF INCOME
0-7	22.2
8	11.3
9-11	12.3
12-(high school graduate)	5.8
13-15 (some college)	3.9
16 or more (college graduate or more)	2.2

Table 5-5: Percentages of Families by Educational Attainment of Family Head Below Poverty Cutoff Level of Income (1972)
SOURCE: U.S. Department of Commerce, *Current Population Reports,* Series P-60, No. 88, Government Printing Office Washington, June 1973.

six persons, 14.3 percent; and with seven or more persons, 22.3 percent. Of course, many large families and persons over 65 may also be members of minority groups living in central cities; the combined effects of these characteristics result in much higher poverty rates.

The relationship between educational attainment of the family head and the incidence of poverty is shown in Table 5-5. As the table indicates, 22.2 percent of families headed by a person with less than eight years of education are in poverty; the percentage falls as education levels increase, with the exception of high-school dropouts.

Finally, it should be noted that the overall poverty gap has decreased over time. In 1959, it was $19.6 billion, in 1966 it had fallen to $13 billion, and by 1972 it had edged down to $12 billion (all of these figures are in 1972 dollars). Government programs have probably closed about half of the poverty gap, and the above amount indicates what remains. Twelve billion dollars is a large sum; however, government income transfers amounted to $100 billion dollars in 1972 (see Table 6-3). There are several reasons why the poverty gap has not been eliminated by this huge transfer. First, many programs are not designed exclusively for the poor, so that much of the aid goes to the nonpoor. Second, some of those who would be in poverty without the government programs are brought considerably above poverty status. For example, a retired person could have investments that yield an income of $1,500 per year, which is less than the poverty cutoff level of income; however, social security and government retirement system checks might put his total income far above the poverty line. Further, many of the government programs do not count toward lowering the poverty gap since they are of an in-kind nature and are not included in the household's money income.

This section has examined the characteristics of the United States poor; these characteristics should not be considered as the causes of poverty per se. Unfortunately, many writers do treat them as such, but, if efficient programs are to be designed, they need to be directed at the true causes of the problem. If the causes are removed, then poverty is alleviated. In many of the cases above, nothing can or should be done about the characteristics of the poor. For example, if people under five feet in height turned out to be poor in large numbers, then it would seem that they should be stretched if they were ever to escape poverty. Similar absurd policies arise from confusing other characteristics with the causes of poverty. People over 65 may be discriminated against and as, a result, be poor; aging itself cannot be reversed, although perhaps discrimination can. This confusion over the causes of poverty versus its characteristics has led to much, probably unwarranted, pessimism regarding the eradication of poverty. The following section develops a classification of the underlying causes of poverty.

Causes of Poverty

Some kinds of poverty can be considered "temporary." For example, during the early 1970s, measured poverty did not decrease and in fact increased as a result of high levels of unemployment. The poverty picture began to improve, as unemployment levels started to drop and the unemployed began to be absorbed back into the work force. Another example of what we are calling temporary poverty would be a family suffering a casualty loss (its uninsured home burned down, for example) or experiencing a loss of income due to illness or temporary disability. The distinguishing attribute of these kinds of short-term poverty is that they are "insurable"—that is, forms of insurance can and do exist to aid the household during the period of temporary poverty until it gets back on its feet. Unemployment compensation, workmen's compensation, health insurance, and other forms of insurance could be provided to "insure" the household against various forms of temporary poverty. (It is assumed in this discussion that the federal government acts to avoid major and prolonged periods of unemployment such as occurred in the 1930s.) The last section of Chapter 6 discusses how the government can do this and the problems involved. Most of the discussion of causes of poverty in this section is concerned with causes of poverty that are more deep-rooted, not temporary, and that do not respond well to policies that lead to full employment. These causes are lack of human capital and discrimination; it will become apparent that these causes are interrelated.

Inadequate Human Capital

Human capital is defined as the acquired skills of an individual, which can be sold, as labor services, to an employer in exchange for income. Several things should be noted about this definition. First, a person may possess unmarketable skills, perhaps because of technical obsolescence; a highly trained craftsman may find himself out of work because his skill is no longer in demand in the economy. These unmarketable skills are not considered human capital, since they cannot be sold.

Second, the definition of human capital refers to acquired rather than innate skills. The causes of poverty listed in this section were chosen so as to suggest ways to alleviate poverty. If a person has an inadequate level of innate skills, he cannot be helped by a program designed to give him more innate skills (a contradiction in terms), but perhaps a program to equip him with a higher level of human capital (acquired skills) could help. A problem arises in cases of "clinical" poverty, where a person may have such a low level of innate skill that even huge expenditures on training and skills acquisition will not enable him to earn an income above the poverty level. In cases such as severe mental retardation and physical handicaps, permanent subsidies to alleviate the symptom of poverty (low level of income) may be efficient rather than futile attempts to augment a person's human capital.

Third an inadequate level of human capital possessed by the breadwinner(s) of a family results in an inadequate standard of living for the entire family, including the children. A breadwinner may possess skills worth $4,000 per year, which will put him above the poverty line if the family has two members, but not if it has nine members. In this context, the adequacy of the human capital possessed by the household's breadwinner(s) depends on whether the resulting income is sufficient to place the entire household above the poverty cutoff level.

Fourth, studies have shown that the process of human capital formation might begin before birth, since the potential for acquiring human capital can suffer from poor prenatal care. Thus, a program for providing better prenatal care to poverty households could be considered as a "human capital" program.

Discrimination

In general, discrimination is a cause of poverty whenever the education and employment opportunities of an individual are restricted on some arbitrary basis. Breadwinners of some families may possess a stock of human capital identical in terms of potential earning capacity to that of others in society, yet be unable to realize the same earnings because of discrimination. Such discrimination in employment opportunities may be based on race, sex, age, religion, ethnic origin, or other attributes unrelated to the productivity of the individual—

including education in the sense that certain employers may require more education than a job really requires (but not *too* much more). In recent periods of unemployment, many highly trained individuals found they were discriminated against because they were "over-trained"; employers were unwilling to hire them for a job if they felt the person would quit whenever an opening occurred in his specialty. With respect to educational opportunities, discrimination may prevent an individual from acquiring an adequate stock of human capital, and so he may end up in poverty. Also, discrimination in housing markets may prohibit people from living near job opportunities, thereby contributing to unemployment and poverty (see Chapter 8).

Other Causes of Poverty

The reader may object to the rather short list of causes of poverty given above, thinking that surely there must be other reasons for the existence of poverty besides lack of human capital, discrimination, and "temporary" poverty. As was mentioned, these causes were designed so that they would yield insight into ways of alleviating poverty. One could easily say that lack of physical capital (wealth) is a cause of poverty; the implication of this statement is that physical assets (or claims to them, like stocks and bonds) should be distributed to the poor, and the political likelihood of such policies being enacted is nil. There are programs for increasing human capital, however, and it is likely that more such programs will be enacted in the future. Interpreted broadly, the list of causes given here covers many more cases than would appear at first glance. For example, a permanent disability might seem to be outside this framework, but it can quite easily be considered a loss of human capital. It may be possible to rehabilitate the individual, that is, equip him with more human capital, in the form of training or a prosthetic device. A surgical operation could be viewed as increasing human capital, if earning capacity is increased by it. If a person is located in an area where jobs are scarce, we can say that his skills are unmarketable owing to location; thus, relocating the person can be thought of as an investment in human capital. With a large family, the breadwinner's human capital may be inadequate to put the family's income above the poverty cutoff level. A program that allows a family to limit its size can thus be viewed as allowing it to maintain a higher level of human capital per household member.

Long-Run Approaches to Reduce Poverty

Before discussing programs for the reduction of poverty, the goals of such programs need to be spelled out. These programs are aimed at both the *symptom* of poverty, which is lack of income, and the *causes* of poverty, which are related to lack of human capital and discrimination. Programs directed at the symptom of poverty are called short-run programs, because the symptom of poverty can be eliminated in a shorter period of time than can the causes. Similarly, programs directed at the causes of poverty are called long-run programs. The symptom of poverty could be eliminated by redistributing $12 billion to all individuals currently below the official poverty line, since $12 billion is the present poverty gap and represents a little less than 1 percent of the United States gross national product. Although such a program would have tremendously adverse effects on the incentive to work (as discussed in the next chapter), it gives us a rough idea of the scope of the problem. The eradication of the causes of poverty would require solutions of a long-run nature. However, there is no clear-cut distinction between short- and long-run programs to combat poverty, since some poverty programs may have ramifications for both the long and short run.

In the following discussion, approaches to poverty will be evaluated in terms of the efficiency criterion. It is assumed that the equity decision—to bring every family up to the poverty cutoff level of income—has already been made. Since the goal has been determined, efficiency, in this context, means achieving the goal by the least-cost means. Thus, long-run programs will be judged in terms of their relative cost measured against the alternative cost of a simple, short-run income redistribution program designed to give each family below the poverty level a cash grant that closes the poverty gap. In some cases, it will turn out that a long-run program aimed at the elimination of the causes of poverty may be most efficient; in other cases, a short-run solution aimed at the symptom of poverty may prove to be the most efficient and least expensive. For example, training programs for individuals over sixty years of age may not be an efficient allocation of resources, since such persons may have only a few remaining years of employment. An income redistribution program is the efficient (least costly) way of reducing poverty in such instances.

Increasing the Stock of Human Capital

Income can be increased by increasing through training or education, both formal and informal, the value of the labor services that a breadwinner sells to an employer for salaries or wages. Increasing the individual's stock of human capital can be looked on as an investment in the same sense as an investment in physical capital such as plant and equipment. Funds are invested (costs are incurred) to increase the stock of human capital and returns (benefits) are received on this investment in the form of increased earnings in the future. Informal learning in the home, formal education, vocational training, and health and rehabilitation programs can all be viewed as forms of investment in human capital.

Informal learning   One of the most tenacious problems associated with poverty is that it tends to be inherited. If the parents in a family have a low level of human capital, this restricts the amount of informal learning that the children of the family acquire. A sociologist might call this cultural deprivation; in our terms, it amounts to a low level of human capital formation in the home, especially in the pre-school years. Associated with this problem is the observation that many of the poor have a short time horizon (do not consider or provide for tomorrow) or have a strong preference for consumption now versus in the future. The next section will illustrate how this would lead an individual to invest less than otherwise in human capital, tending to perpetuate poverty.

Investment in education   Investment in a college education was used as an example of the application of benefit-cost analysis in the last section of Chapter 4. The same approach can be applied to all levels of education and to all types of training. For example, a high-school education could be compared with the alternative of dropping out of school after the eighth grade. The major private cost to the student of acquiring a high-school education is earnings foregone while attending school. If he attends a private or parochial school, there will be additional expenses for tuition. There could also be private costs for books and supplies, if these have to be supplied by the student or his family. The monetary private benefits of this education are the increased earnings that accrue to the student after graduation. The following example will consider a student in a public school system and initially go through the alternatives open to him from a private point of view.

For simplicity, assume that a person who drops out of school after the eighth grade is able to earn $2,400 per year more than if he went on to attend high school for four years between the ages of 15 and 18; however, after age 18, the high-school graduate can earn $2,500 more per year than the person dropping out of school after the eighth grade. (These numbers are close to the actual average earnings differentials.) Assume that all books are free and that living expenses are identical for the student and the worker. Assume further that there is no tuition, since there is a public school. Thus, the private costs of education to the student or his family are $2,400 for the first four years (the foregone earnings); he then receives benefits of $2,500 per year for the rest of his working life. Is this a good investment? Even accepting these numbers, it need not be; however, to see whether it is, the present value of the private costs and benefits must be calculated to determine the net private benefit:

$$\text{present value} = -\$2,400 - \$2,400/(1 + r) - \$2,400/(1 + r)^2$$
$$- \$2,400/(1 + r)^3 + \$2,500/(1 + r)^4 + \$2,500/(1 + r)^6 + \ldots$$
$$+ \$2,500/(1 + r)^{51}.$$

The student's personal discount rate is r. It is assumed that the worker retires at age 65, after working fifty-one years if he does not attend high school and forty-seven years if he does (although he may work part-time during high school, it was assumed that by working full-time, he could earn $2,400 more). The present value at a 10 percent discount rate is about $10,200, an attractive investment from the private point of view. However, the individual may very well view the future in such a way as to warrant a 20 percent rate of discount—placing a much higher premium on benefits to be received now versus in the future. With a 20 percent personal discount rate, the present value of the net private benefits of graduating from high school is minus $200, indicating that dropping out of school is a better choice. At such a high discount rate, amounts in the distant future add very little to the present value. At a discount rate of 20 percent, the present value of $2,500 to be received in fifty years is only about 28¢. Thus, a high personal discount rate leads to lower levels of investment in education than would occur otherwise and can contribute to the persistence of poverty. This factor as an explanation of poverty is highly stressed by some writers.[6]

How would society value additional high-school education? Social costs and benefits of the investment in human capital could be calculated. With a system of public education, the costs would include providing the physical facilities and staffing the school. The benefits might include increased "political awareness" on the part of the population and a "better" citizenry. As a poverty program, the education may increase the person's future income, thereby eliminating the need for other forms of income assistance in the future.

Several comments are in order. First, not all training programs actually increase the level of a person's human capital. In many instances a person receiving training does not pursue the vocation for which the training prepares him. Obviously, our discussion concerns programs that actually increase a person's earning potential. Second, the above discussion assumes that students have the opportunity to avail themselves of additional education, but many barriers may intervene. In the example above, suppose the potential high-school dropout believes that his earnings would be the same whether or not

---

[6]See Edward Banfield, *The Unheavenly City*, Little, Brown, Boston, 1970.

he finished high school, because he has incorrect information. This makes the benefits he perceives equal to zero, and the present value of the investment is necessarily negative (it is a bad choice to stay in school). (The dropout does not actually consult present value tables, of course, but tends to act as if he did, making the same decision.) Programs to provide better information on the private costs and benefits of educational alternatives are required, if a low level of investment in human capital is attributable to individuals underestimating the net private benefits of additional education. This is the basis of the advertising campaign that urges "to get a good job, get a good education."

Another problem was referred to earlier. The present value of the investment in education using a 20 percent rate of discount was negative—a bad investment from the private point of view. Thus, a high preference for present versus future consumption (high personal discount rate) may lead to a perpetuation of poverty. Poor families often rely on the income children can bring in. In such cases, attending school might exact a tremendous hardship on the families. In this context, the costs used in the present value example were too low, if the foregone earnings mean that a family might go without adequate food as a result of school attendance by a teenaged child. Along the same lines, costs might be underestimated because of the mental anguish of simply attending school. An unsuccessful student may have feelings of personal failure constantly reinforced from attending school, thereby increasing his private costs of schooling over what they would be otherwise.

The preceding discussion indicated several potential causes of low levels of educational investment, which in turn suggest several ways to alter the present value of the educational investment to the student and his family so that it will become positive rather than negative. For one thing, the student's effective personal discount rate can be lowered by granting a loan to the student at low interest rates. The National Defense Education Act loan program for college students is an example of this approach. This lower rate of discount increases the present value of the investment. Another approach is to subsidize more of the costs of education, for example, paying the student to attend school. This has not generally been attempted with respect to high-school education, but trainees in other kinds of programs are often paid a stipend. The Job Corps and the WIN programs, discussed later in this chapter, have these features.

In conclusion, there may be a conflict between private and social calculations regarding education, which is the economic justification for public intervention. Support by the public sector of educational programs to prepare individuals for better jobs may be less costly over the long run than provision of welfare payments to individuals who are in poverty because of inadequate human capital. However, low-

skilled individuals may judge the time necessary for additional education or training too expensive in terms of foregone earnings or
effort. As a result, some form of public sector intervention will be
required to insure the individual of increased future earning power
and self-support without future government spending.

Investment in vocational training programs   Investment in human capital may take the form of vocational training programs. Private and
social costs and benefits may be similar to the above example of a
potential high-school student except that tuition may be an added
private cost. However, in recent years many United States companies
have invested funds in support of on-the-job training programs for
their employees. Generally, a company will be willing to make such
an investment if the training is of a sort that enhances the productivity
of the employee and also allows the company to reap some of the
benefits of the training. A company would be wary of teaching basic
office skills, for example, since the employee might take a job
elsewhere if the company tried to keep the employee's salary below
market rates (to recoup the training costs). On the other hand, the
employee might not wish to accept a cut in pay during training in
order to receive the training. Because of these problems, the JOBS
program was set up under the joint administration of the U.S. Department of Labor and the National Alliance of Businessmen. This
program has worked to provide jobs and training for disadvantaged
workers since 1967. One potential advantage of such a program is that
the training is generally for a job that actually exists, rather than for a
hoped-for job; thus, the approach is more likely to result in genuine
human capital formation.

Other programs have grown out of the Manpower Development and
Training Act of 1962 (MDTA). Originally, the idea was to retrain
workers displaced by automation and equip them with new skills.
With the fall in unemployment levels in the late 1960s, the emphasis
shifted to the disadvantaged. The Economic Opportunity Act specifically provided funds for training such individuals. The Job Corps is a
program that provides training to the disadvantaged through residential and, more recently, nonresidential centers. Part of the philosophy
has been to equip the trainee with basic job skills that the disadvantaged youth lacks, such as interviewing for jobs. Yet another program,
aimed specifically at welfare recipients, is the WIN program, which
offers various incentives to accept training and employment. Day care
has been provided under this program; this can be thought of as an
attempt to reduce the costs of employment and training to the
recipient.

These programs cost the federal government about $2 billion in
1972. It is difficult to gauge the effectiveness of various training

programs that have been undertaken. Some of the underlying ideas have merit in that training has been made much more attractive to many potential trainees, but the overall impact on poverty has probably been minimal. Unless jobs are abundant, training can have little effect. Also, training opportunities, particularly under the JOBS program, seem highly responsive to business conditions. When business is in recession, firms are less willing to hire and train the disadvantaged and may lay off previous trainees. Another problem is that some newly trained persons might merely displace others in similar jobs, so that poverty is shifted around rather than reduced. It is essential that training is in areas where jobs actually are available, or it will have little effect. In summary, determining whether specific long-run programs directed at increasing the stock of human capital of low-income individuals are an efficient solution to poverty depends on performing benefit-cost analysis of such programs. Many such programs stemming from legislation of the War on Poverty era of the 1960s have been abandoned, and the apparent ineffectiveness at quickly and significantly reducing poverty has led to considerable disillusionment in recent years. However, this does not imply that all long-run, human capital programs are doomed to failure. The implication appears to be that experimentation with many types of program on a small scale (with careful evaluation using benefit-cost analysis) should precede nationwide implementation. Hopefully, the result would be to increase the probability of widely implementing only those programs that have the largest net social benefits.

Investment in health and rehabilitation programs   The human capital framework can also be applied to investment in health and rehabilitation programs. It is important to consider the efficiency as well as the equity aspects of such programs. If a person receives medical treatment, it may enable him to work, or to work more regularly without extensive government income redistribution programs. The handicapped can sometimes be rehabilitated so that they earn a higher income. Thus, these programs may be viewed as poverty programs in that they increase the level of human capital. Equity aspects are also of great importance here, since society does not desire to deny desperately needed medical care to low-income individuals. Thus, health and rehabilitation programs may be justified on grounds of both equity and efficiency. The federal government has moved extensively into these areas in recent years, principally through the Medicare and Medicaid programs. In one sense, these health-care schemes might be considered as short-run rather than long-run poverty programs since they aid the elderly and have the effect of freeing funds for other uses, much like a short-run cash transfer. These programs will therefore be discussed in the next chapter, which deals with short-run approaches to reducing poverty.

Family Planning and Child Care

Earlier in this chapter it was stated that large family size is strongly related to the incidence of poverty, since a level of human capital adequate to keep a small family out of poverty may not be adequate to keep a large family out of poverty. Thus, future poverty could be reduced by providing incentives and measures to encourage limitation of family size. It has not always been true that a large family size was a cause of poverty. When the United States was primarily an agricultural economy, a large family was desirable and an economic asset, since the children added significantly to the farm's output. It was often said that a farmer's wealth could be measured by the number of sons he had. In a modern urban society, young children generally do not add to the income of the family but do add to the costs, and the costs of raising a child and educating him increase every year as the relative standard of adequate child-rearing increases. Also, high child-care costs associated with large families may result in an inability to utilize the family's existing stock of human capital in the market-place. Parents may be limited in their employment opportunities because of the costs and difficulties of obtaining adequate day-care services. As was previously mentioned the WIN program has provided some day-care facilities and legislation for major day-care programs has been proposed in recent years.

The costs of day care that provides more than mere custody of the child are by no means trivial—at least double the usual cost of maintaining a child in elementary school. Various estimates place the cost at over $2,000 per child per year, unless undesirably high ratios of children to teachers are accepted.[7] If a welfare mother has three children, and we accept these cost estimates for child care, then the most efficient course might be to keep the mother in the home with her children, since her earnings might be more than offset by the cost of the child care. On the other hand, if the mother has no preschool children, then a day-care center that covers the periods when she is at work and the children are not in public school might be an efficient use of resources. There might be many situations where it would be efficient from a social point of view to provide child care and allow welfare mothers to work or enter training programs. At the same time, from the private point of view, the decision to work or acquire training, including the entire cost of day care, might not be a good private decision. In such cases, government subsidization of child care could lower private costs to the point where working would also become desirable from a private point of view.

Impoverished families may want to control family size but may not do so because of inadequate information on, or unavailability of,

[7]Charles Schultze, et al., *Setting National Priorities: The 1973 Budget*, The Brookings Institution, Washington, 1972, pp. 273 - 274.

birth-control devices. Information on contraceptive methods, provision of contraceptive devices, and the recent liberalization of abortion laws may all be considered in part as poverty programs. However, population control is not solely a poverty program. As will be discussed in Chapters 11 and 12, more people also means more pollution, other things remaining the same. For this and similar reasons, national organizations have recently sprung up that advocate population control and a cessation of population growth. One can think of economic approaches to population control that would have an impact on both pollution and poverty; in general, these would involve increasing the private costs of having a child as seen by the family. For example, income tax laws are currently structured so that the larger the family, the larger the number of exemptions the family can claim, thereby lowering the taxes paid on a given amount of income. This provision was no doubt intended to provide more equity in the payment of taxes and to avoid placing high tax burdens on families with many children. From the point of view of limiting family size, it is clear that these exemptions are a mild incentive to increase family size. This is not to say that many families deliberately have more children in order to take advantage of the extra exemptions. However, it may be true that the existence of the subsidies leads some families who are undecided about an additional child to have a child they would not have in the absence of the tax break. The major problem with changing the present tax law is that the impact on the number of births would probably not be very large, but children now living would suffer as a result. A program could be set up that would provide a "reward" for females of child-bearing age who do not have children in a given year or who choose voluntary sterilization. Any program that provides for preferential treatment of those who do not have children may run counter to the objectives of poverty programs in that those who do have children do not receive as much aid.

Combating Discrimination

Discrimination causes poverty. One need look at only a few poverty statistics to see that this is true. Table 5-3 showed that the incidence of poverty among black families is about four times as high as for white families in every category. Among unrelated individuals, poverty rates for blacks are much higher than for whites. One could stop here and feel satisfied that the case had been made, but it is much more complex than that. Whites are on the average better educated than blacks, so part of the problem might be lack of human capital and here, too, discrimination comes in. Blacks and other minority group individuals may be deterred from obtaining the skills necessary to earn an adequate income by denial of equal opportunity to education and training. Also, if a family is poor, the children of the family are quite likely to be poor when they form their own families, since they (for reasons discussed earlier in this chapter) may not have a very high stock of human capital. Thus, discrimination in employment opportunities and discrimination in educational opportunities mutually interact, with the result that poverty is perpetuated.

Discrimination may be embodied in institutional barriers such as laws or customs. For example, entrance to skilled trade unions is often through sponsorship by present members. Since friends and relatives are much more likely to be sponsored than minority members personally unknown to the union members, racial discrimination tends to be perpetuated. Employers in other fields often recruit new employees through present employees, as this tends to boost morale in the work force. Again, this implies fewer opportunities for minority members. Federal government contracts have brought considerable pressure against such practices, which were not necessarily designed to be discriminatory, but have that effect. Trade unions have often been compelled to accept minority members. Many discriminatory laws have been repealed, and antidiscriminatory legislation passed. The U.S. Supreme Court decision of 1954 started the wheels moving toward equality of educational opportunity, yet the implications of this decision are still being battled in local school boards and in federal courts two decades later, indicating that the existence of a law does not insure overnight compliance. Other antisegregation laws have had a great impact on employment opportunities, but few would contend that complete equality for minority groups exists today.

One reason for discrimination in hiring is the erroneous belief that there are just so many jobs and that hiring a woman, say, means that a man somewhere cannot get a job. If the economy is healthy and growing, there are always some skills in short supply. As long as the skills people possess are appropriate to the society in question (and as long as the federal government keeps the economy at full employment), an increase in wages to one person does not imply a decrease in wages to another, or the loss of someone else's job.

One may ask the question, what does it cost to be black? Suppose we look at the black-white income differential and try to discover what it is for people of the same education, ability, and age (those of equal labor productivity). In 1959, the unadjusted income ratio of black urban males to white urban males was 58.3 percent. When adjusted for age, quantity of education, scholastic achievement (quality of education), and geographic region, the estimated income ratio was about 86 percent (that is, blacks with comparable human capital earn about 14 percent less than whites.)[8] This implies that a black can

---

[8]James Gwartney, "Discrimination and Income Differentials," *American Economic Review* (June 1970), 396 - 408.

expect to earn less than a white, even if he has an equal education. Therefore, many blacks cut short the educational process and, as a result, earn even less than the typical white. Lower future earnings because of labor market discrimination means a lower payoff to education, so it may be rational for a black person to choose less education than a white. As was mentioned, employment and educational discrimination are intertwined, and the point here is that employment discrimination and education itself are related. This relationship may go both ways. If employment discrimination were greatly reduced, then the payoff to education would be higher for blacks, and more would go on to higher levels of education. However, there is an offsetting factor. Remember that one of the major costs of education is foregone earnings during the period of education. If a person is subject to employment discrimination, then his earnings will be lower, and so will his foregone earnings if he chooses to be a student. While this factor lowers the cost of education, it does not seem to offset the impact of lower future earnings after the education period is over.

There has been progress in the area of "increasing opportunities," but racial and other kinds of discrimination are still severe. For example, in 1968 the average earnings of white high-school dropouts were higher than the average earnings of nonwhite high-school graduates.[9] This could be due to employment discrimination (by employers or unions) or to discrimination in educational opportunities (a high-school diploma from an inferior school may have much less value than one from a superior school).

REVIEW AND DISCUSSION QUESTIONS

1   Discuss some of the problems associated with the definition and measurement of poverty. Why are these important problems to resolve?
2   Show how discrimination and incentives to invest in human capital are interrelated.
3   Discuss the relationship between one's personal discount rate and investment in human capital.
4   Discuss conditions under which child-care programs are likely to be part of the least-cost means of eliminating poverty.
5   If employer discrimination on the basis of race were eliminated, so would be differentials between white and black incomes. Evaluate.

[9]*Economic Report of the President,* Government Printing Office, Washington, 1969, p. 167.

SUGGESTED READINGS

Banfield, Edward. *The Unheavenly City.* Boston: Little, Brown, 1970.

Economic Report of the President, 1969. "Combating Poverty in a Prosperous Economy," Washington: Government Printing Office, 1969. pp. 151 - 179. (Reprinted in Arthur F. Schreiber, Paul K. Gatons, and Richard B. Clemmer, eds., *Economics of Urban Problems: Selected Readings.* Boston: Houghton Mifflin, 1971.)

Fried, Edward, et al. "Grants for Social Programs: Manpower Training." In *Setting National Priorities: the 1974 Budget,* pp. 218 - 231. Washington: The Brookings Institution, 1973.

Galloway, Lowell E. *Poverty in America.* Columbus, Ohio: Grid, Inc., 1973.

Kain, John. Introduction to *Race and Poverty,* edited by John Kain, pp. 1 - 32. Englewood Cliffs, N.J.: Prentice-Hall, 1969.

Schiller, Bradley. *The Economics of Poverty and Discrimination.* Englewood Cliffs, N.J.: Prentice-Hall, 1972.

Schultze, Charles, et al. "Child Care," In *Setting National Priorities: The 1973 Budget,* pp. 252 - 290. Washington: The Brookings Institution, 1972.

Weisbrod, Burton. "Preventing High School Dropouts." In *Measuring the Benefits of Government Investments,* edited by Robert Dorfman, pp. 117 - 149. Washington: The Brookings Institution, 1965.

Weisbrod, Burton, and W. Lee Hansen. "An Income-Net Worth Approach to Measuring Economic Welfare." *American Economic Review* (December 1968), 1315 - 1329.

6 / Poverty: The Short-Run Approach

While Chapter 5 was concerned with long-run approaches to reducing poverty, this chapter discusses the short-run approach. The term "short run" does not necessarily refer to a short period of time. It means a program that does not address itself to the underlying causes of poverty: lack of human capital and discrimination. It is unreasonable to expect that discrimination will end overnight, and it is impossible to equip people instantly with more human capital. Even if the efficient amount of resources is being allocated to long-run poverty programs, society is still faced with poverty (lack of income) while training is taking place. In addition, long-run programs cannot deal with some cases of poverty, for example, the permanently and totally disabled, who cannot be rehabilitated. Therefore, in some instances, income redistribution programs may be the efficient (least-cost) means of achieving society's equity decision to eliminate poverty.

Cash Versus In-Kind Transfers

There has been a trend toward greater reliance on in-kind income redistribution programs for the poor in the United States. There are several arguments for and against in-kind transfers; an understanding of these arguments is important for the understanding of present programs. Part of the justification for in-kind transfers is a desire on the part of the government to control how the funds are spent by the recipient, the implicit assumption being that the government is a better judge of this than the individual. Some of the support for in-kind transfers can be summarized by the statement: "If we help this person, we do not want the money to go for liquor or some other undesirable thing." Most economists have argued against in-kind transfers precisely because they do violate consumer sovereignty, and it is felt that a cash grant in equivalent amount is more efficient because it raises the family's net private benefits by more than an in-kind transfer (as discussed in Chapter 4). If the poor "cannot be trusted to spend their money wisely" because of a lack of consumer knowledge, then society could provide cash transfers together with consumer education programs to remedy the alleged problems of imperfect information on the part of the poor.

More recently, some economists have favored in-kind transfers on the grounds of positive externalities that are supposedly generated by the consumption of certain commodities, but not others. In this context, increasing the consumption of housing might confer benefits on members of society other than the recipient of the in-kind transfer, while increasing the recipient's consumption of cigarettes is unlikely to benefit anyone other than the user (if, indeed, it benefits him in the long run). It is a question of the magnitude of these indirect benefits. If the positive externalities from increasing certain forms of consumption, like housing or medical care, are sufficiently large to nonrecipients, then in-kind transfers may be efficient.

Certain in-kind programs may be equivalent to cash income redistribution programs. If this is the case, then the in-kind nature of the program is inoperative, and the recipient may as well be given cash, since the results will be the same. The food stamp program, among existing in-kind programs, is probably the one that comes closest to being equivalent to a cash grant. The recipients of food stamps generally would be spending something on food without the program, and the subsidy may in part serve to release for other uses funds that would have been spent on food. Thus, some of the preference for in-kind programs can be traced to a misunderstanding of their true effects. However, it does appear that in-kind programs are more politically feasible than cash programs, even though their results may not differ significantly.

A further potential inefficiency of government income redistribution programs concerns administrative costs. The resources required to make transfer payments (as a percentage of the actual payments) under some programs may be so high as to impair the overall efficiency of the program. For both cash and in-kind programs, identifying the recipients (that is, administratively determining who is qualified to receive transfer payments under a given program) can be a costly administrative task, depending largely on the complexity of the legislation governing the program. In addition, administrative costs may depend on the frequency of payments, whether personal contact between the recipient and the agency disbursing the transfer payment is required, and whether or not the group of recipients changes rapidly over time. For example, one study estimated that the administrative costs of transfer payments to the unemployed under the unemployment compensation program were over 10 percent of the transfer payments because of the complexity of this program with respect to these factors. On the other hand, the administrative costs of cash transfer payments to welfare recipients were somewhat less than 2 percent of the transfer payments.[1] In-kind programs are often more costly than cash programs because there may be enforcement costs in seeing that the in-kind transfers are not resold. Further, when the government produces something there may be less concern with holding down costs than if the same thing is produced in the private market system, where higher costs mean lower profits.

[1]Gary Goetschius and John H. Wicks, "A Note on Administrative Costs of Governmental Transfer Payments," *National Tax Journal* (December 1971), 511 - 514.

The Negative Income Tax: Basic Features

In the last few years, various negative income tax or guaranteed annual income plans have been discussed, and some features of these plans have been incorporated into current income redistribution programs. The original plan was proposed as an alternative to the whole present welfare system, or at least large chunks of it, but political interest in such a sweeping program has declined, at least temporarily. However, since many current poverty programs have been restructured along these lines, the negative income tax and its basic concepts will be discussed first because they are useful in analyzing current programs.

All pure negative income tax plans have three basic features: (1) provision of a minimum income guaranteed to all households covered by the plan; (2) a negative tax rate at which earned income[2] would be taxed; and (3) a break-even level of income above which a household would no longer receive any assistance.

The minimum level of income (guaranteed income) can be set at any level. Take $4,000 as the poverty cutoff income level for a nonfarm family of four (the current official level is somewhat above this, as indicated at Table 5-1, but an even number is taken for illustrative purposes). Also, assume that the goal of society is to completely close the poverty gap; this means that the guaranteed minimum income would have to equal the poverty cutoff level of income ($4,000 in the above case), or else families with no other income would still be below the poverty line. The $4,000 guaranteed income would, of course, have to be adjusted for family size, location, and other factors discussed in Chapter 5, so that all households falling under the negative tax plan would be guaranteed an income just equal to their poverty cutoff income level. If we have properly measured a family's standard of living by its adjusted money income, the program would achieve horizontal equity—all those covered by the program and in the same circumstances would receive equal treatment (an equal subsidy).

The negative tax rate (which is applied to earnings of the recipient) may be varied from zero to 100 percent. Since there are obvious disincentives to work created by a tax rate approaching 100 percent on earned income, ideally the tax rate should be much lower. The key problem is to find a tax rate low enough to provide sufficient incentive to work yet not so low that the program involves unnecessarily

---

[2]Earned income (or "earnings") is income from wages, salaries, commissions, etc., in other words, income derived from working. Other types of income, such as rents received from property owned, dividends on stock, pensions, and interest on savings accounts is "unearned income." A negative income tax plan could easily be designed that would make some or all types of unearned income subject to the negative tax.

high costs to society. A rate often proposed is 50 percent. Plan A in Table 6-1 has a guaranteed minimum income of $4,000 and a negative tax rate of 50 percent. If the family earns $1,000, the transfer from the government would be reduced by $500 (50 percent of the $1,000 earned); thus, the family would receive a total income of $4,500— $1,000 from working plus a transfer from the government of $3,500. An incentive to work is provided, because a family with earnings has a higher total income (earnings plus transfer) than a family without earnings. Similarly, if the family earned $2,000, total family income would be $5,000. In this case, the family would receive $2,000 from working and lose $1,000 out of a potential transfer of $4,000, thus receiving a transfer of $3,000 (50 percent of $2,000 = $1,000; $4,000 − $1,000 = $3,000; $3,000 + $2,000 = $5,000).

At some level of earned income (the break-even level), the family would no longer receive a transfer from the government. When a 50 percent negative tax rate is applied to family earnings of $8,000, the reduction in the transfer payment is $4,000 = 50 percent of $8,000; thus, the family would lose the entire amount of the potential transfer when its earnings reached $8,000. However, families earning between $4,000 and $8,000 would still receive transfer payments, even though their earnings were considerably above the $4,000 poverty line.

The three variables contained in any simple negative income tax plan (with no exempt earnings and with a constant tax rate up to the break-even level of earnings) are related as follows:

$$\frac{\text{guaranteed minimum income}}{\text{negative tax rate}} = \text{break-even level of income.}$$

In the above example, the break-even level calculated by this formula is $4,000/0.50 = $8,000, confirming the break-even level obtained above. There are substantial trade-offs between the three variables; once any two are chosen, the value of the third is determined. With a $4,000 poverty cutoff level, a tax rate of 25 percent requires society to choose between raising the break-even level of income to $16,000 or reducing the guaranteed minimum income to less than the poverty cutoff level. At the present time, a break-even level of $16,000 is greater than average family income in the United States. But, if the poverty gap is to be eliminated, providing an incentive to work by means of a negative tax rate substantially less than 100 percent will result in payments being made to many families whose earnings are above the poverty line. As previously mentioned, several current programs have negative income tax features. If a family participates in several of these programs, it may face negative tax rates approaching or exceeding 100 percent over some range of earnings. A fuller discussion of these problems occurs later in this chapter.

Table 6-1 shows how two other negative tax plans, in addition to plan A, would work. Plan B shows the effect of raising the negative tax rate from 50 percent to 75 percent, while keeping the guaranteed income level for the family at $4,000. The earned income at which the subsidy becomes zero ($5,333) is, of course, the break-even level. Obviously, plan A is more expensive than plan B. Plan C shows part of the Family Assistance Plan that was originally proposed by the Nixon administration, later modified by Congress, and finally shelved. The original plan called for a $1,600 guaranteed minimum income for a household of four, with $720 of earnings exempt from tax and a negative tax rate of 50 percent thereafter. The break-even level of earnings ($3,920) was roughly equal to the poverty cutoff level in 1970. The Demogrant plan proposed by Senator McGovern in the 1972 presidential campaign is a version of plan A. This plan proposed "giving" every man, woman, and child $1,000 per year as a minimum, and taxing earnings at some rate (50 percent in Table 6-1). There is little difference between taxing earnings at 50 percent and reducing transfer payments by 50 cents for each dollar earned, if the program applies to the same people. It should be noted that the Demogrant plan was more comprehensive in coverage than the Family Assistance Plan, which was designed more with a view toward reforming the welfare system than to expanding coverage.

	EARNED INCOME	+SUBSIDY=	TOTAL INCOME
Plan A: 50% negative tax rate			
$4,000 guaranteed minimum income	$ 0	$4,000	$4,000
	1,000	3,500	4,500
	2,000	3,000	5,000
	3,000	2,500	5,500
	4,000	2,000	6,000
	6,000	1,000	7,000
	8,000	0	8,000
Plan B: 75% negative tax rate			
$4,000 guaranteed minimum income	$ 0	$4,000	$4,000
	1,000	3,250	4,250
	2,000	2,500	4,500
	3,000	1,750	4,750
	4,000	1,000	5,000
	5,000	250	5,250
	5,333	0	5,333
Plan C: 0% negative tax rate on first $720	$ 0	$1,600	$1,600
	720	1,600	2,320
50% negative tax rate on earned	1,000	1,460	2,460
income in excess of $720	2,000	960	2,960
	3,000	460	3,460
$1,600 guaranteed minimum income	3,920	0	3,920

Table 6-1: Three Negative Income Tax Plans for a Nonfarm Household of Four

Basically, there is a three-way trade-off at work in negative income tax plans between work incentives, poverty elimination, and cost to the rest of society. Certain programs have been examined in order to determine the cost to the United States taxpayer, and these results indicate the workings of the trade-off. For a plan with a guaranteed income of $3,600 for a family of four (and correspondingly adjusted amounts for other families) and a negative tax rate of 50 percent, the total subsidy cost was estimated to be $14.8 billion. Lowering the tax rate to 33 percent increased the cost to $22 billion, while increasing the negative tax rate to 67 percent lowered the cost to $12.1 billion (in both cases, the guaranteed minimum income remained at $3,600).[3] This seems to indicate that increasing the negative tax rate much above 50 percent does not tremendously reduce the total program cost, while it may have serious work incentive effects. However, lowering the negative tax rate to 33 percent, because of the rapid increase in the break-even level of earnings, greatly increases the cost of the program. It should also be noted that increasing the guaranteed minimum income also tends to increase greatly the cost of the negative income tax plan. With a $4,800 guaranteed minimum income and a 50 percent negative tax rate, the cost of such a program is estimated to be $27.1 billion, or roughly double the cost with a $3,600 minimum. By 1976, the official poverty cutoff level will no doubt exceed $4,800 for a typical family of four, so a program that even comes close to eliminating poverty (as measured) will be expensive. Such estimates should be considered as alternatives to current program costs; when this is done, it appears that a program that "eliminates poverty" will cost perhaps three times what the present set of programs directed at the poor cost. On the other hand, of course, it would do far more toward eliminating the short-run poverty problem.

In summary, the following statements can be made:

1 Decreasing the negative income tax rate, with the same guaranteed income, will:
   a. Increase the incentive to work
   b. Increase the cost of the program to society
   c. Increase the break-even level of income
   d. Eliminate more of the poverty gap (provided that the guaranteed minimum income is less than the poverty cutoff line; if it equals or exceeds the cutoff line, the poverty gap will be eliminated)
2 Increasing the guaranteed minimum income, with the same negative tax rate, will:

---

[3]Estimates by the Urban Institute for fiscal year 1976, as reported in Edward Fried et al., *Setting National Priorities: The 1974 Budget,* The Brookings Institution, Washington, 1973, p. 83.

    a. Increase the cost of the program to society
    b. Increase the break-even level of income
    c. Eliminate more of the poverty gap

The Hours-Wages Form of Negative Income Tax

The severe trade-offs among the key variables of negative income tax plans discussed above come to the forefront when the recipients of the program are the working poor—those who are employed yet, because of discrimination or low stocks of human capital, have earnings below the poverty cutoff level. The fear that a negative income tax plan would significantly reduce the incentives of the working poor (who constitute a large proportion of the total population in poverty) to continue to work may be the main reason why Congress has not adopted a comprehensive negative income tax program. Under most negative tax proposals earnings would be taxed at rates far in excess of the effective rates that very high-income households pay. For example, a household with an income of $100,000 may have a taxable income (income after tax deductions and personal exemptions) of $76,000. The federal income tax on this, under tax rates in effect in 1974, would be $31,020, an effective tax rate of slightly over 31 percent—a rate below that called for in most negative tax plans because of the trade-offs with the guaranteed minimum income and the break-even income level. A worker presently earning $2,000 per year at a low wage might have little incentive to continue working if he became the recipient of a minimum guaranteed income exceeding his present earnings with a high negative tax rate on earnings.

Hours-wages forms of negative income tax plans try to meet this problem of work incentives by making a distinction between earnings that result from high wages and few hours worked and earnings that result from low wages and many hours worked. Lower taxes are applied to earnings resulting from long hours than are applied to the same earnings resulting from fewer hours worked at higher wage rates. Most studies indicate that workers with lesser skills (and lower wage rates)—such as casual laborers, many females, and most teenagers—are more sensitive to work incentives because they have more ability to vary the number of hours they work.[4] For example, a casual laborer may gain employment by standing on a street corner each morning at a "curbside labor market," being hired anew each morning to work on a job lasting only one day. On the other hand, those with greater skills (and higher wage rates) are more likely to be employed in jobs with regular work hours and not be as sensitive to

---

[4]For a summary of the results of some recent studies, see Henry Aaron, *Why is Welfare So Hard to Reform?* The Brookings Institution, Washington, 1973, pp. 36 - 37.

work incentives, since they either work a forty-hour week (with earnings well above the poverty line) or do not work at all (resulting in poverty).

An experiment known as the Graduated Work Incentive Experiment, financed by the United States government, was conducted with several hundred low-income families in New Jersey and Pennsylvania over a three-year period ending in 1971. These families were provided with a guaranteed income ranging from 50 to 125 percent of the poverty cutoff level and subjected to negative tax rates of 30, 50, and 70 percent, in order to determine the work incentive effects of varying guaranteed income and tax rate levels. The results indicate that the negative tax plan had little effect on the hours worked by husbands in families where both husband and wife were present. Hours worked by wives in these families declined by about one-third in white families and about one-half in Spanish-speaking families but were little changed in black families—a result that the research had difficulty explaining. Although the results of the experiment are not completely clear, they tend to indicate that hours worked would decrease in the range of 5 to 10 percent in families subjected to negative tax rates of 50 percent and considerably more for rates above 50 percent.[5]

Table 6-2 shows how a negative income tax plan would work that differentiated the hours and wages that make up earnings. The guaranteed minimum income to the household is $2,400, regardless of the wages and hours that determine the household's earnings. However, as indicated in the top portion of the table, a household whose breadwinner(s) earned $2 per hour would have its earnings taxed at 33⅓ percent (the $2,400 potential subsidy would be reduced by $1 for every $3 earned). As a result of the relatively low tax rate, considerable work incentive (motivation to work more hours) is provided. As can be seen, the break-even level of income would be $7,200, which the household would reach only if the total number of hours worked at $2 per hour by all members of the household totaled more than 3,600 per year. In the case of a household whose breadwinner(s) earned $6 per hour, earnings would be taxed at 66⅔ percent, reducing the potential subsidy of $2,400 by $2 for every $3 earned. As a result, the break-even income is $3,600. While little incentive is provided to work additional hours if total hours are in the range of zero to 600 per year, it is usually the case that employees who are capable of making $6 per hour or more are employed in jobs whose work rules dictate that the individual works full-time (that is, approximately 2,000 hours per year). In such cases, the high tax rates on

[5]Albert Rees, "An Overview of the Labor-Supply Results," *Journal of Human Resources* (Spring 1974), 158 - 180.

earnings up to the break-even level ($3,600 in this case) may have little effect on whether the individual chooses to work a full-time job or not. The result of such a plan is that workers employed for more hours but at lower wage rates than other workers with the same total earnings receive greater subsidies. Of course, if such a plan were implemented, different negative tax rates would have to be developed for all wage rates, not just the two examples in Table 6-2.[6]

While providing a possible solution to the work incentive problem, a wages-hours type of negative income tax plan such as outlined above creates some problems in addition to those associated with regular negative income tax plans. For one thing, such a plan would only apply to that portion of the poor who are deemed capable of working; it would not be of help to a totally disabled individual, for example. The necessity of having to divide the low-income population into those who could potentially find employment and those who could not presents major problems in itself, since high administrative costs may be incurred in making the division. There might be many borderline cases, and value judgments would have to be made, resulting in possible inequities. Also, both hours and earnings would have to be verified to compute subsidy payments, as opposed to just earnings in a regular negative income tax plan. For those below the poverty cutoff line who were not deemed capable of working, another negative income tax plan would have to be provided, which possibly

	HOURS WORKED	EARNED INCOME	+ SUBSIDY	= TOTAL INCOME
Household with low-skilled breadwinner(s) earning $2 per hour ($2,400 guaranteed minimum income, 33⅓% negative tax rate)	0	0	$2,400	$2,400
	150	300	2,300	2,600
	300	600	2,200	2,800
	600	1,200	2,000	3,200
	1,200	2,400	1,600	4,000
	2,400	4,800	800	5,600
	3,600	7,200	0	7,200
Household with higher-skilled breadwinner(s) earning $6 per hour ($2,400 guaranteed minimum income, 66⅔% negative tax rate)	0	0	$2,400	$ 2,400
	150	900	1,800	2,700
	300	1,800	1,200	3,000
	600	3,600	0	3,600
	1,200	7,200	0	7,200
	2,400	14,400	0	14,400

Table 6-2: An Example of an Hours-Wages Form of Negative Income Tax Plan

[6]For a more elaborate example of such a plan, see Henry Aaron, *Why is Welfare So Hard to Reform?* pp. 60 - 62.

would have a higher guaranteed minimum income to close more of the poverty gap of such households. Since work incentives would not concern those not expected to work, the plan could have higher tax rates and a lower break-even level of income compared with the guaranteed minimum income.

Current Short-Run Poverty Programs

Income transfers, viewed here as short-run poverty programs, amounted to $100 billion per year in 1972. Table 6-3 shows these outlays for individual programs. About 85 percent of this amount is financed by the federal government. Most people probably think of "welfare" and, in particular, AFDC (aid to families with dependent children) when they think of income transfers. As Table 6-3 shows, AFDC accounts for less than 7 percent of the total income transfers listed. About 75 percent of the $100 billion is for programs not based on the income of the recipients, that is, programs not directed exclusively at the poor. Social security (OASI) accounts for about one-half of this amount. In addition to the programs shown in Table 6-3, there are other government programs that amount to income transfers. Examples are special tax treatment for certain kinds of expenditures like mortgage interest (discussed in Chapter 8) and subsidies to farmers, which were originally justified in terms of augmenting farm income. Private charity is an additional form of income transfer not flowing through the public sector.

Because the outlays shown in Table 6-3 do not go exclusively to the poor, they do not eliminate the poverty gap, although they do eliminate much of it. In fact, many individuals are pushed above and considerably beyond the poverty line by these programs. As an example, social security payments depend on earnings, but not on nonearned income. A person may have property income that leaves him just below the poverty line, but his social security payment (OASI) pushes him considerably above it.

With the large number of programs, many families are covered by several programs, which results in some serious work incentive problems. For example, an AFDC family is automatically eligible for food stamps and may also be in public housing, have children receiving free school lunches, and be receiving Medicaid. To further complicate matters, many programs vary considerably depending on local government policies. Also, some of these current programs have features of the negative income tax built into them. AFDC, food stamps, public housing, and school lunches all depend on family income. If the family is covered by the first three of these, it is conceivable that, if family earnings increased by $1, benefits from the three programs would drop by 85¢.[7] In other words, the combined negative tax rate would be 85 percent in this case, certainly having an adverse effect on the family's work incentives. Another problem that can adversely affect work incentives is the "notch" effect. If a family earns a certain amount of extra income, it finds that it loses its eligibility for some income-based programs. To compound the problem, loss of eligibility for AFDC, for example, might entail loss of eligibility for food stamps. The effect of a notch is that, in a certain range of earnings income, the negative tax rate can be much greater than 100 percent. For example, it has been shown that a man with a family of four working for the minimum wage in New York City is

	TOTAL OUTLAYS	FEDERAL GOVERNMENT	STATE AND LOCAL GOVERNMENT
PROGRAMS BASED ON RECIPIENT'S INCOME			
Aid to families with dependent children (AFDC)	$ 6.7	$ 3.7	$ 3.0
Old age assistance	2.5	1.7	0.8
Aid to the blind	0.1	0.06	0.04
Aid to the permanently and totally disabled	1.5	0.8	0.7
General assistance	0.7		0.7
Veteran's pensions	2.5	2.5	
National school lunch program	0.5	0.5	
Food stamps	2.0	2.0	
Commodity foods	0.3	0.3	
Public housing	0.8	0.8	
Medicaid	7.0	3.9	3.1
TOTAL	$24.6	$16.3	$ 8.3
PROGRAMS NOT BASED ON RECIPIENTS INCOME			
Old age and survivor's insurance (OASI)	$34.5	$34.5	
Disability insurance	4.0	4.0	
Railroad retirement	2.1	2.1	
Civil service retirement	3.4	3.4	
Other federal employee retirement	4.0	4.0	
State and local employee retirement	3.3		$ 3.3
Unemployment compensation	6.4	6.4	
Workmen's compensation	3.0	0.2	2.8
Veteran's medical care	2.2	2.2	
Veteran's compensation	3.6	3.6	
Medicare	8.5	8.5	
TOTAL	$75.0	$68.9	$ 6.1
TOTAL ALL PROGRAMS	$99.6	$85.2	$14.4

Table 6-3: Outlays Under Public Income Transfer Programs, 1972 (Billions of Dollars)

SOURCE: James R. Storey, *Studies in Public Welfare,* Paper No. 1, U.S. Congress, Joint Economic Committee, Government Printing Office, Washington, April 10, 1972.

[7] J. Storey, *Studies in Public Welfare,* Paper no. 1, U.S. Congress, Joint Economic Committee, Government Printing Office, Washington, April 10, 1972, p. 9.

better off working half-time than working full-time at the same wage rate, provided he participates in programs for which he is eligible.[8]

Welfare Programs

Until 1967, most welfare programs had an implicit tax of 100 percent on earnings. To determine the amount of the monthly check for an AFDC client, a caseworker would prepare an expenditure budget, then subtract the family's resources (earnings and other sources of income from savings, etc.) from the budgeted expenditures. Subject to limitations on maximum payments, the family could get the amount of the difference between the budget and its resources. If its resources increased, for example because earnings increased, the welfare payment was decreased by the full amount of the earnings—an implicit tax of 100 percent on earnings. Since 1967, several deductions from earnings are allowed; generally, these include the first $30 per month of earnings, certain allowable work expenses including child care, and mandatory deductions for taxes and so forth from the paycheck. In addition, one-third of earnings can be deducted. Thus, AFDC presently amounts to a negative income tax plan with a certain amount of exempt earnings and something less than a 66⅔ percent negative tax rate. (Since social security and other taxes are deducted from paychecks, the 66⅔ percent rate applies to take-home pay; thus, the negative tax rate is less than 66⅔ percent of gross pay.) Since there can be a substantial amount of exempt income because of the deductions permitted, it can be quite difficult for one to earn enough income to reach the break-even earnings level, even if one works full-time.

Probably the most serious problem connected with welfare programs is that they can be termed "categorical assistance." This means that one receives assistance if one falls into the categories set by law, but receives nothing otherwise. In some areas, AFDC can go to families with a male present only if he is totally disabled. The reasoning behind this is not novel, stemming from the idea that any able-bodied man should work and if he does work he will not need assistance. Women have traditionally stayed in the home to care for children, so no social stigma was attached to a female-headed family. The problem is whether society really wants to eradicate poverty. Traditional family roles are changing, and a policy that is based on old stereotypes violates horizontal equity in its unequal treatment of equally poor families. Several states have opted to allow AFDC payments to families with males present. In addition to their categorical nature, AFDC programs create equity violations because the level of benefits depends on where one lives. In Mississippi, in 1971, a family of four could get, at most, $60 for basic needs under AFDC, while the

[8]Storey, *Studies in Public Welfare*, p. 10.

comparable amount in Connecticut was $327 per month. This latter amount is fairly close to the poverty cutoff line, but the former is far below it, even after adjusting for differences in living costs between Mississippi and Connecticut.

In addition to AFDC, several other categorical public assistance programs have existed for many years, including aid to the blind, aid to the permanently and totally disabled, and old age assistance. In 1974 these three programs were replaced by the Supplemental Security Income program, which is a negative income tax program. The guaranteed minimum for a married couple is $2,340 per year, with $20 per month of other income received being exempt from tax, and an additional $65 per month exempt if the income is earned. After the exemptions, additional income is taxed at a negative tax rate of 50 percent. Thus, if a couple qualified for the program and had only earned income, the break-even level of earnings would be $5,700. If "other income" came from social security and pensions, the break-even amount of these would be $4,920 per year. This program was designed to replace the state categorical public assistance programs with a national program; the uniform nationwide benefits improve the horizontal equity of these programs over the old ones. Most recipients receive greater benefits under the new program and some receive greatly increased benefits, although some of the increased benefits are cancelled by a provision that recipients are ineligible for food stamps.

Social Security

The most important poverty program in the United States is OASDHI, or social security as it is generally known.[9] According to a study, in 1966, over half of those who were pushed above the poverty cutoff lines by income transfer programs were pushed there by OASDHI. Much of the benefits go to the nonpoor, however, as social security was designed to be self-contributory to some extent, with a person building up credits during his working lifetime. With increases in benefits and rates of contribution, however, one must view the system more as a transfer from those currently working to those retired. Benefits have increased to the extent that the payoff to the contributions of those currently retired has greatly exceeded their contributions. Viewed this way, the OASDHI tax becomes a regressive tax, since it is paid at a constant rate (5.85 percent in 1974 on both employer and employee) up to a maximum income ($13,200 in 1974) and not after that level of earnings. The OASDHI tax rate of 5.85

[9]In OASDHI, OAS refers to the old age and survivor's part of social security; D stands for disability; and H for health (Medicare) insurance. These three parts of the total program are shown separately in Table 6-3.

percent on both employer and employee, with no personal exemptions, means that many low-income employees pay higher OASDHI taxes than federal income taxes. This in turn means that the tax part of OASDHI serves to increase poverty among the working poor, while the benefits financed by the tax alleviate poverty among the retired poor.

An employer generally will take on an employee only if he (the employer) expects to add enough to his revenues to at least equal the employee's wages, including taxes such as OASDHI. Thus, the impact of the tax on a marginal worker is equal to 11.7 percent—the rate the employee must pay (5.85 percent) plus the amount paid by the employer (5.85 percent). The assumption here is that the incidence of the employer portion of the social security tax is shifted onto the employee. The higher costs to the employer brought about by the OASDHI tax may lead him to hire fewer workers, with obvious consequences for unemployment. This argument is similar to that against minimum wage laws, illustrated by Figure 6-1. Assume for simplicity that the number of laborers is the same regardless of the level of wages, giving the vertical labor-supply curve. The demand curve for labor depends on the amount of output a firm expects to get from additional workers. Thus, if a worker is expected to produce addi-

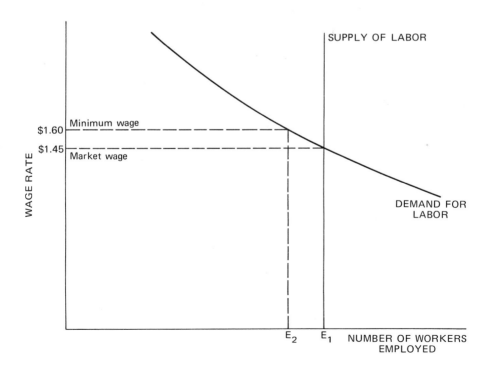

Figure 6-1: The Effect of Minimum Wage Laws on Labor Employment

tional output worth $1.50 to the firm but the minimum wage is $1.60, then the firm will not hire the worker. The popular conception of minimum wage laws is that they are devices that help to alleviate poverty. This is true for workers who keep their jobs. Those who lose their jobs or are not hired are much more likely to be in poverty, since they are unemployed. In Figure 6-1, with no minimum wage, the market wage will be $1.45 and E_1 workers will be employed. At the minimum wage of $1.60, only E_2 workers will be employed, and E_1 minus E_2 workers will be unemployed.

Inner-city black teenagers are particularly affected by minimum wage laws, since they tend to have low levels of skills, which offer low productivity to employers. It should be noted that, under certain circumstances, minimum wages can increase employment. The conditions necessary for this are that an employer be very large relative to a job market, so that in order to hire additional workers, he must raise wages considerably. These conditions are not met in large urban areas.

Figure 6-1 indicates that a minimum wage will cause unemployment. Similarly, Figure 6-2 shows that the social security tax on the employer reduces potential earnings of the employee. Without the tax on the employer, the hourly wage would be $2.12, since this is the

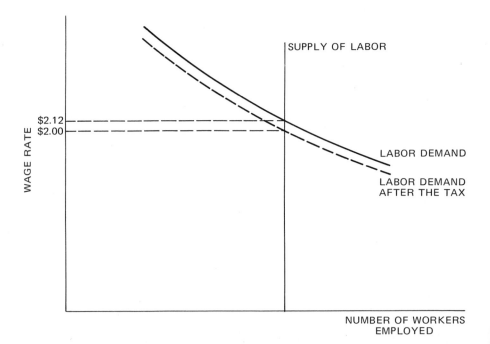

Figure 6-2: Incidence of the Social Security Tax Paid by the Employer

value to the employer of the additional worker. Imposition of the social security tax on the employer does not alter the value of the additional worker; thus, the employer will still be willing to pay a total of $2.12 per hour. However, about 12¢ (5.85 percent of $2.12) now goes to the government, leaving $2.00 for the wage. The worker, too, must pay an additional 12¢ out of the $2.00 per hour be earns. Thus, take-home pay after the tax is $1.88 per hour and it would have been $2.12 per hour in the absence of the social security tax—a tax rate of 11.7 percent on earnings before considering any negative tax rates or other taxes involved.

In-Kind Redistribution Programs

There are several income redistribution programs which provide benefits not in cash, but in kind, mostly housing, medical care, and food. Although public housing for the poor is obviously a short-run poverty program, discussion of that program and other housing assistance to the poor will be taken up in Chapter 8.

Food stamps   The program which probably comes the closest to being equivalent to a cash distribution program is the food stamp program. Food stamps were originally used during the early 1940s, but that earlier program expired; food stamps were revived in 1964 in a different form. Basically, the program involves selling vouchers (that is, a coupon or certificate) to the poor at prices that depend on the household's income level and range from zero to about 80 percent of the face value of the certificates. If someone is in the program and experiences an increase in income, the cost of the food stamps goes up by about 30 cents for every additional dollar in income. Thus, the food stamp program works like a negative income tax plan with a negative tax rate of 30 percent, after some initial level of income is attained. (A family of four receives the stamps free until its income reaches $30 per month.) Benefit levels are the same in all states where the program is in operation with the exception of Alaska and Hawaii, where benefits are slightly higher because of higher living costs. The commodity food program, listed in Table 6-3, is another in-kind food program which has been in operation for some time; however, it is being replaced by the food stamp program.

A family of a certain size receives a designated amount of food stamps ($112 per month for a family of four) and qualifies if its income is below certain specified limits. Many families not qualifying for welfare programs can qualify for food stamps. Stamps are good for any food items that are not imported, but such items as paperwares, cigarettes, and alcoholic beverages cannot be purchased with the stamps. However, reflection would indicate that, provided the family is currently spending quite a bit on food, the food stamps can be used to replace some previous expenditures, freeing money for other purposes, such as cigarettes. For example, suppose you currently spend $20 per week on meat, and someone gives you $20 worth of meat just before you go to the store. You might still buy some meat, but the amount you would buy would be the same as if someone had given you $20 in cash, provided the meat given you is worth $20 to you.

The level of food stamp program benefits has expanded rapidly in recent years, approaching $4 billion by 1975—double the $2 billion in 1972 shown in Table 6-3. Because the requirements to qualify for food stamps are less restrictive compared with welfare programs, one could consider the food stamp program as a guaranteed annual income program. The guaranteed minimum for a family of four under the program is $112, which translates to $1,344 per year. After an initial exemption of $30 of earnings per month, earnings are taxed at a negative tax rate of about 30 percent. This would lead to a break-even level of earnings of about $400 per month or $4,800 per year; however, the maximum allowable income is $373 per month for a family of four, resulting in a notch effect (drop in benefits to zero) as the family's income passes this level. As an antipoverty program, the food stamp plan no doubt closes some of the poverty gap (but not the official gap, since in-kind benefits are not counted). At the higher levels of earnings, some families can even be brought above the line as a result of the program. In fact, if the family also qualified for other programs, it could achieve a living standard considerably above the poverty cutoff line. The main drawback of this program from the point of view of poverty elimination is that the very poor remain very poor even though they receive the stamps free. Unless they receive other assistance, they remain far below the poverty line.

Compared with public housing (discussed in Chapter 8), the food stamp program achieves a much higher degree of horizontal equity, since the benefits of the program accrue to a far greater proportion of the total number of individuals in poverty and potentially could accrue to many more. By 1972, about 12 million persons benefited from the program (or about one-half of the total poor as indicated in Table 5-2) and this number is growing. Compared with AFDC, far more of the poor qualify for the food stamp program. It was already noted that those on AFDC are automatically eligible for food stamps, but many recipients of food stamps receive no other subsidy.

Another food distribution program that is important for families with children is the school lunch program, which provides lunches to school children at subsidized rates for poor families. The outlays by the federal government for this program have also grown rapidly in recent years.

Health programs   Over 20 percent of the government income transfers are for health and disability (see Table 6-3). As discussed in Chapter 5, in one sense these could be considered long-run programs, since they can equip people with increased amounts of human capital. However, they are probably primarily short-run programs, since a large portion of the benefits go to those over 65. Programs such as workmen's compensation and disability insurance are more likely to be long-run programs, since they apply to those of working age. Medicaid goes to the poor, and hence to some extent to future and present workers, but Medicare is primarily for the retired. A major thrust of Medicare and other programs is to provide payments for major nonrecurring expenses that can quite easily leave a family destitute. Part of the public's willingness to provide this sort of in-kind assistance is that it is in the nature of a service, rather than a good that can be transferred or sold to someone else. However, it is still true that part of the effect of providing medical care is to increase the consumption of other goods and services. Those receiving this kind of aid can better afford to buy food and housing (or liquor). Thus, even when the service is not transferable, the program might have some characteristics of a cash grant program.

In terms of equity, Medicare and Medicaid seem to have put medical care within the reach of many who could not pay for such care in the past, and, along with other increases in social security benefits, the programs have reduced the incidence of poverty among the elderly (although it is still high). Medicare is administered through the Social Security Administration, and the benefits are uniform throughout the United States. Medicaid benefits depend on many local rules, and those eligible for other assistance programs (AFDC) are automatically eligible for Medicaid. Benefits vary widely among states, and states are not even required to have a Medicaid program (Arizona and Alaska have none). Thus, there seem to be rather serious violations of horizontal equity. Another problem is that part of the payments to doctors and hospitals by the Medicare and Medicaid programs may simply be taking the place of previous charity. Former charity patients become paying customers, and only part of the increased expenditures on medical care represents an actual increase in such care. In terms of efficiency, if society wishes to increase the quantity of medical care produced, then these additional payments should provide a financial incentive in this direction. However, it takes many years to train new doctors and even more to provide new facilities for their training. If it turns out that a significant portion of social security taxes for Medicare merely increase the price of health services and the incomes of doctors, this amounts to an income transfer from relatively poor wage earners to relatively rich physicians, in which case, the Medicare program becomes in part a poverty program in reverse (while remaining in part a program that transfers income to the elderly in the form of health care).

Maintaining a Tight Labor Market

An approach to poverty reduction which is not directly a poverty program is the use of policies by the federal government to achieve full employment. The maintenance of a tight labor market (that is, very low unemployment) tends to counter both major causes of poverty, lack of human capital and discrimination. As is well known, the unskilled are the last to be hired and the first to be laid off. Maintaining a tight labor market insures that many of the unskilled will be hired and perhaps removed from poverty. In the sense that a person is in poverty because of unemployment (a temporary case of poverty), this can be thought of as a short-run policy. To the extent that low levels of unemployment are maintained long enough to counter lack of training by providing on-the-job training and to counter discrimination, the maintenance of a tight labor market can be thought of as a long-run poverty policy.

In terms of discrimination, when unemployment is high, potential employers can be much more selective in hiring. While this may permit the employer to hire "better quality" labor, it may also enable him to impose unnecessary requirements—a high-school diploma for a janitor, for example. High levels of unemployment also give an employer greater latitude for practicing discrimination in hiring. To the extent that blacks and other minority group members suffer from discrimination, a tight labor market may significantly reduce such discriminatory barriers. From 1959 to 1969, the number of blacks and other minorities below the poverty line fell from about 11 million to about 7.6 million. However, from 1959 to 1961, with rising unemployment, the number of minority group members in poverty rose to 11.9 million. The number of poor whites *fell* during this period.[10] Since a tight labor market means a high demand for employees, employers will have to pay higher wages in order to attract new employees. Rising wages for the unskilled may mean that more people will be able to move above the poverty line.

A tight labor market may also increase the stock of human capital of the poor. Employers may be willing to finance training programs to upgrade workers with skills that are in short supply. The JOBS program seems to follow this pattern. When the labor market is tighter, employers are more willing to provide training to disadvantaged workers.

The federal government uses monetary and fiscal policy to achieve full employment. It is not possible to give more than an outline of these tools in this book, but some important aspects can be considered here. Monetary policy is generally undertaken by the Federal Reserve

[10]U.S. Bureau of the Census, *Current Population Reports*, Series P-60, No. 71 Government Printing Office, Washington, 1970.

System, and it consists of controlling the money supply and interest rates. Fiscal policy refers to the budget of the United States government, whether it is balanced, whether there is a planned deficit, or whether a surplus is planned. Table 6-4 shows how monetary policy and fiscal policy affect the economy, with respect to unemployment and—another problem of the poor as well as everyone else—inflation. It is unfortunate but true that the goals of price stability and low levels of unemployment are often in conflict.

Table 6-4 indicates the following: when inflation is a problem, monetary or fiscal policy can alleviate the inflation, but at the expense of increasing unemployment. This unemployment is not permanent, but is brought about by the transition from a situation of high inflation to one of lower inflation. The transition can be very harsh, however, and may cause unemployment for a year or more. The general pattern after wars, until World War Two, was for the wartime inflation to be followed by a postwar depression. Since then, we have learned how to avoid these depressions, or at least how to make them less severe, through monetary or fiscal policy. Governments are unwilling to simply crunch the economy severely (use contractionary monetary and fiscal policy) in order to control inflation. If they were willing to do so, unemployment would be a greater problem and would lead to greater temporary poverty.

At times, as during the Great Depression of the 1930s, inflation was not a problem (in fact prices fell), so that monetary and fiscal policy could have alleviated a lot of the unemployment without causing inflation. The goals conflict only when the economy is near full employment. Earlier we discussed why unemployment can be a cause of poverty. Inflation can certainly make poverty worse also. If a person is living on a fixed pension, inflation will decrease its value. General-

	CONTRACTIONARY	EXPANSIONARY
MONETARY POLICY	Restrict the growth of money supply, raising interest rates	Increase the rate of growth of the money supply, tending to temporarily lower interest rates
FISCAL POLICY	Raise taxes or cut government spending, or both	Lower taxes or increase government spending, or both
EFFECT ON ECONOMY	Tends to slow inflation, and increase unemployment	Tends to decrease unemployment, and increase inflation problem if economy is near full employment or has been experiencing inflation

Table 6-4: The Effects of Monetary and Fiscal Policy on Inflation and Unemployment

ly, social security payments have been raised by more than enough to adjust for the inflation that has occurred, but other types of pension have not always done so. Further, many older people depend on their savings in order to support themselves, or more correctly, on the interest on these savings. Inflation tends to decrease the value of savings if they are in the form of fixed-value investments (for example, savings bonds).

In recent years, the United States has seen a wide variety of monetary and fiscal policies. One legacy of the Vietnam War was a badly overheated economy. Inflation was the major problem, and unemployment rates were very low in early 1968. At first, contractionary monetary policy was instituted, and the money supply growth was halted. This pushed interest rates up to then historic highs, and no doubt had an effect on the rate of inflation, keeping it lower than it would have been. It was easier to see the increase in unemployment that followed this contractionary monetary policy. Government spending has been held down also in order to deal with inflation. One may wonder why inflation persists in the face of these policies that essentially caused a high level of unemployment. Actually, if control of inflation had been the only goal, a more severe contractionary policy would have ended the inflation quickly. It was the desire to keep unemployment levels fairly low that led to the simultaneous existence of unemployment and inflation. The reader should ask himself if he personally would have preferred more inflation or more unemployment. This dilemma requires an answer through the political process and makes monetary and fiscal policy, in many cases, extremely difficult to use.

REVIEW AND DISCUSSION QUESTIONS

1 Compare and contrast as alternative means of reducing poverty:
   a. manpower training programs
   b. subsidies to help pay for essentials (food stamps, housing, etc.)
   c. direct cash assistance
2 Is the presence of poverty in the United States a problem of inefficiency in the allocation of resources or a question of equity in the distribution of income or both? Explain.
3 Can the poverty gap be completely closed by a negative income tax plan without also redistributing some income to the nonpoor?
4 Propose and defend what you would consider to be an efficient solution to poverty caused by:
   a. a low stock of "genetic" human capital
   b. a high personal discount rate resulting in a low stock of human capital

Be careful to avoid advocating policies that violate consumer sovereignty. Separate long-run from short-run considerations.
5 Describe the essential features of a negative income tax plan with a 30 percent negative tax rate and a guaranteed minimum income equal to 50 percent of the poverty cutoff level of income. Can you suggest another plan which you could justify as superior to this?
6 Is social security a poverty program?
7 Practically all income redistribution programs can be analyzed in similar fashion to a negative income tax program. Explain.
8 Maintaining a tight labor market is both a short-run and a long-run poverty program. Explain.
9 Imagine that you have been named to head a new federal agency called the Office of Poverty Elimination. Your annual budget is any amount up to $30 billion and legislation requires you to eliminate poverty in the statistical sense (every family can receive a check for its poverty gap if it receives no other aid). Outline your long-run and short-run programs.

SUGGESTED READINGS

Aaron, Henry. *Why Is Welfare So Hard to Reform?* Washington: The Brookings Institution, 1973.

Fried, Edward, et al. *Setting National Priorities: The 1974 Budget,* pp. 38 - 100, 101 - 129, 160 - 169. Washington: The Brookings Institution, 1973.

Green, Christopher. *Negative Taxes and the Poverty Problem.* Washington: The Brookings Institution, 1967.

Schultze, Charles, et al. *Setting National Priorities: The 1973 Budget,* pp. 175 - 251. Washington: The Brookings Institution, 1972.

Storey, James. *Studies in Public Welfare.* Paper No. 1, U.S. Congress, Joint Economic Committee. Washington: Government Printing Office, April 10, 1972.

7 / Urban Housing Problems

In Chapter 5, poverty was seen as an inadequate level of consumption of goods and services. If the volume of federal legislation in the last forty years is any indication, society has been more concerned with inadequate consumption of one particular commodity, housing, than with any other form of consumption. Inadequate housing consumption can result from one of two causes: market failure (an efficiency problem), or inadequate income (an equity problem). Since housing is a very large component of total consumption by households (20 percent or more for low-income households), inadequate income will evidence itself in inadequate housing consumption. Further, the special concern with housing may be due to the fact that it is more visible than other forms of consumption, such as food or medical care. It is difficult to tell whether a man walking down the street had breakfast that morning, but if he walks into a dilapidated dwelling he gives, at least in a superficial way, an indication of a low level of housing consumption.

This chapter begins with a discussion of the conceptual and practical problems of defining and measuring housing consumption—a problem similar to that of measuring consumption in general (as discussed in Chapter 5). Given a low level of housing consumption, the next question is one of identifying the causes of this low level of consumption as equity or efficiency. Barriers to the efficient allocation of resources in the housing market are identified along with potential solutions to the problems caused by these barriers.

Measuring Housing Consumption

The measurement of housing consumption is difficult, since it is hard to devise a measure of housing service stated in homogeneous (comparable) units. When discussing poverty, adjusted money income is used as a measure, although poverty is a multidimensional concept. Adjusted money income provides a comparable unit, since dollar amounts can easily be compared with each other. In the case of housing, it might seem like comparing apples with oranges to compare different dwelling units. The value a consumer places on a dwelling unit depends on many quality and quantity characteristics of the structure, the lot, and the surroundings. Among the structural characteristics would be the number of square feet in the dwelling and the type of exterior (wood, brick, or stone). Characteristics of the lot would include the size in square feet and the type of landscaping (if any). Aspects of the surroundings that are important include characteristics of surrounding dwellings, level of public services (such as police protection and schools) provided, and proximity to employment, recreational, and shopping opportunities. Thus, part of the value of a dwelling unit is determined by the factors discussed in

Chapter 2. On the other hand, proximity to certain activities may result in negative externalities that lower the value of a dwelling unit (examples would be noise, air pollution, and traffic congestion). The socioeconomic status of occupants of surrounding dwellings may also be considered important. In total, the measurement of benefits of a given dwelling unit is a composite of the values of all the quantity and quality characteristics of the structure and environment of the dwelling unit.

The U.S. Census Measure of Housing Consumption

In practice, the adequacy of a dwelling unit has been determined by examining only a few features of the physical structure, with no attention being given to environmental characteristics, although these other characteristics may be much more important to the occupants than the physical structure. The U.S. Bureau of the Census has reported on the physical characteristics of housing since 1940, in the decennial Census of Housing. One of the criteria used was *structural condition*; a dwelling was classified as "substandard" if it did not "provide safe and adequate shelter and its present condition endangers the health, safety, or well-being of the occupants." Individuals who surveyed potentially substandard dwelling units were instructed to look for "critical defects," such as holes in large areas of the foundation, walls, or roof; substantial sagging of roofs or floors; external damage caused by storm, fire, or flood; or any combination of lesser defects sufficient to require considerable repair or rebuilding. Any dwelling units of low-quality original construction were also classified as substandard (examples would be tents, huts, or shacks built of inferior materials). Given these vague criteria, census enumerators had to apply considerable subjective judgment, yet the typical enumerator had no expertise in real estate and received only about thirty minutes of training. Furthermore, they were paid on the basis of the number of units evaluated, which was an incentive for spending very little time on each evaluation. Studies by the U.S. Bureau of the Census indicated a low correlation between the evaluation of housing in the 1960 census and a subsequent evaluation of the same units.[1] As a result of these difficulties, the Census Bureau decided not to measure structural condition in the 1970 census.

The other two criteria of housing adequacy are more objective: *plumbing* (the lack of hot running water, a private bath or shower, or a flush toilet in the unit causes it to be classified substandard) and *crowding* (more than one person per room also classifies the unit as

---

[1]Henry Aaron, *Shelters and Subsidies*, The Brookings Institution, Washington, 1972, pp. 25 - 26.

substandard). While these criteria are more objective than assessment of structural condition, they are still very crude determinants of housing adequacy. The number of occupants per room is only a rough measure of crowding, because room size is not taken into consideration; the number of square feet per occupant would be a better measure. Also, the criteria are not stated in terms of intensity, so that an inadequate dwelling is classified along with one judged barely inadequate. Four persons per room is no more substandard than slightly over one per room. Further, the criteria cannot be added to each other to obtain an overall measure of housing inadequacy. A dwelling may be structurally sound but lack an inside toilet; in fact, most dwellings without inside toilets are located in rural areas, where this is a much less important shortcoming than in cities. In 1970, 89 percent of all dwelling units without a flush toilet, 79 percent of all units without a bathtub or shower, and 92 percent of all units without running water were in rural areas.[2] The lack of an inside toilet may be a much less serious defect than major structural problems or excessive crowding of occupants. Basically then, census measures of housing adequacy

CRITERION	1940	1950	1960	1970
Crowding (more than one person per room)	20.3%	15.7%	11.5%	8.2%
Lacking plumbing facilities				
Units without private toilet	40.3	28.6	13.2	5.0
Units without running water or hot running water	n.a.	29.9	12.8	4.8
Units without private bath or shower	43.8	30.7	14.8	5.8

	Number (thousands) of housing units		More than one person per room		Lacking some or all plumbing facilities	
	Total	Black	Total	Black	Total	Black
United States total	68,679	6,180	8.2%	19.9%	6.9%	16.8%
Inside SMSAs	46,295	4,745	7.8	17.8	3.5	7.2
In central cities	22,594	3,838	8.5	17.1	3.5	4.8
Not in central cities	23,701	907	7.1	20.8	3.5	17.2
Outside SMSAs	22,383	1,435	9.2	26.9	19.1	48.9

Table 7-1: Housing Classified as Substandard According to Two U.S. Census Criteria (n.a.—not available)
SOURCES: Bureau of the Census, *U.S. Census of Housing, 1970, General Housing Characteristics, United States Summary,* Final Report HC(1)-AI, Government Printing Office, Washington, 1971. Similar volumes for 1940, 1950, and 1960.

[2]Bureau of the Census, *U.S. Census of Housing, 1970, General Housing Characteristics,* Final Report HC(1)-AI, Government Printing Office, Washington, 1971, Table 10, p. 1 - 53.

suffer from the defect that they do not measure the degree of inadequacy. The label of "substandard" either applies or it does not.

Using U.S. Census measures of housing adequacy, the data in Table 7-1 indicate that significant gains have been made over the thirty-year period 1940 to 1970, in that the percentages classified as substandard have steadily declined in every category. As indicated in the second part of Table 7-1, a greater percentage of dwelling units in SMSAs meet the two census criteria than do dwelling units in the United States as a whole. Also, a much larger percentage of dwelling units occupied by blacks fail to meet the two criteria than is the case for dwelling units occupied by whites.

A Conceptual Measure of Housing Consumption

The preceding discussion implies that it may be impossible to satisfactorily measure housing consumption in practice. However, this measurement can be accomplished at the conceptual level by reference to "housing service units."[3] Each dwelling unit is assumed to yield some quantity of housing service units per given period of time. The number provided by each dwelling depends on all the quantity and quality characteristics associated with the structure and the environment. Thus, two structurally identical houses may yield radically different numbers of housing service units per year. One may yield eighty housing service units, because it is located near an airport with high noise levels and because trash is collected only once a week. The other house may be located on a quiet street with more frequent trash collections and thus it yields 120 service units per year.

One might ask why the market price of housing is not a good estimate of the level of housing service units yielded by a dwelling. It is generally true that dwellings yielding higher levels of service units are more valuable in the market, but a dwelling yielding twice as many service units as another dwelling need not rent for twice as much. Suppose one dwelling yielded one hundred service units and rented for $2,000 per year and another dwelling yielded two hundred service units and rented for $4,000 per year. The price per housing service unit is $20 in either case and the dwelling rents convey the same information about benefits received by the occupants as would the knowledge of the level of housing service units (which we assumed could be accurately measured). However, the critical assumption in this example is that the price per housing service unit is the same no matter what the size or bundle the housing service units come in and no matter what the location of the dwelling. This as-

---

[3]See Edgar Olsen, "A Competitive Theory of the Housing Market," *American Economic Review* (September 1969), 612 - 622.

sumption would be met only if the cost of producing a housing service unit were equal for all bundles of housing, regardless of size or location, and there were no inefficiency in the housing market. In the real world, neither of these conditions is likely to be met, especially the assumption of an efficient market for housing.

With the above definition of housing service units, a standard of housing consumption could be set up by selecting a cutoff level of housing service units for families of a given size. Housing consumption below this level would be considered inadequate, much as adjusted money income below a certain level constitutes poverty (inadequate consumption). For example, if society decides that two hundred housing service units is the cutoff for a family of four, then families of four consuming less than this amount will be considered to live in inadequate housing. This implies a level of housing service of fifty units per person, which will be used for illustrative purposes in the remainder of the chapter. One should note, however, that members of a family engage in collective consumption of some of the services yielded by a dwelling (much like a public good). Thus, a single-person household might require seventy housing service units to achieve society's cutoff level of adequate consumption, and in a large family (over four), fewer than fifty units per person may be required (240 housing service units might be adequate for a family of five).

The Housing Problem: Equity versus Efficiency

Given a definition of housing adequacy, this section deals with the question of why some households occupy inadequate housing. The first part provides a brief and simplified explanation of how the private housing market adjusts to supply housing to individual households based on their housing demands. This is followed by an example of the two basic reasons why a household may live in inadequate housing. Only one of these causes is a housing problem; the other is a symptom of poverty. The ability to distinguish these two causes of low levels of housing consumption is necessary for an economic evaluation of housing policies.

The Operation of the Private Housing Market

The housing market is often considered to be extremely noncompetitive, implying that prices of housing are unresponsive to market forces and that landlords make huge monopoly profits from providing housing, particularly in slum areas.[4] Competition in a market

[4]While the term "slum" can be considered emotional, here it is defined as a neighborhood in which most dwelling units yield less than some specified low number of housing service units.

depends on the number and size of sellers—the greater the number of sellers, the greater the degree of competition, since each seller will control less of the market. What evidence exists seems to indicate that the slum housing market is relatively dispersed in ownership and that the market is relatively competitive. For example, a study in Newark, New Jersey, indicated that over 40 percent of land parcels in slum areas were owned by landlords who owned no other rental property. Fewer than 25 percent of the land parcels were owned by landlords possessing over six parcels.[5] Thus, the housing market is probably more competitive than monopolistic, so that market forces determine a fairly narrow range of rents that can be charged by landlords.

The basic function of the housing market is to match up the existing stock of housing with the existing population (since everyone has to live somewhere). The term "housing shortage" is so widely used it is worthwhile examining what it means. It usually does not mean that families are out on the streets, but rather that, for certain types of housing, the quantity demanded exceeds the quantity supplied. For most commodities, this means that prices will rise until the shortage is eliminated; the same is true for housing. The term is often used in a noneconomic way, however, to mean that, if prices were lower, people would like to have more houses. In this sense, there is a shortage of Rolls Royces.

To gain an understanding of how the housing market operates to allocate the housing stock among households in a city, suppose the housing market were perfectly competitive, so that the price of a housing service unit would be the same regardless of the size of the dwelling or its location. Further suppose that there are no cases of market failure and that the price of a housing service unit is $20, which is the marginal social cost of providing housing services, in constant dollars. All dwellings are occupied and everyone pays $20 per housing service unit. Now suppose a large number of households who occupy dwellings that yield fifty housing service units leave the city for the suburbs and that the same number of households gradually move in, but that these new residents have lower incomes. With these lower incomes each family will be able to afford only forty housing service units at a price of $20 each, for a total outlay on housing of $800. The landlords with vacant units will find they need to lower their rents in order to eliminate vacancies, and if the new residents spend only $800 for rent, they will receive fifty service units for this $800, at a price per service unit of only $16.

However, housing producers cannot profitably provide dwellings yielding fifty housing service units for only $16 per service unit, since the cost to them is $20. They can change the future quantity of

[5]George Sternlieb, *The Tenement Landlord*, Rutgers University Press, New Brunswick, N.J., 1969, p. 122.

housing service units yielded by a dwelling through either maintenance or alteration. In the absence of maintenance, dwellings deteriorate over time, yielding fewer and fewer housing service units.
The producers of housing services at fifty units per dwelling are
losing money, but they will allow the dwellings to deteriorate until
they yield only forty housing service units. At this point, there is no
further incentive to deterioration, since a rent of $800 will provide
$20 per housing service unit, which is the price received by all other
dwelling owners in the city. Thus, the city's housing market adjusts
in time to the demand of the resident population, and this demand is
dependent on the income levels of the residents. The poor do not
desire to live in bad housing, but the private market, even if it is
working efficiently, will not provide "adequate" housing for them.

Inadequate Housing Consumption:
Equity versus Efficiency

The fact that a family lives in inadequate housing (yielding fewer than
fifty housing service units per person per year) is a symptom of the
problem and obviously not the cause. What are the causes of inadequate housing? If resources are efficiently allocated in the housing
market, consumption below the cutoff level is due to lack of income.
In this case the housing problem is fundamentally a problem of
poverty and can be alleviated by increasing a family's income through
the programs discussed in Chapters 5 and 6. However, externalities
and other barriers may inhibit efficient resource allocation in the
housing market. In other words, many families presently living in
inadequate housing could afford adequate housing with their present
incomes, if resources were allocated efficiently in the housing market. The following example is provided to help explain the important
distinction between inadequate housing consumption due to efficiency considerations and that due to equity considerations (lack of
income).

Assume that a family has an income of $4,000 per year and is
willing to spend 25 percent of its income on housing (a widely used
rule of thumb in household budgeting); thus, the family has $1,000
per year for housing. Suppose that resources are not being efficiently
allocated in housing markets (for one or more of the reasons discussed
in the remaining sections of this chapter), so that an adequate dwelling unit, yielding fifty housing service units per person, rents for
$1,500 ($30 per service unit). If the family can afford to spend only
$1,000 on housing, it cannot afford adequate housing. Now suppose
that policies are implemented that achieve efficient resource allocation in housing markets and that the price of a housing service unit
falls to $20. The yearly rental of a dwelling that yields fifty housing

service units will now be $1,000, and the family can afford to live in adequate housing. On the other hand, suppose that when resources become efficiently allocated in the housing market the price per housing service unit falls to only $22. While the family can afford better housing, it still cannot afford adequate housing, which would rent for $1,100 (50 times $22). Thus, some of the inadequate housing consumption is attributable to lack of income—a poverty problem.

It is difficult to explain why society should be more concerned with inadequate housing consumption than with inadequate consumption of food or clothing, if the reason for inadequate housing consumption is simply lack of income. In many ways, society's concern with housing may be the result of a confusion between the two causes of low housing consumption, lack of income and inefficiency in the housing market. Although it would be difficult to assign percentages to these two causes, it is safe to conclude that both considerations are important. The remainder of this chapter discusses some major barriers to efficient resource allocation in housing, which result in prices of housing being higher than otherwise. We assume that society has set a goal of increasing the housing consumption of all households whose consumption is below the socially determined cutoff point so that they are brought above this cutoff. The least-cost way of achieving this goal (an equity objective) is through improving the efficiency of the housing market and providing income redistribution in kind to households whose consumption would still fall short of the cutoff level after efficiency is attained. An alternative to an in-kind redistribution would be a program that would simply augment the incomes of families whose housing consumption is low. Since they would buy more housing along with more of other commodities, poverty programs can be thought of as one type of housing program. However, if society's goal is to increase housing consumption alone, a greater increase can be achieved through a properly designed in-kind program. As discussed in Chapter 4, in-kind programs do not lead to as great an increase in the net private benefits of recipients as money distributions, because they involve violations of consumer sovereignty, but they can achieve a minimum level of housing consumption at the lowest cost, if this is society's goal. Government programs and other alternatives for subsidizing housing consumption are discussed in Chapter 8.

Barriers to Efficient Allocation of Resources in the Housing Market and Some Potential Solutions

The market price of a housing service unit may be higher and the level of housing consumption lower than they would be if the market achieved efficiency and maximized net social benefits. This section discusses several of the more commonly cited potential sources of market failure. In general, these include: the existence of externalities that are not considered in housing market decisions; losses of net benefits to consumers of housing due to imperfect information regarding costs and benefits; and various restrictive practices, which result either in deviations from the lowest-cost means of producing housing or in loss of consumer choice with respect to available housing alternatives. Possible means of eliminating these cases of market failure are discussed. The section concludes with some crude estimates of the amount by which the market price of housing would be reduced if some of these cases of market failure were eliminated.

Externalities and Housing Maintenance and Improvement

The value of a property depends on the amount that has been invested in its construction and maintenance; it may also depend on the condition, as well as the types, of other properties in the neighborhood. This interdependence can lead to inefficiently low expenditures for housing improvements and maintenance. Suppose a homeowner is deciding whether to make certain improvements to his home and chooses not to do so because his marginal private costs exceed his marginal private benefits (the extra cost to him is greater than the value of the additional housing service units generated). Were the improvements to be made, surrounding homes would yield more housing service units owing to the improvement in the neighborhood. For example, the improvements might rid the neighborhood of an eyesore, a dilapidated home surrounded by tall weeds, but the costs would all be borne by the homeowner. The situation is that a positive externality exists—marginal social benefits exceed marginal private benefits—and therefore too little of a commodity (here home improvement) is provided. A similar situation might exist for every home in the neighborhood, so that improvements by any homeowner conferred indirect benefits on his neighbors. It could be that, if every homeowner undertook the improvements, then all would be better off as a result, but it could still remain true that the benefits to each, from his own improvements, would be less than the costs. The difficulty is that the housing market provides no mechanism for achieving the efficient result (everyone fixing up his home).

While the above discussion is applied to homeowners, it can easily be applied to owners of rental housing. Table 7-2 illustrates the above discussion, with respect to a situation where two landlords own adjacent apartment buildings. The cost of improvements (marginal private cost) must be compared with the benefits the landlord receives (marginal private benefits). These will be equal to the value of the additional rentals received over the life of the improvements, or the present value of the additional rental income. (In a competitive housing market additional rental that can be charged would be equal to the increase in housing service units times the price of these service units.) Suppose that, if landlord A makes improvements to his building costing $10,000, the present value of increased rental income would be only $8,000. Under these circumstances he would not make the improvements. But suppose that, if A made the improvements, landlord B could charge additional rents, the present value of which would be $4,000. (The proximity of the improved property makes these higher rents possible.) From a social standpoint, marginal social benefits ($8,000 + $4,000 = $12,000) exceed marginal social costs ($10,000), so the improvements are efficient, adding $2,000 to net social benefits, as shown in row X of Table 7-2.

The second section of Table 7-2 assumes that the same private and indirect benefits would result if landlord B made similar improvements costing him $10,000. The result is the same as in the first case, with net private benefits being a negative $2,000 and net social benefits a positive $2,000, and is illustrated by row Y of Table 7-2. Row Z shows what happens if *both* landlords make the indicated improvements. Both are better off than if neither made the improvements, since net private benefits are $2,000 to each landlord.

Now suppose both landlords understand that they will be better off

	BENEFITS AND COSTS TO LANDLORD A	BENEFITS AND COSTS TO LANDLORD B	BENEFITS AND COSTS TO SOCIETY (A+B)
IF LANDLORD A MAKES $10,000 IN IMPROVEMENTS			
Cost of A's improvements	$10,000	$ 0	$10,000
Benefits (increased rental value) due to A's improvements	8,000	4,000	12,000
X. Net Benefits	−2,000	4,000	2,000
IF LANDLORD B MAKES $10,000 IN IMPROVEMENTS			
Cost of B's improvements	0	10,000	10,000
Benefits (increased rental value) due to B's improvements	4,000	8,000	12,000
Y. Net Benefits	4,000	−2,000	2,000
Z. TOTAL NET BENEFITS IF BOTH A AND B MAKE IMPROVEMENTS (X + Y)	$2,000	$ 2,000	$ 4,000

Table 7-2: An Example of Private and Social Benefits and Costs of Housing Improvements

if these improvements are made, and consider the decision of one of them (landlord A) once again. He knows that landlord B will either make the improvement or he will not. If landlord B does the improvement, landlord A will be better off by not doing the improvement himself (comparing row Z to row Y we see that he receives $2,000 more if he does not undertake the improvements himself). Now suppose landlord B does not undertake his improvements. Then landlord A is on his own, and in the situation illustrated by the first part of Table 7-2. He is better off not doing the improvements by $2,000. Therefore, landlord A is better off by not making the improvements whatever landlord B does. Landlord A's best course of action may be to convince landlord B to make his improvements, perhaps by deceiving B into thinking that he (A) will indeed make improvements; the chances are that he will be unsuccessful, and none of the socially desirable improvements will be made.

Although there is essentially no evidence indicating the magnitude of such unresolved externalities in the urban housing market, various policies exist to correct for such cases of market failure, which implies they are not totally negligible. One possible means of achieving the efficient quantity of improvements or maintenance is for the property owners to sign a legally binding agreement among themselves under which each promises to make certain expenditures. While a lawyer might be hired to draft such an agreement, the geographic extent of the externalities might involve dozens of property owners. When large numbers of parties are concerned, the time and effort involved might become prohibitive, precluding the signing of such an agreement. (The cost of reaching an agreement increases with the number of parties involved.) Further, such agreements might be complicated by the problem of holdouts, discussed below.

Another possible solution to the problem of externalities, short of public intervention into the housing market, would be for one owner to purchase all the surrounding properties. In the example of Table 7-2, if landlord A owned both properties, he would capture all the benefits of his improvements ($12,000) if he undertook the improvements in either one of the properties. The $4,000 that accrued to landlord B now accrues to A, as he has "internalized the externalities" involved (they are no longer externalities), and his decision will be efficient. In the original case he would not do the improvement since his private benefits were exceeded by the private costs. Since he now owns both properties, his private benefits are higher, and when he maximizes net private benefits he also maximizes net social benefits.

Another example of internalized externalities is a shopping center that has a single owner rather than each merchant owning his own store. The actions of one merchant in a large shopping center could impose heavy indirect costs on other merchants that would be reflected in loss of sales and profits. This possibility is avoided with central ownership, since many such actions are violations of the lease agreements and the merchant must abide by the provisions or move out. The control of externalities in housing by such means does not occur as frequently. In neighborhoods made up of single-family detached dwelling units, a developer could build several hundred houses, retain ownership, and lease the houses. However, there are very strong incentives to own one's home as opposed to renting, which increase with the family's income. Lower-income families in the central city are more likely to rent, even if they live in detached housing.

Do these externalities lead to the continuance of slums in areas where improvements would be efficient? They would tend to, but the argument applies with even greater force to upper-income homes, where the external effects would be greater. Applying social pressure to a neighbor who is negligent in caring for his property is common, as are "rewards" for "most improved home." Such nonmonetary considerations are rare in slum situations. An alternative explanation for the continuance of slums is that the housing market is competitive, and low-income people simply cannot afford to pay rent sufficiently high that landlords can profitably maintain a property in nonslum condition. There is controversy among housing specialists over this question, and it remains unresolved.

Attempts to internalize externalities through buying up many contiguous parcels of land is usually thought to be difficult, and in urban areas larger parcels often sell at a higher price per acre than smaller tracts. One reason is the holdout problem. If a property owner discovers that someone is buying up most of the land surrounding him, he may be in a position to hold out for a price several times his previous subjective valuation of the property. Thus, some of the benefits derived from putting together the tract may be eaten up by higher land costs due to holdouts. For example, an insurance company was attempting to acquire a block of land in a major central business district in order to construct a high-rise office building. All the parcels of property were acquired, some through elaborate means to disguise the fact that a single buyer was behind the purchases, with the exception of a small one-man barbershop occupied by its owner. Having gotten wind of the insurance company's attempt to buy the entire block, the barber was able to hold out for $500,000 plus a rent-free barbershop in the new building for life. The fear of failure (because of holdouts) may lead many potential developers to refrain from trying to consolidate properties.

If the property is acquired by the government, on the other hand, the holdout problem can be circumvented by means of laws of eminent domain. Under these laws, the holdout is compelled to sell his property at a legally determined "fair" price, if the land is to be used for a "public" purpose. What constitutes a public purpose may not be entirely clear, but it does not include attempts of private parties to consolidate properties for private purposes, even though this might be justified on ground of efficiency. Although laws of eminent domain might be used more widely, administrative difficulties and potential inequities in determining the fair market value of properties weighs against it. Present "cloak and dagger" methods of acquiring tracts of land, such as dummy companies who represent the true buyer and other techniques of secrecy, may be almost as efficient as the results under wider use of eminent domain.

Housing Finance Costs

Buying a home is the largest financial transaction that most families make in their lifetime. Since very few families have sufficient net worth to buy a home outright, they must borrow in order to finance it, generally through a mortgage loan. The availability and terms of mortgage loans have a significant impact on the number of households who can purchase homes at any one time and on the financing costs incurred. Increases in mortgage loan terms—primarily the interest rate charged—can lead to large increases in the monthly payments required to amortize the loan. For example, an increase in interest rates from 6 to 9 percent raises the monthly mortgage payment by 34 percent for a thirty-year loan. While the government must use monetary and fiscal policy to achieve the broad objective of a stable economy (full employment of resources and stable prices), it appears that the brunt of such policies falls on the housing market through the effects on interest rates and credit availability.

Savings and loan companies account for the major source of residential mortgage money. However, these institutions are restricted from effectively competing with other financial institutions for funds when interest rates rise. As a result, when money becomes tight (interest rates are high), savings and loan companies are usually hardest-hit with respect to availability of credit and they have to restrict the number of mortgage loans granted. The result is that there are large fluctuations in the number of housing units constructed from year to year. This situation of going from "boom " to "bust" and back again is a source of great inefficiency in the housing market.

Various solutions are possible to remedy the large fluctuations in the availability of mortgage funds. One possibility would be to have mortgages with interest rates that went up or down in response to general market interest rates. High interest rates deter potential homeowners, but such persons would be more willing to commit themselves to a long-term contract if the interest rate on the mortgage were likely to fall in the future, and along with it the monthly payment. At present, in times of high interest rates, many potential homeowners defer home purchases in hopes of future lower rates. Mortgages such as suggested above, or mortgages that could be periodically renegotiated, might increase the level of home building in times of high interest rates. The share of available credit allocated to housing would thus be increased in times of credit stringency. If savings and loan institutions could pay higher interest rates to depositors, they would have more mortgage funds available and they could compete better with other institutions. There are other possibilities, among them having a government agency buy existing mortgages (this is done currently through the Government National Mortgage Association), freeing funds for new mortgages, or even directly subsidizing institutions granting mortgages.

The availability of mortgages to individuals seeking homes in certain neighborhoods may be unduly restricted by lending institutions because of practices related to imperfect information. In granting a mortgage loan, the lending institution wants assurance that the value of the property will always exceed the amount of the loan, so that, in the event of default by the borrower, the lender can foreclose and sell the property to cover his loan. Lenders may be reluctant to grant mortgage loans on dilapidated property or on property located in neighborhoods where the level of housing service is declining toward slum levels. If loans on such properties are granted, terms generally include a higher down payment and higher interest rates, to reduce the risk to the lender. Further, the loan may be of shorter duration, inflating the monthly payment. These terms are a great discouragement to purchase, especially to households of low income (reflecting symptoms of poverty such as low-paying or unstable jobs, which add to the reluctance of lenders). In some instances, lenders may refuse to make mortgage loans for areas in the city where slum or near-slum conditions exist—a practice known as "redlining" an area, from the actual or mythical practice of drawing a red line around certain areas on maps.[6] The practice of redlining has also been ascribed to insurance companies in granting fire or casualty insurance.

One of the reasons that lending institutions are reluctant to make mortgage loans that they consider to be risky is the high cost of the foreclosure procedure. Many state laws require slow and expensive foreclosure proceedings, historically enacted to protect farmers against foreclosure of the family homestead as a result of a single crop failure.[7] Such provisions make less sense in a modern urban society. Revision of foreclosure laws would probably result in some reduction

[6]*Building the American City*, Report of the National Commission on Urban Problems, Final Report, Government Printing Office, Washington, 1969, p. 178.
[7]*Building the American City.* p. 460.

in home financing costs, reflecting the smaller costs incurred by the lender in the event of default.

Redlining and rules of thumb practiced by lending institutions in granting mortgage loans reflect risks and uncertainties associated with imperfect information in the housing market. While the practices mentioned above apply especially to slum areas, the rules of thumb used by lending institutions are applied to practically all households seeking mortgage loans. Such rules of thumb are probably based on past experience, but apply to averages rather than specific cases. For example, two often quoted rules of thumb are that the cost of a home should not exceed 2½ times the household's annual income, and that monthly housing outlays should not exceed 25 percent of monthly income. However, many households can manage payments greater than 25 percent of income, and restricting them on this arbitrary basis may violate their consumer sovereignty and needlessly restrict their housing consumption—all because of imperfect information on the part of mortgage lenders. On the other hand, mortgage terms have become much more liberal over time, one of the major reasons for this being government mortgage guarantee programs (such as FHA and VA), which insure lenders against the risk of default.

Among the costs of financing a house through a mortgage, which are usually paid by the buyer at the point of completing the transaction, are "closing costs." These include title search and title insurance, lender's service charges, taxes, and other miscellaneous fees. Many prospective home buyers appear to be unaware of such costs or their magnitude, which must be paid in cash at the time of final settlement of the real estate transaction. Since the down payment might be about 10 percent of the selling price and closing costs are in the range of 2 to 4 percent, closing costs can add 25 percent or more to the amount of cash required to buy a house.

Title search and insurance stem from a problem of imperfect information and are required to protect the lender (and the purchaser) against the risk that the home buyer did not acquire good title to the house (because of prior claims that are unknown and may date back many years). For example, in a California city, an Indian tribe was able to substantiate prior claims to land dating back to the nineteenth century. As a result, those who had "bought" such land and built on it found themselves without good title. Those not covered by title insurance, and their mortgage holders, had to bear the loss of transferring the property back to the Indians. The process of title search involves an attorney searching public records (usually at the county courthouse) relating to sales of the property in question. The costs of title search could be reduced if local governments maintained better records of land transactions. Larger counties could computerize title records so that searches could be conducted in a matter of seconds.

Property Taxes

The property tax (discussed in Chapter 15) is the major source of local government revenue. This tax is levied on the value of dwelling units and usually amounts to somewhere between 2 and 5 percent of the market value of the unit per year. As a percentage of the rent paid, the property tax can be sizeable; when considered in this context the property tax may amount to a "sales" tax on housing of 25 percent or more. To the extent that the price of housing is artificially raised because of this tax, the quantity of resources allocated to the housing market is less than if the revenues were raised in a way that did not increase relative housing prices. However, the impact of the property tax on housing consumption must be examined to see if there are offsetting factors. One offset is that housing is not subject to sales taxation, as are most goods and many services. Another is that the property tax finances some services that are related to property ownership (such as sanitation and fire protection), which would have to be paid somehow by property owners were they not financed with property taxes. Perhaps the most important offsetting factor, with respect to owner-occupied housing, is the income tax advantage (see Chapter 8). After considering all these offsets, the price of some housing, especially rental housing located in the central city, is higher than it would be in the absence of the property tax. Alternative means of financing local government services (discussed in Chapter 15) would eliminate this price distortion in the housing market.

The administration of the property tax is usually considered to be a deterrent to housing improvements. Assessments on property improvements are acknowledged in practice to increase the owner's tax bill out of proportion to the value of the improvements made. For example, assume that an apartment building has a market value of $100,000 and is assessed for tax purposes at $20,000.[8] Now suppose that the owner makes improvements to the building that increase the market value by $50,000 (50 percent). The local property tax assessor may send notice that the assessed value of the apartment building is now $40,000 after the improvements. Thus, the market value increased by 50 percent, but the assessed value, and the tax bill, increased by 100 percent as a result of the improvements. Improvements increase the number of housing service units yielded by a property and allow the landlord to charge higher rents. However, if the landlord's costs (including the additional taxes) increase in greater proportion than rental income, profits may not be great enough to make the improvements worthwhile. In such cases, the property tax serves as a penalty for improving property and provides an incentive

---

[8]The reader who is unfamiliar with the calculation of property tax liabilities is referred to the example in Table 15-3.

to let dwelling units deteriorate (since repairs could lead to greater assessments), possibly until they yield a low enough level of housing service to be classified as slums.

A frequently mentioned solution to this effect of the property tax is to change the existing tax to a "site-value" tax. Instead of taxing both the land (the site) and the improvements (structures), the property tax would be only on the site. As a result, there would be no effect on property taxes from making any amount of improvements, since the site-value tax would be the same whether the lot were vacant or had a 100-story office tower on it. The feasibility of site-value taxation will be discussed in Chapter 15.

Zoning

Many local jurisdictions in urban areas have zoning ordinances that control land use. Practically all zoning ordinances have provisions in common, among them *permitted land uses*. Such uses are usually divided into three categories, dwellings (residential), buildings, and industry, which are often subdivided further, such as dwellings into apartments and houses. Another common provision is some indirect control over population density, either through setting a minimum lot size for a dwelling unit or permitting a maximum number of families per acre. Population density is also constrained by provisions on building bulk, which may require yards along lot boundaries, limit the height of buildings, or limit the proportion of the lot covered by a building. Other zoning ordinance provisions may include minimum house size (stated in square feet), prohibition of signs, landscaping requirements, and provision of off-street parking. In economic terms, the rationale of zoning ordinances is to set minimum standards so as to reduce the externalities associated with land use. For example, if an area is zoned residential, it is not possible for noisy or smelly industrial plants to locate there.

While zoning ordinances may have an efficiency justification grounded in preventing externalities associated with land use, the practice of zoning may result in serious inefficiencies and inequities in the real world. Low-income households tend to be excluded from many suburban areas, and zoning ordinances can easily, though indirectly, be designed to exclude low-income households. All that is required is prohibiting certain land uses, such as mobile homes and apartments, and restricting residential land use sufficiently so that the minimum house price is out of reach of the poor (through minimum house and lot sizes, for example). A survey conducted by the National Commission on Urban Problems showed that 25 percent of metropolitan area municipalities of 5,000 or more population permit no single-family houses on lots of less than one-half acre, and 11 percent of these municipalities have some land for single-family houses zoned for a minimum lot size of two acres or more.[9] Minimum lot size, especially when coupled with minimum house size provisions, easily make it impossible to build new housing in some jurisdictions for less than $80,000. Through such zoning regulations, several jurisdictions effectively achieve segregation on the basis of income, excluding all low-income households. A further incentive to engage in zoning out low-income households is provided by present methods of financing such local services as education and police protection, to be discussed in Chapter 14 under the title of "fiscal zoning." This exclusion of low-income households restricts their choice of housing, and can be a factor contributing to their poverty, since they may not be able to live near places of work—the manufacturing and service establishments that have moved to the suburbs. The impact of restricted housing choice on job opportunities will be discussed in the following chapter.

In addition to restricting the housing choices of lower-income households, zoning may also result in the market price of land being higher in some areas than it would be with an unrestricted market, thus increasing housing prices (since land is a large component of housing cost, perhaps 20 to 25 percent). Zoning can affect land values in several ways; for example, by protecting already developed land from encroaching uses, it enhances property values. The desire to protect their investment is perhaps the major reason why homeowners support zoning and are interested in decisions of zoning boards that would change the classification of certain tracts in their areas. Zoning may also raise the price of land designated for certain uses by restricting its supply (land zoned for apartments, for example). Since zoning decisions can have a very large impact on the values of certain parcels of land, it might well be expected that tremendous pressures would be brought to bear on local zoning boards by both homeowners and developers. It is not surprising that newspapers quite often carry articles reporting payoffs and corruption in zoning cases.

One further point needs to be made regarding zoning and efficiency. The zoning approach is essentially one of prohibiting externalities of land use, but, as Chapter 4 indicated, there is generally an efficient level of negative externalities short of zero. Thus zoning may prevent land from being used in the most efficient way. Some variances (changes in zoning classifications) need to be made in order to achieve efficient land use through time. While bribery cannot be condoned, the market solution to determining whether zoning variances should be granted would be to allow variances on the basis of bribes; if those favoring the zoning change outbid those opposed to it, the variance would be granted. Obviously, if this were to be officially

---

[9]*Building the American City*, p. 214.

sanctioned, then the bribes would have to go to the government rather than to government officials. It would have the advantage that intensity of preferences could be expressed. A zoning change that benefited one person tremendously, yet harmed three trivially, might not be made, because it would be voted down three to one.

The rationale for zoning appears to be that it reduces the negative externalities associated with land use. However, there are about 5,200 governments within SMSAs that have zoning ordinances, and it appears that many jurisdictions play a "zoning game," each trying to maximize its own net benefits, perhaps at the expense of the rest of the urban area. Low-income households are often excluded by this practice, but the poor must obviously live somewhere in the urban area, just as certain land uses (such as sewage plants) must be allowed somewhere in the urban area. While zoning may maximize the net benefits of the local area, costs and benefits to the entire urban area are not necessarily considered, and a fairly convincing case can be made for a zoning authority having jurisdiction over the entire urban area. States could grant such power to metropolitan agencies, since from a legal standpoint zoning is one form of police power that states have delegated to local governments. Metro-wide zoning would not solve all the efficiency problems associated with zoning, only those of the "zoning game," and the present state of knowledge of costs and benefits of various land-use plans leaves much to be desired. Zoning is a heated and controversial issue and will continue to be so, because of the large potential gains and losses that can accrue from zoning decisions. In brief, while zoning supposedly exists to improve efficiency, in some cases it interferes with efficiency and tends to be used for redistributing income among landowners in urban areas.

Building Codes and Housing Construction Practices

The National Commission on Urban Problems defined a building code and its objectives as follows: "A building code is a series of standards and specifications designed to establish minimum safeguards in the erection and construction of buildings, to protect the human beings who live and work in them from fire and other hazards, and to establish regulation to further protect the health and safety of the public."[10] From this definition it would appear that the economic objectives of building codes are some combination of reducing externalities by establishing minimum standards and reducing risks to the house buyer from imperfect information.

Purchasing a house is usually the largest financial decision a family

[10]*Building the American City*, p. 254.

ever has to make and the consequences of a poor choice can be serious. Since very few purchasers of housing are intimately familiar with construction methods and structural characteristics, the purchaser has little way of knowing what he is buying unless he hires a professional appraiser. Building codes are one method of dealing with this problem of imperfect information on the part of purchasers of housing; however, they may not be the best means of handling it (for example, warranties could be required, which would permit the purchaser relatively quick and easy legal recourse in the case of shoddy housing). The ultimate question with respect to imperfect information in the housing market is whether the methods used by the government (including building codes) to counter this cause of market failure result in greater benefits than costs. The following discussion indicates that the costs of building codes, at least in practice, are rather high in relation to the benefits.

Local governments, through the delegation of police power vested in the state, usually have control over the building codes applicable in urban areas. There are four national building codes which are widely recognized and accepted. If all local building codes were in conformity with one of these national codes, many inefficiencies would be eliminated. However, a survey conducted by the National Commission on Urban Problems indicated that only about 15 percent of all jurisdictions of more than 5,000 population had a code in effect that was in close conformity with a national model code. The remaining 85 percent of such jurisdictions either had no building code, did not use a model code, or had failed to keep their code up to date with the model code. The commission examined fourteen specific products or practices about which complaints relating to local building codes are most commonly heard. Most of the products and practices were not prohibited by the national model codes, but lack of local conformity to the national codes resulted in many restrictions. Among the practices examined was the use of plastic pipe in drainage systems as a substitute for iron pipes; this was prohibited by 63 percent of the local governments having a building code. One of the major means of reducing housing construction costs is prefabrication or off-site assembly of roof trusses and plumbing or electrical units. Such units, known as plumbing "trees" and electrical "harnesses," can be manufactured by mass-production assembly techniques, using less specialized and less costly labor than is required by on-site electrical and plumbing work. The commission found that plumbing trees were prohibited in 42 percent of the areas having codes and electrical harnesses were prohibited by 46 percent.

A major barrier to efficient use of resources in house construction is the existence of these restrictions, as well as many other similar prohibitions of products and practices. Many of these techniques involve prefabrication of housing components away from the site of the construction. Were these techniques at odds with acceptable standards, it is hard to see how they would have found acceptance in the national model building codes. Another cost-reducing technique is large-scale building, including modular homes and mobile homes. While building codes, as indicated above, often prohibit certain cost-reducing prefabrication techniques outright, the cost savings associated with the mass-produced manufactured housing that is allowed are negated by local code provisions that require on-site inspection of electrical connections in preassembled panels. The economic feasibility of manufactured homes, which have to be produced in large quantities and sold in large market areas, is partially defeated by building codes. If a manufacturer were to produce a house that met all the code regulations existing in a single large urban or multistate area, the costs would be greater than if he had to meet only one of the model national codes. One study indicated that the additional cost of meeting the local code requirements that exceeded national ones, for a house costing $12,000 (without the lot), was an additional $2,000.[11]

To the extent that "good" building codes are justified as countering lack of knowledge on the part of potential buyers as well as reducing negative externalities, codes which achieved these objectives without prohibiting the use of acceptable products and techniques would be in order. One possibility would be for each state government to impose a uniform statewide building code or require that all local building codes conform with one of the four generally accepted national model codes. This would eliminate many of the barriers to the use of more efficient techniques. If codes were rewritten as far as possible in terms of performance standards, unlike present codes (which often specify certain materials rather than certain technical performance criteria), research in new methods of construction would be spurred.

While building codes may defeat the use of new products and production techniques that could reduce housing costs, the same problems can apply to restrictive work practices associated with building trade unions. The National Commission on Urban Problems classified restrictive union work rules as follows: (1) on-site rules, requiring certain work to be done on the premises and prohibiting or limiting the use of prefabricated products; (2) restrictions against the use of certain tools and devices; and (3) requirements for excessive manpower on the job, including what appear to be irrational limits on the variety of work that certain categories of workers may perform.[12] However, many of the charges examined by the commission concerned big construction projects and not the typical single-family

[11]*Building the American City*, p. 262.
[12]*Building the American City*, p. 467.

house. A large portion of home-builders employ nonunion labor, although nonunion labor may receive the same pay and abide by the same work rules as union labor. The commission found it very difficult to distinguish between a restrictive work practice, as defined above, and requirements that are justified on the grounds of safety, to protect the worker from injury.

It is difficult to determine quantitatively the cost savings that could be achieved from eliminating restrictive work practices, but there are some obvious examples of such restrictions, which imply that costs could be reduced by some amount. The U.S. Supreme Court has held as valid an agreement stating that no union member would handle a prehung door. The primary objective of the provision was found to be preserving and protecting job security of the union; the court held that such an objective was a legitimate subject of collective bargaining, even though the cost of construction was increased as a result.[13] However, the commission concluded that pressures for changing restrictive work practices could be brought to bear by government, since government (at all levels) accounts for about one-third of the total value of construction in the United States. Also, restrictive work practices and local building codes that prohibit certain products and techniques may have the same objectives—protecting union jobs. To the extent that local trade unions control local building codes, the inefficiencies associated with this environment would be eliminated by having more uniform codes or codes conforming to the national model codes, because local influences and vested interests could not then be exercised.

Housing Codes

A housing code is a local government ordinance setting minimum standards pertaining to *occupancy* of dwelling units, i.e., its conditions need be met only by occupied dwellings. Housing codes usually cover three areas: (1) the supplied facilities in the structure, such as toilet, bath, or sink; (2) the level of maintenance, such as leaks in the roof, cracks in the walls; and (3) occupancy, which deals with the amount of space relative to the number of people occupying the unit. The economic rationale for housing codes would appear to be attaining greater efficiency, given the externalities associated with housing. The amount of housing maintenance and improvements may be less than the efficient amount because some of the benefits of the investment accrue to people other than the owner. To the extent that housing codes exist and are enforced, this private market outcome of underinvestment is somewhat proscribed. Property owners are re-

---

[13]*Building the American City*, p. 474.

quired to make maintenance and improvement expenditures, which might not be made in the absence of the code.

Unfortunately, housing codes in the real world do not meet this objective of getting owners to take into account the indirect benefits of their maintenance and improvement projects. As can be seen from the general description of housing codes above, they are similar in standards and inclusiveness to the U.S. Census criteria for evaluating housing quality. Thus, if all jurisdictions had strictly enforced housing codes, there would be little or no substandard housing (as defined by the census) in urban areas. Since a considerable amount of housing is still classified as substandard, the implication is that either the codes do not exist in some areas or else they are not enforced. The answer appears to be both; however, where housing codes exist, their enforcement may not be possible because of a confusion between the equity and efficiency causes of low levels of housing consumption. If codes were enforced, rents for dwelling units that met code requirements would tend to be greater than for the same dwelling units maintained at a lower level of housing service (this was previously discussed in conjunction with the operation of a competitive housing market). If the occupants of such dwelling units do not have the income to pay the higher rents, then code enforcement will tend to put poor people "out in the street." Similarly, if codes are enforced but rents are not raised (or cannot be raised), the landlord may maximize his net private benefits by abandoning the building and leaving it unoccupied, since the costs of meeting code requirements that cannot be recouped with higher rents may be an even more unprofitable alternative.

As the incomes of slum dwellers increase and they can afford to consume a higher level of housing service units, the number of abandoned buildings in central cities would be expected to increase, since many older buildings will be very expensive to upgrade. The increasing abandonment would thus be explained by rising incomes of residents and increasing age of dwelling units. However, it appears that the number of abandoned dwelling units is related to the strictness of housing code enforcement. Since enforcement adds to the costs of maintaining a dwelling unit (it must be maintained at a higher level of housing service units), it can accelerate the process of abandonment of older buildings that are hard to rehabilitate. Further, once a building is vacated, it becomes vulnerable to vandalism and arson. Thus, strict housing code enforcement is likely to have the unintended result of reducing the supply of housing to low-income households.

The situation depicted above also creates the incentive for bribery and payoffs over housing code enforcement. The property owner may maximize his net private benefits by paying off the building inspector not to report code violations rather than making the expenditures to bring the property into conformance with the code. Even in the absence of corruption, it appears that the private costs (to the owner) of violating the housing code are low enough to make violations the rule rather than the exception. Courts tend to treat code violators quite leniently; although jail terms are usually authorized by ordinance, they are seldom given:

> Judicial permissiveness toward recalcitrant landlords is further reflected in the imposition of low or nominal fines. In most instances, a defendant will plead guilty and engage in repairs just before sentencing. In appreciation of this "cooperativeness," the courts will not treat this owner much more harshly than the owner who does extensive repair work without legal delays."[14]

In summary, it appears that most housing codes attempt to require "decent" housing by setting minimum housing consumption standards; however, such attempts fail because they do not treat the cause of much low housing consumption—lack of income on the part of the occupants. One might conclude that the attempt to increase housing consumption through housing codes is a classic example of confusion between equity and efficiency as the cause of the problem.

Racial Discrimination

Discrimination on the basis of race takes two forms in the housing market. First, the market price that blacks pay per housing service unit may be more than that paid by whites (market price discrimination). Second, blacks may incur additional costs, other than higher market prices, which may be related to restrictions in their choice of location and opportunities for ownership (as opposed to renting). Also, a lack of choice may be reflected in the inability to find dwelling units that maximize net private benefits (for example, upper-income blacks may be forced to live in low-quality housing). These nonmarket private costs of racial discrimination include psychic costs (unfriendly treatment by neighbors, threatening phone calls, and vandalism) and transactional costs (the extra time and effort of hunting for a dwelling unit in white-occupied housing areas).

The evidence on market price discrimination is not conclusive. If one were able to perfectly define and measure a housing service unit in the real world, then the price per service unit paid by blacks could be compared with the price per service unit paid by whites. Units yielding the same level of service units could be compared on the basis of black or white occupancy, and the difference would reflect

---

[14]*Building the American City*, p. 287.

market price discrimination. Since the measure of housing service units has not been perfected, empirical studies have shown varying results, depending on the method of measurement of housing service. The results of such studies give estimates ranging from no market price discrimination to blacks paying 10 percent more than whites for similar housing.[15]

Assuming that racial market price discrimination does exist, there must be some mechanism at work in the housing market that achieves this result. Discrimination in the housing market may manifest itself in racially segregated housing, but the existence of racially segregated housing does not necessarily imply racial discrimination. To some extent, such segregation is attributable to segregation on the basis of income, resulting from the housing policies to be discussed in the next chapter. If housing is segregated on the basis of income, and black incomes tend to be lower than white incomes on the average, then blacks will be overrepresented in low-income housing areas (relative to their percentage of the total population). However, the high degree of racial housing segregation is not explainable completely on the basis of income, since there is segregation within each segment of the housing market stratified by income class. Thus, both income and racial discrimination are factors leading to housing segregation.[16]

Suppose that an urban area is totally segregated, with all blacks living in the central city and all whites living in the surrounding suburban jurisdictions. One possible explanation for higher market prices paid by blacks would be the following. Assume that whites do not wish to live near blacks or to sell or rent to blacks in the white segregated area. Further, suppose that black housing demand increases over a period of time as a result of increases in black incomes and migration to the central city by blacks from rural areas. This pressure from the demand side raises housing prices in the black area above those in the white areas. Eventually, prices become so high that some whites living near the frontier are motivated to either sell or rent to blacks. The reasoning so far would indicate that blacks pay more for housing. On the other hand, the entrance of a few blacks into an all-white neighborhood may result in rapid white departure, which increases the supply of housing for blacks and temporarily lowers the price in that neighborhood. In conclusion, there is no generally accepted theory of markets that accounts for a differential in prices paid by blacks and whites, either in the short run (transitional neighborhood) or in the long run (when the racial mix has stabilized). How-

[15]John F. Kain and John F. Quigley, "Housing Market Discrimination, Homeownership, and Savings Behavior," *American Economic Review* (June 1972), 263.

[16]See Table 8-2 for data on the increasing concentration of blacks in the central cities of major urban areas.

ever, any mechanism that results in this price discrimination probably rests to some degree on an aversion on the part of whites to having blacks living among them. Of course, there may also be aversion among blacks to living in proximity to whites, which could also result in housing segregation. Ultimately, the explanation of price discrimination needs to be based on more than this factor, since aversion could lead to segregation without necessarily resulting in price differences.

Differences in opportunities to become homeowners may be one of the nonmarket private costs borne by blacks that ultimately result in blacks paying more for comparable housing. Blacks of given age, family size, income, and other socioeconomic characteristics tend to be homeowners to a lesser extent than similarly circumstanced whites. The costs associated with home ownership are usually lower than the cost of renting similar housing, for reasons discussed in Chapter 8. Thus, to the extent that blacks have fewer opportunities to own their own homes, they will tend to have higher housing costs. One study of similarly circumstanced blacks and whites indicated that, while 41 percent of the whites were homeowners, only 32 percent of the blacks were.[17] One possible reason for this difference is that blacks my be discriminated against by lending institutions when seeking home financing.

The reflection of white preferences in the housing market with respect to having black neighbors is often couched in terms of a "tipping point." If a previously all-white neighborhood reaches some minimum percentage of black residents, a tipping point has been reached, which results in an exodus of the remaining white families. Very few previously all-white neighborhoods have achieved a stable pattern of racial integration. This would seem to indicate that in most neighborhoods the tipping point has been a very small percentage, although normally it is posited to be in the 30 to 60 percent range. If whites expect a neighborhood to tip when a few blacks move in, this expectation in turn helps the neighborhood to tip. Even if no panic selling is involved when blacks first move into a previously all-white neighborhood, since one household out of five changes residence every year, many whites will move out of a transitional neighborhood every year. If whites relocate only in all-white neighborhoods, it is inevitable that neighborhoods containing any blacks will ultimately become racially segregated once again, having moved from all-white status to all-black status.

If society desires to achieve racially integrated housing, such racial preferences and expectations on the part of the white majority need to be dealt with realistically. One possibility would be the use of racial

---

[17]Kain and Quigley, p. 265.

quotas in neighborhoods. For example, the racial percentage in each income class could form the basis for quotas in the neighborhoods of each income class. Once black (or white) percentages reached the levels indicated by the population ratios, then only the other race would be eligible for housing in a neighborhood. Guaranteed quotas would tend to eliminate the tipping phenomenon, since the ratio could not exceed the quota. It should be noted that quotas have been employed by the courts in treating the symptoms of housing segregation—to integrate school systems and faculties. Housing quotas would more directly treat the cause of segregated schools. While a quota system would tend to counter one of the results of racial prejudice, a housing quota system could rank very low in terms of efficiency. Housing choice and the exercise of consumer sovereignty on the part of both blacks and whites would be limited in comparison to a housing market without racial discrimination. However, racial discrimination does exist; therefore, the objective is to choose that policy which ranks highest with respect to efficiency and still achieves the integration goal, given the existence of discrimination.

Another approach to achieve racial integration, which does not involve the potential inefficiencies associated with housing quotas, would be the use of incentives in the form of taxes and subsidies. For example, whites living in all-white neighborhoods could be assessed a "segregation tax" that became lower as the percentage of blacks in the neighborhood rose. Alternatively, subsidies could be granted to families living in integrated neighborhoods. If blacks now bear the brunt of the costs of segregation, then the tax might be more appealing on equity grounds, since it would tend to balance the costs. The question that must be answered is what is the ultimate goal. While the question is complex, at least a large part of the goal is to eliminate the results of discrimination, not to achieve integration per se. Greater integration would seem to help diminish the results of discrimination, but certainly forcing a total integration of housing, where individual choice was suppressed, would not be in society's interest.

Another approach toward greater racial integration would be to promote, rather than attempt to outlaw, the practice of "blockbusting." This is the practice of real estate agents placing one or two black families in a previously all-white neighborhood and then resorting to scare tactics and high-pressure methods to get the remaining white residents to put their homes up for sale "while there is still time." The practice has been condemned by conservatives and liberals alike, and antiblockbusting laws forbid some of the tactics used to induce white homeowners to sell. There is an incentive to engage in these practices because of the large commissions to be made with the rapid turnover of homes; therefore, encouraging the practice would probably be quite effective. Whites living in blockbusted neighborhoods would pay a "tax" on the lowered value of their homes if the practice were confined to only a few neighborhoods, but, if a very large percentage of the blocks in an urban area were "busted," there would be little effect, other than a rapid breakdown of housing market barriers to black families. If there were at least some blacks living in every area, it would not be possible for whites to sell and move to segregated neighborhoods in the urban area. Property values would probably be little changed, except in previously all-white neighborhoods, where they might be somewhat higher, since these properties would now be accessible to more buyers and so there would be greater demand for them. Many of the short-run costs of transitional neighborhoods would be eliminated. It would appear that, while a little blockbusting is a very bad thing, a lot of blockbusting might be a rather good thing. However, it is conceivable, if this happened in one urban area, that the whole urban area could go "all-black," as some central cities are doing (this will be discussed in the next chapter).

In terms of equity, the panic selling of houses on the part of whites at temporarily depressed prices is probably the only major cost of racial discrimination borne by whites, since almost every other cost is borne by blacks. The harassment of homeowners by blockbusting real estate agents who pressure them to sell their houses, also imposes costs on them that society probably considers reprehensible.

Eliminating Market Failure and Reducing Housing Costs: Concluding Note

While many cases of market failure exist in the housing market, it is difficult to determine the amount by which the cost of housing would be reduced if they were eliminated. Many of the causes of market failure discussed above relate to the cost of developing a dwelling unit; however, the costs of housing are probably better evaluated by looking at the costs of occupying a dwelling unit. Estimates of the typical proportion of various components of acquisition and occupancy costs are presented in Table 7-3. The President's Commission on Urban Housing, from which these data are taken, estimated that housing occupancy costs in an efficient market could be reduced by approximately 10 percent,[18] but this is just one "educated guess."

It is unlikely that the elimination of any single cause of housing market failure would result in a large decrease in occupancy costs. For example, debt retirement (representing amortization of the acquisition costs) is estimated to be 53 percent of the total occupancy costs for typical single-family dwelling units (see Table 7-3). The site is 25 percent of acquisition costs, or approximately 13 percent of total

[18]President's Commission on Urban Housing, *A Decent Home*, Final Report, Government Printing Office, Washington, 1969, p. 11.

occupancy costs. Thus, a revision of zoning ordinances, which permitted smaller lot size and resulted in costs of the site being reduced by, say, one-fourth, would reduce occupancy costs by only a little more than 3 percent. Similarly, if local building codes were updated and made uniform, to permit new construction methods, and if restrictive work practices were eliminated, with, say, a 25 percent reduction in labor costs, acquisition costs would be reduced by about 5 percent, but monthly occupancy costs would be reduced by only about 3 percent. On-site labor costs account for a surprisingly low percentage of acquisition costs and hence an even lower percentage of occupancy costs. The bulk of construction costs (materials plus labor shown in Table 7-3) are not those of the "building envelope" (the structural frame and basic enclosing material), but utility systems (plumbing, heating and ventilating, and electrical) and the provision of the interior finish.[19]

In conclusion, although the above numbers are only representative and no definitive estimates of the impact of the various cases of market failure on housing costs exist, it would appear that no single remedy would by itself have a large impact on the cost of housing. However, since the proportion of society's resources devoted to housing is quite large (housing construction is usually between 4 and 5 percent of the Gross National Product), a small reduction in housing acquisition or occupancy costs can translate into billions of dollars on

COST COMPONENT	ESTIMATED PERCENTAGE OF TOTAL COST
Acquisition	
Site (developed land)	25
Materials	36
On-site labor	19
Overhead and profit	14
Miscellaneous	6
	100
OCCUPANCY	
Debt retirement (principal and interest on mortgage)	53
Taxes	26
Utilities	16
Maintenance and repair	5
	100

Table 7-3: Components of Development Cost and Occupancy Cost for Single-Family Housing
SOURCE: President's Commission on Urban Housing, *A Decent Home*, Final Report, Government Printing Office, Washington, 1969, Tables 4-2 and 4-3, p. 118.

[19]*A Decent Home*, p. 118.

a national scale. Also, many households occupy dwelling units considered to yield less than the socially determined minimum number of service units. A relatively small percentage reduction in housing occupancy costs may or may not have a significant impact on the number of households occupying inadequate housing, depending on whether inadequate housing consumption is mostly attributable to efficiency considerations or is merely a symptom of poverty.

REVIEW AND DISCUSSION QUESTIONS

1 The housing problem is that some people reside in inadequate housing. Evaluate.
2 There really is no housing problem; the problem is just a lack of income on the part of people living in inadequate housing. Evaluate.
3 Discuss the adequacy of the U.S. Census of Housing measures of housing consumption. If you were in charge of the census and had sufficient funds, what would you do to measure housing consumption? Why?
4 Are externalities important in housing markets? If so, how would you get them taken into account in making resource allocation decisions?
5 Housing codes should be rigidly enforced, because it would force landlords to provide adequate housing for low-income housing occupants. Evaluate.
6 Ir we build enough new housing, eventually all people will live in adequate housing. Evaluate.
7 The housing problem is that the demand for housing service units is greater than the supply. Evaluate.
8 Zoning laws should be abolished, since the private market determines land use that more closely approaches efficiency better than zoning boards, and without inviting political corruption. Evaluate.

SUGGESTED READINGS

Aaron, Henry J. *Shelters and Subsidies: Who Benefits from Federal Housing Policies?* pp. 1 - 43. Washington: The Brookings Institution, 1972.
Davis, Otto, and Andrew Whinston. "The Economics of Urban Renewal." In *Urban Renewal: The Record and the Controversy*, edited by J.Q. Wilson, pp. 50 - 67. Cambridge, Mass.: MIT Press, 1966.
Olsen, Edgar. "A Competitive Theory of the Housing Market." *American Economic Review* (September 1969), 612 - 622.
Building the American City. Report of the National Commission on Urban Problems. Part III, "Codes and Standards," and Part V, "Reducing Housing Costs." Washington: Government Printing Office, 1969.

8 / Analysis of Housing Programs

Legislation over the last four decades appears to have been more concerned with low levels of housing consumption than with low levels of consumption in general (poverty). Very few of the housing programs that have been enacted appear to have an efficiency objective; in other words, it is not obvious that they are in any way directed at the causes of market failure in the housing market discussed in the previous chapter. Thus, while most housing programs would appear to have an equity goal, political arguments put forth in support of them are usually phrased in terms of efficiency—the supposedly large positive externalities from increasing society's housing consumption. However, there is little sound evidence to substantiate this assumption. Although poor housing has long been alleged to cause poor health, high crime rates, and low levels of educational attainment, this cause-and-effect relationship has not been established satisfactorily. Poor housing goes along with other social ills; however, all of them, including poor housing, are also highly correlated with poverty. Treating one symptom of poverty is not likely to have much effect on another symptom.

As a result of the confusion between equity and efficiency considerations as the cause of low levels of housing consumption, the official goals of present housing policies and programs are not clearly stated. These policies and programs tend to increase housing consumption by subsidizing it in some way, thereby reducing the private cost of this commodity in relation to others. On the other hand, they have done little to eliminate the major sources of inefficiency in the housing market, which would result in the reduction of the private and social cost of housing.

The Basic United States Housing Policy

The major United States housing policy is not explicitly stated in any single piece of legislation. It is the response of the private market system to household incomes that have risen over time with constraints on the number of housing service units yielded by newly constructed dwellings. The outcome has also depended on which income groups received the bulk of housing subsidies to encourage them to move into dwellings yielding more housing service units. While better housing has been provided by this process, it has also resulted in some equity and efficiency outcomes that contribute to such urban problems as poverty and transportation.

The Turnover Process: Construction Standards and Subsidies

If the definition of the housing adequacy cutoff level (in terms of housing service units per person) remains constant over time, the number of households living in inadequate housing would be expected to decline at about the same rate as the number of households below a constant poverty level. As a crude approximation of housing adequacy, the U.S. Census of Housing data in Table 7-1 indicated that inadequate housing has substantially decreased over the thirty-year period from 1940 to 1970. A better indication of the increase in housing consumption in the aggregate is that real per capita housing expenditures more than doubled from 1950 to 1970.[1] While housing consumption would be expected to increase along with the increase in real incomes over time, increases in housing consumption in the United States have been aided by various government subsidies, which have reduced the relative private cost of housing consumption.

A nation's housing policies can be described by two factors: the quality standards (level of housing service units) in newly constructed dwelling units and the income group that receives housing subsidies.[2] For example, one policy would be to permit any sort of dwelling unit and provide no housing subsidies. In this case, one might expect to find tarpaper shacks occupied by the poor, located on the outer periphery of the urban area (where land is cheapest). However, in the United States, high standards for new dwelling units preclude the construction of dwellings yielding low levels of service units. If society has defined the housing adequacy cutoff as fifty service units per person, new dwelling units yielding fifty service units per person could be constructed to provide adequate housing for low-income families. If society has made the vertical equity judgment that all households will be brought above the housing adequacy cutoff level, this would be the simplest and most direct method, given the existing stock of housing at any point in time. However, in the United States, the combined workings of zoning ordinances and building codes result in most new housing construction being of high quality and quantity, yielding a number of housing service units far above that which would be considered minimally adequate. Zoning ordinances often prohibit housing on relatively small lots with a small amount of floor space in the dwelling unit. Similarly, building codes require construction materials and techniques that provide a

[1] Henry J. Aaron, *Shelters and Subsidies*, The Brookings Institution, Washington, 1972, pp. 28 - 29.

[2] Anthony Downs, "Housing the Urban Poor: The Economics of Various Strategies," *American Economic Review* (September 1969), 646 - 651.

physical structure considerably above the minimum criteria of housing adequacy set by the Bureau of the Census.

Given that new housing construction standards result in expensive new dwelling units yielding high levels of housing service units, low-income households presently living in inadequate housing could be placed in new housing only if they were provided with very large subsidies. This is not likely to be politically feasible, since many low-income households would then "leapfrog" over middle-income households in terms of housing consumption. As a result, the vertical equity features of the distribution of housing by income group would probably not be tolerated by the middle-income majority, who would in effect be paying taxes to support someone living in better housing than their own. An alternative subsidy policy is the one primarily followed in the United States: give most of the subsidy to middle- and upper-income groups to encourage them to occupy newer dwelling units yielding higher levels of service units. As a result of the incentive provided to upper-income groups, the housing stock turns over and older dwelling units yielding fewer housing service units become available for occupancy by lower-income groups having the income (either with or without subsidies) to occupy them. This turnover process leaves older dwelling units for occupancy by lower-income families. However, unless subsidies are provided to those at the lower end of the income-distribution scale, their incomes will not be adequate to afford the improved housing that opens up, although incomes have been increasing. The rate at which older but adequate dwelling units are turned over to lower-income families depends on the rate at which new, higher-service-unit dwellings are constructed. In recent years, new residential construction has increased the nation's housing stock by only about 2 or 3 percent annually. At any point in time, therefore, about 97 or 98 percent of the nation's housing inventory consists of "used" housing. While the turnover process creates the supply of housing, if this housing is to yield housing service units above the cutoff level to the new lower-income occupants, the incomes of such families must be adequate to support such housing. If incomes are too low, rents cannot be adequate to maintain the dwelling unit at a high level of housing service.

The process by which housing changes from yielding one level of housing service units to another level is sometimes called "filtering." As a dwelling gets older, the number of housing service units it yields is likely to decline, unless successively larger amounts are spent for maintenance and improvements. This implies that the decline in service units yielded is not purely a result of the passage of time; maintenance and improvements can significantly affect the number of housing service units. Altering maintenance and improvement expenditures in housing is one of the major means by which the housing market matches up the yield of housing service units and the incomes of the occupants. Thus, those who move into older housing must possess incomes adequate to maintain it at levels above the housing adequacy cutoff level; otherwise, filtering will do nothing to increase the proportion of the population in adequate housing. An extreme illustration of the filtering process is provided by some of the mansions of the Victorian era. Once yielding very high levels of housing service to the wealthiest residents of the city, they are now slum dwellings for the urban poor, subdivided into many apartment units. The incomes of their present occupants are inadequate to keep the buildings in a state of maintenance such that they yield enough housing service units to be considered "adequate" by society.

Income Tax Subsidies to Homeowners

The federal personal income tax encourages taxpayers to own the house in which they reside rather than to rent. The amount by which the income tax liability of a homeowner is reduced compared with that of a renter (whose financial circumstances are otherwise identical) can be considered an implicit housing subsidy to homeowners. The homeowner receives favorable tax treatment through three provisions of the federal tax law, as illustrated by the example of Table 8-1. The example takes two taxpayers, who are identical in all relevant respects except that one is a renter and the other one is a homeowner. Both are assumed to occupy identical houses with a market value of $40,000 each. The landlord of the house occupied by the renter receives $4,000 rent from the occupant per year and has expenses associated with the rental property as shown in the top portion of Table 8-1. The landlord has a $10,000 "equity" in the house, which is equivalent to the market value ($40,000) less the principal amount of the mortgage loan ($30,000). The income received by the landlord from renting the property is $700 (net of all expenses), and the landlord must pay income taxes on this amount. Occupancy expenses are assumed to be the same regardless of whether a home is rented or owner-occupied.

The favorable tax treatment afforded the owner-occupant is shown in the lower portion of Table 8-1. Assume that both taxpayers have a net worth (assets minus liabilities) of $10,000. The renter has his $10,000 invested in such assets as savings accounts or bonds, which realize an interest rate of 7 percent and an interest income of $700, which is included as income on his tax return. The $10,000 net worth of the homeowner, however, is his equity in his house, on which he receives no money income and which is thus not included as income on his tax return. The exclusion of this "imputed net rental income" from the owner-occupant's tax return is one of the three tax breaks.

ANNUAL RENTAL INCOME AND EXPENSE GENERATED BY LANDLORD RENTING $40,000 HOUSE	
Gross rental income (10% of $40,000)	$4,000
Rental expenses	
Mortgage interest (7% of $30,000)	2,100
Property taxes (1½% of market value of $40,000)	600
Depreciation (wear and tear and obsolescence)	400
Maintenance and repairs	200
Total	3,300
Net rental income (equal to 7% of equity of $10,000)	700

FEDERAL INCOME TAX LIABILITY, DEPENDING ON WHETHER THE $40,000 HOUSE IS OCCUPIED BY OWNER OR RENTER	RENTER	OWNER
Earnings income	$15,000	$15,000
Money interest income (7% of $10,000)	700	0
Total money income (adjusted gross income for tax purposes	15,700	15,000
Income tax deductions		
Personal exemptions (4 dependents times $750)	3,000	3,000
Mortgage interest (same as above)	0	2,100
Property taxes (same as above)	0	600
Other deductions (charitable contributions, etc.)	2,000	2,000
Total	5,000	7,700
Taxable income	10,700	7,300
Tax liability	1,974	1,247

Table 8-1: An Example of Income Tax Subsidies to Homeowners

The other two are the ability of the homeowner to deduct property taxes and mortgage interest from his taxable income in computing his federal income tax. In summary, the homeowner would have to report as part of his taxable income the imputed net rental income, which is the amount he could have received from renting the house. He would be allowed to deduct all of the rental expenses shown at the top of Table 8-1 as expenses incurred in earning this rental income. The difference, or net rental income, would be added to his taxable income. But the homeowner does not pay a tax on his imputed net rental income and in addition is allowed to deduct mortgage interest and property tax payments from his gross income. Thus, the taxable income of the homeowner is below that of the renter, who has his net worth invested in other assets, by an amount equal to the sum of net rental income, mortgage interest, and property taxes. In the example given in Table 8-1 the result is that the homeowner's taxable income is $3,400 less than the renter's and his resulting federal tax liability is $727 less (using 1973 federal income tax rates). This difference in income taxes paid, $727, is a housing subsidy that achieves the same effect as if the homeowner had paid $1,974 in taxes (the same as the renter) and received a tax-free check from the government for $727, marked "housing subsidy."

With respect to vertical equity, these subsidies provided to homeowners are regressive for several reasons. First, the percentage of households who own homes increases as incomes increase. The lower the income of the household, the less likely it is to have the net worth to make a down payment on a house or to have the financial characteristics (steady employment and credit rating) that institutions rely on in granting home mortgage loans. Second, the higher the income of the household, the greater the absolute amount that such a household is likely to spend on housing. Households with $10,000 per year might live in $20,000 houses, but households with $50,000 would tend to live in $100,000 houses. As a result, the sum of imputed net rental income, property taxes, and mortgage interest increases as income increases—resulting in greater tax deductions, a lower tax liability, and thus a greater housing subsidy. Third, the personal income tax has progressive rates; the higher one's taxable income, the greater the tax savings from each dollar of deductions. For example, in Table 8-1, the homeowner receives tax savings of $727 as a result of the taxable income reduction of $3,400, a saving of 21¢ for each dollar of deductions. However, if the homeowner's money income were $30,000 rather than $15,000, his income tax liability would be reduced by $1,028, a tax savings of 30¢ for each dollar of deductions (using 1973 federal income tax rates).

The total amount of implicit subsidies to homeowners provided by the personal income tax laws was estimated to be $7 billion in 1966 and $10 billion in 1970.[3] This implicit housing subsidy is much larger than the sum of all the explicit subsidies, such as public housing, discussed later in this chapter. With respect to vertical equity, 90 percent of the 1966 subsidy of $7 billion dollars accrued to households with incomes above $7,000 and 70 percent to households with incomes above $10,000 per year. Of the $7 billion subsidy, about $4 billion was attributable to the exclusion of net imputed rental income, and the remaining $3 billion was about equally accounted for by property tax and mortgage interest deductions. The elimination of the $7 billion subsidy would have permitted an overall cut of 12 percent in income tax rates while leaving total tax collections unchanged.[4]

The Turnover Process and Its Relationship to Housing Segregation and Poverty in Urban Areas

Two factors were previously mentioned as describing a nation's housing policies: construction standards and distribution of subsidies by

[3]Aaron, *Shelters and Subsidies*, pp. 55, 66.
[4]Aaron, *Shelters and Subsidies*, pp. 55 - 56, 66.

income group. In the United States, building codes and zoning regulations require very high construction standards, and subsidies go primarily to upper-income groups. Such a housing policy achieves a very high degree of residential segregation on the basis of income. Since only middle- and upper-income groups can afford to live in new dwelling units, lower-income families are forced to live in older dwellings. Construction of less expensive housing that would yield a number of housing service units above the housing adequacy cutoff is precluded by the high-quality standards in construction. Since the central city of the urban area was the first section to be developed, the older dwelling units are located in the central city and rings of successively newer dwellings surround them. Thus, dwelling units for low-income families tend to be located in the central city, while higher-income families are located in outlying areas. Since the average income of black households is less than that of whites, disproportionate numbers of blacks will be found in low-income housing areas. Thus, some of the observed racial segregation is the result of a housing policy that achieves income segregation, given the past and present incomes of blacks versus whites. When this policy is combined with discriminatory practices in the housing market, which reduce the housing choices of those blacks who do have the income to purchase housing outside the central city, a high degree of racial segregation results.

Table 8-2 gives some indication of the racial trends in large urban areas. Between 1960 and 1970, the population of the central cities of the SMSAs in the United States with populations over 1 million

| | 1960 | | 1970 | |
	Population (thousands)	Percentage	Population (thousands)	Percentage
TOTAL WHITE AND BLACK POPULATION				
Inside central cities	30,211	49%	30,048	42%
Outside central cities	31,037	51	40,886	58
Total	61,248	100	70,934	100
WHITE POPULATION				
Inside central cities	24,276	45	21,870	36
Outside central cities	29,666	55	38,672	64
Total	53,942	100	60,542	100
BLACK POPULATION				
Inside central cities	5,587	82	7,657	80
Outside central cities	1,216	18	1,860	20
Total	6,803	100	9,517	100

Table 8-2: Racial Composition of Population in SMSA's with Population of More Than One Million (1960 and 1970)
SOURCE: U.S. Bureau of the Census, *Current Population Reports*, Series P-23, No. 37, "Social and Economic Characteristics of the Population in Metropolitan and Nonmetropolitan Areas: 1970 and 1960," Government Printing Office, Washington, 1971, p. 19.

remained about the same. However, there was a reduction in white central city population of more than 2 million and a corresponding increase in the black population of about 2 million. While the black population of these major urban areas was only 11.1 and 13.4 percent of the total SMSA population in 1960 and 1970, respectively, about 80 percent of the black population resided in the central city in both years (and, obviously, only about 20 percent of the black population resided in the surrounding suburban areas). In numerical terms, the black population of these central cities increased by about 2 million while suburban black population increased by only about one-half million between 1960 and 1970. Of course, such data do not indicate the extent to which this resulted from lack of income or from housing discrimination on the basis of race. In addition, the central city often contains a large part of the total land in the urban area through gradual annexations. If the data in Table 8-2 were only for the area located within a few miles of the central business district, the increasing concentrations of blacks might be even more dramatic.

As discussed in Chapter 2, there are strong economic currents at work that have resulted in the decentralization of jobs from the central city to the suburbs. Thus, segregation of low-income blacks in the central city contributes to the poverty of such households by separating them from the locations of growing job opportunities for which they presently have the skills, especially manufacturing jobs. There are several reasons for believing that the segregation of low-income households may reduce their job opportunities below what would exist if such households were residentially located closer to such job opportunities. The distance factor adds to the difficulty of reaching certain jobs from inner-city black residential areas and may impose costs high enough to discourage job seekers. Also, such households have less information on and less opportunity to learn about jobs that are distant from their place of residence or those of their friends. Although studies of the impact on poverty of segregated housing show varying results,[5] it is safe to conclude that the inability to reside near job opportunities increases the number of segregated households in poverty.

Income Taxation of Rental Property and Slums

Most of the housing subsidies under the existing federal income tax laws are given to homeowners, as discussed above, but rental housing

[5]See John Kain, "Housing Segregation, Negro Employment, and Metropolitan Decentralization," Quarterly Journal of Economics (May 1968), 175 - 198; and Joseph Mooney, "Housing Segregation, Negro Employment and Metropolitan Decentralization: An Alternative Perspective," Quarterly Journal of Economics (May 1969), 299 - 311.

is also subsidized to some extent. Favorable tax treatment is given to investors in buildings, which, in a competitive housing market, results in a lower price per housing service unit to the renter than would exist in the absence of such treatment. Without elaborating on the technicalities involved, the rental housing subsidy from federal tax laws results from the ability of the landlord to take "accelerated depreciation" on his property—tax deductions for depreciation of the improvements (buildings) on the site. If the market value of the property declines less rapidly than the allowable depreciation during the early years of ownership, it will pay to sell the property after a few years and invest in another one where excess depreciation can be taken. The advantage of excess depreciation is that it reduces the income tax liability of the landlord in those years in which it is taken. At the time of the sale, the difference between the selling price and the cost of the property (reduced by the depreciation taken to that point) is taxable. However, this tax is lower for two reasons: first, it has been deferred for several years, reducing its present value; second, gains on the sale of property (if the property is held for more than ten years in the case of real estate) is taxed at half the rate that "ordinary" income is taxed. Since all the tax advantages are gained in the first ten years of ownership under existing tax laws, there is an incentive for owners of rental property to turn over their ownership every ten years.

It is frequently contended that accelerated depreciation helps to create slums (groups of buildings yielding low levels of housing service). If the low-quality housing market is relatively competitive, then the relationship between the rent charged and the number of housing service units yielded by the dwelling unit must be a strong one. The discussion in Chapter 7 of the private housing market indicated that there probably is a strong element of competition in the housing market, including that for low-income housing. Since accelerated depreciation lowers the cost of providing housing, it should lead to improvement in the housing of the poor. Perhaps some of the reason for believing that accelerated depreciation leads to slums is a confusion between depreciation allowable for tax purposes and physical depreciation. Accelerated depreciation for tax purposes does not mean that the buildings "run down" more quickly. Even if low-income housing in major cities is controlled by huge "slumlords" (the evidence seems to be that it is not), there is no logical reason why a tax policy that lowers the net cost of providing housing would lead to worse housing. If slumlords are trying to maximize their incomes, they would more likely provide better housing than worse.

Much of what has been written about slums, their causes and effects, appears to be based on a confusion of equity and efficiency considerations in the housing market. While some slum housing is no doubt attributable to market failure, it is safe to conclude that a large part is attributable to the low incomes of the occupants. As a result, many of the supposed indirect benefits of eliminating slum housing, such as reductions in crime and improved educational achievement, may occur only if poverty is reduced. Since slum housing is one of many symptoms of poverty, it would seem that the line of attack should be through poverty elimination.

Other Housing Programs

Such programs as public housing and urban renewal are usually considered to be the major housing programs in the United States: in fact, the most important housing programs are the implicit ones discussed in the preceding parts of this chapter. In the remainder of this chapter, urban renewal is evaluated with respect to efficiency and equity; this is followed by an evaluation of various programs that explicitly provide low-income housing subsidies, the largest of these being public housing. Federal legislation enacted in 1974 replaced or consolidated many of these programs; some of the important provisions of this legislation are summarized next. Most housing programs do not deal directly with the housing problem (inefficiencies in the provision of housing) but merely with the low levels of housing consumption that accompany low-income households. The recurring question—why subsidize housing consumption at all?—is discussed in the conclusion to the chapter (after an alternative plan for providing low-income housing subsidies, housing vouchers).

Urban Renewal

"Urban renewal," or redevelopment of slum areas, is a local government program encouraged and heavily subsidized by the federal government, which originated the program with the Housing Act of 1949. The local government submits plans for a project to be approved by the federal government. Upon approval, all property in a designated area is acquired by the local government either through negotiation or by condemnation under the laws of eminent domain—paying a "fair value" as determined by independent appraisals. Land assembly is followed by relocation of the tenants (residents and businesses) of the acquired properties. Varying degrees of assistance and relocation allowances are provided. Site clearance and preparation follow; the existing structures are demolished, the site is cleared, and improvements (streets, sewer systems, and other public services and utilities) are made. Site preparation is followed by sale or lease to private developers or transfer to public institutions (such as public housing authorities, public hospitals, or universities). Disposition of the site completes the local government's responsibility under the urban renewal program. The financial role of the federal government is to provide subsidies, which are usually equal to two-thirds of the net project cost. The net project cost is the sum of the gross cost of land acquisition, demolition costs, costs of site improvements and other costs of planning, administration, and interest, minus the price realized from the sale of the land to the ultimate user.

An economic evaluation of urban renewal from an equity and efficiency standpoint must be related to its supposed goals. However, the intent of urban renewal legislation and its goals or objectives are either not clear or are in some cases conflicting. According to the National Commission on Urban Problems, the legislative intent of urban renewal was to improve low-income housing through slum clearance and replacement of slum housing with housing that was deemed minimally adequate for low-income occupants.[6] While this may have been the legislative intent, a more comprehensive listing of the purposes includes the following: (1) removal of slums, (2) eradication of poverty, (3) provision of decent, safe, and sanitary housing in an environment suitable for all, (4) revival of downtown business areas of the central cities, (5) expansion of universities and hospitals, (6) achievement or maintenance of an adequate middle-income component in the central city, (7) attraction of additional "clean" industry into the central city, and (8) enhancement of the financial strength of central city government.[7] Not all these purposes can be dealt with here, but even a brief examination of these various goals reveals that some are couched in terms of equity and some (possibly) in terms of efficiency. Some are aimed at the symptoms of problems, while others are aimed at causes.

From an efficiency standpoint, the actual process of urban renewal results in the simultaneous improvement of adjacent properties within an area containing older and usually low-quality structures. As a result, the indirect benefits of improvement are captured—the area-wide redevelopment overcomes the problems of externalities that prevent individual property owners from making improvements. Further, the urban renewal agency can condemn property through laws of eminent domain, circumventing the holdout problem discussed in Chapter 7. Urban renewal projects could be justified on grounds of efficiency if net social benefits of the projects were positive and greater than those of alternative forms of market intervention

[6]*Building the American City*, Report of the National Commission on Urban Problems, Final Report, Government Printing Office, Washington, 1969, p. 152.

[7]Jerome Rothenberg, *Economic Evaluation of Urban Renewal*, The Brookings Institution. Washington, 1967, pp. 33 - 34.

designed to counter the failure of the private housing market.

The present financing of urban renewal projects provides an incentive to misallocate resources, because the federal government usually subsidizes about two-thirds of the net project costs while local governments make the resource allocation decisions. If the benefits of urban renewal accrue only to the community in which the project takes place, there is no justification on efficiency grounds for the federal government subsidy; those who are receiving all the benefits are not paying the total costs. Since local government planners consider only a portion of the costs associated with the project, they may compare the total benefits of the project with this fraction of the total costs, and thus it often appears that there is a positive net social benefit in cases where it does not actually exist. For example, assume that the social benefits of an urban renewal project are $1 million and the net project costs (assumed to be equal to social costs) are $1.2 million. Net social benefits in this case are negative and the project cannot be justified on grounds of efficiency. However, if the federal government pays two-thirds of the net project costs, the benefits considered by local planners are still $1 million, but the costs are only one-third of the $1.2 million, $0.4 million. From the local point of view the project then appears quite attractive.

Of the eight goals of urban renewal listed above, it is not likely that the first three, concerned with improving the housing stock for low-income people or reducing poverty, are in any way related to urban renewal by itself. To reduce the number of households in poverty, urban renewal would have to achieve some form of income redistribution, which it does not. The removal of slums, given the distribution of income, will not improve the well-being of slum dwellers nor will it result in them moving to minimally adequate housing. In the short run, dwellings are demolished, but the incomes of their former occupants are not increased; thus, there is no reason to believe that they will be able to move into better housing. Instead, if their incomes are not augmented, the former slum dwellers will be forced to seek other substandard housing, creating an increase in demand for such housing, which leads to an increase in rents. Combined with the costs of relocating, the increased cost of inadequate housing may actually decrease the well-being of slum dwellers. Not only does the rent increase adversely affect renters, it provides an incentive to convert existing standard dwelling units into substandard units, either through lack of maintenance or by subdividing larger units. From the standpoint of benefit-cost analysis, many urban renewal projects have been justified on the grounds that they reduce slum housing occupancy and, therefore, the indirect costs of crime, disease, and other social ills that are supposedly the result of slum housing occupancy. However, the preceding discussion indicates that the magnitude of such indirect benefits of slum removal is zero, since the slum (and its indirect costs) are merely relocated within the urban area.

Benefit-cost analyses of specific urban renewal projects that have been conducted to date have generally shown large negative net social benefits. The major reason for this is that structures with a positive market value (used to provide low levels of housing service to low-income households) are acquired and demolished. If the structures had no positive present value in use, then the cost of land acquired for urban renewal purposes would be less, since the land would already be vacant or the structures abandoned, through the operation of the housing market. The market value of these structures is reflected in the net project costs of urban renewal projects and benefits do not seem large enough to offset the costs. The implication of this is that the present use (providing slum housing) of urban renewal sites is the efficient response of the market to the demand for housing by lower-income households and that urban renewal interferes with these market forces, promoting inefficiency.

Urban renewal programs appear to have been primarily directed at the last five of the eight goals of urban renewal. Whether these purposes are in any way related to efficiency objectives is not clear; most of them appear to be subsidies to the central business district and the central city. A survey of over 1,000 urban renewal projects indicated that 67 percent were predominantly residential before urban renewal was initiated and 82 percent of the housing units demolished were judged to be substandard (by census definitions). After urban renewal only 43 percent of the areas were predominantly residential. In acreage terms, there was a shift of 10,700 acres from residential to nonresidential uses, of which 7,000 acres were for public purposes such as civic centers and stadiums.[8] Approximately 400,000 dwelling units have been demolished in urban renewal areas, most of these having been occupied by low-income households. Of the approximately 200,000 dwelling units planned for these same sites, less than 10 percent will be public housing, while over 60 percent will be for upper-income households.[9] From this perspective, urban renewal can be seen as primarily an in-kind redistribution program, which has subsidized the continued viability of the CBD and central city—an attempt to counter the trends of decentralization resulting from technological change. From a standpoint of equity, such subsidies are likely to be regressive, since a majority of urban renewal projects go for upper-income housing, sports stadiums, and similar projects generating benefits that accrue mostly to higher-income people. (Not many low-income individuals hold season tickets to professional football games.) Also, urban renewal projects in the central business

[8]*Building the American City,* p. 162
[9]*Building the American City,* p. 163.

district are likely to improve its physical appearance and result in an increase in the value of land near urban renewal sites (due to the positive externalities of the improved view). Most of these benefits accrue to landowners in the central business district, and such land-owners are likely to be at the upper end of the income distribution.

From the standpoint of local government, which has the authority to decide on the land use to which urban renewal sites will be put, there is obviously a strong incentive to reduce the amount of land used for low-income housing. Converting such land to other uses might bring in greater local tax revenues or reduce the size of the low-income population that has to be provided with welfare-related services financed by local government. Thus, it is not surprising that urban renewal, with a strong element of local control, creates an incentive to remove low-income households rather than to remove slums. As a result, urban renewal projects, overall, have no doubt decreased the well-being of low-income central city residents. This was recognized in late 1967 by the Department of Housing and Urban Development (HUD), which issued a directive that, in the future, urban renewal projects submitted to HUD should primarily provide housing for the poor.

With the Housing and Community Development Act of 1974 (dis-cussed later in this chapter), urban renewal has been supplanted by a new community development program. While some activity that might be described as urban renewal could be funded under this act, the primary focus is on the preservation and improvement of neighborhoods. However, since most urban renewal projects take somewhere between six and nine years from time of inception to completion, it will be several years before this shift in emphasis is seen in practice.

In summary, urban renewal is a prime example of a program whose supposed objectives treat the symptoms rather than the causes of housing problems. The program apparently provides large subsidies for high-income groups when the supposed equity objective is to increase the supply of adequate housing for the poor. However, to the extent that urban renewal legislation was merely the political re-sponse to the lobbying efforts of downtown property owners con-cerned with "saving the city" after World War Two, it could be considered somewhat successful, although very regressive in vertical equity terms.

Public Housing and Other Low-Income Housing Subsidy Programs

There are four existing programs that provide subsidies to lower-income households. All of them are supply-based, meaning that a household qualifies for occupancy in a government-provided housing unit on the basis of income. These subsidies are quite small in magnitude when compared with the major housing subsidy in the United States, the favorable tax treatment of homeowners. Income tax subsidies, primarily benefiting higher-income households, were approximately $7 billion in 1966, while public housing subsidies were approximately $500 million and other forms of lower-income housing assistance totaled less than $500 million.[10] Thus, these supply-based subsidies directed at lower-income households amounted to approximately $1 billion, or less than 15 percent of the income tax subsidies.

As discussed in Chapter 4, supply-based subsidies are likely to result in serious violations of horizontal equity and also entail loss of efficiency. Unless sufficient numbers of such housing units are available, so that all eligible households can become occupants and thus receive the subsidy, then, at each income level eligible for the subsidy, some will receive it and some will not, a violation of horizontal equity. From an efficiency standpoint, since the subsidy is tied to a specific housing unit, the occupant who moves in search of better employment or educational opportunities loses the subsidy and will be unlikely to get another one. Also, the four programs tie subsidies to new construction (except for some public housing that is leased from private owners), which results in the cost of a dwelling unit being more expensive than if low-income households were placed in existing housing units that met minimum adequacy standards. Some of the equity and efficiency features of these four existing programs will be discussed and subsequently compared with alternative forms of housing subsidies that are demand-based (the consumer of housing is given a subsidy, but there is no government provision of housing).

Public housing   In a program originally established by federal legislation in 1937, local governments create housing authorities to construct public housing and obtain federal subsidies. The public housing units are developed, owned, and operated by the local housing authority. The subsidies provided by the federal government are of several forms; the major one is an annual contribution from the Department of Housing and Urban Development (HUD) to pay the principal and interest on bonds issued by the local housing authority to finance the construction costs of the public housing units. Prior to 1969, no federal subsidies were provided for operating costs, but all construction costs were federally subsidized by the annual contribution contract. Thus, an incentive existed to develop housing units that minimized maintenance costs, even if the additional construction costs were greater than the present value of reduced maintenance. As of 1969, federal subsidies for operating expenses not covered by

[10]Aaron, *Shelters and Subsidies*, Table 10-1, p. 162.

rentals were authorized (within certain limits); this form of subsidy offers little incentive for efficient management of public housing projects. Thus, inefficiency has resulted from the lack of incentives for efficient use of resources that were built into the form of the subsidy provided.

Household income required to qualify for public housing is constrained by federal law but the local housing authority has some latitude in deciding the level. The rent paid by public housing occupants cannot exceed 25 percent of their income, the rent must be at least 20 percent lower than private rents for comparable units, and the maximum allowable tenant income is five times the private market rental value of comparable standard housing. Since there is considerable difficulty in determining the rental charge for "comparable" housing in the private market, the local housing authority has considerable discretion in determining the actual money income cutoff level at which a family qualifies for public housing occupancy. If the very lowest-income households occupied public housing, the amount they paid as rent would not cover operating expenses (their payments cannot exceed 25 percent of income). Thus, at least until 1969 (when operating subsidies were authorized), there was an incentive for local housing authorities to rent to the highest-income occupants they could, and the very poor tended to be excluded from occupancy.

The construction cost per dwelling unit of public housing is much higher than would be required to construct dwelling units that would be considered minimally adequate, for several reasons. Public housing projects in major urban areas are mostly located on expensive central city land, since the central city housing authority does not usually have the power to build projects outside its boundaries. The high cost of central city land has led to more intensive land use, and multistory structures have been built, which are more expensive than the lower-density units that could be constructed in the suburbs. Further, concentration of the poor in the central city may be undesirable in terms of access to new jobs that are opening up in the suburbs. On the other hand, public housing residents may rely more heavily on public transportation, so that a central city location is required to keep them from being "stranded." In any case, public housing policies tend to add to segregation on the basis of income, as is the case with private housing policies.

The benefits of public housing to the occupants may be much less than the cost of the subsidies involved, because many of the considerations that determine the level of housing service units yielded by a dwelling are poorly met by public housing, especially such environmental considerations as the level of public services, access to retail outlets, and transportation to jobs. Many observers conclude that the concentration of low-income households, exhibiting all the symptoms of poverty, into large-scale projects tends to encourage antisocial behavior such as window-breaking and other forms of vandalism. An example is the massive (3,500 families) high-rise Pruitt-Igoe project in St. Louis, which was awarded a prize for architectural excellence, but is now partially demolished in order to reduce residential density. Pruitt-Igoe's high vacancy rate apparently resulted from the failure of the project to provide environmental benefits, as opposed to merely meeting (or even surpassing) standards of structural adequacy set down by the Bureau of the Census.

Estimating the cost of subsidies received by public housing tenants is difficult, because some of the subsidy is implicit (like the federal income tax subsidies to homeowners) and does not show up anywhere in a governmental budget. While the federal subsidies actually paid are explicit, the amount of property taxes foregone by the local government as a result of taking land off the tax digest (since the public housing projects are not subject to the property tax) are implicit. There is a further implicit subsidy in that local housing authority bonds are backed by the federal government and thus carry lower interest rates than private corporation bonds. Also, the bonds are exempt from income taxes and this further reduces their interest rate, but not the true cost to society. One estimate of the cost of providing a public housing unit, in excess of rents collected, was $65 per month in 1965. The market value of the public housing unit provided was only $71 per month, for which the tenant paid an average of $44 rent—a subsidy to the tenant of $27, which cost the government $65.[11] Another study estimated the difference between rents paid by tenants and market values at $67 per month in 1966, and the federal subsidy required for interest and principal at $66 per month.[12] Since there are other components to the subsidy, it is safe to conclude that the cost to the government outweighs the benefits to the tenants. There may be positive externalities generated by increased housing consumption; if so, these should be included as social benefits (although, as we have seen, the existence of such benefits is controversial). On the other hand, providing a poor person with a subsidy in kind may not give him the same benefits as a cash subsidy, so the benefits to the tenants are overstated to this extent.

In terms of vertical equity, it seems that the public housing program does quite well. It is estimated that more than half the benefits went to families with incomes under $3,000 in 1966, and 86 percent to families with incomes of less than $5,000.[13] From a horizontal equity

[11]Eugene Smolensky and Douglas Gomery, "Efficiency and Equity Effects in the Benefits from Federal Housing Programs, 1965," in *Benefit Cost Analyses of Federal Programs*, Joint Economic Committee, Government Printing Office, Washington, January 2, 1973.

[12]Aaron, *Shelters and Subsidies*, pp. 123 - 124.

[13]Aaron, *Shelters and Subsidies*, p. 123.

standpoint, however, the story is less satisfactory. Only a small percentage of all households with incomes low enough to qualify for public housing are in fact tenants, since the number of units is limited. As of 1970, 2.5 million people lived in 800,000 public housing units.[14] If all of these had incomes below the poverty cutoff level (some did not), only about one-tenth of all people below the poverty cut-off level would be receiving public housing subsidies, while about 90 percent would receive nothing from the program. Only 2.1 percent of all households with incomes less than $1,000 lived in public housing in 1970, and 6.9 percent of those with incomes between $1,000 and $2,000. The percentages for households with incomes of $2,000 to $3,000 and $3,000 to $4,000 were 5.0 and 3.5, respectively.

Other federal housing subsidies   The federal rent supplement program of 1965 and the homeownership and rental assistance programs of 1968 are all somewhat similar in certain basic respects. They are all supply-based programs, in which the subsidy is received only by the occupants of specific dwelling units that have been constructed under these various programs. Housing projects that qualify under these plans are built by private contractors. Qualification is based on household income and the occupant must pay a certain percentage of his income for rent or mortgage payments, usually between 20 and 25 percent. The difference between the costs borne by the occupant and the cost of providing the housing is paid by federal subsidy. As the occupant's income increases, the amount that he pays increases and the federal subsidy decreases. Unlike public housing, an occupant is not forced to vacate the dwelling unit if his income exceeds a certain level. Instead, he ends up paying the entire costs of his housing.

In terms of efficiency, the homeownership program design created an incentive for excessively high costs. The household qualifying for the program had little incentive to bargain for a good price on the house it was buying, since the amount it paid was a fixed percentage of income, with the federal subsidy making up the difference. Thus, within certain bounds, the amount paid by the occupant did not depend on the price of the house. Also, there were problems of imperfect information on the part of low-income households (some of whom had never owned a house). Some did not realize that maintenance and utility expenses (occupancy costs) were part of the cash outlays of homeownership in addition to mortgage payments (acquisition costs).

As would be expected, the outcomes of these supply-based housing subsidy programs would be similar to those of public housing with respect to horizontal equity. Only a small percentage of all

[14]Aaron, *Shelters and Subsidies*, p. 108.

eligible households in terms of income actually occupy such dwelling units and receive a housing subsidy. The average annual benefit under the homeownership and rental assistance programs is about $830 and the median rent supplement payment is about $1,260.[15] From a vertical equity standpoint, rent supplements are more closely directed at the lowest-income households than are the rental assistance and homeownership programs. Some 93 percent of households receiving subsidies under the rent supplement program had incomes of less than $4,000 in 1969. On the other hand, only 5.3 percent of the households receiving subsidies under the homeownership program had incomes of less than $4,000, while the percentage was 24.2 for the rental assistance program.[16]

The Housing and Community Development Act of 1974

A major piece of housing legislation was enacted in 1974, covering a wide range of housing-related activities. The Housing and Community Development Act of 1974 consolidates several existing programs into a new single program, eliminates some programs, and adds others. This section deals with the two most significant departures from previous policy: the establishment of a single community development program in place of several existing programs and the establishment of a new form of subsidized housing (known as Section 8).

The community development part of the 1974 act terminates several existing programs, including urban renewal and Model Cities Supplemental Grants. In their place, a new program with an authorization of $8.4 billion over a three-year period was created. Some of the more important provisions of the community development section of the act are as follows:

1   There is no requirement for matching grants (such as local governments paying one-third of urban renewal net project costs), so the federal government contribution to local projects can be up to 100 percent.
2   Funds are channeled directly through existing local governments (e.g., the mayor and city council), rather than through separate local agencies (such as urban renewal authorities).
3   Cities and urban counties of a given size are entitled to a certain amount of funds, provided their proposals are consistent with broad guidelines. Thus, while the funding is at the federal level, local projects will be competing with other

---

[15]Charles Schultze, et al., *Setting National Priorities: The 1974 Budget*, The Brookings Institution, Washington, 1973, p. 137.
[16]Calculated from data in Aaron, *Shelters and Subsidies*, Table 8-1, p. 130.

projects in the same area rather than with other localities. The amount of funds to which an area is entitled will be determined by a formula that takes into account the "need" of the area—the extent of poverty, the degree of housing overcrowding, and population.

4   The permissible uses of funds are quite broad, and include the acquisition of property for redevelopment, for preservation of historic sites, for public works; and the construction of neighborhood facilities, such as centers for senior citizens and streets.

5   Eighty percent of the funds are to be distributed to SMSAs, and the remaining 20 percent to nonmetropolitan areas. Areas not entitled to funds by means of the formula may apply directly for a portion of the remaining funds. A further provision allows areas that participated in previous programs (such as urban renewal) not to be immediately cut back to the levels of funding determined by the formula, but this cutback (if one is indicated) will be phased in over a three-year period.

The 1974 act authorizes a new low-income housing assistance program to replace the homeownership and rental assistance programs that now provide subsidies to low-income households residing in private housing. This new form of subsidized housing (known as Section 8) is still supply-based, but has some elements of a demand-based subsidy. Owners or prospective owners of suitable housing (including local public housing authorities as well as private parties) are guaranteed a certain rent per unit, as established in each area. Families pay a certain amount of their incomes for rent, with the difference made up by the government. The subsidy is tied to the individual unit, rather than to a family, as in the case of a true demand-based subsidy (discussed in the next section of this chapter). However, some of the inefficiencies of a supply-based construction subsidy contained in existing programs are eliminated. The guaranteed rent is determined, and then the owner of the housing determines for himself the most profitable mix of construction costs and maintenance costs in the future.

An Alternative to Existing Low-Income Housing Subsidies: Housing Vouchers

The major problem of horizontal equity in supply-based programs is that the number of households who qualify for a subsidy is far greater than the number of available dwelling units. As a result, some households receive substantial subsidies while other households with the same income receive none. Demand-based subsidies for housing, received directly by the household in the form of a "voucher" or coupon to use as it wished, would avoid these horizontal inequities, since all similarly circumstanced households would receive an equal subsidy. From an efficiency standpoint, less violation of consumer sovereignty results from this kind of subsidy than in the case of supply-based subsidies. The household could apply the housing voucher directly toward the rent or purchase of any dwelling unit available on the housing market that provided a level of housing service the family could afford. In the case of public housing and other supply-based programs, no housing alternative is provided to the consumer; the family either lives in the subsidized dwelling unit or does not receive any housing subsidy.

Most proposals for housing vouchers are similar to a negative income tax plan, where the distribution is in kind rather than in cash. First of all, a guaranteed minimum level of housing consumption would have to be established. This might be done by using the results of budget studies such as those of the Bureau of Labor Statistics, which estimate the cost of housing at some level of adequacy for different urban areas in the country and for different-sized households. Given such an estimated expenditure required to achieve minimally adequate housing and assuming that households can spend 25 percent of their adjusted money income on housing, the difference between these two figures would be the dollar amount of the subsidy for each income group. Thus, as in the case of negative income tax programs, the housing subsidy program has a guaranteed minimum amount, even if the family has no income, and the amount of the subsidy is reduced by 25 percent (the implicit negative tax rate) as income increases, up to some break-even level of adjusted money income, at which the housing subsidy would be zero. The tradeoffs between these three variables are the same as those discussed in Chapter 6 for negative income tax programs.

The subsidy could not be paid in cash if the goal were to increase housing consumption. Instead, as with food stamps, the household would pay a certain amount in cash for a voucher worth more if used to buy housing. For example, suppose a household of four living in a given urban area has an income of $2,000 and the guaranteed minimum housing in this urban area has been determined to cost $1,200 per year. If the household is expected to spend 25 percent of its income on housing, then it would have to pay $500 in cash per year for a voucher worth $1,200 (a subsidy of $700). The voucher would be "cashed" with the landlord in the case of rented housing or with the lending institution if the household owned its dwelling unit.

As with any form of income redistribution in kind, the administrative costs (to insure that the subsidy was actually spent on increased housing consumption) would be greater than under an unrestricted cash program. Rent and mortgage payments would have to be verified as part of the administration of such a program. Also, black markets could arise in which individuals would sell housing vouchers for cash or receive "kickbacks" from landlords, since individuals would prefer cash to in-kind transfers, thus defeating the intent of the program.

One of the major difficulties with implementing a housing voucher program is that the demand for housing on the part of the subsidized households would immediately rise, and the supply of housing would not immediately increase. Thus, the initial impact would be an increase in price (rents or house prices), without an improvement in the level of housing service units consumed. While the supply of housing is relatively fixed in the short run, the private market would be expected to respond to the increased demand in the long run by adding to the stock of housing service units (by upgrading existing dwellings and undertaking new construction). To insure that housing vouchers would result in greater housing consumption on the part of lower-income households instead of merely higher prices for the same consumption, voucher plans would have to be implemented slowly. One possibility, suggested by Aaron, would be to gradually tie the subsidy to housing expenditure. Using the example above, the $700 subsidy could be paid in cash in the first year, $500 in cash and $200 in housing vouchers the second year, and so on, until in, say, the sixth year the entire subsidy would be in the form of a housing voucher worth $1,200, for which the family would pay $500.

In general respects, the existing income tax treatment of homeowners is similar to a housing voucher plan, in the sense that the housing subsidy depends on the amount of income and the amount spent on housing. While this existing plan provides implicit subsidies, mostly to higher-income households, of about $10 billion, the dollar amount of subsidies provided to lower-income families through a voucher plan would likely be less. For example, it has been estimated that the following housing voucher plan would have cost approximately $5 billion in 1967. Housing vouchers would be provided to all families with incomes below the break-even point, the guaranteed minimum housing expenditure would be in the neighborhood of $1,000 to $1,600 (depending on local housing costs) for a family of four, and households must spend 25 percent of their income for housing. More than 12 million individuals would have received some amount of housing subsidy.[17]

A Concluding Note

While housing vouchers could be designed to reduce the inequities and inefficiencies associated with present housing subsidy programs

[17]Aaron, *Shelters and Subsidies*, pp. 169 - 171.

directed at low-income households, the recurring question still exists: why subsidize housing at all? There is little evidence that indirect benefits are generated by housing consumption as opposed to other forms of household consumption. Most forms of governmental intervention into the housing market do not appear to be directed at the real housing problem—the various sources of inefficiency in the housing market. Instead, practically all of them involve some form of income redistribution in kind that appears to be justified more on grounds of political feasibility than on grounds of economic rationale. However, while in-kind distribution may be the most politically feasible way to provide better housing for the poor, in fact most such subsidies go to upper-income groups, owing to the provisions of federal income tax law. Eliminating the income tax advantages of homeownership would be one of the most politically infeasible acts conceivable, since so many households receive benefits from the provisions, and these tend to be the most vocal and politically active segment of society.

Government programs have attempted to increase housing consumption through various forms of subsidy rather than trying to reduce the price of housing through countering the causes of inefficiency in the housing market. However, improving the physical and structural characteristics of housing consumed by low-income households may deal with only a small part of the "housing problem." The major benefits received by the occupants of housing may not stem from the dwelling unit itself but from where it is located— the environmental characteristics. As long as certain neighborhoods are filled with housing occupants who exhibit the major symptoms of poverty (such as crime and other antisocial behavior) and the level of public services provided by the local government (such as schools and trash pickup) is low, housing adequacy, in its structural sense, may be a misplaced emphasis (together with the confusion of equity versus efficiency as a cause of the "housing problem").

REVIEW AND DISCUSSION QUESTIONS

1   Why is a greater proportion of the central city population in major urban areas poor than is the suburban population?

2   Explain the process by which housing vouchers given to lower-income households could result in better housing for the poor. Could such a program substitute for urban renewal, housing-code enforcement, and land-use restrictions that are presently aimed at eliminating inadequate housing?

3   Discuss how present housing policies would lead to income and racial segregation in urban areas, even in the absence of racial

discrimination in housing markets. Do such housing policies aggravate the poverty problem?

4 The destruction of slums by urban renewal and other public programs only results in the birth of new slums elsewhere. If so, why?

5 Explain why most housing subsidies in the United States go to middle- and upper-income households.

6 Can subsidizing housing consumption be justified on grounds of efficiency?

SUGGESTED READINGS

Aaron, Henry. *Shelters and Subsidies: Who Benefits from Federal Housing Policies?* Washington: The Brookings Institution, 1972. Chapter Four, "Taxes and Housing," pp. 53 - 73. Chapter Seven, "Low Rent Public Housing," pp. 108 - 126. Chapter Eight, "Housing Assistance Programs," pp. 124 - 144. Chapter Ten, "Home Delivery: How and for Whom?" pp. 159 - 173.

Building the American City. Final Report of the National Commission on Urban Problems. Part II, "Housing Programs." Washington: Government Printing Office, 1969.

Davis, Otto. "Reflection on the Urban Crisis." In *Our Cities in Crisis: Review and Appraisal,* edited by Paul Gatons and Richard Wallace, pp. 39 - 56. Atlanta: Georgia State College, Bureau of Business and Economic Research, June 1968. (Reprinted in Arthur F. Schreiber, Paul K. Gatons, and Richard B. Clemmer, eds. *Economics of Urban Problems: Selected Readings.* Boston: Houghton Mifflin, 1971.

Downs, Anthony. "Housing the Urban Poor: The Economics of Various Strategies." *American Economic Review* (September 1969), 646 - 651.

Fried, Edward, et al. "Helping People Buy Essentials: Housing." In *Setting National Priorities: the 1974 Budget,* pp. 129 - 145. Washington: The Brookings Institution, 1973.

Report of the National Advisory Commission on Civil Disorders. Chapter 16, "The Future of the Cities," pp. 215 - 226. Washington: Government Printing Office, 1968. (Reprinted in Schreiber et al.)

Rothenberg, Jerome. *Economic Evaluation of Urban Renewal.* Washington: The Brookings Institution, 1967.

Transportation problems are among the most misunderstood of all those that face urban areas. Widely held conceptions of the situation are not in accord with the facts. For example, the urban transportation problem is often considered to be synonymous with the problem of peak-hour traffic congestion stemming from journey-to-work trips by commuters employed in the central business district (CBD). However, in larger urban areas, a relatively small percentage of the work force is employed in the CBD, although people tend to view it as being nearer to 50 percent than the actual figure of, maybe, 15 percent (see Chapter 2). Another popular notion is that rail rapid transit is a panacea that will simultaneously solve problems of traffic congestion, central city decay, and air pollution. We do not wish to imply that rail is never the efficient answer, but rather that all alternatives should be considered. It is the purpose of this chapter to apply economic reasoning to the urban transportation problem. We shall begin by presenting some statistics on transportation in urban areas, to have a background against which to consider potential solutions to these problems. Then the extremely important (but widely ignored) concept of short-run efficiency in transportation will be examined. In the next chapter, long-run problems and potential solutions will be explored.

An Overview of Transportation in Urban Areas

At the outset it should be mentioned that certain kinds of transportation in urban areas will be neglected to some extent in our discussion. Transportation on foot and in elevators is important but outside the scope of this chapter. Similarly, a very large percentage of commuting trips could be handled by bicycle; however, this mode is not discussed, since the trend in countries where bicycles have been used extensively has been toward other modes such as autos. (Europe is approaching the United States in numbers of autos owned per capita.) A more serious omission is that trucks will not be extensively discussed. Trucks are obviously an important part of the transportation picture, but their omission does not radically change the conclusions of the chapter. More trucks mean more congestion if they travel during peak periods, but the congestion would be similar if there were simply more cars. This chapter will focus on the main modes of passenger transportation in urban areas—automobiles and the alternatives under the heading of public transit.

Public Transit

A casual glance at Table 9-1 indicates that the transit industry has been declining rather steadily for the last thirty years. The only

| | RAILWAY | | | TROLLEY | MOTOR | GRAND |
YEAR	Surface	Subway and elevated	Total	COACH	BUS	TOTAL
1940	5,943	2,382	8,325	534	4,239	13,098
1945	9,426	2,698	12,124	1,244	9,886	23,254
1950	3,904	2,264	6,168	1,658	9,420	17,246
1955	1,207	1,870	3,077	1,202	7,250	11,529
1960	463	1,850	2,313	657	6,425	9,395
1965	276	1,858	2,134	305	5,814	8,253
1970	235	1,881	2,116	182	5,034	7,332
1972	211	1,707	1,918	144	4,505	6,567

Table 9-1: Total Passengers Carried on Transit Lines of the United States, 1940 - 1972 (Millions)
SOURCE: *Transit Fact Book: 1972 - 3,* American Transit Association, Washington, 1973.

apparent exception are buses, but this is due to the fact that buses were substituted for trolleys (called surface railways in the table) during the period; however, the total of these two modes declined. The rise in public transit usage between 1940 and 1945 is attributable to World War Two, during which automobile use was curtailed due to decreased private market supplies of gasoline, tires, and new automobiles. Some of the reasons for the decline of public transportation have been alluded to in previous chapters—the relative decline of the CBD and the general trend toward decentralization, which have resulted in lower population densities in urban areas. Another reason has to do with how people spend their incomes as these incomes go up. We would not expect families to buy more and more potatoes as they move into higher and higher income brackets. Their higher incomes allow them to buy foods they consider more desirable, and probably most families would buy fewer rather than more potatoes. A similar situation exists with regard to transportation. As people's incomes go up, their ridership on public transit goes down, since they have a greater range of choice. An auto may be out of reach to a poor person, forcing him to rely on public transit, but, as his income increases, he may abandon public transit for an auto. The higher levels of income that people have enjoyed since World War Two have enabled many to opt for nonpublic transportation.

Despite the magnitude of the trend away from public transit, there has recently been an increased level of activity concerning new systems and expansions of old systems, much of it sparked by the Urban Mass Transportation Act of 1964 (UMTA). Thus, it would be inappropriate to dismiss public transit as simply a moribund relic of the past. Although mass transit performs a minor, and decreasing, role in the transportation picture of urban areas, it is still important, particularly in large urban areas. Some of the reasons for the increased interest in rapid transit may be the decline in ridership itself, which has led to declines in levels of service in some areas. Another reason may be that the huge outlays for highways do not seem to have done much to solve the problems of traffic congestion (the section on the short-run transportation problem will examine this carefully), contrary to the hopes of some. Environmental concerns have no doubt played a role here also. Finally, many people are opposed to the auto on various grounds, among them that the auto is incompatible with their idea of the city of the future, or that individual transportation is "not in the public interest." These may be a few of the reasons why interest in public transit has increased in recent years, in the face of more and more desertions by former riders.

Auto Transportation

Table 9-2 shows the trend of auto registrations and usage since 1940. Unless energy shortages lead to a reversal of this trend, autos will be more important in the future than they are now. (The main impact of the energy problem on auto ownership seems to be toward smaller rather than fewer cars.) While public transit ridership declines as incomes increase, the opposite is true of auto ownership and thus auto riders. On the other hand, a person can only drive one car at a time. As Table 9-2 shows, passenger car registrations continue to rise (at least up to 1970), but after some point in time the increase in registrations may merely reflect the increase in population. The trend toward auto ownership per se is probably over, except for very low income groups. Future increases in registrations will be due mainly to population increases and increases in two- and three-car families.

Regardless of what anyone prefers to believe about transportation in urban areas, it is already dominated by the auto, as Table 9-3 shows. The trips that depend most heavily on public transit (journey-to-work trips) are shown for 1970 in SMSAs over 250,000 population; how-

YEAR	AUTO VEHICLE MILES IN URBAN AREAS (BILLIONS)	PASSENGER CAR REGISTRATIONS (THOUSANDS)	POPULATION PER CAR REGISTRATION
1940	129.1	27,466	4.8
1950	182.5	40,339	3.8
1960	284.8	61,682	2.9
1965	378.2	75,241	2.6
1970	494.5	80,388	2.5

Table 9-2: United States Passenger Car Registration and Vehicle Miles in Urban Areas, 1940 - 1970
SOURCE: U.S. Bureau of the Census, *Statistical Abstract of the United States: 1973*, Government Printing Office, Washington, 1973, pp. 545, 547.

JOURNEY-TO-WORK TRIP MODE	SMSA RESIDENTS WORKING	
	In central cities	Outside central cities
Private automobile (driver)	60.7%	73.0%
Private automobile (passenger)	10.6	11.4
Bus or streetcar	11.6	3.2
Subway or elevated train	6.3	0.2
Walked to work	6.0	6.8
Worked at home	1.5	2.5
Other, including railroad and taxi	3.3	2.4
	100.0%	100.0%

Table 9-3: Journey-to-Work Trips by Mode in SMSAs over 250,000 Population, 1970
SOURCE: *1970 U.S. Census of Population, Journey to Work,* PC(2)-6D, Table 2.

ever, an even larger proportion of other than journey-to-work trips are by auto. Thus, data on all trips, including shopping and leisure ones, would show even more dependence on the auto. The blunt conclusion is that the automobile is almost the whole show in United States urban areas, and public transit plays a supplementary role, rather than the other way around.

The Short-Run Problem: Efficient use of Existing Transportation Facilities

Resource allocation decisions made in the past have resulted in the existing stock of transportation facilities in urban areas. It will be shown that the market system leads to inefficient use of these facilities because of negative externalities. Unfortunately, few outside the economics profession have realized that the gross misuse of existing facilities not only lowers present net social benefits but also distorts planning for future facilities. To take a somewhat frivolous example, suppose an auditorium could only be entered through a revolving door that turned extremely slowly, and that officials in charge of the auditorium had previously come to the conclusion that only such doors could be used. Huge lines of people waiting to use the door would imply (to the officials) that more doors were needed to accommodate the people. This installation of new doors would be quite costly, but, if officials were committed to using only revolving doors, and only ones of the slow-turning type, then more doors would be needed (a long-run decision). However, it might be possible to consider other alternatives, such as oiling the existing door, or putting another type of door in the entrance, so that the lines of people would be eliminated. This is rather similar to the situation in transportation, where certain alternatives are not seriously considered, even though they could greatly reduce the apparent need for additional facilities.

The Congestion Problem

Traffic congestion is defined here as a level of usage of an existing transportation facility at which the social costs of additional users exceed the private costs of these users—a divergence between private and social costs, or a negative externality. There are several ways in which congestion can occur, but the type we will analyze first has to do with the fact that additional cars on a road reduce the average speed of the cars on the road. In Figure 9-1 the level of use of the facility is measured on the horizontal axis, with the units of this axis determined by the transportation mode under consideration. They could be the number of trips completed over a given stretch of highway in a given period of time, the number of passengers on a bus or rail car, or the number of takeoffs or landings in some time period at an airport. The analysis here pertains to auto transportation, since this is the major mode of passenger transportation in urban areas (however, this does not imply that the analysis does not apply to other modes). Thus, the number of trips per hour along a highway is on the horizontal axis, in this example, the number of trips per hour along a one-mile stretch of three lanes traveling in one direction.

The number of trips per hour (or other time period) will depend on both the number of cars on a stretch of road (density) and their average speed. Table 9-4 shows the number of trips per hour that can be achieved when various numbers of cars on the road travel at the maximum safe speed attainable (this is assumed to be 70 miles per hour if there is no congestion, although a speed limit of 55 miles per hour would not change either the qualitative conclusions or the maximum capacity of the road).

The basic idea is that, if there are more cars on the highway, average speeds drop after some point. The reader may be inclined to think of this in another way—that slow speeds tend to make cars closer together; it is important to keep in mind that causation runs from density to speed rather than the other way around. It may seem that, during especially slow times, more imbecilic and meandering drivers enter the road, but probably the proportion of such drivers decreases during rush hours. Speeds are slower because there are more cars on the road. In Table 9-4 the maximum number of trips per hour (7,000) obtains when 200 cars are on the one-mile segment of highway, traveling at an average speed of 35 miles per hour. If more cars enter the highway, the number of trips drops below 7,000; for example, if there are 300 cars on the road, speeds fall to 20 miles per hour and the

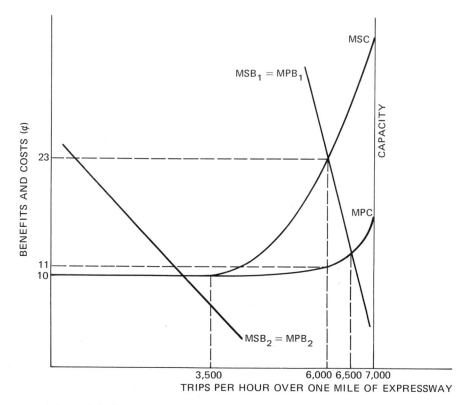

Figure 9-1: Benefits and Costs of Highway Use

number of trips falls to 6,000. In the extreme case shown, cars are creeping along at 1 mile per hour and, although there are 720 cars on the road, the number of trips per hour drops to only 720. Densities on this order are often approached on urban expressways during peak hours of use. It should be obvious that, if the usage of the expressway is restricted so lower densities will prevail, more trips per hour (greater flow) will result. Thus, to achieve efficiency, use of the facility should be rationed at least to the point where the flow is maximized and the capacity of the highway is not being exceeded.

Thus, we have a rather paradoxical result. To increase the number of trips, we must decrease the number of cars allowed on the road at any one time. The use of expressways is thus not unlike what happens when people push and crowd to get through a narrow door. The flow of people through the door is impeded by these actions (an obvious reason for requiring fire drills in public schools). It should be kept in mind that this result applies to situations of extreme congestion and that impeding entry will not increase flow unless the capacity of the

TRIPS PER HOUR OVER ONE MILE OF EXPRESSWAY	=	DENSITY (NUMBER OF CARS ON EXPRESSWAY)	×	AVERAGE SPEED (MILES PER HOUR)
1,750		25		70
3,500		50		70
6,000		100		60'
7,000		200		35
6,000		300		20
4,800		400		12
3,000		500		6
720		720		1

Table 9-4: The Relationship of Flow, Density, and Speed

facility has been exceeded. However, capacity is usually exceeded on urban expressways during some times of the day, so this is not an unusual case.

Figure 9-1 portrays the social and private costs and benefits associated with the use of an expressway during two different times of the day. The MSB curves represent the summation of the individual marginal private benefit curves of all individuals who have a desire to use the expressway at these two different times of the day. MSB_1 may represent a time when relatively large numbers of commuters are using the highway (but not enough to exceed capacity flow of 7,000), and MSB_2 may represent an "off-peak" time of day such as ten o'clock in the morning. MSB_1 is greater than MSB_2 for two reasons: (1) there are a greater number who wish to use the facility during times when many people are commuting to and from work, and (2) the private benefits of peak-time journey-to-work trips are considerably higher than, say, shopping trips, which can be made at almost any hour of the day. A person can lose his job if he consistently fails to arrive at work on time, but not getting to a grocery when planned is far less costly.

In Figure 9-1, the MPC curve is horizontal at a constant 10¢ per trip up to expressway flows of 3,500 trips per hour. These costs of 10¢ per mile include operating costs of the auto and the value of the time of the auto's occupants. Remember that these are marginal costs of using a particular highway and refer to additional trips. Suppose a family owns an auto for purposes of shopping, recreation, and so forth. Using a highway on a particular day for a commuting trip does not incur extra costs of depreciation, since the car is owned already and depreciation is almost totally dependent on the age of the car. Only costs that increase because of the trip should be included as marginal costs; gas and oil and repairs that depend on the number of miles driven should be counted, but not depreciation. Let us assume that these marginal costs of operating a vehicle amount to 4¢ per mile, although mileage per gallon will vary somewhat with speed.[1] A larger cost will be the value of time of the occupants. Suppose the driver and his passengers value their travel time at $2.80 per hour and that, on average, there are 1.5 persons per car. Thus, total hourly travel-time private costs are $4.20 per car ($2.80 × 1.5). Traveling over a one-mile stretch of highway at 70 miles per hour will take one-seventieth of an hour, which is worth 1/70 of $4.20, or 6¢. Thus, the private cost of using the highway when there is no congestion is 10¢ (6¢ time cost plus 4¢ operating cost). When average speeds drop to 35 miles per hour, the time costs double to 12¢, since the trip takes twice as long; thus, the marginal private cost becomes 16¢. If traffic is creeping along at 1 mile per hour, the time costs become $4.20 and swamp operating costs (4¢) in magnitude.

The MPC curve in Figure 9-1 is upward-sloping beyond flows of 3,500, because the high densities result in increased travel time and higher travel-time costs. Also, as indicated in Table 9-4, the capacity of the expressway is 7,000 trips per hour. If densities exceed this, then the flow decreases, but travel time per car continues to increase even though fewer trips are made. The MPC curve in Figure 9-1 would become backward-bending, if this segment of the curve were drawn in the figure past a flow of 7,000. For example, from the figures in Table 9-4, a flow of 6,000 can be achieved with a density of 100 cars traveling at 60 miles per hour, which would result in MPC of 11¢ (4¢ operating cost per mile plus one minute of travel time valued at 7¢ per minute). However, if densities increase to 300, the capacity of the expressway (a flow of 7,000) is exceeded and the flow is back to 6,000; travel time is now tripled to three minutes, since cars are achieving speeds of only 20 miles per hour. As a result, the cost of a trip under these conditions is 25¢ (4¢ operating cost per mile plus three minutes of travel time valued at 7¢ per minute). Thus, there are two MPCs at a flow of 6,000: 11¢ and 25¢. In other words, the MPC curve is backward-bending because it has more than one value for a given flow as measured on the horizontal axis. In a sense, the backward portion of the MPC curve is not truly a marginal curve. It shows the cost incurred by an additional car that enters the road, but does not show the cost of making an additional trip, since the extra car will decrease the number of trips. (The backward portion of the MPC curve is not shown in Figure 9-1 to avoid confusion in the subsequent discussion.)

It is admitted that there are difficulties in measuring the value people place on their time, but some value must be placed on it, since

---

[1]The Federal Highway Administration estimated the total cost of operating a three-year-old car for 11,500 miles per year to be about 14½¢ per mile. Of this, gasoline cost about 2¢ and other marginal costs seemed to be about 2¢. Reported in *Statistical Abstract of the United States: 1973*, Government Printing Office, Washington, 1973, p. 550.

it is a limited resource (there are only twenty-four hours in a day). An often used assumption is that a person's hourly wage net of income taxes is a fair approximation of the value he places on his time. In any case, it is unlikely that travel time would be valued any higher than this, since wages are taxed while travel time is not. If a person could work one more hour because he saved an hour previously spent in traffic, then the amount that he earned per hour after taxes would be a measure of the value of his time. In the example at Figure 9-1, we have chosen $4.20 as the value of time to the driver and the occupants of a typical car, which, on average, probably contains about 1.5 persons. This figure would obtain if both driver and passenger made a gross wage of $4.00 per hour and social security contributions and income taxes were 30 percent of gross wages, resulting in an after-tax wage rate of $2.80.

In Figure 9-1, no congestion exists at times when 50 or fewer cars are on the road (that is, fewer than 3,500 trips per hour are being made), since, as indicated in Table 9-4, all cars can maintain the maximum permissible speed of 70 miles per hour. In other words, there is no divergence between private cost (10¢) and social cost at these densities. However, if more than 50 cars are on the road, additional entrants onto the expressway incur higher private costs, since they cannot drive at 70 miles per hour and so use greater amounts of time. Thus, MPC is increasing for densities in excess of 50 cars. However, not only do the marginal private costs increase, but the additional entrants slow down other drivers, thereby imposing indirect costs on them. The individual driver does not take into consideration that his entry slows other drivers, but considers only the fact that *his* costs are higher than he would like.[2] As more and more drivers enter the highway, the number of trips increases, up to the point where the capacity of the highway is reached (200 cars, or 7,000 trips per hour); beyond this point, additional cars will reduce the number of trips per hour while private and social costs per trip continue to increase.

The Efficient Level of Congestion

Consider the level of usage of the road indicated by MSB_1 in Figure 9-1. During the time of day represented by MSB_1, drivers will enter

---

[2]In this discussion, we have assumed that the driver actually knows his own private costs but does not perceive the social costs of his actions. One could argue that he does not know his private costs very well either, but all that is being said here is that he will tend to equate MPB and MPC to the best of his knowledge. The better his knowledge of his costs and benefits, the better he will do. Further, he may indeed know that he will slow down other cars. The question is whether he does anything about it, and the answer to this question is generally in the negative.

the highway until the average rate of speed and number of cars are such that 6,500 trips are made. At this level, MPB = MPC, so net private benefits are being maximized; however, marginal social costs exceed marginal social benefits, which implies inefficiently high usage. From the standpoint of society (which is just the drivers as a group in this example), the efficient number of trips is 6,000 per hour at this time of day, since this is the flow where MSB = MSC. Thus, we have a situation of negative externalities leading to an inefficiently large quantity of a service (level of usage), because individual motorists, maximizing net private benefits, do not take the externality into account.

Furthermore, during the peak of the rush-hour traffic periods in the morning and the afternoon, the MSB curve would be to the right of the MSB_1 curve in Figure 9-1. Since the capacity of the highway is 7,000 trips per hour, if the number of cars on the highway during the peak hour exceeds 200, the total flow is decreased, yet individual motorists will be equating marginal private benefits and marginal private costs at densities exceeding 200. As previously discussed, for example, at a flow of 6,000 that results from densities of 100 cars traveling at an average speed of 60 miles per hour, the MPC of the one-mile trip is 11¢; however, at a flow of 6,000 that results from a density of 300 cars, at an average speed of 20 miles per hour, the MPC of the one-mile trip is 25¢. If the number of motorists trying to enter the expressway during the peak period is such that densities reach 400, the average speed of 12 miles per hour will increase the private costs of the trip to 39¢. Yet the demand for the use of the facility is sufficiently large during the peak-hour period that many motorists may maximize net private benefits subject to a private cost of 39¢. When this happens, the divergence between private and social costs becomes extremely large and traffic congestion far exceeds the efficient amount. In either the time period represented by MSB_1 or in cases where the number of cars on the road exceeds its trip capacity, the number of cars on the road must be restricted in order to achieve the efficient flow at which marginal social benefits and marginal social costs are equated. As previously stated, in no case could the efficient level of usage at a given time of day result in such high densities that average speeds were reduced to the point where the trip capacity (maximum flow in Table 9-4) was exceeded.

In contrast to the peak-period conditions discussed above, consider MSB_2 in Figure 9-1. The level of usage at the time of day represented by MSB_2 is low enough that additional cars do not slow down the flow of traffic, and no negative externalities of congestion result. At this level of usage, MSB = MSC, so both net private benefits and net social benefits are maximized.

Achieving Short-Run Efficiency: Rationing Use of Existing Transportation Facilities

Why is not a flow of 6,000 achieved during the time period represented by MSB_1 in Figure 9-1 instead of 6,500—that is, why are transportation facilities used beyond the efficient level during some times of the day? Highways are "common property resources" (owned in common by the public rather than by individuals) and can be used by anyone at any time.[3] Thus, anyone owning a car can enter the highway as he desires. There is no incentive to stay off unless the marginal private costs incurred by him exceed the marginal private benefits he receives from making the trip. The higher the level of congestion is, the higher are the marginal private costs, but not high enough to lead to efficiency. Individual users entering the road do not take into consideration the indirect costs of traffic congestion they impose on other drivers on the road. Achieving efficiency requires some kind of management. The use of the road must be rationed when congestion exists, but only at those times of the day when it does. When fewer than fifty cars are on the road, with the result that fewer than 3,500 trips per hour are made (as in the case of MSB_2 in Figure 9-1), there is no divergence between social and private costs, and individual decisions lead to efficiency. When congestion prevails, some form of rationing must be imposed if there is to be efficiency.

Rationing by Prices

If the marginal social benefit curve and the marginal social and private cost curves shown in Figure 9-1 could be estimated, use of the road could be rationed by charging a price (toll) designed to achieve the efficient level of usage. Suppose we could make marginal private costs equal to marginal social costs at all levels of usage. Then the *new* net private benefits would be maximized at a level where MSB = MSC, since MSB already equals MPB and now MSC = MPC. The price that will equate MPC and MSC is the difference between these figures. Thus, in Figure 9-1, at the time of day represented by MSB_1, the price required to make the motorist incur all the costs of his activity would be 12¢, the difference between the MSC of 23¢ and the MPC of 11¢. Once the marginal private costs, including the toll, are 23¢, the toll leads to efficiency, since it was designed to make MPC equal to MSC.

---

[3]There are several other kinds of common property resource, including the environment, which will be discussed in Chapters 11 and 12.

An example   Note carefully that the price charged the motorist depends on the time of day he travels. Different prices should be charged at different times of the day in accordance with the divergence between MPC and MSC. Table 9-5 shows an example of the tolls required on an urban expressway for a trip of about eight miles. This is probably more typical of urban expressway trips than the example of Figure 9-1 and was chosen to provide the reader with a feel for the kind of tolls that might actually be established with a view toward approximating efficiency. The toll here is not precisely efficient, but comes as close to efficiency as possible, while not varying the charge by less than 50¢ or the time periods by less than one hour. Since no peak-hour tolls exist in the real world, this is an informed guess of what might be expected if expressways were rationed by the price mechanism. Column 2 shows the number of trips per hour in the time period given in column 1, in the absence of any toll. The use of the expressway is highly peaked, with both morning and evening rush hours. Column 3 shows the peak-hour tolls required to approximate efficiency, and column 4 shows the number of trips per hour after the imposition of the toll. Notice that the toll depends on the level of use established *after* the toll is imposed. For example, the level of usage at 6:00 to 7:00 P.M. prior to the toll was 1,500 trips per hour, which is sufficiently low to result in no divergence between private and social cost. However, imposition of tolls at earlier times would lead some drivers to make later trips; thus, a toll of 50¢ is now required at this hour to keep the level of usage at the efficient (more or less) level of 1,800. Without this toll, usage would be (inefficiently) above 1,800. The total number of trips during the peak hours in the morning and evening has been reduced by the toll because the higher private cost of driving an auto during this time of day has resulted in car-pooling, switching to public transit, and other actions on the part of individual motorists. If the expressway under consideration in Table 9-5 had a usage during a peak hour that exceeded its capacity, the imposition of a toll would lead to an increase in trips during this time, as discussed at Table 9-4 for densities in excess of 200 cars.

The example shows that the level of the toll depends on the time of day, but, more basically, it depends on the demand for the use of the facility. Efficient tolls can be designed to closely approximate the divergence between marginal social cost and marginal private cost. Note carefully that *efficient tolls have nothing whatever to do with paying for the construction of the road.* Efficient tolls ration use of the road to more efficient levels, and the proceeds of the toll could potentially be used for anything. Present tolls often are imposed for the purpose of retiring and servicing bonds and do not vary by time of use, but there is no reason for future tolls to be of this type.

To conclude, urban expressways (as well as other types of transportation facilities) are common property resources, and users of such

1 Time of day	2 Trips per hour without any toll	3 Peak-hour toll	4 Trips per hour after imposition of toll
Midnight-6 A.M.	200	$ 0	200
6 A.M.-7 A.M.	1,000	0	1,400
7 A.M.-8 A.M.	3,000	1.00	2,500
8 A.M.-9 A.M.	4,000	2.00	3,000
9 A.M.-10 A.M.	1,800	0.50	1,700
10 A.M.-3 P.M.	1,500	0	1,500
3 P.M.-4 P.M.	2,000	0.50	2,000
4 P.M.-5 P.M.	3,000	1.00	2,500
5 P.M.-6 P.M.	4,000	2.00	3,000
6 P.M.-7 P.M.	1,500	0.50	1,800
7 P.M.-8 P.M.	1,300	0	1,400
8 P.M.-Midnight	1,000	0	1,000

Table 9-5: An Example of a Schedule of Peak-Hour Tolls on an Urban Expressway

resources often impose indirect costs on other users. If a price is set that is equal to the indirect costs imposed on other users, then private decisions will tend to be efficient. The toll price will depend on how heavily the facility is in demand at different times of the day. In periods of light use, no indirect costs are imposed, and assessing a toll during these periods will cause the facility to be underused. As demand rises, so does the efficient toll. In extreme cases of congestion, an additional vehicle will actually cause the number of trips to decline, but an efficient toll will prevent such overuse. Efficient tolls will smooth out the peaks of use, but will not generally eliminate congestion. Rather, it will be lowered to efficient levels.

Other types of congestion and price rationing   Before discussing some of the problems associated with implementing a price rationing system in the type of congestion discussed above, it should be noted that price rationing could alleviate congestion caused by bottlenecks in transportation systems.[4] Any time a facility is used to the extent where additional users impose costs on other users, a toll or other method of rationing can lead to a more efficient level of use. Suppose there is a heavily used bridge that connects a suburban area to a central city. A toll on such a bridge could be set so that users would bear the costs of their activity (someone who uses the bridge during a heavy peak makes all those behind him wait longer than if he had not used it then). A diagram such as Figure 9-1 would be appropriate to analyze this situation as well as the one where density led to lower speeds. Below some level of use of the bridge, no toll would be

[4]See William Vickrey, "Congestion Theory and Transport Investment," *American Economic Review* (May 1969), 251 - 261.

appropriate, since no congestion would occur (at 3:00 A.M. for example). As congestion (queuing, or waiting in line) rises, the appropriate (efficient) toll rises also.

In Figure 9-1 the number of trips per hour is measured by counting the number of vehicles rather than the number of riders. It is crucial that the toll be on a per vehicle basis. A widely publicized policy used on the Golden Gate Bridge in San Francisco collects tolls on cars containing one or two people but lets cars with three or more occupants enter without paying a toll, provided a nominal monthly charge is paid. The inefficiencies of this policy are easy to point out. Each car, regardless of the number of passengers, adds the same amount to the congestion level, so an an efficient toll must be the same for all cars at the same time of day. Although there may be some incentive to form a small car pool, there is no incentive to add additional members, which there would be with an efficient toll. Secondly, the efficient toll needs to be high enough to cover the indirect costs per car. (Such a toll would drastically reduce the number of cars trying to enter the bridge during the peak.) Further, the toll must vary according to intensity of demand for the facility. It appears that the idea of tolls as a rationing device has been picked up by those who do not understand that the purpose is to achieve efficient usage, not to punish drivers or certain classes of drivers (those without passengers, for example) per se. The value of an efficient toll is that people would be induced to voluntarily double up and form car pools, in accordance with the private costs to them of doing so. For some, this would not happen, but a single driver would pay a high toll that could not be shared with passengers. Finally, it should be noted that the case of a bottleneck in transportation differs from the case of congestion due to density; the efficient level of a queue waiting to get across a bridge may be essentially zero, since the number of vehicles crossing may be the same regardless of the length of the queue. In this case, any queue constitutes overuse (except for a small queue of varying length that guarantees the bridge will be used to capacity).

Potential effects of price rationing   If prices were charged to ration existing highway facilities, what might be some of the effects? There are usually several alternative routes available to the motorist for the journey-to-work trip, often consisting of an expressway and various street routes. In addition, there may be some form of public transportation available, such as bus or rail rapid transit. It would undoubtedly be more difficult to ration the use of streets by prices than limited-access highways, since cars can enter and exit from streets at a very large number of points. Thus, if it were administratively feasible to apply price rationing only to the expressways in an urban area, there would be incentives for previous users of the expressways to shift to congested streets or public transportation. The increased use of streets would certainly result in increased congestion on those streets. Public transportation might then be more attractive, since the relative costs of operating an auto would be increased relative to public transportation (unless the buses relied heavily on congested streets as opposed to rationed expressways). Costs of using the expressway would be raised because of the toll, and costs of alternative streets would be increased because of the increased congestion. On the other hand, many people tend to value travel time rather highly; travel time on the expressway may be sufficiently decreased to make many drivers greatly prefer the toll road to the streets, and to prefer the expressway with the toll on it to the toll-free expressway.[5]

The extent to which drivers would switch from an expressway because of a toll would depend on the private benefits and private costs to individual motorists. A key factor is, of course, the value of time to the individual. A person with a very high value on his time would choose the expressway and pay the toll, since this would be the least-cost way for him to make the trip. A person with a lower value of time would tend to choose other alternatives.

The relatively high cost of peak-hour trips (in terms of congestion tolls on expressways and increased congestion on side streets) would tend to discourage nonessential trips during peak periods. For example, housewives would probably refrain from making shopping trips to the central city during peak hours (they do already to a great extent, but the toll would be a further deterrent). The elimination of nonessential trips may be of considerable importance in reducing peak-hour congestion. There are many other users who could shift their time of usage to a nonpeak hour, and a pricing mechanism would encourage this.

A more important potential effect of price rationing would be the formation of car pools. There have been many exhortations to get people to form car pools and some government offices have required employees to register for participation in car pools. During World War Two people were required to participate in order to conserve fuel for the war effort, as a part of the rationing system. These arm-twisting activities are strong evidence that people often find it in their private interest to refrain from forming or joining car pools (that is, their net private benefits are maximized by driving alone). Otherwise, there would be no need to persuade or coerce them to "pool," since they

---

[5]Note that this situation is similar to that in early 1974 over the buying of gasoline. Prices were held below the prices that would have eliminated the shortages. Thus, long lines of cars at gas stations greatly increased the true cost of gasoline. If someone had to wait in line for one hour to buy ten gallons of gas at 50¢ per gallon, the true cost to him would be perhaps $10, if his time is valued at $5 per hour. Suppose the price rose to 70¢ per gallon and, as a result, the queue vanished. Now the cost of the gasoline is simply the price of 70¢ times 10, or $7, a considerable saving over the $5 gasoline plus $5 time cost.

would do it on their own. The effect of a toll would be to reduce the relative costs of forming a car pool (or increase the relative costs of driving alone). A toll during peak hours could easily amount to $5 per day for a round trip; splitting this five ways with a car pool of five people would substantially reduce the toll on a per rider basis. Remember that it is absolutely crucial that the toll be on a per car basis, or this advantage of pricing will be lost. For some trips, the marginal benefits to a driver may be sufficiently high that it is to his advantage to drive alone and pay the toll. Even a small incentive to form car pools is likely to have a significant effect on traffic congestion, however, since the national average number of occupants per car during peak-hour journey-to-work trips is about 1.3 persons. In Los Angeles, average peak-period auto occupancy is 1.2 persons and between 85 and 90 percent of all vehicles are occupied only by the driver.[6] Doubling the number of persons per car would cut the number of vehicles in half, if the same number of people used the facility. It is important to recognize that, without price rationing, efforts to encourage car pools are not likely to have much effect. Suppose a large campaign did indeed induce people to form car pools in unprecedented numbers. This would temporarily reduce congestion on the expressways, but it would reduce the cost of using the expressways in peak hours. Therefore, some drivers would shift from other times and modes and drive during the peak. Congestion would return, although not quite as bad as before, and much of the effect of the car pools would be counteracted. In fact, this situation is much like what would happen if new rapid transit facilities were constructed, or new expressways built. Temporarily, congestion would be reduced, but as drivers adjusted to the new situation, congestion would return.[7]

If this argument seems implausible, consider the situation in almost every urban area that has added to its investment in expressways. In Atlanta, with the opening of a new section of the circumferential highay, peak-hour congestion on another freeway became much less and was a widely discussed topic. However, within a few months, congestion on the freeway had returned to its previous peak-hour level. If a rail rapid transit facility were opened, some, but only a minority of, previous drivers would switch to the new mode. This would no doubt have an effect similar to opening some new freeways, in terms of congestion on the old expressways. In general, the short-run problem of traffic congestion cannot be solved unless it is squarely faced. Long-run solutions will not solve short-run traffic problems.

[6]U.S. Department of Transportation, *Preferential Treatment for High Occupancy Vehicles,* Federal Highway Administration, Washington, January 1974, p. 16.

[7]See Anthony Downs, "The Law of Peak Hour Expressway Congestion," *Traffic Quarterly* (July 1962), 393-409.

Criticisms of price rationing   Even when the principle of price rationing of transportation facilities has been accepted, objections have been made on the grounds that the costs of administering such a pricing system would be prohibitive. The objection is that administrative costs would more than offset the increase in net social benefits obtained from more rational use of the transportation system. Probably the vision that many people have is of a four-lane highway converging to a single tollbooth manned by an octogenarian and massive congestion induced by collecting tolls. Even if tollbooths were the only method of pricing expressways, many present toll roads build a "reverse bottleneck" at the booths, so that three lanes are served by maybe ten tollbooths. Further, tolls are often collected by automatic devices so there would not be the necessity of hiring collectors to work only during the peak hours.

The reader may be familiar with electronic guidance systems that would enable cars to be operated without the control of a driver. Electronic impulses are transmitted from the vehicle to a buried cable and back again. Tolls could be assessed in a similar manner. Transmitters in the cars would communicate with roadside units that would record the time of day and the particular vehicle passing by that point. Existing technology would allow these data to be collected and the auto owner billed monthly, much like the present system of collecting for long-distance telephone calls. (Actually this system would be simpler than that used by the telephone company.) The system could be installed at a place where there are presently tollbooths, and the installation of the electronic units in cars could be voluntary, with nonequipped cars going through the booths. Those appropriately equipped could pass the booth without slowing down, using special lanes. Why would others not by-pass the booths? For the same reason they do not go through red lights. A siren could go off and alert police that an unauthorized car had gone through. A simple device carried by the police could tell which car it was (it could test cars to see whether they emitted signals). No doubt, frequent users of the expressway would want to get the units installed on their cars, so that they could reduce their travel times. The total cost of the system would be quite low and could easily be paid for if efficient tolls were enacted. Various estimates indicate that the capital costs of the electronic identifier units for the auto plus the roadside units and computer hookup would average less than $100 per car, with nominal annual operating costs thereafter.

Another objection that has been raised is the difficulty of measuring the dollar magnitude of the indirect costs of congestion in order to determine the appropriate charge. There are indeed conceptual difficulties in placing a value on travel time, but, from a pragmatic point of view, if a congested expressway has no toll, then a gradual imposition of tolls would move the system toward efficiency. If a particular expressway is used beyond capacity (that is, so many cars on it that trips decline), then a toll could be set to at least eliminate that problem with a large gain in efficiency. As the example in Table 9-5 indicated, if tolls are placed only on present peaks, then people may drive just early enough to avoid the toll, thereby causing a new peak, for which another toll may be required. When by trial and error the overall schedule of tolls is found, peaks will be flattened out, as in the example of Table 9-5.

Considerable political resistance may be encountered in attempts to use prices to ration roads. People are not sufficiently familiar with the use of price mechanisms in this context, and it has traditionally been considered the right of anyone with a valid driver's license to use the road any time he so desires.[8] A moment's reflection will convince the reader that using price to ration peak-hour usage is familiar in other situations, for instance, in the pricing of long-distance telephone calls (they cost more during the peak, that is, business hours). Golf courses usually charge more on weekends, when demand is heavier. It costs less to fly on a commercial airline during certain (off-peak) hours. Thus, peak-hour pricing is nothing new; what is new is the application of this widely used device to a facility traditionally considered "free."

Price rationing and equity   The most severe criticisms of price rationing of transportation facilities have been that it would adversely affect low-income families or that low-income individuals would be priced off the road. It is contended that, in achieving an efficiency goal, we would violate equity objectives. In one sense, the argument is plausible, since some low-income individuals would no doubt be priced off the facility, but it may be possible to meet this objection with only a minor loss in efficiency. The trip patterns that result in the greatest levels of congestion tend to involve middle- and upper-income people, as will be discussed in the next chapter. Thus, relatively few low-income individuals would be priced off the road. For those that are, special cards could be issued to exempt them from the toll. With relatively few of these people, there would be little efficiency loss.

The tolls collected could be used in any way except rebating them to a substantial number of drivers on the basis of the trips made (this would negate the beneficial effect of the toll). If equity objectives were to receive high priority, then a possible use of the toll would be for the benefit of lower-income people. As suggested above, benefits went to some of the poor (those who drove during rush hours) but not the rest;

[8]It is interesting to note that in the early part of the nineteenth century it was considered the right of anyone to use *any* roads, even if they were privately owned. Early railroad trains often had to stop because people considered the railroad right-of-way a private road and would drive wagons down them.

this is a violation of horizontal equity. A program that benefited a larger portion of the poor would be more equitable. This general approach has rather wide applicability. It is often true that efficiency goals can be attained at the same time as equity goals. In the example of Table 9-5, about $600,000 per mile of expressway would be collected each year, and these funds could be used to accomplish equity goals. A major problem now is that any program that moves toward greater efficiency generally adversely affects various people, and may adversely affect the poor. This should not put the kiss of death on efficient programs, however, since most programs can be altered so equity problems are corrected. On a basic level, if it is felt that income is not fairly distributed, then programs should be enacted to redistribute income to the desired pattern. Then, if a program to achieve greater efficiency had adverse equity effects, the overall redistributive structure could be altered to correct for this.

Consider the following example. Suppose a certain bridge constitutes a bottleneck in the transportation system, so that, if someone arrives at the bridge at 8:00 A.M., he has to wait in line for thirty minutes to cross the bridge. Suppose further that a toll of $1.50 would be sufficient to eliminate any excessive queuing, but it is not imposed for fear of injuring the poor who may have to cross the bridge. A way to make sure no one is worse off as a result of the toll would be to construct a parking lot next to the entrance to the bridge. Someone would have the option of either paying a toll at 8:30 or arriving at 8:00 as before, waiting in the lot for thirty minutes (a situation identical in cost to the nontoll situation), and then proceeding across the bridge without paying any toll. The system would eliminate excessive queuing and would not make anyone worse off, although it is rather absurd. Few people would want to wait around while other cars passed over the bridge, particularly if the bridge were used by downtown commuters. Lower-income commuters might find it to their advantage to take a bus across, as this mode would be considerably faster than before; thus, people could only gain as a result of imposing the toll. The idea of the parking lot was used mainly to show the potential efficiency gains to peak-hour pricing, without sacrificing equity objectives.[9]

Other Forms of Rationing

There are other methods of rationing the use of roads. One is the use of simple physical controls, for example, installing traffic lights on the entrance ramps of urban expressways so that the total number of cars on the road during peak hours is reduced. The use of physical controls does not allow the expression of consumer preferences to the same

[9]This example was first suggested by William Vickrey.

extent as tolls. Some potential users will be blocked from entry who would be willing to pay a peak-hour charge. On the other hand, there will be some users of the road who were fortunate enough to get on the road, but who would not be willing to pay a peak-hour charge (the suburban housewife driving downtown for a shopping trip, for example), because the benefits of using the road at that time of day are less than the costs (the social costs, or the private costs including a toll). Thus, physical controls provide lesser incentives for efficient use of the expressway, because users are not required to take into account the total costs of their actions, including indirect costs. Since individuals do not bear the total costs of their actions, there is little inducement to form car pools or eliminate nonessential peak-hour trips. Physical controls can restrict the usage of an expressway sufficiently to eliminate overcrowding, but they cannot achieve the same degree of efficiency as tolls. They can achieve the right number of users, but the individual users making up this total will not be the right ones (those receiving the greatest benefits). Another problem with physical controls is that traffic may back up on side streets as people wait in line to get on expressway ramps. With an efficient toll, this would seldom occur.

The congestion problem would be reduced by any device that switched expressway use from peak to nonpeak hours. Many suggestions have been made, such as staggering work hours of establishments in the CBD or prohibiting trucks from using streets during certain hours. As in the case of physical controls, there are varying degrees of inefficiency associated with such measures. Businesses that depend heavily on maintaining face-to-face contacts with those in other business firms located in the CBD would be adversely affected if forced to keep other hours. Similarly, trips made by some trucks into the CBD during the day may be more valuable than others. Therefore, enactments to prohibit all trucks or force all business firms to introduce staggered hours are likely to be inefficient.

An indirect form of price rationing would be peak-hour pricing of parking facilities. As it is now, many forms of downtown parking are subsidized, encouraging more cars to come into the CBD than would do so otherwise. Many companies provide parking for employees, and on-street and off-street parking provided by the city is often priced below the social cost of providing it. The basic problem is not so much that parking is provided below cost as that the charges do not vary in such a way as to decrease the congestion problem. If higher rates were charged for parking during peak hours of highway use, there would be an effect similar to collecting a toll for the use of streets and highways during peak hours. To truly replace the concept of highway tolls, additional fees would have to be charged to those cars that left the parking lots during the evening peaks. As it is now, most lots charge lower rates to those staying all day (that is, those who tend to travel during peak times). Owners of parking lots are unlikely to be willing to change their pricing practices voluntarily, so an alternative would be for the city to impose a tax on cars entering or leaving parking lots during peak hours. A significant problem is that the tax should apply to all parkers, even those in private parking spaces. Further, much of the traffic through the CBD does not ever park but merely passes through, perhaps letting off a passenger or simply going to another destination. A parking tax would not ration use by such motorists, since such trips would not be affected by parking fees. Thus, while the use of peak-hour taxes to ration parking appears to be an interesting alternative to the use of tolls per se, it would be difficult to administer in an equitable manner. The use of car pools would be encouraged, as with tolls, but other inefficiencies would dilute the impact of the program. It might be noted that current underpricing of parking often leads to increased traffic congestion, because cars form lines to get into parking lots and cruise around looking for a parking space on city streets. Pricing that more properly reflected the social costs and benefits would eliminate much of the congestion associated with this "mobile parking."

Another form of rationing is the state and federal excise tax paid by motorists on gasoline (also higher gasoline prices per se). Anything that raises the cost of operating an auto will tend to discourage its use, and may lead some people to get rid of a second or even a first car. The problem being considered here is traffic congestion; to be efficient, the tax would have to vary according to time of day and week. Although gasoline taxes increase the private costs of operating a vehicle, they do not vary according to time of day (not much anyway, although driving in heavy traffic means lower gas mileage and higher gasoline taxes per mile). Therefore, gasoline taxes would be expected to have a limited effect on peak-hour highway use, unless they were raised to astronomical levels.

In contrast to the strategy of increasing the private costs of auto operation, another tactic would be to decrease the private costs of alternative modes. Atlanta, for example, has reduced fares to 15¢ on its bus system and zero fares have been tried in downtown Seattle. The effect would be to increase the number of public transit riders and reduce the number of people driving cars, to some extent; however, since the basic short-run inefficiency is not dealt with under such a program, the impact is likely to be minimal. In other words, if highways are still operated so that drivers do not take into account all the costs of using the facility, then it is not possible to achieve efficient utilization.

In conclusion, the reader should keep in mind that the underlying goal is to achieve or at least move toward efficient use of transportation facilities in the short run. Since highways are common property resources, in which additional users impose negative externalities on previous users after some level of usage is reached, they tend to be overused. This theory not only tells us that the highways are over-used, it also indicates by how much they are overused; conceptually at least, we know that there is some efficient level of usage. Further, it appears that some form of pricing is the best way of achieving efficient use. The idea that any policy that reduces the use of autos is as good as any other policy should be rejected. Because transportation facilities are overused, one should not conclude that the goal is to limit usage per se; rather, the goal is to limit usage in an efficient manner.

Potential Long-Run Effects of Short-Run Policy

Altering transportation costs in the short run will tend to affect long-run location decisions of households and business firms. The advantage of proximity to other business firms is one of the key reasons why urban areas exist, and transportation costs will influence the form of the urban area. Generally, a lowering of transportation costs will allow households and firms to locate further out from the CBD, which has been the general pattern in recent years. Raising transportation costs would tend to reverse the pattern, at least as a first approximation. Peak-hour pricing of expressways would not raise all transportation costs, however. Private costs, including tolls, would increase during periods when congestion existed, but only if the congestion in the absence of the toll did not lead to overuse of the expressways. In cases of extreme congestion, tolls can actually lower the costs to individual drivers, if decreased travel-time costs more than offset the congestion toll. Thus, the effect on households is not clear. Businesses likewise may find suburban locations more or less attractive, depending on how the tolls affect their costs.

Suppose outlying business firms used expressways only during off-peak periods to maintain contact with other firms, but that employers in both downtown and outlying locations employed people who commuted during peak times. Further, suppose that the peak-hour tolls had the effect of increasing the relative costs of commuting to the CBD during peak times. Downtown business owners would find that, in order to retain workers, wages would have to be increased to counter the additional costs of commuting. Another alternative would be to change hours of work so that employees could avoid peak-hour tolls, the increased time costs on alternate streets, or the increased time spent in commuting for those who shift to public transit. Finally, business firms could choose to relocate in the outlying region and avoid these increased labor costs. Downtown businesses could make their own decisions based on the costs to them, which would be closer to social costs than the present ones. Firms would *choose* the best alternative for them, unlike proposals for coercing firms to stagger work hours, etc. Those firms that depend very heavily on face-to-face contacts would probably pay higher wages and not alter working hours, while firms that could more easily do so would migrate outward or stagger work hours.

The prognosis is by no means clear. Peak-hour tolls could have the effect of enhancing the CBD or causing further movement of jobs away from it. The most likely outcome would be that the effect of peak-hour tolls would not be great enough to substantially alter the present trend toward job decentralization in urban areas.

Efficient Pricing of Other Modes of Transportation

Thus far the discussion has centered on efficient pricing of highways, with a brief mention of the idea that parking was probably underpriced also. In general, if demand for a service is highly peaked (that is, very intense only during certain times of the day, week, or year), a higher peak charge is required for efficiency. Someone who adds to the demand for a service during a peak puts a strain on the capacity of the system and may impose costs on other users. Someone who uses a facility when it is not being as heavily used by others does not strain the capacity of the system and is unlikely to impose substantial externalities on others by his use.

Peak-time (rush-hour) users of a public transit system strain its capacity in that more buses or trains are necessary to handle the peak load, while during off-peak times buses and trains may run mostly empty. The implication for efficient pricing is that fares should be higher during the peak times and lower during off-peak times. As a numerical example, suppose that the marginal cost per passenger in an off-peak time was 10¢, but that the average cost of providing a trip for the whole day was 60¢. Charging more than 10¢ during off-peak times would be inefficient, since it would cause usage to be less than when MSC = MSB. Likewise, charging 60¢ or less during the peak would not be efficient, because peak-time users add to the strain on the system and cause additional investment to be made in equipment. A fare of 75¢ might be required to take account of the true cost of using the transit system during a peak time.

Rail rapid transit lines are subject to higher relative peaks in usage than highways, since their use is substantially for commuting. The implication is that these facilities should be subject to higher fares during peaks and lower fares during off-peak times. On the other hand, a proposal is often made that transit fares be subsidized, particularly during peak times, so traffic congestion will be diminished as people shift to transit. Considering the long-term trend of ridership of transit discussed earlier in the chapter, it would appear that such a policy might temporarily reverse the trend toward fewer and fewer riders and also temporarily alleviate highway congestion. but this will reduce the relative cost of driving a car and lead others to increase their use of the roads. This is like the situation mentioned above, where building new expressways does not seem to have much of a long-run impact on traffic congestion.

REVIEW AND DISCUSSION QUESTIONS

1   A bridge leading into a major CBD charges 50¢ per vehicle to cross the bridge, but there is no charge for vehicles with three or more passengers. Is this an efficient solution to the peak-hour congestion problem?
2   Why is rationing by prices likely to be superior to other forms of rationing transportation facilities during peak periods?
3   If peak-hour congestion tolls were implemented, the congestion caused by lines of cars waiting to pay the toll would offset most of the efficiency gains, thereby defeating the purpose of such tolls. Discuss.
4   Is traffic congestion inefficient? If so, why?
5   Peak-hour congestion tolls would have to be so high that only the very rich would get to their place of work in the CBD. Evaluate.
6   Why has public transit ridership plummeted in the last thirty years? In answering, do not invoke irrationality on the part of commuters (or yourself).
7   Why do not more people drive in car pools? Would car-pooling solve the peak-hour congestion problem?

SUGGESTED READINGS

Downs, Anthony. "The Law of Peak Hour Expressway Congestion." *Traffic Quarterly* (July 1962), 393 - 409. (Reprinted in Anthony Downs. *Urban Problems and Prospects*, pp. 176 - 191. Chicago: Markham, 1970.)
Vickrey, William. "Pricing in Urban and Suburban Transport." *American Economic Review* (May 1963), 452 - 465.

10 / Urban Transportation: The Long Run

The previous chapter discussed the short-run transportation problem: the efficient use of existing transportation facilities. A pervasive problem was that these facilities seemed to be underpriced, particularly in the case of urban highways during peak hours. This chapter is concerned with the efficient allocation of resources to additional facilities—the long-run problem. It was noted earlier that short-run policies may have substantial long-run repercussions. It is also true that inefficiency in the short run makes long-run planning more difficult, and can cause perverse long-run decisions to be made. As an example, consider the supply and demand of anything. Suppose the price is held too low (below marginal social cost) or that a higher price is needed to achieve short-run efficiency. At a higher price, there may be no shortage at all, but, if planning is undertaken based on an "artificial" shortage, then the expected result would be overinvestment. In the case of transportation, pricing of highways during peak hours would greatly alter the present picture of highway congestion and the "need" for new facilities, since, except for about twenty hours per week, there is tremendous excess capacity. Heavy use in spite of peak-hour tolls would be a good indicator of the need for additional facilities, but current heavy use in the absence of tolls is an unreliable indicator. Unless present facilities are used more rationally, it is difficult to determine the amount of additional investment actually required for efficiency. All that can be said now is that the efficient amount is less than is apparently needed, while we do not have tolls. If existing facilities were more efficiently used, it is clear that the apparent need for more facilities would be reduced and in some cases eliminated.

In all resource allocation decisions, costs and benefits must be considered. In the case of investment in new transportation facilities, future benefits and the relative costs of providing various levels of services will need to be estimated. The next section will consider future demand for transportation in urban areas, in particular, demand for the journey-to-work trip. The following section will consider the relative costs of providing these benefits through alternative modes of transportation. Next, the question of subsidies for transportation and the impact of such subsidies on the income distribution will be considered, followed by a discussion of transportation problems of lower-income inner-city households. Finally, a suggested plan for transportation in urban areas will be presented, and the potential benefits and costs of this plan will be compared with costs and benefits of present transportation plans, in order to tie together the various aspects of the long-run urban transportation problem.

Estimating the Benefits of Transportation Investment

The total benefits of transportation facilities stem from all the different uses to which they are put. There will be benefits received from using the facilities for shopping and leisure trips, and for the movement of goods within and between urban areas, but the major benefits from transportation facilities in urban areas have been, and probably will continue to be, those related to the journey-to-work trip. Since the most intensive use of the transportation facilities at present is for these journey-to-work trips, provision of adequate capacity to handle them will generally provide capacity that is more than adequate for other types of trip. Thus, the primary focus will be on the journey-to-work trip, with reference to other kinds of demand when relevant. It should be noted that future changes in such factors as communication and production technology may perhaps reduce the relative importance of the journey-to-work trip sometime in the future.

Future journey-to-work transportation requirements depend in large part on the future location of jobs and people in the urban area. As discussed in Chapter 2, there has been a considerable trend toward decentralization. As a result, employment in CBDs has not increased substantially, and, as a percentage of the total employment in SMSAs, it has fallen. However, the CBD is still an important employment center; and, since employment in that area is heavily professional and white-collar, the impact of journey-to-work trips to the CBD is magnified in that many of these employees live in the suburbs and commute relatively long distances.

Suppose we divide the urban area into two parts: (1) the central business district (CBD) and the adjoining low-income residential ring, and (2) everything else, that is, the remainder of the central city plus the suburbs. Since there are two destinations and two areas of departure, there will be four possible commuting patterns for the journey-to-work trip. First, there will be some who live in or near the CBD and also work there, although these will be relatively few in most urban areas. The second pattern is what is ordinarily thought of as commuting—from the outlying area into the CBD. To have a name for this pattern, we shall call it "downtown commuting." Since jobs in the CBD tend to be white-collar and professional, this trip pattern would be filled mainly by middle- and upper-income groups.

Another pattern is known as "cross-commuting," from one part of the outlying area to another point in the outlying area. (There is of course some cross-commuting within the city core, but this is not as extensive as the other type.) Probably the intensity of congestion for downtown commuting is greater because of this pattern, since many cross-commuting trips pass through or near the CBD. This might be expected since most urban transportation facilities are built radially, radiating from the CBD in "hub-and-spoke" fashion. With the construction of nonradial expressways, such as beltways or circumferential highways, more cross-commuting trips can be made without going via the CBD. The cross-commuting pattern is probably the most heterogeneous with respect to income, since outlying jobs exist at all skill levels.

A third pattern, "reverse commuting," involves commutation from homes near or within the CBD to jobs in the outlying area. Since the poor tend to live in large numbers near the CBD, it would be expected that this type of commuter is likely to be at the lower end of the income distribution, commuting to a low-skill job at an outlying location. An important aspect of this kind of commuting is that it is in the opposite direction to the heavy flow, so it adds little to congestion problems and puts little strain on the transportation system. In some cities, buses travel into the CBD filled with downtown commuters and make the return trip with fairly large loads of reverse commuters, some of these being domestic workers. The evening trip reverses this pattern. It must be pointed out that the present systems of buses and highways were designed, or at least evolved, as radial systems to take care of the downtown commuting pattern. Accordingly, it can be quite difficult to get to certain outlying destinations. A person may have to travel into the CBD and then transfer onto another bus heading out, greatly increasing the length of his trip.

The relative importance of these trip patterns will depend on future locations of jobs and people; hence, so will benefits of transportation investments. An investment designed to accommodate present patterns may not be efficient if future trip patterns change significantly. For example, suppose enough rail and highway facilities were built so that an urban area would be free of congestion at all times of the day for all trip patterns (this might be accomplished at a cost of $100 billion for a city of 1 million inhabitants). Assuming the urban area does not grow substantially in the future, but that the present decentralization trends continue, much of the capacity will be unused in future years, even during peak times.

As was discussed in Chapter 2, changes in transportation, production, and communications technology have played an important part historically in determining the spatial distribution of economic activity in urban areas; future technological changes may result in further changes in location of jobs and people. It is possible, for example, that many future journey-to-work trips will be eliminated by communications technology. Certain jobs may be performed by the worker at his residence, such as research work by lawyers and other professionals; a trip to the library might be replaced by sitting down at a computer terminal that links the professional with libraries in all parts of the country. The use of telephones has already obviated the need for many face-to-face contacts in business. Lower-cost "picture-phones" that transmit television pictures as well as voices may eliminate the need for even more of these face-to-face contacts, which are a primary reason for the CBD location of many firms. Thus, the location of jobs at the place of residence could potentially result in a decline in commuting, particularly downtown commuting, and this would lower the estimated benefits of transportation facilities serving primarily the CBD.

The location of jobs and people and the resulting benefits from transportation investment are determined in part by the transportation investment itself. A prime example would be the new regional shopping centers that have located along the urban sections of the interstate highway system, often near both circumferential and radial interstate highways. Business firm and individual residence decisions are made with close consideration of the availability of transportation facilities. While it is often felt that improved transportation to and from the CBD will encourage growth of the CBD, it seems that other outlying areas are stimulated to a much greater extent, since access to the CBD can be obtained at a greater distance from it. Individuals can locate their residences further out and take advantage of large lot sizes, while still retaining access to the CBD. In fact, the post - World War Two experience is generally one of increasing journey-to-work trip distances, with total travel times remaining about the same over the years because of improved transportation facilities. It should not be assumed that, since transportation investments in part determine location decisions, the starting point should be some "ideal city" and transportation investment should attempt to guide the growth into that pattern. For one thing, the outcome of an investment in transportation may be opposite to that expected (many thought that the interstate highways would revitalize the CBD and thwart urban sprawl). Also, not all outcomes are equally efficient (an example of an inefficient outcome would be spending what is necessary to remold a contemporary United States city into its nineteenth-century counterpart).

The Cost of Alternative Transportation Modes

While it is difficult to assess accurately the future benefits from investments in transportation, it is possible to look at the supply side of transportation and consider the question of which mode will provide a given level of benefits at the lowest cost. Riding on a crowded bus is not equivalent to making the same trip in a chauffeured limousine; thus, comparisons between modes must be made carefully. To simplify matters, assume that the benefits measured above refer only to trips from various points to other points. A trip from Scarsdale, New York, to Times Square is assumed to confer $x worth of benefits on a person, regardless of the transportation mode taken. Given these benefits, the question becomes which mode will achieve these benefits at least cost, thereby maximizing net benefits. In other words, differences in privacy, flexibility, convenience, and other such amenities will be considered as much differences in the cost of making the trip as time-cost differences. Thus, the limousine trip will be thought of as providing the same benefits as the bus trip; however, from the point of view of, say, a bank president, the total costs, including time and amenity costs, are lower with the limousine, and, thus, the net benefits are higher with the limousine. One could divide benefits and costs in other ways, but net benefits would be the same regardless. Many observers have commented to the effect that commuters were insane if they drove their cars rather than take an available bus, which may involve lower cash outlays. In the framework here, the choice of the car is rational if the total costs of taking a bus (including time and amenity costs) are higher than the costs of driving a car.

To illustrate this idea, let us consider an example showing the relative costs of taking a bus versus driving a car. Table 10-1 shows the relative out-of-pocket costs and other costs for the two modes and is based on the following assumptions. First, the person owns a car for other purposes, so it is available for making the trip. Were this not the case, costs for the auto mode would be higher than shown here, since they would include all the costs of operating the car, which would have to be purchased for the purpose of making the trip. In Chapter 9, these marginal costs were estimated to be about 4¢ per mile. The

	AUTO	BUS
OUT-OF-POCKET COSTS		
Operating costs at 4¢ per mile (trip of ten miles each way)	$0.80	
Parking	2.00	
Bus fare		$1.00
TOTAL	$2.80	$1.00
TIME COSTS		
Waiting time at bus stop (5 minutes each way)		10
Walking time: home to bus stop (5 minutes each way)		10
Walking time: bus stop to job destination (7 minutes each way)		14
Walking time: parking lot to job destination (2 minutes each way)	4	
Time spent in vehicle making twenty-mile round trip	50	70
Total time, door-to-door	54	104
Value of time at $4 per hour	$3.60	$6.93
TOTAL TRIP COSTS (OUT-OF-POCKET PLUS TIME)	$6.40	$7.93

Table 10-1: An Example of Relative Private Costs of a Journey-to-Work by Bus Versus Auto

typical case for most families is that the car is already owned and only marginal costs need be considered. Second, it is assumed that, on the average, a person has to wait five minutes at a bus stop for each trip. Buses usually do not run on a time schedule that is accurate to the minute; if the rider were to risk trying to get to the bus stop at the precise minute of expected arrival, frequently the bus may have already passed. Therefore, the rider normally would arrive early enough that the probability of missing the bus would be relatively small. Further, assume that the rider must walk for five minutes in order to get from his home to the bus stop and seven minutes from the bus stop to his destination, compared with two minutes from the parking lot to his destination were he to drive his auto. Finally, assume the rider values his time at $4 per hour. As shown in Table 10-1, out-of-pocket costs are lower for the bus; however, when the cost of the person's time is considered, the auto is the cheaper mode.

As indicated in Table 10-1 the auto mode is $1.53 cheaper per day if time costs are considered. If parking is provided by the employer, then the difference rises to $3.53. Further, costs such as comfort and flexibility were not considered, and it would seem that these would make the auto mode even more attractive for this particular commuting trip. Even if all costs of operation of the car are included (about 16¢ per mile) and parking is provided by the employer, the auto mode involves lower total private costs. It should also be noted that fares are a small part of the total cost of commuting via the bus. In the example of Table 10-1, even if the fares were eliminated, the auto would still be a lower-cost mode in terms of total private cost. It should be mentioned that not everyone values his time at $4. If a person values it more highly, the advantage of the auto becomes even greater. If a person values his time at less than $4 per hour, then it is certainly possible that the bus would become the lower-cost mode. A person's hourly earnings tend to be closely related to the value placed on his time (as discussed in Chapter 9); on this basis, we would expect lower-income people to favor buses while higher income-people would tend to favor the auto.

The quadrupling of the price of imported crude oil in 1974 resulted in significant increases in the price of gasoline. This led to much recent discussion of the potential impact on automobile use in urban areas and on urban spatial form. One implication of the example of Table 10-1 is that it would take large increases in the price of gasoline to have a signficant impact on the relative attractiveness of the auto for journey-to-work trip purposes, especially for high-income auto users. Of the few studies available, the indication is that, in the short run (with existing stock of automobiles of given miles per gallon and other factors as given), a doubling in the price of gasoline would lead to somewhat less than a 20 percent decrease in gasoline usage. In the longer run (when consumers can adjust to smaller car sizes, changed residential and job location patterns, and other factors), the indication is that a doubling of gasoline prices would lead to about a 50 percent decrease in gasoline usage.

A transportation facility may yield benefits for many different types of trip requirements. Since the journey-to-work trip results in the heaviest usage of the transportation facilty, the following analysis will be primarily concerned with the cost of providing for that requirement. However, the costs of providing for *all* trip requirements are the ultimate concern, and consideration must be given to the mode's ability to provide for other types of trips during off-peak hours. A rail transit system may provide for rush-hour commuting much better than it provides for shopping trips, for example. In general, the choice is not between single modes for the entire transportation system, but rather what mix of various modes will best serve the transportation function. In very large urban areas, for example, a combination of rail, bus, and auto transport will probably be the lowest-cost way to provide transportation. Since these modes already exist, the real question is the efficient amount of investment in additional facilities. (Remember that efficiency implies an amount of investment where marginal social benefit equals marginal social cost.) Therefore, the lowest-cost mix of modes will need to be considered for several different levels of service. In practice, this should mean that benefit-cost analysis of various modes should be undertaken for each segment of the transportation network, and the appropriate level of service (the efficient level) provided for each segment.

Given the present state of transportation technology, there seem to be four basic modes that serve to move people from place to place in urban areas (a fifth mode, jitneys, will be discussed later in this chapter):

1 Rail transit
2 Highways for primary use of autos
3 Rapid bus systems using special lanes or conventional highways
4 Conventional bus systems

The second mode was the primary focus of government investment during the postwar period, although the first mode is currently receiving greater attention. The third mode has been tried on an experimental basis, although it is generally ignored by planners or merely given lip service. The fourth mode is the inheritor of the trolley system—the principal means of mass transportation in the latter part of the nineteenth century and the beginning of this century (although initially these were usually privately owned, rather than being established as a result of government policy).

The selection of a particular mode depends on its relative costs, and the "best" mode in one urban area is not necessarily the best in another. These costs include:

1 Fixed-investment costs, including land acquisition and construction costs for highways and rail lines, and costs of equipment (such as trains, autos, and buses)
2 Operating costs, including out-of-pocket costs (such as fuel, repairs, and personnel) and imputed costs (such as the value of passengers' time spent in traveling, convenience, and amenity factors)
3 Indirect costs, including congestion and pollution costs

The following discussion will broadly compare each of these costs for the four transportation modes mentioned above. However, any investment decision relies on the sum of all these costs (the social costs) for various modes providing comparable trip benefits.

Rail Transit

The mode that has received the greatest attention in recent years has been rail rapid transit. Several new rail systems have been planned and are under construction, and the new BART system in San Francisco is now carrying passengers. Rail rapid transit can carry very large numbers of passengers along a route at relatively high speed (potentially higher than any of the other modes). From the point of view of costs, the most obvious is a very high fixed-investment cost. The MARTA system in Atlanta initially was projected to have a capital cost of $1.4 billion; by the time it is actually completed, the cost will probably be much higher. A rail system proposed for Los Angeles would have a capital cost of approximately $7 billion. In Atlanta, although some of the capital costs are for conventional bus portions, the MARTA system is to be built around a rail network. To get a feel for the magnitude of the cost, at the time the voters approved MARTA, there were about 1.4 million people in the Atlanta SMSA, so the fixed-investment cost came to about $1,000 per person in the SMSA.

An obvious arithmetic calculation would show that the initial fixed-investment costs per rider decline as the number of riders increases. Doubling the number of riders will cut the fixed cost per passenger in half. Thus, the key to whether rail rapid transit is the most efficient mode is whether there are enough riders.

Operating costs are relatively low for rail rapid transit, at least for the journey from one station to another. Other costs that must be considered are the cost of getting to the station and time spent waiting for a train. The fastest rapid transit in the world will not attract a rider who has to spend excessive time in getting to and from the transit line. For short trips in or near the CBD, conventional buses may prove "cheaper," because using rapid transit may involve transferring from buses anyway. The amenity costs for rail rapid transit are probably low relative to bus systems, but higher than for auto transportation. Many people value privacy as well as comfort, and the auto provides more of this. Additionally, rail rapid transit does not offer the flexibility of the auto mode. One must follow the schedule and route; if trains are not very frequent, time will be wasted (although perhaps made up by the speed of the train), and one can seldom change his route in order to attend to other matters on the way home. In terms of actual cash outlays, most systems project that fares will barely cover operating expenses. It would seem that benefits as seen by the users are equal to only a fraction of the costs of the system (all the capital costs, and probably some of the operating costs, will have to be provided by means of subsidies). There is another possibility, namely, that higher fares could cover all the costs of the system; but these high fares would discourage usage to an inefficiently low level. In other words, a low fare may lead to both efficiency and losses for the system, while a higher fare will cut the losses, but will be inefficient. The experience of the industry seems to indicate that, regardless of the fare charged, the system will not be able to cover all of its costs; thus, it would seem that the only justification for rail rapid transit would be in the realm of indirect costs.

In terms of pollution costs, it is fairly clear that, given present technology, rail is superior to other modes. Trains generally run on electricity, and, if this is produced in a clean manner, very little air pollution will result, unlike other modes. In terms of congestion costs on highways, provision of new transportation facilities of any kind will tend to temporarily reduce traffic congestion, as people leave cars for rapid transit. During the referendum in Atlanta, a widely held belief on the part of supporters of rapid transit was that enough other drivers would shift to rapid transit so that they personally could drive in less congestion. It seemed that few supporters wanted to use the rail rapid transit personally. As previously discussed, additional capacity means that private costs are lower for all modes, and lower congestion on highways leads more people to become drivers, as long as an efficient short-run policy is lacking. The probable result of the additional capacity would be that the peak period would be shortened somewhat, but peak congestion would not be perceptibly alleviated once people adjusted to the new situation.[1]

Highways for the Use of Autos

This mode is probably the cheapest when the number of trips along a route is relatively low and flexibility is required. Most noncommut-

---

[1]See Anthony Downs, "The Law of Peak Hour Expressway Congestion," *Traffic Quarterly* (July 1962), 393 - 409.

ing trips probably can be handled most economically in this way, even in urban areas. During periods of heavy use, however, highways become inefficiently congested, and the apparent picture is that, to handle the traffic, far more highways are needed. The first step should be obvious by now—do something to improve the short-run efficiency of the system, so that planners will have at least some idea of the true transportation needs rather than the present distorted picture. Given the present endowment of transportation facilities, marginal costs are relatively low, at least during off-peak times. The highways are there already and most people would have autos, even if they did not use them for journey-to-work purposes. The only costs in this situation are the operating costs for the vehicle and the value of the occupants' time. Since trains are potentially faster than autos (at least for trips of several miles), the time costs of the actual trip may be higher for the car, but, if time must be spent in waiting, this advantage of rail may be lost. As the volume of traffic along a route increases, either congestion results or very large investments in highways must be made (assuming an inefficient short-run situation). Thus, additional autos impose additional congestion or capital costs on the system. There will be some point, then, where the costs of this mode will be quite high, depending on the density of use along a particular route. If rail rapid transit is compared with autos, for relatively low densities the auto will be less costly, and beyond some point rail will be the least-cost mode. The problem is where this point is. According to Meyer, Kain, and Wohl, it is quite high; the only cities in the United States with sufficient densities along routes are New York and possibly Chicago, both places where rail facilities already exist.[2] The key is the level of usage. In order to take advantage of the superior features of rail, densities must be very high along a corridor; very large numbers of people must be traveling from points along the corridor to other points along it, perhaps to the CBD. The present trend toward lower-density living and the relative decline of the CBD indicate that rail will be even less advantageous in the future. Although bus ridership has declined faster, ridership on rail has also declined somewhat. As densities along particular routes fall, the auto becomes relatively more attractive.

In terms of indirect costs, autos rank the poorest of any mode. As discussed in Chapter 11, with present technology and pollution abatement incentives, autos cause a large percentage of the air pollution experienced in urban areas (although pollution control legislation of recent years has improved matters somewhat). Many autos have only a driver and no passengers, so the pollution per person is higher than with fuller cars or buses or rail rapid transit. Indirect costs

---

[2]John Meyer, John Kain, and Martin Wohl, The Urban Transportation Problem, Harvard University Press, Cambridge, Mass., 1965.

of congestion are high with the auto mode of transportation, if highways are not rationed during periods of heavy use. Again, it must be emphasized that short-run efficiency would greatly reduce the indirect costs of congestion of this mode. Since the private costs of operating an auto would include the indirect costs of congestion, if peak-hour tolls were implemented, the private choice of mode would be closer to the efficient choice. For example, in Table 10-1, the private costs of the auto mode would then include a congestion toll, which would make the bus the lower-cost mode for some motorists.

Rapid Bus System

There are many forms a rapid bus system could take, with resulting differences in fixed-investment costs. The system with the highest capital costs would be one that constructed special busways for the exclusive use of buses. The cheapest systems would utilize existing expressway and other road facilities either by reserving some lanes for the exclusive use of buses (either all day or during peak-hour periods) or merely by running buses on expressways or other road facilities that had been price-rationed during peak periods. In the latter cases, capital costs would approach zero, other than for the equipment (buses). In the former case, special busways are about equal to the costs of rail transit; however, they may have other advantages. For example, suppose ridership continues to decline so that the line is abandoned at some time in the future. A busway or special bus lane could be used for other forms of traffic, while rails would probably not have an alternative use.

Operating costs for a bus system are probably somewhat higher than for a rail system, since trains use fewer operators per passenger mile or can even be operated by computer. Fuel costs would probably be higher with buses when compared with trains, but lower than for cars. Time costs of passengers would be similar to existing rail systems, particularly when waiting and transfer times are considered. Bus speeds of 70 miles per hour are possible, and rail transit seldom surpasses this, although rail speeds are potentially higher. In amenity costs, buses rank only slightly below rail transit, at least potentially. The popular conception of buses seems to be that of antiquated vehicles packed with derelicts swaying through the worst sections of town and asphyxiating some of the passengers, while the popular conception of rail is a monorail streaking through the sky into a city of the future. In fact, there need be little difference in the comfort levels of these modes. Rapid buses would be more like the newer intercity buses currently in operation. Much of the objection to buses seems to be based on the idea that they would operate along congested routes, so that they would be quite slow. Almost any desired speed could be attained if buses ran on special busways, or lanes reserved for buses on existing roads, or on roads rationed to sufficiently low densities during peak periods. A proposal will be presented later in the chapter for a rapid bus system that is based on the present highway system and combines a short-run system of rationing with a rapid bus system.

Summary of Comparative Costs

Figure 10-1 shows the probable relative social costs of various modes, as these costs depend on the density along a corridor (and resulting passenger trips generated). The diagram is not meant to be precise, but rather to illustrate the previous discussion. At low levels of usage, the sum of the costs for the auto mode is the lowest. At some inter- mediate level of usage, rapid bus is probably efficient, and, at high densities, rail becomes the least-cost mode. In terms of the three journey-to-work trip patterns discussed earlier in this chapter, only along corridors radiating from the CBD is it likely that origin and destination densities (primarily downtown-commuting trips) will

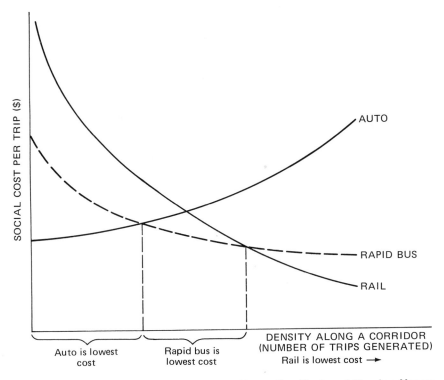

Figure 10-1: Relative Social Costs of Alternative Modes at Varying Usage Levels

ever be sufficiently high to justify rail. For most cross-commuting trips and many reverse-commuting trips, origin-destination patterns may be so dispersed that auto will be the least-cost mode.

There will probably be the alternative of using the auto even if other modes are available, but these other modes may not always be available. If drivers are not bearing all the costs of using highways, then the cost to them will be below the social costs shown in Figure 10-1. Thus, rail and rapid bus (as well as conventional bus, which is not shown) may appear relatively more costly. Efficient pricing of existing highways would allow better comparisons to be made, and would lead some drivers to switch modes. Simply increasing the capacity of highways will not lead to short-run efficiency, and drivers will still bear less than the full costs of their activity unless short-run efficiency is achieved. If this is achieved, then we would expect a greater demand for the other modes.

Transportation Subsidies

Relatively large transportation subsidies to various modes have been provided over the years by the federal government. The first part of this section deals with problems of efficiency associated with these subsidies. The second section considers the equity outcomes of these subsidies, since they are not likely to affect all income groups equally.

Efficiency Aspects

The largest subsidies have been provided for highway construction. Under the Federal Aid Highway Act of 1956, the federal government undertook to pay 90 percent of the cost of constructing the 42,500-mile interstate highway system. At the end of 1972, all but 5,000 miles of the system was either completed or under construction. Of the total, about 7,000 miles were in urban areas. Some of the urban mileage provides links with other parts of the interstate system; however, much of it is radial expressway construction designed for downtown commuting. In terms of the dollar amount of total interstate highway construction subsidies, urban expressway mileage accounts for a much larger proportion of the dollars than of the miles, because the value of land and improvements demolished for the right-of-way is much more expensive than in rural areas. The 90 percent federal contributions to such highway construction are financed through the Highway Trust Fund, which derives its revenues from federal taxes on gasoline, oil, tires, tubes, trucks, and buses.

Federal subsidization of 90 percent of construction costs is likely to promote inefficiency unless 90 percent of the benefits accrue to the nation as a whole. The 90 percent share was chosen so that local areas would be willing to construct the highways—the idea being that a large part of the benefits fall on nonresidents. This may be true for rural stretches of the interstate system, but is less likely to be true in urban areas, where the main use of expressways is for commuting and other purposes by residents of the urban area. To the extent that benefits fall on local areas, subsidies distort investment decisions. Suppose a local area would not approve a $500 million addition to the highway system; if the federal government paid $450 million of the tab, then the local government might approve it. Even if benefits to the local area were only $100 million, the local cost of $50 million would be more than covered, and the project would appear to increase the net benefits of the local area. Suppose that, in addition, positive spillovers to other areas amounted to $40 million more. The project would be undertaken, even though total benefits of only $140 million would be generated at a cost of $500 million. Another problem with the funding of highways is that they are paid for through gasoline and other taxes on vehicle operation. Since the primary burden on the transportation system is caused by peak-hour users, these users are subsidized by nonpeak users, since gasoline taxes do not vary appreciably according to the hour of use. Additional capacity has been built primarily to accommodate peak-hour users, and all users have paid for it. If peak-hour tolls were established in urban areas, a possible use of these tolls could be to replace gasoline taxes to some extent, so that taxes were matched more closely to benefits.

In comparison with highways, rail and bus services have not historically received large public subsidies and have relied upon user charges as their primary source of revenue. While it can be argued that highway investment has received substantial subsidies and motorists are not made to incur all of the costs of using an auto for journey-to-work trips, this does not necessarily imply that equivalent subsidies to other modes of transportation should be made so as to decrease the apparent attractiveness of highway use. Instead, the subsidy to auto transportation should possibly be eliminated, so that no significant subsidies are given to any transportation mode. The effect on the relative attractiveness of alternative modes would be the same. At any point in time, we should take the existing stock of transportation facilities and try to achieve greater efficiency in the short run. Then, additional investments should be made if they are efficient. The heavy investment in urban expressways may have been a mistake, but we cannot return to a state where these expressways do not exist and then decide on the most efficient system. We are "stuck" with it, and efficiency now depends on using it efficiently while considering efficient additions to the system. Thoughts of "getting even with" highway interests should not dominate current planning.

While the efficient approach would be to implement congestion tolls and otherwise make motorists incur the full social costs of their decision to use the auto mode (thereby eliminating heavy subsidization of any transit mode), the approach being taken by the federal government appears to be the opposite—to provide subsidies to other (nonauto) transportation modes so as to reduce their private costs to a level where they would be better able to compete for ridership with the automobile. Under the Urban Mass Transportation Administration (UMTA), the federal government pays two-thirds of the capital cost of urban mass transportation projects. These grants are made directly by the Department of Transportation to local governments on a case-by-case basis. Four major kinds of grant are made for: (1) conventional bus system equipment purchases; (2) purchases of cars and other equipment on rail transit lines; (3) building completely new rail systems and extensions, such as Atlanta's MARTA and Washington's METRO; and (4) funds for local governments to buy out privately owned transit companies, mostly bus lines.

All of these grants are for capital expenditures as opposed to operating expenditures. As a result, they tend to bias local transit decisions toward choices involving high capital costs relative to operating costs, which may not necessarily be the transit choice that results in the lowest social cost and is, thus, the efficient one. With respect to existing transit systems, for example, suppose you were operating a bus line that was losing money and you were subsidized to buy new buses (that were cheaper to operate than the old buses), but could receive no subsidy for operating expenses. There would be an incentive to replace buses sooner than otherwise. A study has shown that, in the case of Cleveland and Chicago, this wasted 23 percent of the subsidy.[3] With respect to new transit systems, such capital grants bias decisions toward rapid rail, which has the highest capital costs of any mode discussed earlier in this chapter but relatively low operating costs per passenger. This may be a major reason why many urban areas in the United States have in recent years put forth proposals for expensive rail systems, when it appears that the same trip demands could be met at a small fraction of the costs of rail systems by other modes, primarily rapid bus systems, which involve relatively low capital costs but probably higher operating costs than rail.

Because of the incentives to make inefficient local decisions provided by existing mass transit grants for capital expenditures, it has been suggested that federal grants for nonauto transportation be given for either capital or operating expenses. However, if UMTA grants were to finance some portion of all operating expenses, this would provide little incentive at the local level to run operations at least cost.

---

[3]W. Tye, "The Capital Grant as a Subsidy Device: The Case Study of Urban Mass Transportation," in *The Economics of Federal Subsidy Programs*, part 6, Joint Economic Committee, 93rd Congress, 1973.

Instead, operating subsidies could be established to pay a certain amount per passenger trip or a certain percentage of passenger revenues collected at the fare box.

Operating subsidies are often advocated as the only feasible way to divert riders from automobiles during the peak hour. However, the fare may be a relatively small part of the total private costs of making a journey-to-work trip, and reduced fares may not have much of an impact in increasing public transit ridership. As an illustration, consider the example of Table 10-1; if operating subsidies were provided so that the bus fare was reduced from $1.00 to zero, the rider would not switch from his auto, since the private costs of the auto trip are still less than the private costs of the bus trip with a zero fare. Studies tend to support the contention that public transit ridership is relatively insensitive to reductions in fares. For journey-to-work trips, a 1 percent reduction in fares may result in only about a two-tenths of 1 percent increase in ridership. On the other hand, if, instead of subsidizing fares, the subsidy were used to improve transit service and decrease the private costs of travel time, a 1 percent decrease in travel times might result in more than a 1 percent increase in ridership.[4] Similarly, a study of Chicago public transportation estimated that public transit fares would have to be negative (that is, people would have to be *paid* to take public transit) in order to induce at least 50 percent of commuters by car to switch to bus or rail transit.[5] Thus, the implications of these studies, as well as the example in Table 10-1, are that the value of time is the major private cost of transit choice (swamping out-of-pocket costs) and that the auto is generally superior in this respect. Subsidizing public transit is not likely to get people out of their cars and is likely to be an inefficient approach to solving peak-hour congestion, since it treats symptoms rather than the cause (failure to ration usage of the transportation network during periods of peak usage).

In summary, the federal government has provided billions of dollars of subsidies for construction of urban expressways that mainly have local benefits and it is now moving in the direction of providing similar subsidies for other transit modes that also have primarily local benefits. The apparent premise is to lower the private costs of nonauto modes to a level where there would be substantial diversion of riders from automobiles for peak-hour journey-to-work trips. The efficient approach would be to eliminate *all* transportation subsidies and make the rider incur the full social cost of his transportation mode choice.

[4]For example, see Tom Domencich and Gerald Kraft, *Free Transit*, Heath, Lexington, Mass., 1970.

[5]Leon Moses and Harold Williamson, Jr., "Value of Time, Choice of Mode and the Subsidy Issue in Urban Transportation," *Journal of Political Economy* (June 1963), 247 - 264.

The first step would be to achieve efficient use of existing transportation facilities. This would provide planners with useful data on the need for additional transportation facilities. In some cases, the apparent need for additional facilities would vanish, since existing transportation systems have large amounts of excess capacity during all but a few hours of the week (peak-hour congestion periods). In the absence of large federal subsidies, if sufficient taxes or user charges cannot be raised within the urban area to finance, say, a rail transit system, then it is probable that the costs of such a system outweigh the benefits. The same would be true for additions to the highway network or any additional transportation investments. The fact that a local government is unwilling to undertake the investment should not be a signal for the federal government to step in, as this may be inefficient. In fact, the heavy subsidization of radial expressways may have led to an inefficient amount of decentralization of jobs and people in urban areas over time, since travel times to outlying areas were lowered, no doubt flattening the rent gradient (see Chapter 2).

Equity: Distribution of Costs and Benefits from Transportation Investments

A given transportation investment usually results in net benefits that change the distribution of income among members of society. If those who benefited from such transportation investment also paid all of the costs, there would be no income redistribution; however, as discussed above, large transportation subsidies have in fact been provided. Thus, the transportation system redistributes income, possibly in significant amounts and in ways that society would deem undesirable on closer examination.

Previous investments in radial expressways in urban areas appear to benefit primarily the middle- and upper-income groups who constitute the downtown-commuting pattern. Circumferential highways may benefit all groups that engage in cross-commuting, and these come from all income ranges. Also, as discussed above under highway subsidies, much of the total dollar subsidy for highways has gone to build extra capacity in urban areas for peak-period use. To the extent that there is a relationship between income group and peak-hour users, the subsidization of peak-hour users by nonpeak motorists who have paid federal excise taxes into the Highway Trust Fund to construct such additional capacity may also have resulted in significant income redistribution between income groups.

The construction of expressways radiating from the CBD may impose significant costs on the low-income residents of inner-city neighborhoods through which such rights-of-way pass. Most of these costs are not compensated for when property is acquired for rights-of-way. The costs for low-income residents who are actually displaced by highway construction are similar to those briefly discussed in Chapter 8 with respect to urban renewal projects. They include the time and money costs of searching for alternative residential locations, which may be less convenient with respect to existing employment, resulting in increased costs for journey-to-work trips. As demonstrated by recent controversies in several major urban areas concerning the construction and placement of urban expressway projects, neighborhood quality may deteriorate as a result of an expressway. The displacement of stores may reduce shopping opportunities. Expressways, unless they are constructed on stilts above ground level, usually block off a number of local streets that formerly crossed the route, resulting in increased transportation costs and decreased accessibility for the residents of the neighborhood. Also, the residents of neighborhoods that have expressways running through them incur indirect costs in such forms as traffic noise and increased air pollution.[6]

Radial rail lines are most useful for bringing people from outlying areas into the CBD; the further one lives from the CBD, the greater is the likelihood of using a nearby rail line. Since higher-income people tend to make the downtown-commuting trip, it may be that most of the benefits of a rail system accrue to higher-income households; also, some of the costs may be financed by local taxes, which are regressive. For example, in the case of the BART system in San Francisco, the annual payments required to pay interest on and retire the principal amounts of the bonds issued to finance the capital costs of the system are estimated to be about $78 million. With an annual expected one-way passenger volume of 60 million, this amounts to a capital cost per round trip of $2.60. If a downtown commuter make 250 journey-to-work trips per year, he receives a subsidy of $700 per year. Since most of the capital costs of the BART project were financed by local taxes rather than UMTA grants, the distribution of net benefits from the BART rail system are likely to be quite regressive, assuming that most downtown commuters are from higher-income groups and that local taxes tend to be somewhat regressive (see Chapter 15). Subsidized investments in a radially oriented rail system are also likely to result in substantial benefits for those who own land in the CBD, since the system has the tendency to improve accessibility to the CBD. To the extent that such land is owned by those in higher-income groups, the benefits accruing to nonriders are also likely to be regressively distributed.

In terms of horizontal equity, not all of those in the same income

---

[6]For a detailed discussion of costs imposed on residents from highway construction, see Anthony Downs, "Losses Imposed on Urban Households by Uncompensated Highway and Renewal Costs." in Anthony Downs, *Urban Problems and Prospects*, Markham, Chicago, 1970, pp. 192 - 227.

group are likely to use any given transportation investment to the same extent. Although subsidized public transit fares are advocated on the grounds of not pricing the poor out of transportation, reduced fares are not likely to benefit all low-income groups equally. At the same time, they reduce the price to all users, thereby providing subsidies to any higher-income users as well. If society wished, for some reason, to provide income redistribution in kind through increasing transportation consumption (as is the case with in-kind housing programs), the only type of program likely to achieve horizontal equity would be to provide low-income households with transportation vouchers that could be applied to the cost of transportation by any mode, including payments on purchase of an auto.

The Low-Income Transportation Problem

As discussed in Chapter 2, there has been a steady decentralization of manufacturing and service jobs to suburban areas over time. Since low-income households tend to remain concentrated in the inner city while new job opportunities for which they have the skills are moving out, low-income journey-to-work trip distances and costs are likely to be increasing. Table 10-2 presents some recent data on journey-to-work trip patterns of low-income inner-city residents in six major urban areas. The table indicates that cross-commuting within the central city is the major journey-to-work trip pattern but that reverse commuting is already of considerable importance (and is likely to increase in importance as the job-decentralization process continues).

Earlier sections of this chapter indicated that the auto is usually the superior mode of transportation in terms of time savings, privacy, convenience, and flexibility for most journey-to-work trips, as well as shopping and recreation (leisure) trips; however, automobile ownership is expensive. The costs of automobile ownership as a percentage of income for low-income households make auto transit an unfeasible choice for many such households. This is implied in relevant statistics: in 1972, about 41 percent of households with incomes below $3,000 owned autos, while 93 percent of households with incomes over $25,000 owned one or more autos.[7] Since many low-income residents (especially blacks) of the urban area reside in the inner portions of the central city, conventional bus systems plus occasional reliance on taxis are the predominant transit modes. However, conventional bus systems tend to be radially oriented. Thus, in many cases, to get from a residential location in the central city to a job

[7]U.S. Bureau of the Census, *Statistical Abstract of the United States: 1973*, Government Printing Office, Washington, 1973, Table No. 542, p. 332.

| | JOB LOCATION | | |
CENTRAL CITY	Within inner-city neighbor-hood of residence	Within balance of central city	Suburbs
Atlanta	24.5%	55.5%	20.1%
Chicago	23.3	55.4	21.3
Detroit	31.4	42.3	26.4
Houston	41.4	48.8	9.8
Los Angeles	15.3	49.7	35.0
New York City	22.4	68.1	9.6

Table 10-2: Work Locations of Inner-City Residents of Six Major Central Cities
SOURCE: Roberta V. McKay, "Commuting Patterns of Inner-City Residents," *Monthly Labor Review* (November 1973), 44.

location in either another part of the central city or a suburban area, the worker must take a bus to the CBD and then transfer to a second bus, traveling a distance that may be twice that required to make the same trip by automobile. Also, a journey-to-work trip by bus during peak hours involves encountering the congestion of the CBD and results in a relatively large amount of travel time compared with cross-commuting by auto. Going back to the example of Table 10-1, even though the poor do not value their travel time as highly as those in higher-income groups (since time costs are related to wage rates), the total amount of time involved in making a journey-to-work trip by radial routes may result in total time costs that discourage employment. For example, the time costs of a four-hour round trip for a person who values travel time at $1.50 per hour are $6.00, which may be as much as or more than travel-time costs incurred by many in higher-income groups, owing to the shorter travel times of other modes or other trip patterns.

Conventional bus transit may impose other costs, besides heavy time costs, on low-income users. If the demand for certain trip patterns is low, service may be provided on an infrequent basis—only at peak hours between suburban job locations and the CBD. Unless the worker catches the bus exactly at closing time, he may not be able to get home or has to find some other mode of transportation, possibly incurring high costs. Such inflexibility in trip times may result in the worker being unable to accept lucrative overtime work and discourage the employer from hiring the individual because of the limitations of his working hours. It is not surprising that often such workers only use public transit for a sufficient time to be able to make a down payment on a car or find another worker to car pool with. For those individuals who never get hired or are discouraged from seeking employment by the heavy costs of the journey-to-work trip by bus, public transit may be a deterrent to employment and thus be related to the poverty of households residing in the inner city.

While low-income households rely heavily on conventional radially oriented bus systems for their transportation in the absence of auto ownership, changing the bus trip patterns might be quite costly relative to the demand for such trips. Setting up the system on a grid basis, with buses traveling along north and south streets and making connections with buses on east and west streets, would allow shorter trips to be made in some cases. Of course, if radial lines are still heavily demanded, these could be continued. While providing grid patterns does generate benefits, these benefits seem to be less than for radial lines. The question is whether such service could be provided more economically with modes other than running nearly empty buses. Some alternatives that have been tried are "call-and-ride" systems, where buses or taxis pick up riders when they telephone in to a central office. This assumes a telephone is accessible, which may not be the case for many poor persons. A possibility might be to provide call boxes at bus stops, so that a person could go to a stop and call for a ride there.

An alternative that is still used in a few scattered areas is the jitney system. At one time in this country's history (about 1915), there emerged a large and growing jitney industry.[8] The idea was quite simple, and it operated without government assistance (or approval, since it was universally suppressed by government statutes). Anyone with a car (a Model T at that time) could enter the business of carrying passengers; he generally would run it like a taxi, except that rates were lower and passengers were picked up until the car was full (sometimes with passengers on the running boards). Some drivers would travel along special routes, and others would wait until they picked up the first passenger to determine the route, which was then posted on the windshield, and would travel that route while picking up passengers and letting them off at their destinations. During special events, jitneys would show up in hopes of attracting passengers; Eckert and Hilton show evidence to the effect that, when it rained, more jitneys would come out (unlike present bus and taxi systems). The jitney system can be thought of as the private market system response to the demand for transportation in urban areas. One tremendous advantage today would be that workers driving to work could take on paying passengers, although current regulations generally prohibit this. Why were jitneys suppressed? The main reason was that they attracted passengers away from trolley companies, which had considerable political influence. It can be assumed that the jitneys provided better service if they were able to do this, so there is at least a prima facie case that suppression was a mistake. Apart from historical interest, jitneys might be considered as a very good way of providing

---

[8]See Ross Eckert and George Hilton, "The Jitneys," *Journal of Law and Economics* (1972), 293 - 325.

transportation, particularly in poverty areas, where people are more heavily dependent on buses and cabs. Reducing the prohibitory statutes would make it feasible for ghetto car owners to supplement their income by providing jitney service, perhaps on a part-time basis or during periods of unemployment. Auto insurance regulations that do not allow for paying passengers could be modified to make this more feasible. In many cases, it would be easier to arrange than car-pooling, in that a driver might pick up a passenger or two on his way to work without requiring them to travel to his house to pick him up on alternate days.

A Proposal for Public Transit in Urban Areas

In order to integrate the various strands discussed in this and the preceding chapter, a specific proposal will now be presented for public transit in a typical major urban area (say, an SMSA in the 1-to 3-million population range). The features are as follows: (1) short-run price rationing of expressways; (2) integration of present conventional bus systems into a rapid bus system; (3) allowing buses to enter expressways without paying congestion tolls; and (4) allowing jitneys to operate. Price rationing of existing expressways would greatly reduce congestion and allow much higher speeds to be maintained by both buses and autos. If tolls were collected efficiently (perhaps electronically, as suggested in Chapter 9), then the collection of tolls in itself would not impede traffic. Buses would become much more attractive relative to the auto mode than they are now. Currently, bus trips are much slower than auto trips, because buses not only have to fight it out on congested roads with autos but also make many stops and usually travel more circuitous routes. Buses on rationed expressways would travel much faster than at present and would reduce the advantage of the auto driven on congested routes. While such buses would continue to be slower than autos on expressways, high tolls would have to be paid by autos. As a result, the difference in the relative private costs of bus versus auto would be significantly reduced. Buses could operate with fares at present levels but offer much better service; thus, more people would be attracted to them because of their relative lower private cost. For example, in Table 10-1, suppose that on a price-rationed expressway the bus could make the twenty-mile round trip in thirty-five instead of seventy minutes. Travel-time costs by the bus mode would be reduced by $2.33, while auto costs would be increased, either by paying a peak-hour toll to travel faster than at present or by traveling more slowly on congested alternate routes. As a result, the private costs of the bus mode relative to the car would now be low enough for many people to switch from auto to bus, even taking account of such intangible factors as privacy, which are not included in Table 10-1.

Since buses could achieve much higher speeds with this system, they would become more like rail transit systems in this respect. The advantage of the bus is that it could travel through residential areas and pick up passengers, serving as its own feeder, and then enter the expressways and travel to the destinations at high speeds (nonstop in cases where it was providing service to the CBD). The total travel time of the passengers could be competitive with that by rail. Existing bus systems would become more or less feeder-plus-express buses that use the expressways for part of the trip. There may be sufficient demand for certain trips, so that buses could function as "shopper specials" looping the shopping district or provide for other such specialized trip demands. For many cases where buses are currently used (the most unprofitable lines, no doubt) jitneys would fill the transportation demands. If only a handful of passengers make a certain trip, some kind of jitney arrangement would be cheaper than sending a bus there. Perhaps one person could drive and pick up the others, or a jitney operator could pick them up and take them to their destination, which might be a bus stop located at a point where a bus would enter the expressway.

The advantages of the system briefly outlined above are that it would provide transportation services to the urban area at a much higher level than it is presently getting. At the same time, since it would mainly use existing facilities, the cost would be moderate, only a fraction of the cost of a rail system, and it could be established in relatively short order, as contrasted to a rail system. Finally, if cities continue to follow the decentralization trends of recent years, this system would be much easier to adapt than one predicated on a reversal of present decentralization trends. It is often stated that a rail system should be built because it is the "most modern" kind of system. It is our contention that, for most SMSAs in the United States, the system outlined above would be more modern than rail, in that it would make the best use off existing technology and would be far more efficient.

REVIEW AND DISCUSSION QUESTIONS

1 In what respects can peak-hour highway urban users be said to be subsidized by (1) off-peak highway users and (2) taxpayers in general? How could such subsidies be removed? What would be the major consequences of their removal?

2 The automobile will go down in history as the most wasteful and

extravagant form of urban transportation ever devised. Evaluate.

3 The efficient way to reduce peak-hour traffic congestion is to pay people to take public transit, so that fewer people would make their journey-to-work trip by car. Evaluate.

4 Why is it reasonable to assume that substantial federal subsidies to urban areas to build public transit facilities are likely to result in a misallocation of resources?

5 Why are the benefits of rail transit systems likely to be regressively distributed?

6 The reason that poor people use public transit proportionately more than higher-income people is that they place a lower value on their travel time. Evaluate.

7 Think of your journey-to-work (or school) trip or that of someone in your household, and attempt to determine the out-of-pocket and travel-time costs of this trip for car and public transit, as done in Table 10-1.

8 If our cities are to survive, traffic congestion must be eliminated. Evaluate.

9 Suppose the Supreme Court ruled that regulation of local transportation was unconstitutional, so that anyone could operate a jitney if he wished. Discuss the effects on existing public transportation systems and taxi companies.

10 Discuss the efficiency of the following programs to reduce urban traffic congestion:
    a. build more urban highways
    b. put a heavy tax on gasoline
    c. build rail rapid transit systems
    d. mandate car-pooling

SUGGESTED READINGS

Domencich, Tom, and Gerald Kraft. *Free Transit.* Lexington, Mass.: Heath, 1970.

Dyckman, John. "Transportation in Cities." *Scientific American* (September 1965), 163 - 174. (Reprinted in Arthur F. Schreiber, Paul K. Gatons. and Richard B. Clemmer, eds. *Economics of Urban Problems: Selected Readings.* Boston: Houghton Mifflin, 1971.)

Eckert, Ross, and George Hilton. "The Jitneys." *Journal of Law and Economics* (1972), 293 - 325.

Fried, Edward, et al. "Investing in the Physical Environment: Urban Transportation." In *Setting National Priorities: the 1974 Budget*, pp. 238 - 252. Washington: The Brookings Institution, 1973.

Hilton, George. *Federal Transit Subsidies.* Washington: American Enterprise Institute for Public Policy Research, 1974.

Kain, John. "A Reappraisal of Metropolitan Transport Planning." Talk delivered to the Seminar for Urban and Regional Research, February 21, 1969, at the University of Washington. (Reprinted in Schreiber et al.)

Meyer, John. "Urban Transportation." In *The Metropolitan Enigma,* edited by J.Q. Wilson. Garden City, N.Y: Doubleday, Anchor Books, 1970.

Meyer, John, and John Kain. "Transportation and Poverty." *The Public Interest* (Winter 1970).

Meyer, John, John Kain, and Martin Wohl. *The Urban Transportation Problem.* Cambridge, Mass.: Harvard University Press, 1965.

11 / The Urban Pollution Problem

A definition of pollution is followed by a discussion of the case of market failure that results in it being an economic problem. In order to evaluate policies for reducing pollution levels, the sources, trends, and social costs of air, water, and other forms of pollution are considered. This is followed by a discussion of the extent to which various types of pollution are attributable to urbanization. The last section of the chapter defines the efficient level of environmental quality and presents a set of criteria for evaluating alternative policies to achieve this goal.

Pollution: Definition and the Problem

Pollution results from overusing the environment for waste-disposal purposes, as defined in the first part of this section. The environment is a scarce resource that has alternative uses. The pollution problem is the inefficient level of use of the environment for waste-disposal purposes that results from the case of market failure.

Definition of Pollution

Pollution results from the excessive discharge of effluents (wastes) into the environment. The production and consumption activities of an economy convert matter from one form to another in order to increase the benefits received from its use. For example, iron ore is converted to steel and the steel is converted through manufacturing processes into useful items like automobiles. When individuals have finished using the automobile for transportation purposes, the original iron still remains, even though the car is abandoned in a junkyard and the iron has reverted to a hunk of iron oxide. Matter is never really consumed; it is merely converted from one form to another, and some of these conversions do not result in any benefit to society. Much of the matter society uses is converted to gas and released into the atmosphere; in other cases, it is released in the form of liquids that end up in our watercourses or in the form of solids left on the land. In summary, matter is neither created nor destroyed, except for very small amounts in nuclear reactions. The production and consumption activities of an economy convert rather than destroy material substances that come from mines, farms, and forests, pass through the economic system, and finally reach consumers. The mass of inputs to production must be matched by the mass of outputs of residuals. It should be noted that energy is also released into the environment in the form of heat and noise, and this discharge can also become excessive.

The discharge of effluents or residuals is not necessarily pollution, however. Pollution is defined as *a level of effluent discharge sufficient to overload the capacity of the environment* to assimilate it. This definition implies that the emission of effluents into the environment does not necessarily result in environmental pollution. The smoke from a campfire in the middle of a large forest will not result in pollution, since the environment has the capacity to assimilate this amount of smoke. However, a similar fire in an urban area may àdd to pollution, since that environment may already be overloaded from other waste discharges.

The Efficient Level of Pollution

Contrary to what was said in most economics textbooks of several decades ago, the environment is not an example of an unlimited resource. Although most of society may have only recently realized it, the environment and its assimilatory capacity are limited, as are all other resources. When the assimilatory capacity of the environment is exceeded, there is a cost associated with discharging effluents, which is incurred because the environment generates many important benefits in addition to serving as a receptacle for waste. These alternative uses of the environment include the support of human and plant life, recreational benefits, and a supply of inputs into consumption items such as food and lumber. Thus, pollution (the discharge of effluents at a level that exceeds the assimilatory capacity of the environment) alters the environment to some extent and reduces the alternative benefits that could be received. In this context, the pollution problem is one of efficient use of all the potential functions of the environment so that net social benefits are maximized.

At the present time, the environment is not used efficiently; the level of effluents discharged into it results in social costs (from foregone alternative uses) that are greater than the (marginal) social benefits of using the environment as a receptor for effluents. The main reason for this inefficiency is the failure of the market to ration the environment's use, because negative externalities exist. The environment is a common property resource, meaning that individual property rights (defining which individuals have the right to use the environment for specified purposes) have not been adequately established and enforced. The market system can efficiently allocate commodities between competing uses when property rights to resources are defined and enforceable. With full right of ownership, the owner of a resource can prevent others from using, benefiting from, or damaging it without making compensation to him. In the case of the atmosphere and other environmental resources, these are common property resources over which private property rights cannot be well defined and enforced. Given this lack of private property rights and any other form of restriction on use, any individual or business firm has the "right" to use the environment as he sees fit. In this situation, the price charged to individual users of the environment is zero. As a result, there is an incentive for them to carry their use to the level at which marginal private benefits are zero, since net private benefits are maximized when marginal private benefits equal marginal private costs (which are zero because no price is charged for the use of the environment). However, while those parties using the environment as a "wastebasket" incur no private costs by this use, costs are incurred by society—foregone alternative uses of the environment—which accrue as negative externalities (impaired health, lost recreational opportunities, and other costs). As is the case with all unresolved negative externalities, the market-determined outcome is a level of use that is greater than the efficient one.

The definitions of pollution and the pollution problem are illustrated by Figure 11-1. The example takes an electrical generating plant that discharges sulfur dioxide into the air as a by-product of generating electricity. The MPC curve is equal to the costs of electricity incurred by the producer, assuming he uses a production method that minimizes his production costs, subject to his ability to discharge residuals into the atmosphere at a zero price. Indirect costs are imposed on others from the effluent discharge, as indicated by the divergence between marginal private and social costs. While

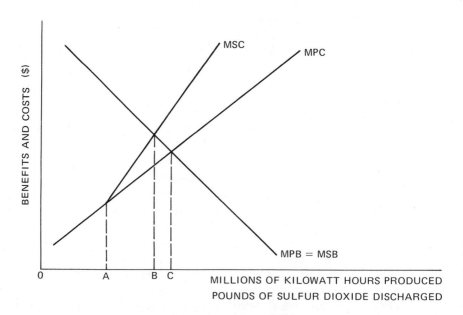

Figure 11-1: Pollution and Inefficiency: An Example

effluents are discharged into the environment at production levels below OA kilowatt hours, the level of discharge does not result in *pollution*, since the capacity of the environment to assimilate this level of sulfur dioxide emissions has not been exceeded. While pollution occurs at production levels greater than OA, the *pollution problem* stems from the fact that OB would be the level of production and effluent emission that would maximize net social benefits (given the existing production methods), yet the market-determined outcome is production level OC. Thus, an inefficient level of pollution exists in this case because the environment is being "overused." Net social benefits would be maximized at a level of OB and the pollution problem would be eliminated; however, pollution would still exist, since sulfur dioxide emitted at this level exceeds the capacity of the environment to assimilate it, and some indirect costs would be incurred.

Pollution: Types, Sources, Trends, and Costs

After a brief discussion of the basic determinants of pollution levels, this section provides an overview of types of effluents and their effects (such as the social costs of damage to human and animal health and corrosion of exterior surfaces). Also, some data on major sources of various pollutants and trends in pollution levels are included. Obviously, efficient solutions to the pollution problem necessitate knowledge of the damage of various pollutants and the dollar magnitude of these indirect costs. Most of the major sources of pollutants, in terms of both quantity and the order of magnitude of their indirect costs, have been identified; however, estimates of the indirect costs of these effluents individually and in conjunction with each other are not known. For example, considerable effort has been directed toward identifying the human health problems associated with air pollution and the costs of this reduced health. While there is little question that air pollution tends to increase the incidence and seriousness of a variety of respiratory diseases (such as emphysema, lung cancer, tuberculosis, and bronchitis), evidence on how the incidence of such diseases varies with the level of air pollution (or more precisely, with the level of specific effluents in the air) is not well established. Acute exposure to air pollution (short periods of high levels of air pollution) has been shown to significantly increase death rates in several areas, among them London, England (the "killer fogs"), New York City, and Donora, Pennsylvania.

Obtaining empirical evidence on precise relationships between effluent levels and human health damage (as well as other effects of effluents) is extremely difficult. While data may show a correlation between pollution levels and morbidity and mortality, these relationships may be spurious in that the level of air pollution may be correlated with a third factor, which is the "real" cause of the health problem, such as eating and exercise habits. While the problem is difficult, an efficient environmental policy in the long run requires that resources be allocated to research to determine the social costs and benefits associated with different levels of environmental quality.

Determinants of the Level of Pollution

The quantity of effluents discharged into the environment is related to population size and per capita income. As population and income grow, so do the production and consumption of goods and services, and more effluents are discharged into the environment. The amount of pollution also depends on what is produced and consumed and the resulting residuals—some can easily be absorbed by the environment or recycled through the economy, while others cannot. Thus, both the quantity and type of residuals are important in determining the level of pollution. In addition, the location of residual discharge is important. Since pollution does not exist until the capacity of the environment is exceeded, some forms of pollution in the United States would be significantly reduced if the population and location of economic activity were more evenly spaced across the country. However, as discussed in other chapters of this book, there are advantages to clustering economic activity in urban areas. The growth of urban areas has resulted in a concentration of jobs and people in a relatively small portion of the total United States land mass. As urbanization and the resulting concentration of population continue, a larger proportion of the residuals and by-products from production and consumption are discharged into a smaller proportion of the environment. Certain types of pollution are primarily urban problems, and so pollution is one of the major offsets to the advantages of concentrating economic activity in urban areas.

Air Pollution: Types and Effects

Although a large number of substances pollute the air, the present state of knowledge indicates that approximately five to ten of these substances account for most of the indirect costs of air pollution and are thus the important pollutants from an economic standpoint. Five of them, which have received the attention of legislation to date, will be discussed below: carbon monoxide, hydrocarbons, nitrogen oxides, sulfur oxides, and particulates.

Carbon monoxide   By combining with hemoglobin in the blood
stream more rapidly than oxygen, inhaled carbon monoxide reduces
the capacity of the blood to transport oxygen to the body's tissues. The
major effects of relatively short periods (a few hours) of inhalation of
carbon monoxide, at levels that may occur at street level in certain
cities, are impairment of mental and physical functions, with symptoms including headaches and dizziness. High concentrations can
result in death. Little is presently known about the costs to human
health from long-term inhalation at levels below those that result in
the short-term symptoms noted above.

Hydrocarbons   The primary effect of hydrocarbons is their interaction with oxides of nitrogen in sunlight to produce photochemical
smog, for which Los Angeles is famous. Hydrocarbons have no
known directly harmful effects, although it is speculated that some
hydrocarbons may be carcinogenic (cancer-inducing). Photochemical smog results in eye irritation and may make it more difficult for
people to breathe, especially those already suffering from respiratory
diseases such as emphysema and asthma. Smog also results in damage to plant life.

Nitrogen oxides   Oxides of nitrogen are primarily of concern because
of their role in the formation of photochemical smog discussed above.
In addition, nitrogen dioxide has been found to be harmful to the
lungs in man and has resulted in health impairment in animals,
including pulmonary injury and increased susceptibility to bacterial
infection. Effects on plants in the form of leaf damage and growth
reduction have been established, and there is some evidence that
higher human mortality rates are associated with continuous exposure to nitrogen oxides.

Sulfur oxides   Sulfur dioxide and sulfur trioxide emitted into the
atmosphere react with moisture in the air (or in the lungs) to form
sulfurous and sulfuric acid, respectively, which can cause severe
pulmonary reactions when human beings are subject to acute exposure (high level and short duration). Sulfur oxides may also result in
damage to painted surfaces and other materials, as well as damage to
plant life. Chronic exposure (low level and long duration) has major
health effects and is associated with higher mortality rates.

Particulates   Particulates are a heterogeneous mixture of solid and
liquid particles suspended in the air; many of these are so small in
diameter that they cannot be seen with a good microscope. These very
small particles act as carriers for other pollutants and produce more
serious health effects than larger particles, which are intercepted in

the nose and throat. Particulate matter may have a large, though not well-established, influence on the weather through its effect on cloud formation and precipitation. While chronic exposure to particulates in general appears to be associated with higher death rates, as well as other effects on people, plants, and animals, much concern has been expressed recently over specific particulate substances, such as asbestos and lead, which appear to be potential health hazards even at very low concentrations. Long exposure to asbestos in industry produces the lung-scarring disease, asbestosis. Lead poisoning has been recognized for centuries; the symptoms of chronic lead poisoning include weakness, apathy, lowered fertility, and miscarriage. Atmospheric lead is a major contributor to the level of lead in the bloodstream, but there is no sound evidence at the present time as to what constitutes normal versus toxic levels of lead in the blood and the effects of nontoxic levels on health.

In summary, the effects of various pollutants and their interactions are not well understood at present. A National Academy of Sciences conference on the health effects of air pollution reviewed the existing evidence in 1973. Among the conference's conclusions, emerging evidence seemed to indicate that the health effects of a mixture of pollutants may impair health more than any primary pollutant alone. Also, there is a difference in human lung cancer incidence between rural and urban areas that is not attributable to cigarette smoking, but definitive evidence is lacking that this is caused by the pollutants discussed above.[1]

It should be noted that any substance emitted into the air in sufficient quantity will result in indirect costs. The carbon dioxide expelled by human and animal breathing can form carbonic acid when combined with moisture in the atmosphere and lead to more rapid deterioration of buildings. The list of major pollutants above was compiled to include those that presently seem to exist in sufficient concentrations to cause significant indirect costs. At some time in the future, other substances may join the list, even though they are considered harmless now. The point is that pollution results from the discharge of any substance in an amount that overloads the assimilatory capacity of the environment. The situation is much like the definition of toxicity. Any substance is toxic in sufficient amounts, although the amount required to cause death varies, depending on the body's capacity to assimilate it. A very small amount of arsenic is fatal, but a large amount of water is also fatal if ingested in a short period of time.

[1]*Conference on Health Effects of Air Pollution: Summary of Proceedings* (prepared for the Committee on Public Works, U.S. Senate, by the National Academy of Sciences), Government Printing Office, Washington, 1973, pp. 8 - 9.

SOURCE	CARBON MONOXIDE	PARTI-CULATES	SULFUR OXIDES	HYDRO-CARBONS	NITROGEN OXIDES
TRANSPORTATION	111.0	.7	1.0	19.5	11.7
Motor vehicles	96.6	.4	.3	16.7	9.1
Gasoline	95.8	.3	.2	16.6	7.8
Diesel	.8	.1	.1	.1	1.3
Aircraft	3.0	.1	.1	.4	.4
Railroads	.1	—	.1	.1	.1
Vessels	1.7	.1	.3	.3	.2
Nonhighway use of motor fuels	9.5	.1	.2	2.0	1.9
FUEL COMBUSTION IN STATIONARY SOURCES	.8	6.8	26.5	.6	10.0
Coal	.5	5.6	22.2	.2	3.9
Fuel oil	.1	.4	4.2	.1	1.3
Natural gas	.1	.2	—	.3	4.7
Wood	.1	.6	.1	—	.1
INDUSTRIAL PROCESS LOSSES	11.4	13.3	6.0	5.5	.2
SOLID-WASTE DISPOSAL	7.2	1.4	.1	2.0	.4
MISCELLANEOUS	18.3	3.9	.3	7.3	.5
TOTAL	149.0	26.1	33.9	34.9	22.8

Table 11-1: Estimated Emissions of Air Pollutants, Nationwide, 1970 (Millions of Tons per Year)

SOURCE: Nationwide Air Pollutant Emission Trends, 1940 - 1970, U.S. Environmental Protection Agency, Research Triangle Park, N.C., January 1973.

Air Pollution: Sources and Levels

The estimated quantity of emissions of the five primary air pollutants and their major sources in 1970 are listed in Table 11-1. Gasoline-powered motor vehicles (primarily automobiles) account for over 64 percent of all carbon monoxide emissions. Even though vehicular travel is fairly evenly divided between urban and rural areas, traffic in urban areas accounts for 64 percent of total motor vehicle emissions, since driving speeds tend to be slower. In addition, essentially all industrial emissions, aircraft emissions occurring below 3,000 feet, and a majority of emissions from fuel combustion and refuse disposal occur in urban areas.[2] The combustion of coal and industrial-process losses account for most particulate emissions. The majority of coal combustion is for purposes of generating electricity; steam-electric plants emitted 3.6 million tons of particulates. Industrial-process losses are the largest category of particulate emissions, and nearly half of this amount was generated by the sand-, stone-, and rock-processing industries (such as cement plants).[3] Over one-half of total

[2]*Nationwide Air Pollutant Emission Trends, 1940 - 1970,* U.S. Environmental Protection Agency, Research Triangle Park, N.C., January 1973, p. 17.

[3]*Nationwide Air Pollutant Emission Trends,* pp. 16, 22.

sulfur oxide emissions are from the combustion of coal to generate electricity in approximately 1,000 power plants in the United States. Of the 26.5 million tons from fuel consumption in stationary sources, steam-electric production accounts for 19.4 million tons, industrial combustion 4.9 million tons, and the space heating of homes and businesses the remaining 2.2 million tons.[4] With respect to hydrocarbons, motor vehicles account for about one-half of total emissions. Nitrogen oxide emissions result almost exclusively from fuel consumption in mobile and stationary sources.

In summary, transportation contributed more pollution than all other sources together when measured by total weight of effluents, with most of this attributable to the automobile. Carbon monoxide alone, primarily from the automobile, almost equals the weights of the other pollutants combined. However, the peak level of automobile pollution has already passed, as older cars are replaced by newer ones with the pollution-control devices that were first required in 1968 models. Emissions from solid-waste disposal have also declined over time, probably through reduction in open burning at municipal dumps. Particulate emissions are heavist in urban areas with heavy industry and coal combustion for electricity and industrial purposes; for example, Chicago is estimated to have particulate emissions of 450,000 tons per year, while Los Angeles has about 10 percent of this amount (47,000 tons).[5]

While the data in Table 11-1 give a rough approximation of the major sources of air pollution, nationwide emissions are a very poor indicator of the status of air quality, because this depends strongly on the location of emission sources. Further, the weight of the various effluents is poorly related to the indirect costs associated with air pollution. Other things being equal, a ton of sulfur dioxide is much more harmful than a ton of carbon monoxide. While generally accepted estimates of the costs of air pollution do not exist, one rough estimate of the indirect costs of the five pollutants listed in Table 11-1 indicates that carbon monoxide accounts for 48.1 percent of the total weight of effluents, but only 3.2 percent of the indirect costs. The percentages of the total indirect costs for the other pollutants are as follows: particulates, 45.8 percent; sulfur oxides, 31.8 percent; hydrocarbons, 6.3 percent; and nitrogen oxides, 12.9 percent. As a result, the contribution of transportation (primarily the auto) is 50.7 percent by weight but only 19.3 percent with respect to costs, since most of the auto effluents are carbon monoxide and hydrocarbons, which have low indirect costs per ton. On the other hand, fuel combustion (primarily coal-fired electrical generation) accounts for 21.2

[4]*Nationwide Air Pollutant Emission Trends,* pp. 5, 13.
[5]*Nationwide Air Pollutant Emission Trends,* p. 16.

percent of the weight but 40.8 percent of the costs.[6] Again, this estimate of the indirect costs does not take into consideration the geographical distribution of pollution sources, to be discussed later.

Water Pollutants

Probably the most useful classification for discussing water pollutants is degradable versus nondegradable residuals. Degradable residuals are reduced in weight by the biological, physical, and chemical processes that occur in the waters receiving them. The most common forms of degradable residual are organic materials such as human sewage or pulp-mill wastes. When a degradable effluent is discharged into clean water, bacteria in the water feed on the effluent and decompose it into its basic components of nitrogen, phosphorus, and carbon. As part of the process, the bacteria use up some of the dissolved oxygen in the water. As long as the quantity of the effluent does not exceed the assimilative capacity of the watercourse, the used-up oxygen will be replaced (through reoxygenation) from the air that is dissolved by moving water and by the photosynthesis of aquatic plants. The most common measure of the impact of various degradable effluents is the amount of oxygen required to achieve complete decomposition of the material. Biochemical oxygen demand (BOD) is used as a common denominator, measuring the number of pounds of oxygen required to decompose degradable materials.

If the BOD requirements of effluents are sufficient to result in a permanent reduction of the level of dissolved oxygen in a stream, many species of fish will be unable to survive. Very low (or zero) oxygen levels will kill most fish and result in wastes being decomposed without oxygen, producing foul odors and black, bubbly waters. The dissolved oxygen content of a watercourse (and thus its assimilative capacity for degradable wastes) depends not only on effluent discharge but on other considerations such as stream flow and water temperature. Thus, the discharge of waste heat (such as heated water from coal-fired and nuclear electricity-generating plants) has an adverse impact on the dissolved oxygen content of a watercourse. Colder fluids can dissolve more gases, as one discovers if he opens a warm bottle of beer.

Nondegradable residuals are not decomposed by bacteria in the water, and usually the only change that occurs is dilution and settling. These residuals include various inorganic chemicals, salts, silt, and other substances. Relatively high concentrations of such residuals in watercourses produce toxicity, cloudiness, unpleasant taste,

[6]Council on Environmental Quality, *Environmental Quality: Fourth Annual Report*, Government Printing Office, Washington, 1973, p. 328.

and other forms of water-quality deterioration. Some heavy metals, such as mercury, are absorbed by plant life and work their way up the food chain, until they may become concentrated at poisonous levels in higher-order species such as tuna. Pesticides (such as DDT), radioactive wastes, and other nondegradable residuals enter watercourses and can result in severe health problems as well as other potential indirect costs.

Reliable data on the sources of various types of water-borne effluents and their magnitude are essentially nonexistent. However, several estimates of degradable residuals (in terms of BOD) have been made. For example, the Environmental Protection Agency estimated the BOD of degradable residuals before treatment (for 1968) to be about 38 billion pounds. Households accounted for 8.5 billion of this but after sewage-plant treatment the amount actually discharged into watercourses was probably only about 3 billion pounds. On the other hand, manufacturing wastes are not usually treated to the same extent as household wastes and manufacturing accounted for a total BOD of 29.7 billion pounds, the major contributors being chemicals (14.2), paper (7.8), and food products (4.6).[7] Actually, these figures greatly understate the total BOD of all economic activity in the United States, since many sources of water effluents are nonpoint sources or sources that are not readily identifiable. (The term "nonpoint" refers to the fact that some effluents do not emanate from a single point, such as a pipe from an industrial plant.) Nonpoint sources of water effluents include agriculture (run-off from croplands and feedlots) and natural resource exploitation (lumbering).

For the large number of nondegradable residuals that cannot be measured by a common denominator such as BOD, no comprehensive data exist at present. However, estimates of industrial effluents in the Southeastern region of the United States for phosphorus, nitrate, heavy metals, and solids indicate that the three industrial sources contributing heavily to degradable effluent emissions are also the major contributors of nondegradable effluents.[8]

From the standpoint of the indirect costs of water pollution, the problem would not appear to be as serious as air pollution. For one thing, it is much more difficult to avoid air pollution than to avoid water pollution. While air pollution has direct impacts on human health, there appear to be three major benefits of improved water quality: recreation (greater use of watercourses for boating, fishing, and swimming); improvement in commercial fishing; and reduced costs of municipal treatment and purification of water that is taken from rivers. Although such benefits are easy to identify, they are difficult to quantify. However, what scant evidence exists indicates

[7]Environmental Protection Agency, *Cost of Clean Water*, Vol. II, March 1971.
[8]Council in Environmental Quality, *Environmental Quality*, pp. 280 - 281.

that lost recreational opportunities are the major cost of low water quality.

Other Pollutants

Solid-waste residuals, ranging from litter to abandoned automobiles, create potential pollution problems. Water drainage from dumping sites can pollute streams and incineration of solid wastes can result in air pollution. Further indirect costs are imposed by solid waste per se—the ugliness of littered highways and auto junkyards. Nationwide, approximately 200 million tons of solid wastes are collected each year from household, commercial, and industrial activities, or approximately one ton per person in the United States. In addition, there are agricultural wastes and uncollected residuals such as roadside litter.

Radioactive wastes from the disposal of spent atomic fuel (from electricity generation) present a difficult disposal problem because of their long life and potentially high indirect costs. Such wastes buried several hundred feet underground generate relatively high temperatures and could remain active for perhaps thousands of years. Methods of disposal have to be carefully planned and maintained for very long periods of time.

Noise is also a pollutant. The most significant source of noise is transportation—airplanes, automobiles, trucks, buses, and railroads. Tire noise and motor noise from road traffic is probably the primary source, with heavy trucks generating a significant proportion of this noise. Decibel levels are the common measure of noise levels and the major indirect cost of noise is permanent impairment of hearing. Other indirect costs that have been identified include interference with conversation, sleep, and other human activities and possible lasting psychological effects in people exposed to high decibel levels over a long-term period.[9]

Pollution as an Urban Problem

It would appear that most of the major environmental problems in the United States today are concentrated in major urban areas. While there appears to be a relationship between air, water, and other environmental-quality factors and the degree of urbanization, this does not imply that concentration of jobs and people in urban areas is necessarily the cause of environmental problems. This section briefly discusses possible relationships between urbanization and pollution in order to determine the extent to which pollution is an urban problem.

[9]Council on Environmental Quality, *Environmental Quality: Third Annual Report,* Government Printing Office, Washington, 1972, p. 132.

Water Pollution

Although the evidence is scant, it is not obvious that concentration of pollution sources in urban areas results in greater indirect costs from a given level of effluent discharge than if these sources were more geographically dispersed. Since it appears that the major indirect cost of water pollution is foregone recreational opportunities, this form of externality might be reduced by concentrating pollution sources in urban areas. Although this would heighten the pollution levels in the urban areas, other watercourses relatively near these same urban areas could be left in a more pristine state for recreational purposes by urban residents and the indirect costs might be lower than if all watercourses were equally polluted. As mentioned earlier, reliable knowledge of the sources of water pollutants and their indirect costs does not presently exist. Some of the major sources of water pollution are nonpoint sources, most of which do not exist in urban areas and are thus not related to urbanization. Also, the cost of treating effluents that flow through sewer systems may be less per unit for the large volumes generated in urban areas than if such effluents were more evenly distributed geographically, with many smaller treatment plants. In summary, while urban watercourses are usually the most polluted, this does not necessarily imply that the social costs of pollution would be lower if the sources of pollution were more evenly dispersed throughout the water shed.

Air Pollution

While water pollution is not obviously an urban problem, air pollution definitely is. The indirect costs of air pollution are probably much more serious than those of water pollution in that they have many important effects on people. Water pollution mainly curtails recreational activities, but air pollution costs include impairment of health, reduction of life expectancy, soiling of clothing and exterior surfaces, physical deterioration of structures, reduced visibility, and damage to plant life. While urban water pollution costs are generally avoidable by seeking alternative recreational opportunities, urban air pollution affects most people most of the time, and the costs of avoiding it are quite high, including the possible sacrifice of current jobs and homes in order to move to rural areas with lower air pollution levels. In other words, there is no good available alternative or substitute for polluted urban air, as there is for polluted urban water.

While the nationwide amount of effluents discharged into the air (as shown in Table 11-1) would probably be little affected if the population and industry were more dispersed, the amount of pollution would be much lower. Pollution occurs only when effluent emission in an environment exceeds a certain level. Since urban airsheds account for only a fraction of total airsheds in the country, and since effluents are disproportionately discharged into them, greater pollution results in urban areas. Prevailing wind patterns and terrain in a given area determine the boundaries of an airshed, which is analogous to the boundaries of a watershed or a river valley. For example, the urban airshed in Los Angeles is well defined by the prevailing westerly winds off the ocean and the inland mountain ranges, which result in an assimilative capacity less than it would be if the wind patterns and terrain were different. The upper boundary of the airshed is a ceiling that results from lack of vertical mixing of air. Air temperature during the day normally decreases with altitude, permitting warmer air near the ground to rise and disperse the effluents in it. However, when temperature increases with altitude (an *inversion*), the air near the ground is not able to rise, and effluents concentrate in the air at ground level. The intensity and duration of an inversion depend on how rapidly the earth cools at night and warms in the morning. Inversion conditions that develop over a city during the night frequently last until three or four hours after sunrise, so that pollution from the morning traffic peak may be held over the city until late morning. Similarly, ground cooling may produce the beginning of an inversion at peak-hour traffic time in the evening, sometimes holding this pollution down until morning. These horizontal and vertical dimensions of airsheds determine the level of effluent concentration in urban areas, given the level of effluent emission. In the case of Los Angeles, thermal inversions occur approximately three hundred days a year, preventing effluents from escaping upward, while the prevailing westerly winds trap them against the mountains to the east of the city, so they back up over the Los Angeles area rather than dissipate horizontally. Were the emissions equal to those in Chicago (which has a much greater assimilative capacity), the death rate in Los Angeles would probably rise dramatically.

In conclusion, urbanization is a direct cause of air pollution problems, because the nationwide total amount of effluents is concentrated in urban airsheds, which are only a fraction of the total airsheds in the United States. As a result, indirect costs of air pollution are greater, since greater dispersal would allow emission into airsheds not overloaded at present. Further, air pollution costs probably increase faster than effluent levels, so that doubling effluent levels would more than double the indirect costs of pollution. Therefore, evenly distributing effluent emissions would greatly reduce pollution costs. In many cases, air pollution would not exist without urbanization, since pollution occurs only if effluent discharges overload the capacity of the environment. Table 11-2 presents levels of concentrations, by size of urban area, of three of the five major air pollutants shown in Table 11-1. While these concentrations do not continuously rise with size of urban area (because of differences in

	POLLUTANT CONCENTRATION (MICROGRAMS PER CUBIC METER)		
POPULATION	Particulates	Sulfur dioxide	Nitrogen oxides
Nonurban	25	10	33
Less than 10,000	57	35	116
10,000-25,000	81	18	64
25,000-50,000	87	14	63
50,000-100,000	118	29	127
100,000-400,000	95	26	114
400,000-700,000	100	28	127
700,000-1 million	101	29	146
1-3 million	134	69	163
More than 3 million	120	85	153

Table 11-2: Concentration of Air Pollutants by Size of Urban Area, Annual Averages, 1970
SOURCE: Council on Environmental Quality, *Environmental Quality: Second Annual Report*, Government Printing Office, Washington, August 1971, p. 243.

airshed characteristics, errors in data estimation, and other factors), in general, the larger the urban area, the greater the concentration of effluents in the urban airshed. For example, in 1970, for urban areas with 3 to 5 million population, the levels of particulates and sulfur dioxide were approximately five and seven times greater, respectively, than the levels of these effluents in nonurban areas of the country. Since these were annual averages, daytime and seasonal peaks were not reflected, yet such peaks probably result in the greatest costs of pollution. Thus, the difference in levels may understate the difference in the indirect costs of air pollution.

Other Forms of Pollution

In addition to air pollution, urbanization is a contributing cause of the indirect costs associated with other forms of pollution, especially noise. Most noise pollution problems are associated with transportation vehicles and facilities, which tend to be concentrated in urban areas (airports, for example). It is likely that the geographic dispersion of noise sources would reduce the associated indirect costs, since not only are noise sources concentrated in urban areas, but so are the people who are afflicted by the noise levels. As a result, the indirect costs are greater than if the same level of noise were emitted in an area inhabited by fewer people.

Achieving Efficient Use of the Environment

A statement of the efficiency criteria applied to environmental quality, in both the short run and the long run, is followed by a brief discussion of alternative methods for reducing pollution levels. Finally, some considerations involved in achieving the efficient level of environmental use are presented.

The Efficient Level of Environmental Quality

Figure 11-2 portrays the social costs and benefits associated with achieving a given level of environmental quality, in both the short run (MSB_S and MSC_S) and the long run (MSB_L and MSC_L). Of course, this graph abstracts from the real world the problems of identifying and measuring the social costs and benefits associated with various levels of environmental quality. Defining "environmental quality" itself is difficult, since such a definition implies an aggregate measure of the concentration of many and varied types of effluents in the air and water, as well as noise and other forms of pollution. The short run is defined here as a time period long enough to implement the best existing technology for controlling pollution, that is, the least-cost means of achieving a given level of environmental quality, given the present state of knowledge. As previously discussed, the pollution problem is a case of market failure in which the level of environmental quality attained through decisions in the market is less than the efficient level, because users of the environment do not take into

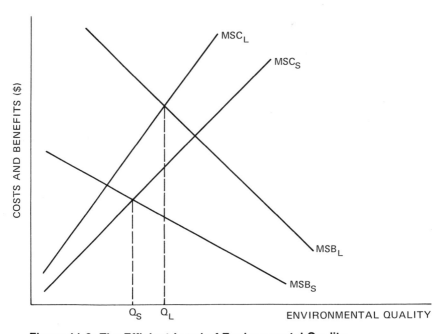

Figure 11-2: The Efficient Level of Environmental Quality

account the negative externalities associated with their actions (as shown in Figure 11-1). Thus, the short-run efficient level of environmental quality (Q_S in Figure 11-2) is a higher level than actually exists today with major unresolved cases of market failure.

In the long run, the benefits to society of a given level of environmental quality will probably increase, as implied by the long-run MSB curve lying above the short-run MSB curve. The basis for this speculation is that environmental quality appears to be a "superior good," for which demand grows as income increases. The more affluent a society becomes, the greater the demand for improved environmental quality. For example, as incomes increase and working hours decrease, more households can take vacations in the mountains and at the beaches; thus, the deterioration of such natural resources is likely to evoke more widespread concern than in the past, when fewer households could enjoy them. The superior-good aspect of environmental quality suggests why belching smokestacks were welcomed a generation ago as indicators of economic progress and prosperity, while today they are symbols of the pollution problem. As more information becomes available about the costs imposed on individuals by low levels of environmental quality, preferences regarding environmental quality are likely to change, shifting the MSB curve upward in the long run.

While it is likely that the MSB curve will shift upward in the long run, it is not obvious what sort of shift will occur in the MSC curve, where there are opposing forces at work. Since the assimilatory capacity of the environment is limited, the level of effluents associated with increasing affluence (increased production and consumption) would increase over time, other things being equal. Thus, the resources required to achieve a given level of environmental quality would also increase over time. However, other things are not equal: the technology for reducing effluent emissions might advance, so that they could be controlled at lower cost than is presently possible. The net result is difficult to predict. Thus, while the long-run MSC curve lies above the short-run MSC curve in Figure 11-2, it could in fact turn out that it will lie below it, if technological innovation is a strong enough force. In any case, the relative shifts in both the long-run benefit and long-run cost curves will determine the efficient level of environmental quality in the long run, which, as shown in Figure 11-2, is a higher level (Q_L) than in the short run (Q_S). Most observers do agree that the long-run efficient level of environmental quality is likely to be higher, although their reasons may differ.

Basic Alternatives for Reducing Pollution Levels

In order to achieve a given level of environmental quality at least cost, all options for reducing pollution levels must be considered. Either a reduction in the level of residual discharge into the environment or a reduction of the environmental costs of a given level of residuals will achieve a lower pollution level.

Reducing levels of residual discharges   One obvious but probably socially unacceptable method of residuals reduction is by cutting back production and consumption in the economy. In the heat of the argument, this approach is frequently mentioned by "environmentalist" factions; most arguments of this nature appear to be looking solely at the benefits of doing so and not considering the costs. As an example, the construction of the Alaskan oil pipeline had been delayed for several years because of environmental considerations, but, when the Arab oil embargo was imposed in late 1973, the pipeline was quickly approved. Society perceived the foregone benefits of a reduced energy supply as being greater than the potential environmental costs. While the approach of reducing consumption has a high cost associated with it in the short run (foregone benefits), in the long run such a policy could be implemented without reducing standards of living, through reducing population growth (this very long run policy will be discussed in the next chapter). However, the level of residuals discharged into the environment can be reduced by various means without reducing the output of the economy. Changing production methods to make more use of material inputs to produce a given output, thereby reducing residuals, is one such method. Closely akin to this is the recovery of materials through recycling efforts. Also, the composition of output can be changed—for example, if the auto is the major source of pollution, alternative modes of transportation may result in less pollution—and existing products could be made more durable—if the useful life of an automobile were longer, there would be fewer discarded autos to dispose of.

Reducing the environmental costs of residual discharges   The form of residuals can be changed through various methods of treatment. For example, residuals in the form of air pollutants can be changed into solids or liquids. However, such treatment does not cause them to disappear. If the amount of sulfur dioxide emitted from smokestacks is reduced by means of abatement equipment, there will be some offsetting increase in the amount of the residual in another form (liquid or solid) that must either be disposed of or recycled. While the treatment of effluents to change their form does not change the total amount of residuals, it can reduce the costs imposed on the environment. Sulfur dioxide emitted into the air may result in greater disposal costs (including indirect costs) than if it is collected from stack gases in the form of a solid and disposed of in some less harmful way, such as burial or perhaps recycling. (The term "collecting" may mean changing the sulfur dioxide into another compound.)

Given the type and quantity of residuals discharge, the amount of pollution caused by disposing of them may be lessened by altering the time or place of such discharges. As discussed in a previous section, air pollution is largely caused by urbanization, since the concentration of jobs and people results in a concentration of pollution sources in urban airsheds, overloading their capacity . If the total exhaust emissions of autos in the Los Angeles area were more evenly distributed among several airsheds outside of the Los Angeles basin, the resulting concentration of effluents and level of pollution (the level of the indirect costs) would be less. Alternatively, given the existing level of urbanization, land-use policy could be designed to control future locations of industrial emitters of effluents, perhaps locating them downwind of major population centers.

Since the assimilatory capacity of the atmosphere varies not only with characteristics of airsheds but also with the time of day or year, the timing of effluent discharges may also be an important determinant of the costs imposed on the environment. For example, if peak-hour traffic emissions occurred during times of the day when thermal inversions only rarely occurred, the emissions would be cleared away from the ground rather than being trapped by thermal inversions. Also, high smokestacks, which discharge effluents into the air at places where air circulation is better than at ground level, may reduce costs because of quicker dilution and dispersal of the effluents.

Achieving a Given Level of Environmental Quality at Lowest Cost

Achieving the efficient level of environmental quality, in either the long or the short run (as shown in Figure 11-2), implies that the level will be achieved at least cost; otherwise, the marginal cost of achieving a given level will be above the MSC curve. In other words, an efficient allocation of resources implies using the smallest amount of resources that will achieve a given environmental goal; otherwise, the resources used to achieve the last few units of environmental quality have a more efficient use elsewhere, generating greater benefits. Certain implicit criteria are behind what has been discussed in this chapter regarding pollution problems, their causes, and potential means of reducing them. These criteria are briefly discussed below as the source of a framework to be applied to pollution problems in Chapter 12.

As discussed at Figure 11-1, the pollution problem stems from greater than efficient use of a common property resource, for which the market fails to ration use. Individuals using the environment do not take into account the indirect costs of their activities. Thus, an efficient pollution policy requires that polluters be faced with the social costs of their production and consumption decisions—the private costs they already incur plus the indirect costs associated with their use of the environment as a receptacle for wastes. With respect to Figure 11-1, this means that polluters need to be faced with the MSC curve rather than with the MPC curve, so that they will maximize net social benefits. If a policy results in marginal private costs being equated with marginal social costs, then outcomes which maximize (the new) net private benefits will maximize net social benefits as well, since the negative externality will be taken into consideration. In other words, the use of the environment for effluent disposal purposes needs to be rationed in a manner such that those who receive the greatest benefits from using it for disposal purposes do so and pay a price equal to the opportunity cost (foregone benefits) of the lower environmental quality involved.

Second, pollution policies must be technologically neutral to provide the incentive for individual polluters to seek the least-cost means of reducing emission levels. Depending on the costs and benefits involved in different situations, the least-cost means of reducing pollution in some cases may be the treatment of effluents to convert them from gases to solids, whereas in other cases it may be building a higher smokestack. Thus, pollution policies should not foreclose any of the potential means of reducing pollution levels.

Third, knowledge of the costs and benefits involved with pollution are far from perfect today and there is a cost involved in generating information on them. Thus, other things being equal, the pollution policy that minimizes information requirements and has fewer "transaction costs" (the manpower, time, and effort required to make a decision) will be preferred. Since any pollution policy involves some form of market intervention to correct for the cases of market failure that result in inefficient use of the environment, there will always be resource costs involved in the administration of such a policy. However, the costs of administering alternative policies may vary considerably.

Fourth, water, air, and other forms of pollution cannot be considered separately and in isolation. This stems from the fact that matter is not destroyed, but merely changed in form. If the amount of residuals discharged into the air is decreased, it is likely that greater amounts will have to be disposed of via water or solid-waste treatment. As a result, reducing air pollution levels may not bring significant progress toward achieving an efficient level of environmental quality—a reduction in air pollution may be offset by an increase in water pollution. Thus, the administration of pollution control policies requires that all environmental consequences be taken into account.

The next chapter evaluates existing and proposed public policies for reducing pollution to the efficient level. Achieving pollution reduction at the lowest resource cost possible is the primary criterion for evaluating alternative policies, and the criteria discussed above will be used in making these evaluations. Suggested readings on pollution are listed at the end of Chapter 12.

REVIEW AND DISCUSSION QUESTIONS

1 Explain why pollution externalities require some form of public intervention to increase net social benefits. Under what conditions would reducing these negative externalities make society worse off?
2 Is pollution caused by urbanization?
3 What causes air pollution to be a more serious concern to society than water pollution?
4 What information is required to determine the efficient level of pollution?
5 We should strive to achieve pure water and pure air, returning watercourses to their original state and avoiding the discharge of effluents into the air. Evaluate.
6 Why are the problems of traffic congestion and pollution conceptually similar?

12 / Urban Pollution: Evaluation of Alternative Policies

The first section of this chapter discusses alternative methods of public intervention to ration the use of the environment so as to correct for the market failure that re- sults in inefficient levels of pollution. These approaches are evaluated in terms of the criteria discussed in the last section of Chapter 11. Then comes a discussion of which groups in society are likely to receive the benefits and incur the costs of im- proved environmental quality—equity considerations. Existing and proposed governmental legislation to control water and air pollution is then evaluated with reference to the framework developed before. Emphasis is placed on automobile pollution control policy because of its importance in major urban areas. The chapter concludes with some implications of rationing the use of the environment (achieving improved environmental quality) with respect to living standards, population, and urbanization.

Rationing the Use of the Environment

Achieving the efficient level of environmental quality at lowest social cost first involves setting the environmental standards to be achieved. This implies a reduction in emission levels from those that exist at present; thus, the use of the environment for waste-disposal purposes must be rationed by some form of public intervention into the mar- ketplace. Several rationing alternatives are discussed; the lowest-cost means of achieving a given reduction in emissions is likely to be the imposition of effluent fees (charges on those using the environment for waste-disposal purposes). The implementation of effluent fees in theory and practice will be discussed in some detail.

Establishing the Standards

The government could establish standards on several bases. In some cases, standards have been set for inputs, such as the sulfur content of coal burned in Chicago (to reduce the level of sulfur oxides emitted per ton of coal burned). However, such standards may not succeed in accomplishing the ultimate goal, an efficient level of environmental quality. While they may reduce the amount of residuals per unit of *input*, consequent changes in production methods may bring about a change in the amount of this input used for each unit of output, so that emissions per unit of *output* might be as great as ever. Increases in output could also add to emission of effluents, so that the overall level of environmental quality might not be improved. Similarly, standards could be set in terms of emissions, limiting the amount of pollutants that a given polluter can discharge into the environment. This sort of standard may not change the level of pollution in the long run either, since the number of polluters might increase. Thus, the only standards that relate directly to the goal of achieving efficient use of the environment are those set in terms of ambient levels of effluent concentration, where the term "ambient" refers to the overall quality of the environment, not just the quality near a specific pollution source. (Cases of high effluent concentrations near the source may be examples of negative externalities, but such cases can probably be best resolved through lawsuits.)

If the costs and benefits associated with the use of the environment as a disposal for wastes were known (as shown in Figure 11-2), it would be possible to determine the quantity of various types of pollutants that could be emitted per unit of time into the environment while maintaining the efficient level of environmental quality. Since this precise knowledge of the costs and benefits and of the resulting efficient levels of environmental quality is not available at the present time, it is unlikely that the current determination of environmental standards, through the political process, will fortuitously set the standards at the efficient level. All we really know about the efficient level of environmental quality is that it is a higher level than presently prevails and that it does not imply zero pollution. The following discussion of alternative means of rationing the use of the environment to achieve predetermined ambient standards is concerned with achieving a given standard at lowest cost, whether the standard is set at a level that achieves efficient use of the environment or is based on a "best guess" of the efficient level. In other words, while it would be ideal to be able to determine the efficient standards, the likelihood of this is slim given the present state of knowledge, but the secondary criterion of achieving any given standard at lowest cost is still applicable.

The Least-Cost Form of Rationing:
A Numerical Example

Once ambient standards have been established, they will have to be translated into total quantities of the various major effluents that can be emitted per time period in order not to exceed the concentrations established by the standards. Table 12-1 presents a simple example to illustrate the basic alternatives available and the costs of these alternatives in achieving an ambient standard. It is assumed in the table that there are three industrial plants (X, Y, and Z), which are the only sources of sulfur dioxide emissions in the airshed. The level of emissions that maximizes the net private benefits (profits) of the three firms, if they do not have to pay for the use of the environment, is shown in row A. Row B shows the marginal cost of reducing emissions of sulfur dioxide by one ton per year for each of the three firms. The example implies that the marginal cost of pollution abatement is constant—that the marginal cost of the first ton of abatement is the same as for the hundredth ton. While this is not likely to be the case in the real world, the example would be considerably complicated by introducing a complete schedule of marginal costs for each firm, and the assumption of constant marginal cost does not detract from the general conclusions. The marginal cost is assumed to be the least-cost alternative for reducing emission levels; as discussed in Chapter 11, this may involve any one of a number of alternatives, including a change in the production process or the installation of pollution abatement equipment to reduce the sulfur dioxide content of gaseous emissions. The marginal cost of abatement for each of the three firms is significantly different, illustrating the real-world fact that abatement costs are not likely to be the same for all polluters because of differences in the outputs being produced, the production technology being employed, and other considerations.

Assume, as shown by the total column in rows C, E, or G, that it has been determined with the best information available that the net social benefits of ambient air quality would be maximized in this specific airshed if total sulfur dioxide emissions were 300 tons rather than the existing 600 tons. (In the real world there would also be standards set for levels of other effluents allowed.) The question

	FIRM X	FIRM Y	FIRM Z	TOTAL
A Tons of sulfur dioxide emitted into airshed per year with no environmental rationing	100	200	300	600
B Marginal cost of reducing sulfur dioxide emissions by one ton per year	$ 10	$ 15	$ 20	—
C Reduction in emissions required to achieve standard with equal absolute reduction policy	100	100	100	300
D Cost of achieving standard with equal absolute policy (B × C)	$1,000	$1,500	$2,000	$4,500
E Reduction in emissions required to achieve standard with equal proportional reduction policy	50	100	150	300
F Cost of achieving standard with equal proportional policy (B × E)	$ 500	$1,500	$3,000	$5,000
G Reduction in emissions required to achieve standard with selective reduction policy	100	200	—	300
H Cost of achieving standard with selective reduction policy (B × G)	$1,000	$3,000	—	$4,000

Table 12-1: The Costs of Alternative Means of Achieving a Given Reduction in Emission Levels

becomes what form of rationing will achieve this result at least cost. Three approaches are illustrated in Table 12-1. The first approach requires each polluter to reduce the amount of sulfur dioxide emitted by a fixed amount, the total of which adds up to an overall reduction of 300 tons. Since there are only three polluters, this would require each firm to reduce its emissions by 100 tons, as shown in row C. Given the marginal cost to each of the three firms of achieving a one-ton reduction in emissions (row B), the total cost of this equal absolute reduction approach to achieving the ambient standard is given in row D, which is equal to row B multiplied by row C, or a total of $4,500.

An alternative approach that is frequently mentioned for rationing the use of the environment is the equi-proportional approach. Since the quantity of sulfur dioxide permitted by the ambient standard (300 tons) is one-half the total amount of emissions that occur in the absence of rationing, the equi-proportional approach requires that each polluter reduce its quantity of emissions by one-half, as shown in row E. Since the three polluters discharge significantly different amounts of the pollutant, the quantities of effluent cutbacks will differ. Multiplying required cutbacks by the marginal cost of abatement for each of the firms gives the total costs of abatement via the equi-proportional approach as $5,000 (shown in row F).

However, neither the equal absolute nor the equi-proportional approach to rationing the use of the environment achieves the ambient air quality standard at lowest cost of resources, because the marginal cost of reducing sulfur dioxide emission is significantly different for the three firms. The least-cost approach to achieving the 300-ton reduction requires that those firms that can achieve reduction at the lowest cost do so while other firms are allowed to have higher emission levels than those permitted under the other two approaches. In other words, if all polluters could achieve a reduction in sulfur dioxide emissions at the same marginal cost per ton, any method of rationing the use of the environment would result in the same cost of achieving the required reduction of 300 tons of effluents. However, this is an unrealistic assumption, and the least-cost approach requires differential treatment of polluters. Thus, in the example of Table 12-1, if the pollution control authority had perfect knowledge of the marginal costs of abatement of each firm shown in row B, it could require that firms X and Y eliminate all of their sulfur dioxide emissions while letting firm Z continue to emit at prerationing levels. This selective abatement policy would result in the ambient air quality standard being achieved at the total lowest cost of the three alternative approaches to rationing, as shown in Row H ($4,000).

Achieving the least-cost approach in the example of Table 12-1 required that the pollution control authority have perfect knowledge of the amount of sulfur dioxide emitted and the marginal cost of achieving a given reduction in emissions to each firm. In the real world, this knowledge is not obtainable by the pollution control authority, and there may be hundreds, if not thousands, of sources of each of the major pollutants in a given airshed. The administrative costs of attempting to gain information about the least-cost alternative of each polluter for each of the major pollutants would be prohibitive, but even this statement assumes that such information could be acquired at some cost. In fact, it might not be possible to get the information, regardless of costs, because each polluter would have an incentive to overstate his costs of achieving effluent reductions in order to be exempted from controls on his discharges, while other polluters would have to take up the slack and bear greater burdens in the achievement of the ambient air quality standard. In addition, the equity outcome of the selective abatement approach shown in Table 12-1 will be objectionable to firms X and Y, who have to bear all of the costs of achieving the ambient standard while firm Z, the worst polluter, bears no costs. The next section discusses a means of achieving the least-cost outcome in Table 12-1 that is practicable from the standpoint of information costs and enforcement of the standard and is also more appealing on grounds of equity.

Achieving the Least-Cost Form of Rationing: Effluent Fees

To illustrate the use of effluent fees to ration the use of the environment, the first part of this section employs an example based on Table 12-1. This is followed by a rather detailed discussion of the effects and major advantages of effluent fees compared with other mechanisms. The concluding part of this section discusses some considerations for implementing effluent fees in the real world.

An example   With reference to the example of Table 12-1, the effluent-fee approach to rationing the environment requires that polluters pay a price for using the environment for waste disposal, which is set at an amount that will achieve the ambient standard (as translated into quantity of emissions). In the example, suppose an effluent fee were established for sulfur dioxide emissions within the range of $15.01 and $19.99 per ton. Firms X and Y would maximize net private benefits subject to the effluent fee by eliminating emissions of sulfur dioxide, since their marginal costs of abatement (in row B) are less than the effluent fee and thus abatement is the lower-cost alternative. On the other hand, the marginal cost of abatement to firm Z is $20 per ton, which is greater than the amount of the effluent fee; hence, firm Z would continue to emit effluents at the rate of 300 tons per year and pay the effluent fee to the control authority. The implementation of an effluent fee has achieved the ambient air quality standard, since emissions have been reduced to 300 tons, and it has done so at least cost, $4,000. This result is no different from a selective abatement policy in which the pollution control authority, with complete knowledge of abatement costs for the polluters in an airshed, determined which firms would be permitted to emit what quantity of sulfur dioxide. Since this sort of information is never available in the real world, the least-cost selective abatement result cannot be achieved on this basis. The effluent-fee approach to rationing the use of the environment accomplishes the objective of selective abatement with a minimum of information. The pollution control authority does not need to know the costs of abatement for all polluters. All it needs to determine, probably through trial and error, is the amount of the effluent fee for each of the major effluents; the appropriate fee will result in a quantity of emissions that achieves the predetermined level of ambient environmental quality.

The effect of effluent fees in the long run   In the example of Table 12-1, it was presumed that the ambient standard was a short-run standard. With reference to Figure 11-2, the efficient level of environmental quality in the longer run is likely to be higher because of the availability of new technology that will reduce the costs of achieving any given ambient standard. The effluent fee is not only the superior approach in the short run, achieving a given standard at lowest cost, it is also superior in the long run, since it provides an incentive for polluters to continue to search for alternative production methods that will result in lower emissions and thus lower fees. In Table 12-1, it was assumed that marginal costs of abatement were constant over the entire range of emissions, but a more plausible assumption is that the marginal cost of abatement increases with the amount of abatement; thus, the imposition of effluent fees is likely to result in partial abatement by all firms, as opposed to total abatement by some firms and none by others. As a result, all firms will be paying some amount of effluent fees, since no firm will be at a zero level of emissions, given the costs of achieving complete abatement. The continuous payment of effluent fees provides an incentive to all polluters to keep searching for lower-cost methods of pollution abatement, which would lead to lower fees in the future as effluent emissions fell. Thus, an effluent fee of an amount that achieves the short-run ambient standard also provides incentives for further reductions in the long run without the necessity of further adjustments in the standard. With an effluent fee that remains in effect at constant rates, the amount of effluent fees collected with decrease (and so will the amount of effluent), because it will be more profitable to decrease emission levels by incurring additional abatement costs than to continue to pay the same level of effluent fees.

The effect of effluent fees on market resource allocation   By putting a price on the use of the environment for waste disposal, the effluent fee will change the relative prices of various commodities in the market to reflect the opportunity cost of their production and consumption. With no price attached to environmental resources, commodities that impose heavy costs on the environment are underpriced by the amount of the indirect costs, compared with commodities that do not impose such costs on the environment. Figure 12-1 shows the type of changes in prices of commodities, and in quantities produced and consumed, as the result of imposing an effluent fee to reflect the indirect costs of using the environment. MPC_u are the marginal private costs to the producer of the commodity when market failure exists. Net private benefits are maximized (but social benefits are not) at the quantity Q_u and market price P_u, since the indirect costs of the unabated sulfur dioxide emissions represent a negative externality not considered by the market. However, once the pollution control authority establishes an effluent fee, to ration the use of the local airshed to the quantity of emissions that achieves the ambient air quality standard, the costs of the producer will increase. Since it is presumed that the MPC_u curve represents the lowest cost of production, given that the environment has a zero price, any change that the producer makes is going to increase the costs over the unabated amount. MPC_s is the least-cost alternative to the producer in the short

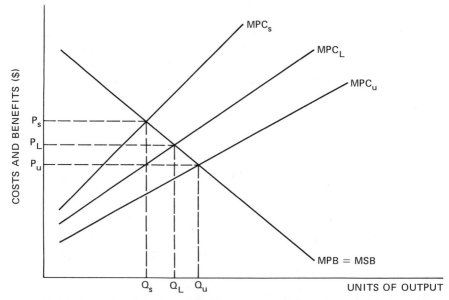

Figure 12-1: The Effect of Effluent Fees on the Output of the Polluter over Time

run, given existing abatement technology and methods. This curve represents the sum of private production costs, including abatement costs, and any effluent fees paid as the result of failure to eliminate emission completely. The quantity of output that maximizes the producer's net private benefits is now reduced to Q_s and the price increased to P_s. The result of the effluent fee has been to decrease the output of commodities that impose significant costs on the environment and increase the output of commodities that do not involve significant environmental damage, since the latter prices will be lower.

However, the effluent fees provide the producer with a continual incentive to seek even lower-cost alternatives in the long run, as better abatement technology and methods are developed and implemented. Thus, MPC_L represents the least-cost combination of producing the output, incuding abatement costs and any effluent fees paid for emissions, in the long run. Notice that the effluent emission per unit of output is lower in the long run, since the only way to reduce costs is through implementing a reduction in emissions, thereby avoiding effluent fees. By providing an incentive for further reduction in effluent emissions in the long run, the effluent-fee approach results in an output of Q_L and a price P_L, which is lower than existed just after the imposition of the fees. In both the short run and the long run, imposition of the effluent fees leads to higher prices and lower quantities of those outputs that contribute heavily to pollution. The higher prices brought about by the effluent fees lead to lower quantities being bought in the market, this in itself tending to reduce pollution. Further, in the long run, pollution is reduced even more as new abatement methods are employed, and quantities recover toward the preabatement levels. As an example, as discussed at Table 11-1, the coal-fired generation of electricity is the major contributor to sulfur dioxide emission levels. After implementation of effluent fees, the price of electricity would increase, providing an incentive for users to reduce electrical consumption wherever possible. Residential users might economize by installing better insulation in their homes and by reducing their consumption of electricity for air conditioning and heating. Thus, an increase in the price of electricity would provide an incentive to curtail use of electricity and expand use of insulation materials.

A frequently mentioned criticism of the effluent-fee approach to rationing the use of the environment is that many of the major polluters are large business firms with substantial market power who would simply pass on the effluent fee to their customers and not make the effort to reduce the amount of effluents emitted. This criticism lacks economic logic in several respects. First, if a firm can raise its price and pass on the effluent fees with no effect on quantity produced or profits, this implies that the firm could have increased its prices and profits before the imposition of the fees. If business firms strive to maximize profits, then they are somehow supposed to have been lax in this objective until the imposition of the effluent fees, which somehow snaps them back to their original objective. One conclusion is clear. Businesses cannot pass on effluent fees without losing profits unless they were previously not maximizing profits. Second, the demand curve faced by the business firm is not vertical, as would be implied by the ability to increase prices without decreasing quantities. A price increase will lead to a reduction in quantity sold, so even if no effort is made to reduce effluent discharge, the discharge will diminish because a smaller quantity will be sold. The incentive to reduce emission levels depends on the cost of paying the effluent fee versus the cost of reducing emission levels. As discussed at Table 12-1, once the reduction in quantities of effluents required to achieve a given ambient air quality standard is determined, effluent fees can be set at levels that bring about the desired emission reductions. There must be some level of fees that will provide an incentive sufficient to achieve the desired reduction in emissions; if not, then as a beginning all government revenues could be derived from effluent fees, and further uses could easily be determined. The history of the American economy indicates that firms do not usually pass up opportunities to reduce their costs. Even in the case of firms with a substantial share of the market, a strong incentive exists to reduce emission levels if the cost of doing so is less than the amount of effluent fees that would be avoided. While avoidance of most taxes and fees is frowned upon, the underlying purpose of this fee is to induce producers to avoid it by reducing emissions. Once the price of an output in an industry has been raised by the imposition of an effluent fee, every producer has an incentive to lower his marginal private costs by substituting abatement for the payment of fees in order to earn high profits while the industry price is still high. As more firms substitute abatement for effluent fees, output prices will fall, and firms continuing to pay the effluent fees will not be able to compete.

Other advantages of effluent fees   Rationing the use of the environment with effluent fees meets the criteria introduced in the previous chapter for achieving a given level of environmental quality at least cost. First, the costs of using the environment for disposal of residuals are placed on the polluter, thereby getting him to take into account the indirect costs of production. Effluent fees are technologically neutral, not biased toward any one of the possible alternatives for reducing pollution levels on the part of each individual producer. As shown in the example of Table 12-1, they achieve rationing of the environment with minimum information costs, not requiring that the costs of abatement for each polluter be known, but still achieving the least-cost means of pollution abatement through individual responses to the effluent fee. Effluent fees can also consider water, air, and other forms of pollution together, since they can be applied to all known major sources of effluents at whatever rate is required to achieve predetermined ambient environmental standards.

In conjunction with the criteria for achieving the least-cost form of rationing, it is worth noting that effluent fees are the only means of rationing that does not require setting a time deadline for meeting a standard. When the environment is rationed by setting emission standards for various polluters through the issuance of permits or other means, the polluter is forced to meet the standard by the time deadline. This may lead to the hasty implementation of high-cost alternatives, although a much lower-cost method may be developed a year after the deadline has to be met (or may presently exist, but the polluter does not have time to find out about it). As a result, the deadline tends to violate the criterion of technological neutrality. This problem with deadlines will be discussed subsequently in relation to automobile pollution abatement policy. The problem of time deadlines forcing premature abatement decisions is avoided only by a policy of effluent fees, since the individual polluter always has the option of paying the fees as opposed to choosing an abatement alternative.

An alternative that is often considered to be a good substitute for effluent fees is the creation of a market for pollution rights. In the example of Table 12-1, suppose the pollution control authority determined that emissions of sulfur dioxide had to be reduced to 300 tons per year to achieve the ambient environmental quality standard set. The pollution control authority could hold an auction in which the "rights" to emit 300 tons of sulfur dioxide were sold to the highest bidder. In this case, firm Z would bid the highest for all 300 tons of pollution rights, bidding more than \$15 per ton but less than \$20. Neither firm X nor firm Y would bid this high, since their pollution abatement costs are lower. While the result is the same for the example of Table 12-1 as with the effluent-fee approach, in the real world, the pollution rights market implicitly involves setting a time deadline and not allowing emission levels in excess of the rights sold, although a much lower cost abatement alternative may be on the horizon. The pollution rights market approach provides an incentive for local polluters to exert political pressure to have the ambient standards lowered and resulting emission levels increased; the problem is lessened with the effluent-fee approach, since the polluter always has the option of paying the fee as opposed to reducing emission levels.

While direct-control approaches to pollution regulation involve setting emission standards for each individual polluter, the costs of administering such a scheme are likely to be quite high. Not only is a large amount of information required about the abatement costs of each polluter, there are also high costs involved in enforcing the determined emission standards. Since a violation of pollution regulations is usually a criminal offense, it is necessary that the prosecution of such offenses proceed through the court system, which is time-consuming and costly. To the extent that fines for exceeding emission standards are lower than the costs of abatement, polluters have an incentive to stall via legal maneuvers and extended negotiations with pollution control authorities, haggling over the level of emission standards.

Not only do effluent fees minimize the costs of information required to achieve the least-cost means of abatement, it is likely that the enforcement and regulation costs of this approach are also smaller than those involved in a system of direct controls. An effluent-fee system could operate in a way similar to the existing income tax system, in which individual polluters would be responsible for determining their levels of effluent discharge and for reporting these, along with appropriate effluent fee payments, to the pollution control authority. Dischargers would have to install monitoring equipment and the accuracy of this equipment and the amount of discharge of effluents would be subject to audit by the pollution control authority in much the same way that income tax returns are subject to audit. As opposed to the direct-controls approach, there is little latitude for bargaining over emission standards or engaging in stalling tactics. As a result, administrative costs are reduced and it must be remembered that these are as much a part of the costs of abatement as are the costs of recycling or investing in pollution control equipment. As is the case with the income tax system, the effluent-fee approach would primarily rely on voluntary compliance subject to audit and penalties for failure to comply. As a result, the costs of administering and enforcing such a system are likely to be smaller than for alternative methods of rationing the environment.

Implementing effluent fees in the real world   Pollution control authorities equal in geographic area to the dimensions of the airsheds and watersheds, would be established for the entire nation in similar fashion to the presently existing air- and water-quality regions established under federal legislation. To avoid political pressure being brought to bear by major local polluters for relaxed environmental quality standards, the federal government might have to set the local standards of environmental quality and levels of effluent fees. This would help insulate local pollution control authorities from local political pressures. Having identified the major types of effluents and the reduction in emission levels required to achieve the ambient standards in the air- and watersheds, the pollution control authority would set effluent fees for each of the major air and water effluents at a level based on the best available estimates of the rate required to achieve the desired level of effluent discharges.

Having identified all pollution sources of any significance, the pollution control authority would require the installation of such monitoring equipment as presently exists for measuring the amounts of the various major effluents. The authority could either provide each polluter with standardized monitoring equipment to insure uniformity and accuracy or could certify certain monitoring equipment as meeting its standards for accuracy. To the extent that accurate and relatively inexpensive monitoring equipment for certain types of effluents does not presently exist, the nationwide implementation of effluent fees would create a tremendous incentive in the marketplace for the development of such equipment. In cases where monitoring equipment does not presently exist, the pollution control authority could require that periodic samples be taken and analyzed in lieu of continuous monitoring. In terms of compliance, the authority would take periodic samples itself to check against the amounts of various pollutants reported.

Once the fee rate was set for the various effluents (after some initial trial and error), there would have to be some legally established guarantee that the rates would not be changed for a minimum period of time. Otherwise, the incentives provided by effluent fees for polluters to seek the least-cost means of reducing pollution levels would be defeated. Polluters who expected effluent fee rates to go up or down significantly in the near future would have less incentive to reduce pollution levels until the fee uncertainty was resolved. If rates were lowered, the abatement might be more costly than paying effluent fees, while, if rates were raised, abatement equipment might be less costly. Thus, some guarantee would have to be given that effluent fees would remain in some relatively narrow range for some specific period of time.

While effluent fees could effectively resolve most sources of the pollution problem, there would still probably be a role for the administrative-legal approach that has been extensively used. For example, the indirect costs associated with some pollutants may justify totally banning their discharge on the basis of maximizing net social benefits. Among such pollutants would be radioactive wastes and the discharge of heavy metals (such as mercury), which work their way up the food chain, into the watercourses. Conceptually, effluent fees would work in such cases (if they were set extremely high, like the tax on the transfer of machine guns), but an equivalent approach is simply to ban extremely harmful effluents.

Equity Aspects of Improved Environmental Quality

Achieving the efficient use of the environment for waste-disposal purposes would have significant impacts with respect to the distribution of social benefits and costs among business, labor, and households in different income groups. This distribution of net social benefits will depend on the means employed to ration the use of the environment as well as the reduction in pollution levels by type of effluent and geographic area affected.

Effects on Business and Labor

As discussed in Chapter 11, the failure of the private market to efficiently ration the use of the environment stems from its being a common property resource, which results in a lack of enforceable property rights. In the absence of such property rights, business firms and other polluters have used the environment to dispose of wastes *as if* they had the property rights. Any form of public intervention into the market to correct for negative externalities involves some interference with these existing de facto property rights. Any government appropriation of wealth that is considered to be private property raises a major equity conflict. For example, if a pollution control authority establishes emission standards for various polluters, even though the polluters are not made to pay for their use of the environment, their unlimited right to use the environment in this way has been restricted. This equity conflict may be the major reason that, while economists have been advocating the superiority of the effluent-fee approach for many years, there has been little political enthusiasm for it. The implementation of effluent fees would result in a major wealth and income redistribution, since polluters would now have to pay for the use of the environment. The effluent-fee approach results in a direct and obvious redistribution of income from polluters to those who use the environment for purposes other than waste disposal, and polluters have a vested interest in preventing this outcome. Effluent fees would probably hit polluters harder than any other approach to rationing the use of the environment, because in the absence of effluent fees, the permitted amount of use of the environment is still priced at zero (unlike the effluent-fee approach), even though the polluters have to incur abatement costs in getting emissions down to the allowed level. Given the strong political and lobbying influence of certain industries, it is not difficult to understand the political difficulties associated with legislation to ration the environment by the use of effluent fees.

Any form of environmental rationing that increases the costs of polluters, such as effluent fees, will have effects on costs, output, and profits, as indicated by Figure 12-1. Increased costs are likely to reduce profits and, in some cases, the business firm faced with the full costs of its production activity (including the indirect costs) may be in a position where the least-cost alternative is simply to go out of business. This would be especially true in the case of industries that are major pollution sources, where some of the industrial plants are old and use obsolete technology. In such plants the costs of abatement could be prohibitive, leading them to shut down. To the extent that the output of some business firms is reduced or that some polluters go out of business, pollution abatement will result in a certain amount of unemployment in some industries.

From an equity standpoint, society may decide to provide subsidies for the dislocations caused by pollution control policies. Subsidies that cover the costs of abatement are likely to result in major inefficiencies (as discussed in the next section of this chapter, which evaluates current pollution programs). Any industrial plant that has to shut down because of an efficient pollution control program is likely to be an inefficient producer; subsidizing such plants would merely tend to subsidize inefficiency. However, subsidies to labor to cushion the impact of unemployment brought about by pollution control programs could be justified on equity grounds and would not subsidize inefficiency. Such programs could be directed at the goal of achieving the re-employment of labor through some combination of retraining and relocation allowances as well as unemployment compensation.

Effects on Households in Different Income Groups

To the extent that costs of pollution abatement are reflected in higher prices for commodities (as discussed at Figure 12-1), the vertical equity outcome with respect to income is likely to be somewhat regressive, since lower-income households tend to spend a greater percentage of their income on goods and services and save less than higher-income households. With respect to the distribution of benefits from improved environmental quality, the major benefit of better water quality, as previously discussed, is recreational opportunities. Higher-income households are predominant users of many types of recreational facilities, especially those that require additional equipment (such as boats and water-skis) and long-distance travel for their enjoyment. On the other hand, when watercourses going through central cities are significantly improved, the large concentration of low-income people near such watercourses may enjoy increased benefits through expanded opportunities for water-based recreation.

The distribution of the benefits of improved air quality are likely to be more progressive, since, at least in urban areas, the major improvements are likely to occur in central cities heavily populated by the poor. The concentration of air pollutants tends to be much higher in the inner city than in outlying portions of the urban area. Given the

geographic distribution of households by income and the concentration of air pollutants in various parts of the urban area, inner-city
lower-income households are currently exposed to higher air pollution levels, as indicated by the data in Table 12-2 for three major urban
areas. Thus, improvements in air quality in urban areas are likely to
have their greatest impact on low-income households.

An Evaluation of Major Existing Pollution Programs and Alternatives

The major federal legislative acts pertaining to air and water pollution
are evaluated with respect to efficiency in this section. The criteria for
achieving efficient use of the environment discussed at the end of the
preceding chapter are employed, and these legislative programs are

INCOME ($ THOUSANDS)	SUSPENDED PARTICULATES	SULFATION
Kansas City		
0-3	76.7	.22
3-5	72.4	.20
5-7	66.5	.18
7-10	63.5	.17
10-15	60.1	.15
15-25	57.6	.14
25 and over	58.1	.12
St. Louis		
0-3	91.3	.97
3-5	85.3	.88
5-7	79.2	.78
7-10	75.4	.72
10-15	73.0	.68
15-25	68.8	.60
25 and over	64.9	.52
Washington, D. C.		
0-3	64.6	.82
3-5	61.7	.82
5-7	53.9	.75
7-10	49.7	.69
10-15	45.5	.64
15-25	43.2	.58
25 and over	42.0	.53

**Table 12-2: Air Pollution Exposure Indices by Income for Three Urban
Areas**
SOURCE: Council on Environmental Quality, *Environmental Quality: Second Annual Report*,
Government Printing Office, (Washington, August 1971), p. 195.

compared with alternative policies. Special emphasis is placed on automobile pollution policy because of its importance to the pollution problem in major urban areas.

Water Pollution

The major piece of water pollution legislation is the federal Water Pollution Control Act Amendments of 1972. A general evaluation of this act is followed by a discussion of the difficulties associated with its main purpose—subsidizing polluters to reduce the amount of effluents they discharge into watercourses.

General evaluation   The 1972 legislation provides for the continuation of certain policies implemented in previous years and adds several important new ones. The law's basic regulatory requirement is that "point-source" dischargers, such as industrial firms and municipal sewage plants, must obtain a permit specifying allowable amounts and types of effluents and a time schedule for achieving compliance with the limits specified in the permit. With reference to the discussion at Table 12-1, the Environmental Protection Agency (EPA) will have to determine an ambient water-quality standard to be achieved by some future date. Whether this ambient standard will be the efficient level of environmental quality or not will depend on knowledge of the costs and benefits involved and whether such information is exploited in determining the standard (see Figure 11-2). Once the ambient standard is fixed, the question is whether the various policies of selective abatement to be applied to point sources of effluents will achieve this standard at lowest cost. The 1972 Water Pollution Amendments do not use effluent fees but authorize the establishment of emission standards for various pollution sources. EPA is to issue "effluent guidelines" for major types of pollution sources and the permits issued must be consistent with these guidelines. Instead of being based on the benefits and costs involved, the emission standards are intended to be based on what the best existing technology will achieve. Rather than achieving an ambient environmental quality standard through some form of rationing, the legislation appears to reverse this process by setting emission standards to be achieved by a certain date, based on the best existing abatement technology, so that the water-quality level achieved will be whatever the emission standards achieve. In addition to the industrial emission standards, municipal treatment plants must achieve secondary water-treatment standards (defined below) by 1977.

Also by 1977, industrial pollution sources must comply with EPA's effluent guidelines prescribing "best practicable control technology currently available." Stricter effluent limitations for both industry and municipalities will be required in individual cases if best practicable technology or secondary treatment is inadequate to meet ambient water-quality standards, which are set on the basis of water uses, such as the propagation of fish and recreation. This implies that the ambient water-quality standards will vary by watershed or by watercourse within the watershed. By 1983, municipalities must provide "best practicable waste treatment technology" and industries must comply with effluent guidelines prescribing "best available technology economically achievable" that will result in "reasonable further progress" toward the goal of eliminating the discharge of effluents.

These 1972 Water Pollution Control Act regulations leave a lot to be desired with respect to achieving an efficient level of environmental quality at lowest cost. For one thing, the long-range goal of total effluent elimination is obviously inefficient, since (1) pollution becomes zero at a positive level of effluent discharge, and (2) the efficient level of pollution is zero only if abatement costs are zero. It appears that short-run standards will be indirectly determined by whatever is considered to be the level of abatement that can be achieved with present technology. Such terms as "best practicable" and "best available" defy definition. The result of such legislation is likely to be a continuation of past regulatory enforcement policies, which entailed endless negotiation with polluters in order to determine what was possible. Since abiding by a regulation will increase the costs to a polluter, it is frequently less costly to hire attorneys and tie up the enforcement of pollution permits for as long as possible.

With respect to the criteria for achieving an environmental quality standard at least cost, the selective abatement policy approach of the 1972 act outlined above is not likely to be the least-cost alternative. The information required to achieve least-cost selective abatement does not exist, and the legislation is not designed to achieve least-cost abatement even if such information did exist. The enforcement and regulation costs will be high because each polluter is handled on an individual basis with respect to the effluent levels and timetable specified in the permit. Since all of the costs of using the environment are not placed on the polluter, he has an incentive to avoid these costs by prolonging negotiations and stalling with respect to the time by which the emission standards are to be achieved. Such abatement policies are not likely to be technologically neutral, since the emission standards are set on the basis of present technology and involve a time deadline. It is always possible that a much lower-cost alternative for reducing emission levels will develop soon after the deadline; thus, the time deadline restricts the options available. The goals for 1983 of making "reasonable progress" toward elimination of all effluent discharges implies a "spaceship" economy, in which all residuals are recycled. As mentioned above, the marginal social benefits of achieving very high abatement levels are likely to be much lower than the resource costs of achieving them.

The inefficiency of subsidies   Major sources of inefficiency in the federal water pollution control legislation of recent years are the subsidies provided to local governments for the construction of sewage-treatment plants and those provided to industry in the form of tax breaks for investment in pollution abatement equipment. Beginning in 1965, the federal government paid up to 55 percent of the cost of local sewage-treatment plant construction costs. The maximum subsidy has been increased to 75 percent by the 1972 amendments and the amount of subsidies authorized is $18 billion over a three-year period. As mentioned above, the 1972 legislation requires that municipal sewage plants achieve secondary treatment by 1977. Primary treatment is a process of filtering and settling that can remove approximately 40 percent of the BOD from human sewage and various percentages of other materials. Secondary treatment (combined with primary treatment) can remove between 85 and 95 percent of the BOD, while tertiary treatment can remove as much as 99 percent.

With respect to the criteria for achieving the least-cost means of abatement, the subsidy program has many inefficiencies associated with it. First, the subsidies are not technologically neutral in that the subsidy is provided only for the construction of plants, while lower-cost alternatives may exist, such as pumping wastes up- or downstream or into another watercourse where the dissolved oxygen content is sufficient to assimilate the waste. Second, the requirement that all municipal sewage plants achieve secondary treatment may be inefficient given the differences within and among watersheds. For example, within a watershed, least-cost abatement might be achieved by primary treatment at some discharge points and tertiary treatment at others, resulting in an ambient standard equal to that achieved by overall secondary treatment. Third, subsidies for construction of treatment plants provide no incentive to operate them efficiently. Local governments can reduce their costs by operating the plants inefficiently, since they bear none of the costs of the environmental deterioration. Although better sewage-treatment plants are being built with the subsidies, there is no guarantee that the BOD content of waste discharges will be lowered enough to warrant the costs, especially when the plants may not be operated efficiently.

Somewhere between 40 and 50 percent of the wastes handled by municipal sewage-treatment plants are from industrial sources. When the costs of sewage treatment are subsidized, industry indirectly receives a substantial subsidy through reduced sewer rates. Since the environmental costs are not borne by the polluters, they have no incentive to seek the least-cost means of reducing their pollution levels. On-site treatment, a change in production methods, or other alternatives are less costly in many instances than paying the full costs of treating the wastes at a municipal sewage-treatment plant. Also, the allocation of treatment plant construction subsidies among geographic areas has not been in relation to the severity of water pollution problems. In some cases, treatment plants have been built downstream from major industrial locations, so that the treated water discharged by the treatment plant was of higher quality than the water in the river into which it was discharged. As a result, the improvement in ambient water quality is much less than if the subsidy had been applied to locations, especially large cities, where the treatment of wastes would have resulted in the greatest benefit.

Similarly, tax subsidies have been given to industry for investment in water pollution abatement equipment. Many of the same difficulties applicable to sewage-plant subsidies apply to this form of subsidy, such as providing minimal incentive to seek the least-cost form of abatement. In general, the provision of subsidies to reduce the costs of abatement to the polluter are likely to be inefficient. Although the subsidies reduce the costs of abatement to the polluter, he is still better off achieving no abatement, since his costs are going to be increased by any abatement, as long as the subsidy is less than 100 percent. Even if subsidies were stated so that they were technologically neutral (that is, a reduction in emissions no matter how achieved) polluters would have a very strong incentive to overstate their initial emission levels in order to receive large subsidies for very small improvements in abatement. In an extreme case, it could even become profitable to start a business to "produce" effluents, in order to collect large subsidies for reducing this production. In summary, subsidies are likely to be an inefficient approach to achieving environmental quality standards because they fail to meet the criteria for achieving least-cost abatement.

The 1972 legislation at least attempted to correct the inefficiency associated with subsidizing the waste treatment of industrial pollutants dumped into local sewer systems. Industry that uses the local sewer system is now required to pay its share of construction costs and also to pay higher sewer rates to reflect the treatment costs of its discharges. How this will be precisely worked out has not been determined; however, the rationale is good in that it places the costs of treatment on the polluter and will provide some incentive for industry to decide between higher sewer charges and other means of reducing discharge levels.

The alternative to the unpromising approach of administrative granting of effluent permits and subsidizing certain abatement methods that has been taken by the federal government is the use of effluent fees levied on polluters. Such a bill was introduced in Congress in 1969. It would have set national effluent fees for BOD and other major effluents; however, the bill did not get out of committee, apparently reflecting the major equity conflicts associated with placing the costs of pollution on the polluters.

Air Pollution

The major piece of air pollution legislation is the Clean Air Act Amendments of 1970. The Clean Air Act required the establishment of national ambient air-quality standards to "protect public health" and the achievement of these standards by 1975. The EPA is responsible for administering the act and is permitted to grant time extensions of up to three years if methods of abatement to achieve these standards are "not available." In addition, higher environmental quality standards to "protect aesthetics, property, and vegetation" (referred to as secondary standards) must be established and achieved within a "reasonable time" as determined by EPA. In early 1971, EPA established the primary and secondary national ambient air-quality standards required in the act for the five major pollutants listed in Table 11-1 plus photochemical smog, which is formed by the interaction of two of the five pollutants, hydrocarbons and nitrogen oxides. Each state was then required by the act to submit plans to EPA for achieving these air-quality standards. Considerable delays in submitting and approving the plans have resulted and time extensions for meeting the standards have already been granted.

In addition to requiring establishment of ambient air-quality standards, that act also established emission-quality standards for automobiles for the three major automotive pollutants: carbon monoxide (CO), hydrocarbons (HC), and nitrogen oxides (NO). These standards required that 1975 new car emissions of CO and HC be 90 percent below the 1970 standards and that 1976 new car emissions of NO be 90 percent below 1970 emission standards, at which time no NO emission standards existed. However, the act permitted a one-year extension of the time deadline, if EPA determined that such an extension is "essential to the public interest or public health and welfare of the United States." Such an extension was granted in 1973. Automotive emissions standards were first established for 1968 vehicles. In subsequent years, as the number of pre-1968 autos still on the road decreased, the quantity of auto emissions has also decreased. However, while automotive emissions have been decreasing in recent years, it is not expected that these emission standards plus pollution controls on stationary sources of emissions (such as electrical generating plants) will be sufficient to achieve the primary ambient air-quality standards by the 1975 deadline for thirty-seven urban areas of the United States. As a result, EPA required the affected states to include transportation controls in the plans they submitted for achieving the ambient standards. These transportation control plans involve two basic approaches—reducing the number of miles driven, through expanded public transit or car pools, and reducing emissions per mile such as through auto emission inspections and maintenance of abatement equipment on older vehicles. Some of the initial proposals for restricting the use of autos in affected urban areas would impose severe constraints on the existing transportation systems and life styles. For example, an initial proposal for the Los Angeles area would have curtailed gasoline sales (and resulting auto use) by 82 percent from May to October, the period when the temperature inversions that trap pollutants in the Los Angeles basin are most prevalent. Obviously, such proposals have been met with numerous objections, illustrating that after some point the social costs of improving the environment greatly exceed the benefits, particularly if least-cost methods are not used.

While there is little question that a relationship exists between high concentrations of the five pollutants for which ambient standards have been set and human health, it is not at all certain at this time what the shape of the benefit curve from reducing these pollutants is. In other words, referring to Figure 11-2, the marginal social benefit curve in terms of improved human health, plant life, and other effects of air pollutants is not well known. The benefits from controlling the primary automotive pollutants (HC, CO, and NO) may be much smaller than some have estimated, except for a few urban areas where the concentrations of these pollutants is relatively high, at least during certain times of the day. For example, it is believed that the natural production of hydrocarbons, carbon monoxide, and perhaps nitrogen oxides far exceeds that from manmade sources.[1] As a result of more recent information on nitrogen oxides, EPA has decided to ask Congress to reduce the nitrogen oxide emission standards of 90 percent reduction by 1976, described above. Neither the benefits associated with the ambient air-quality standards nor the social costs of achieving these standards are well known. To achieve an efficient level of environmental quality, as discussed at Figure 11-2, we need to know both social benefits and social costs. Given the paucity of research in that area, it is unlikely that the current levels set by EPA approximate the efficient level of environmental quality.

However, even if one were to assume that EPA's ambient standards are based on the best information available as to the efficient level of environmental quality, the selective abatement approach that has been followed to achieve these standards is unlikely to be the least-cost means. The major component of this selective abatement procedure has been to establish emission standards for automobiles. Given the importance of this part of the overall strategy for achieving the

---

[1]National Academy of Sciences, *Report by the Committee on Motor Vehicle Emissions*, Washington, 1973.

ambient air-quality standards (especially in urban areas), the next section will evaluate the automobile pollution control policy established under the Clean Air Act and some potentially lower-cost alternatives.

Automobile Pollution Policy

The automotive emission standards for CO, HC, and NO set by the 1970 Clean Air Act can be considered as one of the forms of selective abatement used to achieve the ambient air standards specified by EPA. The question of whether the emission standards set for automobiles are a part of the least-cost method of selective abatement will not be dealt with here. Given the inadequate information that existed when the automotive emission standards were set, it is more than likely that some combination of abatement from all sources, perhaps involving less stringent auto standards, would be the least-cost means of achieving the ambient quality standards. For one thing, Congress set the standards, not on the basis of the costs and benefits involved, but rather on the basis of the highest level of abatement that was predicted to be technologically feasible at the time that the emission standards were to be met. The social costs and benefits of technologically feasible emissions standards may be very different from those of standards that maximize net social benefits.

The means of abatement used to achieve the automotive emission standards are not technologically neutral because of the time deadlines involved; as a result, the standards are not likely to be achieved by the least-cost means of abatement. There is always the possibility that some method will be available in the future that can achieve a given level of abatement at much lower cost. In the case of the auto, United States manufacturers planned to meet the 1975 and 1976 standards of the Clean Air Act by putting catalytic mufflers in the exhaust systems of cars. However, the National Academy of Sciences (NAS) has estimated the annual increased operating costs of achieving the 1976 standards with catalyst systems at about $270 per car per year relative to a standard 1970 model auto. This includes the cost of the hardware (the catalyst system) prorated over the first five years of the car's life, plus increases in operating and maintenance costs. One of the major components of the $270 per year is the increased fuel consumption that results from abatement with the catalyst system. On the other hand, the NAS found that a recently developed alternative, called the dual-carbureted stratified-charge engine, can probably meet the 1976 emission standards with additional annual costs per car of approximately $70.[2] The difference between the $270 and $70 per year is mostly attributable to the increased fuel consumption and

[2]Report by the Committee on Motor Vehicle Emissions, p. 4.

was estimated with gasoline prices in effect in late 1972. Of course, gasoline prices have increased substantially since 1972, and this would lead to an even greater cost difference. While the difference of $200 per car per year perhaps does not sound like a substantial one, when multiplied by the approximately 100 million cars in the United States, the difference in total annual costs is on the order of $20 billion per year. This $20 billion annual cost difference would be realized once all cars not equipped to meet 1976 standards were off the road, which would take place approximately ten years after the standards were implemented, this being the average life of a car.

With respect to the criteria for achieving the least-cost means of abatement, the establishment of emission standards to be met by a certain date does not place the indirect costs of automotive pollution on the polluter until the standards are met. Thus, an incentive is created to delay implementation of the standards, since auto manufacturers can make greater profits if they do not have to incur the costs of abatement devices, thereby reducing sales because of higher prices to consumers. Also, the auto manufacturers have an incentive to meet the standard by a method that results in the lowest costs to themselves, but may not result in the lowest social cost, since the maker incurs only the cost of the hardware and not the increased operating costs of the vehicle. The catalyst system also requires maintenance by the automobile owner to remain effective in reducing emissions. It becomes ineffective if the owner uses even one tankful of leaded gasoline. Yet the price of unleaded gasoline is higher than leaded gasoline of the same octane rating; thus, the owner would maximize net private benefits by purchasing leaded gasoline and increasing the emissions of his auto, shifting the costs onto others. Even pre-1976 auto emission control equipment significantly increases fuel consumption and decreases performance, providing an incentive for the automobile owner to have the abatement equipment disconnected.

The incentives discussed above make designing a policy to achieve given emission standards at lowest social cost rather difficult. One implication is that incentives must be provided for both the producer and the consumer of the automobile. An effluent fee placed on the producer would provide the incentive for seeking means of reducing automotive emissions whenever the cost of abatement was less than the reduction in effluent fees that would accompany an emission reduction. Placing an effluent fee on the auto user to attempt to induce him to install abatement equipment is not likely to achieve least-cost abatement, since the user has fewer options at his disposal than the manufacturer in terms of hardware. However, an effluent fee on producers has no effect on cars once they leave the factory, so that, in addition to providing incentives for manufacturers to build low-emission cars, owners need incentives to keep the auto tuned for low emission levels after it leaves the factory. An effluent fee on the auto owner would provide an incentive for maintenance. One possible way to assess the fee would be by monitoring the three major automotive effluents in connection with the annual safety inspection that is required in many areas. Emission tests are already becoming a requirement in some places. For example, beginning in 1974, autos in Chicago are required to submit to an emissions test. Instead of requiring some minimum level of abatement, fees could be charged based on emissions per mile, multiplied by the number of miles driven annually (obtained from annual odometer readings). The resulting fee could be differentiated according to whether the auto was driven in an urban airshed or a rural area. It is important that the fee not vary according to size of car or age of the vehicle. One hundred pounds of CO impose the same costs whether they come from one large limousine or one-hundred motor scooters. If older vehicles cause more pollution, a uniform fee would provide an incentive to buy a newer and cleaner car.

Effluent fees on auto owners would provide incentives to reduce fee payments through several routes. First, there would be an incentive to have more frequent tune-ups (at least just before the test, so that in practice semiannual inspections might have to be required). Second, an incentive to drive fewer miles would exist, since the effluent fee is based on annual mileage. Some of the options here include moving closer to the place of work, forming car pools, and using public transportation. Also, consumers would demand cars with lower effluent discharge, giving an incentive to auto manufacturers to build such cars. On the other hand, there would be an incentive to disconnect the odometer cable, so that miles driven would not register, and this may create problems in the implementation of auto effluent fees. Effluent fees placed on auto manufacturers (on the basis of estimated emissions over the expected life of the vehicle) generally would be passed on to the consumer, which would discriminate against consumers who operate their vehicles in areas where pollution is not a problem (like rural areas). Further, effluent fees on the producer cannot distinguish between heavy and light users in terms of miles driven per year, but this is not too important since autos that are driven fewer miles per year tend to be driven for more years. The main drawback to the implementation of effluent fees at the present time is the lack of a relatively simple, foolproof, reliable diagnostic instrument for measuring the emission levels of the three effluents. The incentive to develop such an instrument did not exist until recently, so perhaps one will become available in the near future.

In summary, without any regard for whether the standards for auto emissions established under the 1970 Clean Air Act are those that would be appropriate for achieving the efficient level of ambient air quality, the policy established to date appears to substantially deviate from one that would achieve the standard at lowest cost. The incentives that have been created are not those that would be required to meet the criteria for achieving least-cost abatement. A combination of effluent fees on both auto producers and consumers is required to achieve the appropriate incentives. However, such a fee system would have to be carefully designed to achieve the appropriate incentive structure.

Some Long-Run Implications of Rationing the Use of the Environment

Pollution is a classic case of failure of the private market. Externalities from production and consumption have increased as population and living standards have risen. Yet little has been done about these increasing indirect costs because the private market system has provided no means of taking them into account. Since the environment has traditionally been regarded as a common property resource, its users have often overused and abused it, to the point where its use must be rationed. An appropriate system of effluent fees meets the criteria of achieving environmental quality standards at lowest possible cost, and is thus the most efficient means of rationing in most cases. Effluent fees make the polluter bear the indirect costs of his activity and provide incentives to seek efficient solutions in the long run. There follows a brief discussion of some long-run implications of rationing the use of the environment.

Standards of Living and Population

The argument is frequently presented that improved environmental quality will result in a decrease in our standard of living. Certainly, the composition of output will change, since resources will have to be allocated to reducing pollution levels and output of heavy polluters may be curtailed. Thus, improved environmental quality may come at the cost of smaller cars and changing urban spatial form and population concentration. To some, such changes may imply a decreased standard of living. Traditional measures of economic well-being, such as per capita income or the aggregate measure of economic performance, gross national product (GNP), are far from perfect indicators of the welfare of society. While GNP records goods and services that add to our standard of living, it fails to take into account the indirect costs not reflected in market transactions. Further, some increases in GNP may reflect deteriorations of true standards of living, as in the case where rampant crime leads to increased police expenditure, which is recorded as an increase in GNP. Recall the basic definition of efficiency: if resources are allocated efficiently, then society's benefits (true standard of living) are maximized. Since pollution is a case where benefits are not being maximized, correcting for this inefficiency cannot help but increase society's benefits, and for most people, the true standard of living must increase, whether or not this increase in well-being is measured by an increase in GNP. As with any change of this magnitude, however, benefits and costs are not equally distributed, and some individuals may be worse off. On the whole, however, society's benefits and standard of living increase substantially if pollution is controlled.

As previously mentioned, one means of reducing the level of residuals discharged, other things being equal, is to curtail the growth in the number of consumers by population control. While the United States has recently achieved birth rates that would result in zero population growth sometime in the next century, reduction in population growth in the United States is likely to have little impact on pollution by itself. The increase in GNP is attributable more to increases in per capita standard of living than to population increases. For example, the generation of electricity is the major source of sulfur oxide emissions; 90 percent of the increase in electricity consumption in the last thirty years is due to increase in per capita consumption and only ten percent to population increase.[3] On the other hand, in a large part of the world, increases in GNP are attributable to increases in population rather than to increases in per capita consumption. Thus, in low-income countries, population control is a major component in the strategy of increasing environmental quality.

Urbanization and Urban Form

As will be discussed in Chapter 16, there are many economic advantages to the concentration of economic activity in cities; however, this concentration directly contributes to some forms of pollution, especially air pollution. Thus, policies that result in producers and consumers individually bearing the costs of their environmental use will probably provide an incentive to counter the existing market incentives for urbanization. To some extent, these policies will also counter the forces resulting in the spatial separation of place of residence and place of employment within urban areas and the superiority of the auto as the transportation mode that supports this decentralization of jobs and people. When the indirect costs of using the environment have to be taken into account, individuals will tend to live closer to the work place and choose travel modes other than the auto.

[3]"A Disposable Feast," *Resources*, No. 34 (June 1970), 1; adapted from a paper by Hans Landsberg, presented at an environmental teach-in in Pittsburgh, April 1970.

REVIEW AND DISCUSSION QUESTIONS

1 Effluent fees are an ineffective way of rationing the use of the environment to achieve the efficient level of pollution, since the fees levied on polluters will just be passed on to consumers in the form of higher product prices and there will be no reduction in pollution levels. Evaluate.

2 The Externality Motorcycle Corporation produces vehicles that emit a level of noise exceeding 100 decibels. What should be done to determine whether public intervention is required? If intervention is required, what should be the basic goal? Describe and define what you would consider to be the efficient public policy for achieving this goal.

3 If use of the environment had been rationed by effluent fees in the past, there would be little concern over pollution problems today. Evaluate.

4 Educating the public on the subject of ecology is the best way to eliminate the negative externalities of pollution. Evaluate.

5 Why is the present automobile pollution abatement policy likely to be inefficient? (Note: this sets emission levels for hydrocarbons, carbon monoxide, and nitrogen oxides that auto makers must meet by certain dates.)

6 Both the benefits and the costs of reducing pollution are likely to be distributed regressively. Discuss.

7 Why are subsidies to polluters to reduce their pollution levels likely to be inefficient?

8 Reducing pollution requires the use of resources that could have been used to increase standards of living. Evaluate.

SUGGESTED READINGS

Ayres, Robert U. "Air Pollution in Cities." *Natural Resources Journal* (January 1969), 1 - 22. (Reprinted in Arthur F. Schreiber. Paul K. Gatons, and Richard B. Clemmer, eds. *Economics of Urban Problems: Selected Readings.* Boston: Houghton Mifflin, 1971.)

Council on Environmental Quality. *Environmental Quality.* Washington: Government Printing Office. (Published annually since 1970. The best single source of information on environmental data and legislation.)

Gerhardt, Paul H. "Incentives to Air Pollution Control." *Law and Contemporary Problems* (Spring 1968) 358 - 368. (Reprinted in Schreiber et al.)

Mills, Edwin. "Economic Incentives in Air Pollution Control." In *Ecology and Economics: Controlling Pollution in the 70's*, edited by Marshall Goldman, pp. 142 - 148. Englewood Cliffs, N.J.: Prentice-Hall 1972.

Revelle, Roger. "Pollution and Cities." In *The Metropolitan Enigma*, edited by J. Q. Wilson, pp. 96 - 143. Garden City, N.Y.: Doubleday, Anchor Books, 1970.

Teller, Azniel. "Air Pollution Abatement: Economic Rationality and Reality." *Daedalus* (Fall 1967), 1082 - 1098.

13 / Crime

The benefit-cost framework developed in earlier chapters can also be applied to the analysis of crime. A potential criminal considers the expected private benefits of a crime (perhaps money or property) as well as the expected private costs (for example, the opportunity cost of time spent in prison). However wrongful his act in the eyes of society, the criminal can be viewed as rationally choosing to commit an amount of crime that maximizes his net private benefits. The implication is that crime prevention can be viewed as the attempt to lower the private benefits of the criminal or to raise his private costs, thereby lowering the amount of crime where net private benefits are maximized. Another implication is that, if certain members of society have lower opportunity costs than others (the chronically unemployed forego little income while incarcerated), they will tend to choose to commit greater amounts of crime, regardless of moral and other noneconomic considerations. The social benefits and costs of crime must be determined if society is to achieve the efficient level of crime (in terms of allocation of resources to crime prevention). Surprisingly, driving a vehicle under the influence of alcohol (DUI) appears to be the crime with the highest social cost.

A crime is an illegal activity. While certain laws make sense on economic grounds, such as the prevention of negative externalities through the outlawing of murder, other laws may be based on cultural or religious grounds quite unrelated to economic efficiency or equity. Our approach is pragmatic. Regardless of the initial reasoning behind certain laws, the existing body of criminal law defines the criminal act.

Crime as an Economic Problem

An examination of crime statistics indicates that most crime is economically motivated, in the sense that the objective of committing the crime is to acquire property (including money) in order to enhance the criminal's standard of living. Is the amount of crime (the crime rate) increasing over time? While official statistics indicate a large increase, this is still a difficult question to answer, for reasons discussed subsequently. Do we have too much crime? There is some efficient level of crime, perhaps less than the present level, but certainly greater than zero. The social costs and benefits of crime must be determined in order to achieve the efficient allocation of society's resources to crime prevention. Once efficiency is attained, attempts to lower the amount of crime further would decrease society's benefits—additional costs would exceed the additional benefits generated.

Amount and Types of Crime

Unfortunately, available data on crime and other aspects of the criminal justice system are quite inadequate. The only major reporting source for crime statistics is the FBI *Uniform Crime Reports* (UCR). The UCR annually present data on only seven crimes that are generally referred to as "index crimes." These seven crimes, for which data are presented in Table 13-1, are commonly classified into violent crimes (crimes against persons) and property crimes. The violent crimes are willful homicide, forcible rape, aggravated assault (assault with the intent to maim or kill, whether or not a dangerous weapon is used), and robbery (the taking of property from a person by use or threat of force with or without a weapon). The three property crimes do not involve threats or actual injuries to persons; they are burglary, auto theft, and larceny over $50 (theft of property). Of the 3,413 index crimes per 100,000 population in SMSAs in 1972, 493 were violent crimes and 2,920 were property crimes (as shown in Table 13-1). Thus, property crimes make up about 86 percent of total index crimes. Also, robberies are about 49 percent of total violent crimes; since violence or potential violence is likely to be incidental to obtaining money or property in a robbery, it can be concluded that at least 93 percent of the seven index crimes involve taking some form of property, including money. Thus, most crimes considered "serious" by the FBI involve economic motivations.

While adequate crime data exist only for the seven FBI index crimes, these particular crimes do not necessarily include those with the highest economic cost or those most frequently occurring. From the standpoint of society, the crimes that probably concern people most are those that affect their personal safety at home, at work, or on the streets. The most frequent and serious of these crimes against persons are the four violent crimes included in the FBI crime index. Knowledge of the number of nonindex crimes depends on arrest statistics, which understate the number of crimes, since many may not result in arrests. On the basis of arrest statistics, "victimless crimes" account for a large proportion of total arrests. As opposed to crimes against persons or property, victimless crimes involve some form of illegal behavior (such as indecent exposure or the sale of liquor to minors). Drunkenness accounts for almost one-third of all arrests, with disorderly conduct ranking second (accounting for more than 10 percent of total arrests). None of the FBI index crimes against persons ranks in the top ten arrest categories and the three index crimes against property only account for somewhere between 10 and 15 percent of total arrests.

Is the amount of crime or the crime rate increasing over time? This is a difficult question to answer for several reasons. The FBI has been collecting data on the seven index crimes since 1930; based on these

GEOGRAPHIC AREA	TOTAL INDEX CRIMES	CRIMES AGAINST PERSONS					PROPERTY CRIMES		
		MURDER	RAPE	AGGRAVATED ASSAULT	ROBBERY	AUTO THEFT	LARCENY ($50 AND OVER)	BURGLARY	
Total United States	2,830	9	22	187	180	423	883	1,126
Total SMSAs	3,413	10	27	212	244	552	1,028	1,341
Cities								
Over 1 million (6)	5,100	22	47	405	787	1,008	968	1,863
500,000 - 1 million (21)	4,890	19	52	332	453	998	1,212	1,825
250,000 - 500,000 (31)	4,755	17	40	289	376	858	1,206	1,970
100,000 - 250,000 (96)	4,173	11	27	246	219	687	1,276	1,708
50,000 - 100,000 (254)	3,219	6	19	165	132	480	1,163	1,253
25,000 - 50,000 (481)	2,825	5	15	145	102	389	1,102	1,066
10,000 - 25,000 (1,224)	2,281	4	12	129	55	244	944	894
Under 10,000 (2,972)	2,068	4	12	143	45	203	872	789
Suburban areas (SMSAs excluding central city)	2,364	5	17	128	72	288	891	963
Rural areas	1,084	7	11	109	16	70	364	508

Table 13-1: FBI Index Crimes per 100,000 Population in the United States, by Geographic Area (1972)

SOURCE: Federal Bureau of Investigation, *Uniform Crime Reports for the United States, 1972*, Government Printing Office, Washington, 1973, pp. 61, 102 - 103. Numbers in parentheses are the number of cities falling in each given population-size category.

reported data, the crime rate has been increasing. For example, between 1960 and 1970, the number of index crimes per 100,000 population increased from 1,126 to 2,907, or an average annual increase of 9 percent.[1] However, these data are subject to many qualifications. In 1965, the President's Commission on Law Enforcement conducted a survey of households, which indicated that a large number of index crimes are not reported to the police and are thus not included in the above data. The amount of crime against persons from the survey was almost twice that shown by the UCR and property crimes were more than twice the UCR levels.[2] In some cases, increased crime rates can have positive connotations. For example, one of the measures of success of programs designed to encourage women to report rapes is an increase in the number reported.

The UCR are based on voluntary reporting by police departments in the United States. The methods by which local police departments collect data are often inconsistent. For example, before 1950 the New York City police department allowed precincts to handle and record complaints directly. In 1950 the department switched to a central reporting system through which citizens had to route all calls. In the first year, robberies "increased" 400 percent and burglaries 1,300 percent because of the change in procedures. Also, what is considered to be a crime may change over time (e.g., prohibition of alcohol in the 1920s) and, as discussed, the FBI crime reports cover only a small number of total crimes, so that it is difficult to reach conclusions as to how much crime has increased, and even whether it has increased. However, if the UCR data on crimes against persons are at all reliable, these crimes have been increasing over time, and these are the crimes of most concern to most members of society. Thus, there has been an increasing emphasis on crime as a social problem in recent years.

The Efficient Amount of Crime: Social Benefits and Costs

Disregarding the costs of reducing crime, people always prefer less crime to more; however, if those concerned about crime are willing to sacrifice some private consumption in return for an increase in resources allocated to crime prevention, then the present amount of crime is greater than the efficient amount. There is some efficient level of crime, perhaps less than the present level, but certainly greater than zero, since for crime to be eliminated would require almost all of society's resources. As a minimum, people would have to

[1]Federal Bureau of Investigation, *Uniform Crime Reports for the United States, 1970,* Government Printing Office, Washington.

[2]President's Commission on Law Enforcement and Administration of Justice, *The Challenge of Crime in a Free Society,* Government Printing Office, Washington, 1967, p. 21.

be isolated from each other so that there would be no potential victims. Determining the efficient amount of crime requires knowledge of the social costs and benefits associated with various amounts of crime prevention, and hence levels of crime. The social benefits of crime reduction are equivalent to reductions in the social costs that result from lesser amounts of crime.

What should be included in the calculation of costs of crime to society and, thus, potential benefits from crime prevention? The cost of crimes against persons is obviously difficult to measure, especially if the crime is murder. One way to approach this measurement problem is to estimate the loss of production caused by crime. For example, if an aggravated assault causes a loss of work to the victim, at least part of the cost of the crime can be measured by the loss in wages. There may also be measurable costs in the form of medical expenses and unmeasurable costs such as pain suffered by the victim and his family. There may be permanent injury and a reduced ability to work (a loss of human capital), in which case the present value of future wage losses must be considered.

The value of property destroyed or stolen can be more easily measured than the cost of crimes against persons, but there are conceptual problems in the use of such figures. Arson results in the destruction of physical capital, and thus society's total resources are reduced by the value of that capital. The theft of money or property, however, may be looked on as a forced redistribution of income or property, similar to an arbitrary tax. There is obviously property loss to the victim, but there may at first appear to be no *net* loss to society as a whole, just a forced transfer of property from one member of society to another. There are real losses, which take the form of the value of resources diverted to activities and devices designed to prevent the forced transfer. In addition, losses may take the form of smaller production of goods and services, if potential theft reduces the incentive to acquire property. Thus, theft may reduce the amount of work effort and savings.

Those who are not direct victims of criminal acts may also be adversely affected. For example, shoplifting results in an increase in the prices paid for goods and services (and thus a decrease in purchasing power), because business firms must recoup losses of merchandise or cover additional costs of security or insurance. Insurance rates may be higher because of automobile and other property theft. Automobile safety violations that result in accidents increase the insurance rates of those not involved in the accidents.

What is the magnitude of these social costs of crime? As indicated above, there are conceptual problems associated with estimation of such costs. In 1965, the President's Commission on Law Enforcement estimated that the "cost" of crime in the United States was about $21 billion. As a measure of the social costs of crime, this estimate is very crude. For example, some social costs are not included, such as the pain and suffering of crime victims. On the other hand, the estimated dollar value of forced transfers is included in this amount, which, as indicated above, may not be a true cost to society but rather the involuntary transfer of property from one person to another. Estimated costs of crimes against persons (primarily loss of earnings due to the destruction or impairment of human capital) were about $815 million. The dollar magnitude of property crimes was estimated to be about $4 billion; most of this is forced transfers and not genuine social costs. The FBI index property crimes accounted for less than one-sixth of this amount, while employee theft, embezzlement, and other crimes involving business, which appear in relatively small numbers in police statistics, loom very large in dollar volume. Direct stealing of cash and merchandise, manipulation of accounts and stock records, and other forms of these crimes, along with shoplifting, make up the majority of the $4 billion. One real cost included in this amount is $300 million for property destroyed by arson and vandalism.

The amount estimated by the commission for "driving under the influence" was $1.8 billion. Most of this is probably due to the social cost of damage to human and physical capital and is therefore a real economic cost. Assuming that this $1.8 billion is a true measure of the social costs of driving under the influence of alcohol, the amount is greater than the estimate for all seven index crimes combined. The estimated net profits associated with the provision of illegal goods and services (victimless crimes) is $8 billion. The extent to which this amount is a real economic cost would be difficult to determine. As discussed above, most of the FBI index crimes appear to be economically motivated. Similarly, from the standpoint of the social costs of crime, most of the social costs appear to stem from economic motivations.

Crime prevention costs include both the public costs of the criminal justice system and additional costs incurred by individuals to avoid being victimized by crime. Public expenditures for all levels of government and for local government for 1960 and 1971 are shown in Table 13-2, and it can be seen that total money expenditures for all governments and for local government more or less tripled during the eleven-year period. Even after deflating the 1971 expenditures to dollars of 1960 purchasing power, they more than doubled. About 85 to 90 percent of all police costs are for salaries and wages, with a fairly small percentage spent for equipment and research; the relatively high proportion of labor costs is one reason why criminal justice system costs have grown so rapidly (the reasons are discussed at Table 14-3). Not all police expenditures are for crime prevention; 10 to 15 percent of local police time is spent on traffic control. In 1965, the commission estimated that about $4.2 billion were expended in the criminal justice system for crime prevention. The commission

	1960 EXPENDITURES		TOTAL 1971 EXPENDITURES ($ MILLIONS)	1971 EXPENDITURES DEFLATED TO 1960 DOLLARS		NUMBER OF FULL-TIME EQUIVALENT EMPLOYEES, 1971 (THOUSANDS)
	Total ($ millions)	Per capita		Total ($ millions)	Per capita	
ALL GOVERNMENT	$3,349	$19	$10,513	$7,688	$37	862
Police	2,030	11	6,165	4,508	22	529
Judicial	597	3	1,358	993	5	118
Prosecution	NA		491	359	2	45
Indigent defense	NA		129	94	—	4
Correction	722	4	2,291	1,675	8	180
LOCAL GOVERNMENT	2,289	13	6,621	4,842	23	578
Police	1,612	9	4,488	3,282	16	403
Judicial	424	2	911	666	3	80
Prosecution	NA		295	216	1	26
Indigent defense	NA		51	37	—	2
Correction	253	1	857	627	3	67

Table 13-2: Public Expenditures and Employment in the Criminal Justice System   NA, not available
SOURCE: Computed from data in U.S. Bureau of the Census, *Statistical Abstract of the United States, 1973*, Government Printing Office, Washington, 1973, pp. 13, 155, 354.

also estimated that approximately $2 billion of resources were allo-
cated to private costs of crime prevention in 1965. This includes
amounts spent for burglar alarms and other protective equipment,
night watchmen, and the administrative cost of theft insurance
programs.

In addition to determining the efficient amount of crime, there is
the question of efficiently allocating crime prevention resources both
within the criminal justice system and between public and private
inputs. In other words, the level of crime that maximizes net social
benefits must be achieved by the least-cost means. Subsequent sections of this chapter discuss the problem of achieving crime prevention by the least-cost means, after first discussing the extent to which
crime is an urban problem and developing a framework for determining the effects of changes in public and private inputs on the level of
criminal activity.

Crime as an Urban Problem

As Table 13-1 shows, the rates for each of the seven index crimes are
higher in SMSAs than in the United States as a whole. Also, the index
rate is higher for large central cities than it is for suburbs, although
there are substantial differences in this ratio, depending on the type of
crime. In most cases, the ratio of large central city crime rates to rural
crime rates is higher yet. For example, in the case of robbery the crime
rate for the six central cities of more than 1 million population is
forty-nine times the rate in rural areas. The data in Table 13-1 indicate
that the index crime rates usually decline from the large central cities
to the suburbs to the small towns to rural areas, but they decline much
more rapidly for crimes against persons than for property crimes.
However, the data in the table mask great differences between
neighborhoods within an urban area. Table 13-3, which shows the
incidence of index crimes and the number of patrolmen in five
Chicago police districts in 1965, indicates much larger variations in
rates for crimes against persons than in property crime rates. One
low-income black district had thirty-five times the violent crime rate
of the high-income white district; on the other hand, the highest
property crime rate of the five districts is only 2.5 times higher than
the lowest. Also, the intensity of police patrols was much higher in
the high-crime districts, raising the possibility that the social costs of
preventing crime in some neighborhoods might exceed the social
benefits of reduced crime. Some studies have shown a positive relation between increased police patrols and the crime rate; while this
may seem paradoxical, one explanation is that increased patrols bring
about an increase in the amount of *reported* crime, since they allow a
greater proportion of crimes to be discovered.

The apparent relationship between crime rates and urbanization may be due to the concentration of wealth, people, and poverty in urban areas, although no convincing evidence for this exists. Urban areas contain a large proportion of the affluent individuals in society; and the higher the community's income the more goods there are, and the more valuable are the goods available to be stolen. Thus, theft becomes more profitable in urban areas than in other places, where the potential income from theft is not as great. A similar consideration is that population densities are higher, so that there are more potential targets in a given area and more offenses can be committed in a shorter period of time. While urban areas provide a concentration of better criminal opportunities, people with low stocks of human capital and other poverty characteristics also tend to be concentrated there (see Chapter 5), and, as will be discussed in the next section, crime and poverty are related. In summary, the higher crime rates in urban areas may be explainable by better criminal opportunities and more potential criminals. In any case, the available crime data indicate that the major part of the national crime problem is concentrated in urban areas and in the central cities of these urban areas.

Costs and Benefits of Crime from the Criminal's Viewpoint

Economically motivated criminal behavior can be analyzed with the use of the cost-benefit framework developed in Chapters 3 and 4. What affects the amount and type of crimes committed by criminals? The benefits to the individual criminal are the expected gains (income) from committing criminal acts. Depending on the criminal's preferences, the private benefits may be greater or less than the income received from the crime. The private benefits will be higher if the criminal receives satisfaction from committing the crime itself ("ripping off the establishment"). They will be less if the individual feels guilty about spending his illegally obtained income. The benefits from each additional criminal act (marginal private benefits) are weighed against the expected costs of the act (marginal private costs). If MPC exceeds MPB and the criminal is rational and has full knowledge of the costs and benefits involved, he will be deterred from committing a crime.

The cost side of the decision to commit an additional crime includes consideration of a number of factors. These include the opportunity cost of foregone legal wages, the income that the criminal could obtain from employing his skills and abilities in a legal occupation. Also there are the "occupational" costs associated with the crime: the risk of being arrested, of being convicted and receiving

	HIGH-INCOME WHITE DISTRICT	LOW-MIDDLE-INCOME WHITE DISTRICT	MIXED LOW- AND HIGH-INCOME WHITE DISTRICT	LOW-INCOME BLACK DISTRICT 1	LOW-INCOME BLACK DISTRICT 2
Index crimes against persons	80	440	338	1,615	2,820
Index crimes against property	1,038	1,750	2,080	2,508	2,630
Patrolmen assigned	93	133	115	243	291

Table 13-3: Incidence of Index Crimes and Patrolmen Assignments per 100,000 Residents in Five Chicago Police Districts (1965)
SOURCE: *Report of the National Advisory Commission on Civil Disorders,* Government Printing Office, Washington, 1968, p. 134.

some form of punishment, as well as the legal costs of defense, the nonmonetary cost associated with loss of freedom if confined, and decreased future legal earnings from having a criminal record. A possible offset to these costs is the "free room and board" received while incarcerated.

Table 13-4 provides a numerical example of the most important private costs and benefits considered in making the decision to commit an additional crime. The criminal act under consideration is the armed robbery of a branch bank that will yield $6,000; thus, the marginal private benefits are $6,000, assuming that the private benefits to the two individuals, Dick and Paul, are equal to the money gained from the criminal act. How would they know how much money they would obtain from the robbery? They would not. However, based on information from various sources (such as acquaintances who have robbed banks), they would place an expected value on the take from the robbery, and might conclude that on the average it will be $6,000. This assumes that their information is correct about the private benefits involved. Newspaper stories about bank robberies generally report that an "undisclosed sum" was taken. Presumably this discourages potential bank robbers by minimizing their information and increasing the degree of uncertainty associated with the potential take.

With respect to the private costs to Dick and Paul of robbing the bank, the example assumes that they would be treated equally and would incur equal risks under the criminal justice system. In other words, the example assumes that the probabilities of arrest and conviction for the two men are identical, as is the expected punishment. However, Dick possesses a large stock of human capital from which he can legally obtain an income of $50,000 per year, while Paul is a high-school dropout possessing skills for which he could realize only $3,000 per year. The probability of arrest in this example is 0.5 and the probability of being convicted, once arrested, is 0.6. Thus, the probability of being arrested and convicted is 0.3 (0.5 times 0.6). While Dick and Paul would expect to receive a sentence of ten years if arrested and convicted, on the average they would serve three years for committing such a crime, since there is only a 0.3 probability of arrest and conviction (ten years times 0.3 = three years). While the expected time to be spent in prison is three years for both Dick and Paul, the private costs to Dick are much higher than the private costs to Paul because of the differences in the foregone earnings from legal occupations while in prison.

The undiscounted private costs to Dick are equal to the expected time in prison times the annual foregone legal earnings while in prison ($50,000), or $150,000. Similarly, the undiscounted private costs to Paul are equal to three times $3,000 per year, or $9,000. Thus, for both individuals, the undiscounted private costs exceed the pri-

	DICK	PAUL
PRIVATE BENEFITS		
A. *Expected value of money received from armed bank robbery*	$ 6,000	$6,000
PRIVATE COSTS		
Probability of being arrested	0.5	0.5
Times		
Probability of conviction	0.6	0.6
Times		
Expected sentence	10 years	10 years
Times		
Annual foregone earnings from legal occupation while in prison	$ 50,000	$3,000
Equals		
B. *Undiscounted private costs*	$150,000	$9,000
PERSONAL DISCOUNT RATE	5%	20%
C. *Present value of private costs at these personal discount rates*	$115,826	$3,773
UNDISCOUNTED NET PRIVATE BENEFITS (A — B)	−$144,000	−$3,000
PRESENT VALUE OF NET PRIVATE BENEFITS (A — C)	−$109,826	$2,227

Table 13-4: Marginal Private Benefits and Costs of a Specific Criminal Act

vate benefits. However, to make a rational decision, costs and benefits need to be converted to their present values. Assume that Dick has a personal discount rate of 5 percent, while Paul is much more present-oriented and has a discount rate of 20 percent (which may account for his small investment in human capital and resulting low income from a legal occupation, as was discussed in Chapter 5). The present value of the private benefits are equal to $6,000 for both men since they will occur now (in the present). Assuming that, if they were convicted, sentences would begin one year from the present (the date of the robbery) and run for ten years. In Dick's case, the present value of foregone legal earnings of a ten-year sentence ($50,000 for ten years discounted at 5 percent) is equal to $386,087 ($113,913 less than the undiscounted amount of $500,000). Multiplying this discounted amount by 0.3 yields the discounted private costs of $115,826 (the present value of private costs), and subtracting the present value of expected benefits we get a present value for net private benefits of minus $109,826 (Table 13-4). In Paul's case, the present value of foregone legal earnings of $3,000 for ten years, discounted at 20 percent, is $12,578 ($17,422 less than the undiscounted amount). Multiplying this by 0.3 yields the present value of private cost of

$3,773 and resulting discounted net private benefits of *plus* $2,227, as shown in the table. Thus, to maximize net private benefits, Dick would not commit the bank robbery, but Paul would.

One implication of the above example is that economically motivated crimes would be related to the causes and symptoms of poverty. Individuals, such as Paul, who have low stocks of human capital or are discriminated against in the labor market have much less to lose from committing crime than individuals with higher legal earnings opportunities. Thus, one would expect to find more criminal activity conducted by those members of society with lower opportunity costs of committing crime (minority groups, the young, the poor), and these lower opportunity costs are related to the causes of poverty. Another poverty-related cause, discussed in Chapter 5, is that individuals with higher personal discount rates would not be willing to make investments in human capital because of the negative present value of net private benefits. In the case of Paul above, the net present value of the private benefits of committing the bank robbery were positive. However, if his discount rate were lower (say 5 percent), then the present value of net private benefits would be negative, and he would not commit the bank robbery. Thus, a higher personal discount rate reduces the opportunity costs of committing crimes, because the costs occur in the future and less weight is given to future costs by people with high personal discount rates.

Economic Approaches to Crime Prevention

Since the number of economically motivated crimes depends on the private costs and benefits to the criminal, a reduction in crime depends on increasing the private costs or decreasing the private benefits of crime, thereby decreasing the net private benefits of criminal acts. The private benefits and costs of criminal activity depend on the actions of potential victims of crime, the allocation of resources to criminal justice system activities (police, courts, and corrections), and economic conditions. This section discusses ways in which these factors determine the net private benefits of crime and the resulting crime rate. Also, possible policies for decreasing the net private benefits of crime are considered.

The basic economic approach to crime reduction outlined above can be contrasted with traditional approaches such as changing the moral values of criminals so that the psychic costs of committing crimes (feelings of guilt) are increased, with a corresponnding reduction in net private benefits from criminal activity. This sort of approach assumes that a person is either "good" or "bad" and that perhaps a "bad" person will reform and become "good," no longer committing crimes. In other words, the psychic costs of criminal activity are assumed to be essentially infinite in the case of "good" persons and very low for "bad" people. The economic approach avoids the moral issues by examining the net private benefits of criminal activity for individuals. If the net private benefits for the "bad" person are reduced to the point where they are negative, then he will not commit the crime. (On the other hand, if the net private benefits are high enough for the "good" person, he *will* commit a crime—everyone has his price.)

It should be noted that the economic approach to crime prevention is applicable to many crimes that may not be economically motivated in the strict sense. For example, in the case of driving under the influence, there is no apparent motivation to gain income from the crime. However, it may be that the intoxicated person weighs the costs and benefits of driving (as best he can) while drunk against such alternatives as leaving his car and calling a taxi, retrieving the car later. If the costs of drunken driving are not sufficiently high (in terms of jail sentences, fines, and license suspensions), then drunken driving may be the alternative that maximizes the individual's net private benefits, since he stands to save taxi fares, etc. Thus, the economic approach to crime prevention has applicability to any crime for which it can be presumed that the individual is not wholly irrational and to some extent weighs the benefits and costs of his activities.

Victims

Potential crime victims can make it more difficult for potential criminals by "hardening the target" in a variety of ways. As previously stated, the Commission on Law Enforcement estimated 1965 expenditures of $2 billion for burglar alarms and other protective equipment, night watchmen, and other private inputs on the part of potential crime victims. This greatly underestimates the social costs of individual crime prevention methods. For example, people may use taxis instead of walking through certain neighborhoods, may take roundabout routes to their destinations, or may travel at inconvenient times of the day in order to avoid robberies and muggings.

Retail stores have the choice of hardening the target by having most merchandise enclosed in glass counter cases. The traditional department store conducted its business in this manner, with clerks behind the counters; increasing labor costs have made it more profitable to switch to the large-volume, low-labor-cost, "discount house" type of retailing operation. While this reduces the number of clerks required to achieve a given sales volume, the more accessible merchandise increases the risk of shoplifting. Thus, in the retailing case, the target is easier than it could be, with resulting higher losses to retailers in the form of shoplifting, but this cost is more than offset by the reduced costs of labor. The implication is that to reduce shoplifting losses would not be profitable. A similar situation exists with respect to employee thefts. The additional costs of more elaborate security arrangements apparently more than offset the decrease in employee thefts that would result. As another example, business establishments handling large amounts of cash can reduce the potential sums to be gained by armed robbery by hiring an armored car service to pick up their cash more frequently for bank deposit thus reducing the average cash balance and the potential loss from robbery.

Auto thefts could be reduced if all people locked their cars when not in use. Approximately 40 percent of all auto thefts involve cars with the keys left inside. While for most car owners the time spent locking the car appears to increase their net private benefits (or they would not do it), for the rest the insurance coverage against theft may lead them to exercise less care. Insurance premiums are naturally higher because of this, but the increase in rates to a single careless individual because of his own actions may be minuscule, since the additional premium cost is spread over all insurance holders. While police recover most stolen autos (approximately 85 percent), considerable police resources are devoted to recovery of stolen cars, and these resources could be diverted to other uses if drivers had a greater incentive to harden the target. For example, if police charged a fee to owners for auto recovery that was not reimbursed by the insurance company (similar in concept to fees charged when autos are towed away for parking violations), more potential victims of auto theft would have a greater incentive to make it more difficult for thieves to steal their cars and a reduction in auto theft would result.

There are many similar interactions between victims and the criminal justice system with respect to decreasing the net private benefits to criminals and reducing crime rates. Appropriate incentives are required to obtain the efficient quantity and combination of private and public inputs. As another example, if there was a large increase in patrolling by the police force, business firms would not have to spend as much for locks and burglar alarms. However, it is probably much cheaper to install locks on each building than to spend enough for police patrolling to make locks unnecessary.

The Criminal Justice System

In terms of the example of Table 13-4, the criminal justice system influences the value of the three variables that affect the private costs of criminal activity. Police activity affects the probability of arrest, and, to a much lesser extent, the probability of conviction through the collection and presentation of evidence. The courts (including the prosecution function) affect the probability of conviction. Corrections (prisons, fines, the parole system, etc.) determine the expected punishment.

Police   The quantity of police resources and the alternative police activities among which these are allocated affect the crime rate through deterrence and determine the probability of arrest for various types of crime. As indicated in Table 13-2, police expenditures account for over half of all public sector resources devoted to the criminal justice system and approximately 70 percent of all criminal justice expenditures by local governments. Little research has been done on the efficient allocation of police resources. Ideally, these resources should be allocated so as to minimize the total social costs of crime to society. That is, the police would devote more attention to generating arrests for those crimes that result in the greatest social costs, so as to maximize social benefits obtained from police activities. And if the social benefits and costs of police activities were known, the quantity of police resources that maximize net social benefits could be determined.

The major police activity is patrol—the movement around an assigned area, on foot or by vehicle, of uniformed police. In most police departments more than one-half of the manpower is allocated to this function. A principal purpose of patrol is deterrence, discouraging people who are inclined to commit a crime from doing so because of a fear of arrest. The maximum reduction in crime achievable this way might be attained by placing a policeman on every street corner; however, it is unlikely that this would maximize net social benefits, since the additional costs would be enormous.

To determine the efficient level of patrol and resulting deterrence, knowledge is required of the extent to which crimes of various kinds can be deterred. Little is known on this subject; intuition would indicate that "crimes of passion," where emotion overwhelms reason, are less likely to be responsive to deterrence than economically motivated crimes, such as burglary. Efficient patrol also depends on knowledge of when and where crimes are most likely to occur. Some studies have indicated that patrol man-hours could be reallocated among days of the week and hours of the day to achieve better response to calls for assistance. Further, there is little knowledge of the effectiveness of alternative patrol techniques, such as foot patrol versus motor patrol, one-man versus two-man patrol, etc. However, in motor patrol assignments, most departments have shifted from two- to one-man patrol cars. Since salaries consume about 90 percent of police budgets, the switch to one-man patrol cars could cut costs per patrol car nearly in half, and allow the police budget to support more cars. However, police officers greatly prefer two-man patrols, because of protection and camaraderie during patrol hours; therefore, the switch to one-man patrols may have to be accompanied by an increase in pay, reducing the cost savings somewhat.

As mentioned above, labor costs account for most of police spending; there has been little substitution of capital equipment for labor in the police function over time, although technology cannot solve all problems. For example, all cars could be implanted with a radio transmitter that would allow police to trace all stolen autos electronically; the cost of this would no doubt be prohibitive, and professional auto thieves would soon learn to disconnect such devices. On the other hand, a study of the Los Angeles police department indicated that the time required for police to respond to calls was critical in determining the probability of arrest. The average response for emergency calls was 4.1 minutes for cases in which the police were able to make an arrest, while it took 6.3 minutes for cases that involved no arrest.[3] Thus, it appears that response time is a critical factor in increasing the probability of arrest for many crimes. In this case, technology could have a large payoff—automatic car-location devices, by which a computer keeps track of all cars on patrol, are available at relatively low cost. A call for assistance can then be routed to the car closest to that location.

When patrol fails to prevent a crime or apprehend the criminal soon after the commission of a crime (or better yet, in the act), the police must rely on investigation. In many cases, fingerprints are important clues to determining a suspect, but there is no practical method of classifying and tracing single latent fingerprints by a manual search of local, state, or national files unless a suspect's name is known. The development of computer technology that would permit matching up a single print from files of millions of prints would greatly increase the effectiveness of police investigation. At the present time the social costs and benefits of developing such technology are unknown.

An increase in police resources in only one jurisdiction (the central city) may increase the private costs of crime in that jurisdiction, but may result in the criminal's movement to adjoining jurisdictions (suburbs) without any reduction in overall crime. This may in fact have been the result of the billions of dollars that the Law Enforcement Assistance Administration has pumped into the nation's major central cities since 1967 in an effort to reduce crime. The FBI crime index indicates that cities of over 250,000 population experienced a decrease of 7 percent in robberies between 1971 and 1972, while suburbs experienced a 9 percent increase.[4]

In summary, while the police are an integral function of the crimi-

[3]President's Commission on Law Enforcement and Administration of Justice, p. 248.
[4]Federal Bureau of Investigation, *Uniform Crime Reports, 1972*, Government Printing Office, Washington, 1973, pp. 9 - 22.

nal justice system and the resulting crime rate, little is known at present about the efficient allocation of police resources. One reason for this is that police budgets provide for almost no research, possibly because the output of the research could be considered a "public good," in which the research of one police department would benefit all law enforcement agencies in the country. Thus, while police departments hope that other departments will conduct research, they see the benefits of their own research as being too small relative to the costs. Federal government financing of research related to the allocation of police resources might result in large social benefits.

Courts   The private costs of committing crime are tied to the probability of conviction and the determination of the punishment as decided in the court system. While a large number of those arrested for less serious offenses are either convicted or released within twenty-four hours of their arrest, those arrested for more serious offenses are usually either required by the court to post money bail for their release pending trial (the amount of bail depending on the severity of the crime) or are detained in jail. The usual method of posting bail is to pay a fee, between 5 and 10 percent of the bail, to a bail bondsman who posts the bail for the full amount to the court. One's ability to post bail depends on income. A study in New York, where the bail bondsman's fee is 5 percent, showed that 25 percent of arrested persons were unable to furnish bail of $500 (i.e., raise $25 for the bail bondsman's fee), 45 percent could not furnish $1,500, and 63 percent failed at $2,500. Thus, money bail tends to discriminate against the poor, who are unable to post bail and must remain in jail until their case is completed. Since confinement often means foregone earnings as well as loss of freedom, the bail system tends to make crime more costly for those of lower incomes than it does for those able to post money bail and avoid these pretrial confinement costs.

Most defendants who are convicted—as many as 90 percent in some jurisdictions—are not tried; instead, they plead guilty, often as the result of "plea bargaining" between the defendant's lawyer and the prosecutor about the charge or the sentence. Plea bargaining is the response of a court system that does not have the capacity to bring most cases to trial. From the prosecutor's viewpoint, the acceptance of a negotiated guilty plea to a lesser charge or a lower recommended sentence will maximize his net private benefits in the sense that his limited resources can be more profitably used in seeking convictions in more important cases. From the defendant's viewpoint, he must weigh the net private benefits to be received from going to trial versus the pretrial bargain. In the case of plea bargaining, the defendant's costs of legal defense will be less and the punishment will usually be less if he accepts the "deal" than if he is tried and convicted of the original charge. This must be weighed against the probability he assigns to being found guilty via trial and the additional defense costs incurred. Prosecutors would be expected to offer better deals the more crowded the court system is, since they need a larger percentage of the defendants to accept the pretrial bargains. In terms of the example of Table 13-4, the criminal who anticipates plea bargaining if arrested may assign a high probability to conviction but expect a lesser sentence (and smaller private costs) than in a situation where all cases went to trial.

Since higher-income individuals who are arrested place a higher value on their time and have the resources to avoid pretrial confinement and hire competent legal defense, it is likely that the court system would work in favor of those with higher incomes. To attempt to achieve horizontal equity in the court system (where everyone has a right to equal treatment), there is no price charged to a defendant for having a court trial; however, since courts are not priced, dockets become overcrowded, and in some cases a court's docket may be filled three to five years in advance. For the low-income person who is arrested for a serious offense and sent to jail because of his inability to post bail, the alternative to plea bargaining may be months of confinement even in the case of innocent defendants. At the same time, a higher-income defendant is not confined and his ability to pay for better legal defense may result in a lower probability of conviction or a lower expected sentence, as the result of either a trial or pretrial bargaining. Further, the higher-income person's resources allow a sentence to be appealed to higher courts, postponing the serving of the sentence for years, if not reversing the conviction. In the case of Table 13-4, suppose that both Dick and Paul are out on bail for three years before they are convicted. The present values of their expected sentences are reduced to $100,055 and $2,184, respectively, indicating that promptness of conviction and sentencing have a significant impact on the costs of crime. The percentage reduction in private costs is about 14 percent for Dick and 42 percent for Paul, indicating that the costs to persons with high personal discount rates (present-oriented people) are greatly reduced by delaying punishment; that is, the deterrent effect of prison terms is greatly reduced if the sentencing is delayed.

The courts are also instrumental in determining the procedures under which arrests and convictions are conducted. One of the most controversial topics of recent years has been civil liberties under criminal law. The greater are civil liberty protections in terms of searches, arrests, and other rights of the accused, the higher the costs of apprehending criminals and obtaining convictions. It appears to some members of society that increasing the probabilities of arrest and conviction, while reducing individual civil liberties, is the least-cost means of reducing crime. However, as the probability of a guilty person being punished is increased by reducing civil liberties, so is the probability of an innocent person being convicted. Thus, society must decide whether it wishes more civil liberties or more convictions. According to court decisions in recent years, the choice has been in favor of greater civil liberties.

Corrections A survey conducted by the President's Commission on Law Enforcement gave the first accurate data on the number of offenders under correctional authority on an average day (in 1965). The survey found that the number was 1.3 million, of whom one-third were in institutions (jails and prisons) and two-thirds were "in the community" (on probation or parole). For juvenile offenders, the average cost per offender per year in institutions was $3,613, while for those in the community the cost was $328, less than 10 percent of the institutional cost. The cost relationship for adult offenders was similar, $1,966 for those in institutions versus $198 for those on parole or probation.[5] As indicated in Table 13-2, the total corrections costs in 1970 were about $2.3 billion.

From the standpoint of decreasing crime through increasing the private costs of criminal activity, the choice between imprisonment and release into the community involves greatly different costs to the criminal justice system. The costs are also greatly different for a convict. Probation and parole result in much lower private costs to both offenders and to the corrections system. Imprisonment reduces the crime rate in several ways, most of which are obvious. First, it removes the offender from society temporarily, preventing him from committing crimes. Second, imprisonment might deter some potential criminals by increasing the expected private costs of crime. The private costs of imprisonment can be increased in two ways: by increasing the length of the sentence or by making prison life less pleasant (solitary confinement, thumbscrews, etc.). Society would consider the latter approach as cruel and unusual punishment, so it will not be examined further here.

The first approach, increasing sentence lengths, may have major drawbacks in addition to using more of society's resources. The potential offender may not consider a fifteen-year sentence much different from a ten-year one, since the additional years occur far in the future, and must be discounted back to the present. In terms of the example of Table 13-4, Paul's *undiscounted* private costs would be increased by 50 percent if the sentence upon conviction were increased to fifteen years. However, the *present value* of this increase in costs is only $435, an increase of 12 percent in private costs. (The increase for Dick would be $39,869, or 34 percent.)

[5]President's Commission on Law Enforcement and Administration of Justice, pp. 160 - 161.

Undoubtedly, many types of criminal act could be substantially curtailed by large increases in the severity of punishment, but the punishment must fit the crime in the eyes of society. If the penalty for stealing hubcaps were increased to a mandatory ten-year prison term, the probability of conviction for this offense would be greatly reduced, since judges and juries would tend to find a defendant innocent in order to avoid the stiff punishment, or perhaps find him guilty of a lesser crime. Also, the punishment should fit the crime from an economic standpoint—crimes that involve the largest social costs should carry the largest penalties, thereby increasing the marginal private costs of such crimes. In fact, more severe penalties for lesser crimes might lead to an increase in social costs; if armed robbery and murder carried the same penalty, then the robber might find it advantageous to kill the victim, since dead men tell no tales, and, even if they did, there would be no increase in penalty. Thus, while the number of robberies might decline in response to the higher penalty, the number of murders might increase, resulting in higher overall social costs of crime.

In the example of Table 13-4, the major difference between the private costs to Dick and Paul was the foregone legal earnings while imprisoned. Thus, crime might be reduced by increasing the opportunities and income that the individual can obtain from legal employment. Education and training programs within prison (rehabilitiation) could enable an ex-convict to get a new start in legal employment, if he has learned more than how to make license plates or do large batches of laundry. Reducing crime through rehabilitation of criminals in this manner appears to be an insignificant goal of the correctional system, in that 95 percent of prison costs are for custody and only 5 percent for rehabilitation.[6] In fact, prisons often serve as a socially undesirable school. Prisoners learn the skills of crime from fellow inmates. If the inmate's opportunity costs of committing crimes are not increased via an increase in his stock of legal human capital (training and skills acquired in prison for a legal occupation), he may come out with greater criminal skills than when he went in, which increase his net private benefits from committing crimes. Thus, an ex-convict may be a greater menace to society than a criminal who is never caught. In terms of federal and state prison inmates, the President's Commission on Law Enforcement estimated that only 5.3 percent of inmates had some college education, compared with 17.8 percent for the whole United States population. At the other end of the human capital scale, 14.4 percent of inmates had four or less years of schooling compared with 6 percent for the population as a whole. Thus, economic reasoning leads one to conclude that those

[6]Ramsey Clark, *Crime in America*, Simon and Schuster, New York, 1970, p. 48.

with less human capital are those who have lower opportunity costs for committing crimes and are therefore more likely to commit them.

Given the above situation, it would appear that considerable reductions in crime rates could be achieved by increasing the stocks of legal human capital through training and education programs. To a considerable extent, crime is a symptom of poverty and countering the causes of poverty should lead to reductions in crime. However, it is not possible to conclude that rehabilitation could significantly increase the opportunity costs of potential criminals. For example, if most criminals have very high personal discount rates (like Paul in Table 13-4), the incentives to make investments in human capital are small, and such prisoners might just "go along with" training programs while acquiring little human capital. Also, it is possible that some prison inmates have strong preferences for committing crimes as opposed to legal occupations. In these instances, rehabilitation programs may have little impact. However, since very little has been tried in the way of substantial rehabilitation programs affecting large numbers of criminals, there are no obvious answers.

Economic Conditions

As discussed in Chapter 6, a full-employment economy decreases the incidence of poverty. The few economic studies that have been conducted on the subject show that crime increases when unemployment goes up or when wage rates for unskilled workers decline. Thus, when economic conditions change the incidence of poverty, they also change the incidence of crime. This is as expected—an increase in legal earnings amounts to an increase in the opportunity cost of crime, and economic conditions, such as the unemployment rate, determine these legal earnings.

Changes in the relative prices of various commodities affect the net private benefits of stealing these commodities. If the price of a commodity increases relative to the cost of stealing it, we might expect an increase in thefts of such items. For example, the demand for black walnut lumber for use in furniture veneers has been high relative to the supply of such lumber, and a large top-quality black walnut tree can bring as much as $15,000 at a lumber mill. As a result, the economic motivation for stealing such trees has increased along with the price. The activity is sufficiently profitable that sophisticated methods have been used, such as the use of airplanes to spot trees during the day. "Tree rustlers," armed with chain saws silenced with auto mufflers, then go on to the prospected properties in the middle of the night, saw down large tree trunks, and winch them onto trucks to be sold to sawmills.[7] Also, in times of economic downturn, the arson

---

[7]"The Tree Rustlers," Time, April 16, 1973, pp. 62 - 63.

rate increases. A business firm that is failing to turn a profit may be worth more burned to the ground (with the collection of fire insurance proceeds) than if the assets of the failing business were sold. When gasoline was in short supply in late 1973, there appeared to be an increase in the number of autos reported stolen and later found burned. One insurance investigator commented, "It appears that some people have a big gas hog that they can't unload so they've decided to collect insurance on it."[8]

In summary, criminals, victims, the component parts of the criminal justice system, and economic conditions are all interrelated with respect to decreasing rates of crime. Determining the least-cost means of achieving the efficient amount of crime involves resource allocation decisions in all sectors affecting criminal activity. In the numerical example of Table 13-4, an increase in the probability of being arrested from 0.5 to 0.75, or an increase in the probability of being convicted from 0.6 to 0.9, results in an increase in private costs (undiscounted) of 50 percent. Other means of increasing the private costs of crime include hardening the target and increasing the potential criminal's lawful earnings. It is likely that least-cost attainment of the efficient amount of crime will involve a combination of these approaches and others.

"Victimless Crimes" and Organized Crime

Criminal activity that is generally termed "organized" has extensive direct and indirect effects on members of society. Organized crime is primarily concerned with supplying goods and services that are prohibited or strictly regulated by society, but for which many people have a demand. These goods and services include gambling, loan-sharking, prostitution, and narcotics. While there may be a justification in many cases for laws restricting the sale of these goods and services, restriction is sometimes based solely on grounds of morality. Morality—as the basis of prohibition—cannot be justified economically, since it involves a violation of consumer sovereignty. Prohibition can be justified on economic grounds only if negative externalities result from the consumption of these goods and services, and the efficient level of consumption can best be achieved by prohibition. Frequently, it appears that a good or service is prohibited because of a potential externality in its use. For example, consuming alcohol provides benefits to many people or else they would not drink it. The moderate consumption of alcohol in one's own home would not appear to result in an externality; however, if one becomes drunk and then drives a car, there is a probability that this consumption-

[8]"Fanning the Flames," *Wall Street Journal,* February 21, 1974, p. 1.

related act will result in a negative externality. In this case, the appropriate public policy approach probably rests with more rigorous apprehension and conviction policies related to driving under the influence, not with the abolition of alcohol, which would involve a needless violation of consumer sovereignty. (Similarly, the potential of accidental electrocutions should not lead to the prohibition of the use of electricity.)

The greater the amount of goods and services that are made illegal, the greater the amount of criminal activity that one would expect with respect to supplying these commodities. The difficulty here is that outlawing supply does not make the demand for the commodity vanish. The best example of this in the United States is provided by the Prohibition era of the 1920s, when the sale of alcohol was made illegal. While prohibition was probably motivated by a desire to protect people from alcoholism (as well as from the pleasures of moderate consumption), it had a quite different effect. Because there was still a tremendous demand for alcohol, Prohibition made multimillionaires out of suppliers of alcohol such as Al Capone but certainly did not eliminate the consumption of alcohol. Because of the lack of government control over the production of the illegal alcohol, some consumers purchased and consumed low-quality alcohol that resulted in severe illness or even death. In addition, large amounts of the resources of the criminal justice system were allocated to try to decrease the supply of illegal alcohol. The widespread public acknowledgement of the failure of prohibition to efficiently resolve the externalities of alcohol consumption ultimately led to its repeal. Alcoholism, drunken driving, and other results of the use of alcohol are serious social problems in the United States and many other countries, resulting in billions of dollars in social costs annually in the form of lost lives, reduced work productivity, and property damage. However, prohibition does not appear to be the efficient means of reducing such social costs.

Many crimes involving the consumption of illegal goods and services are considered to be "victimless" crimes; the provision of such commodities does not affect anyone other than the producer or the consumer. Gambling is one possible example of a service that does not result in consumption externalities. Society has apparently been unwilling to come to grips with the issues involved in victimless crimes. For example, there have been presidential commissions to study both pornography and marijuana. In both cases the commissions concluded, on the basis of their review of the evidence, that it was difficult to justify banning the consumption of either commodity on grounds of externalities. At the same time, the commissions recommended that supply continue to be illegal while demand be made legal (possession by users in small quantities would not be illegal). In some cases, the original rationale for outlawing a commodity may have been that a potential consumer had to be protected from himself. Of course, this is a deliberate violation of consumer sovereignty; however, the problem may be one of imperfect information, in which the consumer was not aware of the total private costs to himself from consuming a commodity (e.g., thalidomide taken by pregnant women, which resulted in deformed babies). In cases of imperfect information it may sometimes be more efficient to provide information to the public than simply to ban the commodity's use. For example, it is generally agreed that cigarette consumption increases the risk of incurring respiratory diseases such as emphysema and lung cancer. The government in recent years has provided information to the public regarding the hazards of cigarette smoking, including a requirement that a warning label be placed on all cigarette packages. In 1960, per capita cigarette consumption was 4,171; by 1965 it had increased to 4,258, even though a major government report linking smoking and lung cancer had been published a year earlier. In 1972, per capita consumption was 4,040,[9] a rather modest drop in light of the intensive antismoking campaigns, the labeling requirement on the hazards of smoking, and the banning of cigarette commercials from television and radio. However, if the government were to attempt to reduce the social costs of cigarette smoking by outlawing the sale of tobacco, this is unlikely to be an efficient solution. Ultimately, the doctrine of consumer sovereignty boils down to whether an individual has a right to kill himself (or incur a risk of death), through heavy cigarette consumption, being overweight, obtaining no physical exercise, or in any other manner that reduces one's life span without imposing negative externalities on others.

In summary, organized crime exists to supply commodities that have been made illegal but for which a demand exists. Prohibition may or may not be the efficient solution to problems of imperfect information or externalities associated with these commodities. In any case, the social costs of prohibition are high in terms of diverted criminal justice system resources and the extra resources that go into the provision of the commodities themselves (sale of illegal commodities is obviously a more costly and complicated procedure).

In many large central cities, there appears to be an almost annual police department scandal. Usually, this is the discovery that some members of the police force have been taking bribes from organized crime not to report on various illegal activities or to pass on "interesting" information. It is probably quite difficult to run a gambling or prostitution operation without some help from police. From the

---

[9]U.S. Bureau of the Census, *Statistical Abstract of the United States, 1973*, Government Printing Office, Washington, 1973, p. 720.

policeman's standpoint, the willingness to accept a bribe can be analyzed in the same way as the private costs and benefits of committing a crime as illustrated in Table 13-4. The benefits are the increased income from accepting the bribe, and the policeman may not feel quilty (incur psychic costs) about accepting it if he has preferences (as do many of the population) that there is nothing socially harmful connected with gambling or prostitution. The costs are those associated with getting caught, being busted from the police force, and other forms of punishment involved in criminal prosecution. If the bribe is sufficiently large for the net private benefits to be positive, then the policeman will be "on the take." From the standpoint of the "organization" the payment of the bribe is worthwhile if it costs less than the reduction in private costs involved in a greater probability of arrest. From the number of scandals reported, it would appear that there are many instances in which the policeman and organized crime both maximize net private benefits by the acceptance and payment of a bribe. This is one of the ways in which victimless crimes result in higher resource costs in the criminal justice system. If these victimless crimes were "decriminalized," i.e., made legal through repeal of laws, the incentives for police payoffs would be significantly reduced. In addition, all other things remaining equal, fewer resources would have to be devoted to crime prevention, since fewer activities would be considered crimes.

The illegal supply and consumption of one good, heroin, has been considered one of the major crime concerns of large central cities, since it is widely stated that heroin addiction is directly related to the amount of robbery and theft. Policies related to this special case of organized crime's provision of an illegal commodity are treated in the next section.

Heroin Addiction and Drug-related Crimes

The supply of heroin that is illegally consumed in the United States derives primarily from opium grown in Turkey and other countries, which is converted to morphine base and shipped to France. There it is transformed to heroin in small illegal laboratories and shipped to the United States either directly or indirectly. It is difficult to prevent the shipment of heroin into the United States because it is easily transported and concealed and has great value relative to its weight and volume—a kilogram of heroin (2.2 pounds) may have a retail value close to one-half million dollars. The production and distribution of heroin in the United States is presumably controlled by organized crime. For one thing, the lengthy distribution chain from the opium field to the retail market on the street requires considerable business expertise and resources. However, organized crime is not usually directly involved with the actual retailing on the street. The more transactions, the greater the risk of discovery; organized crime reduces this risk by handling the importation and wholesaling functions, where the number of transactions are smaller but the size of each transaction larger. The "pusher" on the street is not usually a member of the organized crime group and is the one who incurs the greatest risk of arrest, since he is involved with the end of the distribution chain where the number of transactions is the greatest. The larger the distribution chain, in terms of number of people, the smaller the amount of information possessed by any one individual. Thus, organized crime attempts to reduce the probability of being apprehended by elongating the distribution chain.

The retail price of heroin on the street is related to a number of demand and supply considerations. On the supply side, if more resources of the criminal justice system are devoted to intercepting imported heroin, apprehending pushers on the street, or increasing the probability of arrest at any point in the distribution chain, the costs to the supplier will be greater and the final price higher. To the extent that police can be bribed, as discussed above, the costs of doing business may be reduced. On the demand side, the more addicts there are, the higher the price, other things being equal.

Because the supply of heroin is illegal, its market price is considerably higher than the resource cost of producing it if it were legal. As a result of the higher illegal price, the income required by a heroin addict to support his habit is much larger than it would be with a legal supply. A typical heroin addict needs about $40 per day to support his habit, or over $14,000 per year. Even if the addict has a stock of human capital that potentially could support such an expensive habit, the effects of heroin addiction probably impair his human capital to the extent where he can no longer make the legal income that he could before the addiction took place. Therefore, illegal alternatives must be considered to generate income sufficient to support the habit. In most cases, these are robbery or theft (perhaps heroin retailing or prostitution), although a considerable amount of criminal activity is required to bring in enough income. Since a fence will pay only about one-fourth to one-third of the retail value of merchandise, a $40-a-day habit may translate into robbery and theft of $150 per day. If all heroin addicts were millionaires, society probably would not be overly concerned with heroin addiction, since they could support their habits without resorting to illegal activities. In fact, however, the addict population tends to be of the lowest income groups, and so is likely to turn to crime. As a result, although there are no good available data, it is generally believed that heroin addicts account for a large part of property crimes (and related crimes of violence) in the large central cities of the United States.

A major implication of the above discussion is that, if the price of heroin were lower, the addict would have to commit less income-producing crime to support his habit. For example, if the cost of producing heroin sufficient to support a typical habit were $1 per day, most addicts could support their habits without resorting to crime, and so crime rates would probably drop. While the drug-related crime would be drastically decreased in the short run, in the long run the lower price of heroin might provide the incentive for more people to become addicted. Although the amount of crime per addict would be reduced, the greatly expanded addict population might cause increased crime rates in the long run, particularly if the price of heroin increased again.

Answers to the problem of heroin addiction and drug-related crimes are not easy to produce. Conceivably, income-producing crime related to addiction could be essentially eliminated if the government provided heroin addicts with enough heroin to satisfy them at a zero price and also provided them with a guaranteed minimum income to provide them with other costs of living. However, the social costs of a large and unproductive addict population would be high. Alternatively, some sort of "price discrimination" system might be devised whereby "veteran" addicts could obtain heroin at low cost, but the price for new users, not yet addicted, would be kept high. The low price to addicts would tend to eliminate drug-related crime, but the high price to new users would tend to deter new addictions. Establishing such a policy is fraught with difficulties, among them the possibility of resale by veteran addicts and the difficulties of distinguishing between veterans and novices.[10]

Another approach that has been implemented rather extensively in recent years is the provision of a substitute for heroin, methadone. Apparently, methadone is not a perfect substitute for heroin—the addict does not get the thrill of the "rush" as when injecting heroin—but it does meet the physiological demands of the heroin addict. An addict who converts to methadone supposedly can hold down a job with little impairment of human capital. Still, much controversy surrounds methadone programs, and will continue to do so until better data are obtained. At present, most addicts on methadone must come to a governmentally operated clinic to receive their doses, and methadone cannot be easily purchased. Thus, there are private costs to using methadone, including the time spent going to a clinic, which usually requires periodic urine tests to see whether the user has reverted to the use of heroin or other hard drugs. A more permissive methadone policy, which lowered the private costs to the

[10]For a discussion of some possible means of price discrimination with respect to heroin users, see Mark Moore, "Policies to Achieve Discrimination of the Effective Price of Heroin," *American Economic Review* (May 1973), 270 - 277.

addict of converting to methadone, would possibly encourage a greater decrease in the heroin addict population. However, methadone is addictive too, and at the present time little is known about the social costs of long-run methadone addiction.

While there are no easy answers to the problem of heroin addiction, there is some recent evidence that the problem in the United States has peaked and is on the downswing. This may be attributable to better information about the costs to the potential drug addict in using heroin, to changing preferences in the population that has produced most of the addicts (young, male, low-income), to the efforts of the criminal justice system in increasing the private costs of users, or to the widespread implementation of methadone programs. No one can really say at this time. However, addiction to heroin and other opiates is nothing new. In the United States in 1900, it was estimated that one out of four hundred in the population (much higher than the present percentage) were addicts. The normal dosage in those times would be lethal for the average heroin addict of today.[11]

Equity Aspects of Crime and Crime Prevention

Preceding sections have pointed out several relationships between crime and income of the criminal. In this section several points related to crime victims and income, as well as criminals and income, are discussed from an equity standpoint.

The Probability of Being a Victim

The probability of being a victim of one of the FBI index crimes against persons or property is related to one's income, as indicated by the data in Table 13-5 for six of the seven index crimes. There are probably several explanations underlying this relationship. The higher one's income the more wealth he is likely to possess and thus the greater the criminal's potential gain from committing crimes against his property. On the other hand, if one has a low income and lives in a low-income neighborhood, it is likely that higher criminal activity flourishes in that neighborhood because of the lower opportunity costs of his neighbors in committing crime. Thus, close proximity to larger numbers of potential criminals increases the probability of being the victim of crime.

The allocation of resources within the criminal justice system will also determine the probability of being a crime victim. Table 13-6 presents an example of the probability of being a victim, which varies

[11]Ramsey Clark, *Crime in America*, p. 67.

because of different criteria for assigning police to patrol duties in two neighborhoods of a local government. The total population is 20,000, of whom 10,000 live in a low-income area and 10,000 in a high-income area. Given the police department's resources as determined by the local government's budget, assume that the police chief has 100 patrolmen to assign to the total area. One equity criterion would be to assign an equal number of police to each area, so that the number of patrolmen per capita would be the same in both areas. In the first section of the table, the assignment of patrols on an "equal input" basis results in total crimes of 1,000 and the probability of being a victim nine times as high in the low-income district, since there are nine times as many crimes committed per capita.

The second section of Table 13-6 shows the resulting crime rate if the police chief decides to employ another equity criterion in assigning patrols. In this case, the number of police are assigned to the two districts so as to equalize the crime rate ("equal outputs"). However, equalizing the crime rate, and the resulting probability of being a victim, results in 400 more crimes being committed in the total area. Neither one of the patrol allocations above is likely to be efficient. As previously discussed, achieving an efficient allocation of police resources subject to a limited budget requires minimizing the social costs of crime with these resources. If all crimes impose the same social costs, then minimizing the amount of crime will achieve the efficient allocation. (This assumption of equal costs per crime is used in this example for simplicity.) The efficient allocation of the limited police resources is indicated in the third part of Table 13-6; this results in 950 total crimes, which is lower than for either of the other two approaches of equal inputs or equal outputs.

| | INCOME OF CRIME VICTIM | | | |
FBI INDEX CRIME	$0 - 2,999	$3,000 - 5,999	$6,000 - 9,999	$10,000 and over
Total	2,369	2,331	1,820	2,237
Forcible rape	76	49	10	17
Robbery	172	121	48	34
Aggravated assault	229	316	144	252
Burglary	1,319	1,020	867	790
Larceny ($50 and over)	420	619	549	925
Motor vehicle theft	153	206	202	219

Table 13-5: Victimization by Income: Six FBI Index Crimes, 1965 (Rates per 100,000 Population)
SOURCE: President's Commission on Law Enforcement and Administration of Justice, *The Challenge of Crime in a Free Society,* Government Printing Office, Washington, 1967, p. 38.

	TOTAL PATROL AREA	LOW-INCOME DISTRICT	HIGH-INCOME DISTRICT
Population	20,000	10,000	10,000
Equal inputs			
Total police	100	50	50
Police per capita	.005	.005	.005 .
Crimes	1,000	900	100
Crime per capita	.05	.09	.01
Equal outputs			
Total police	100	99	1
Police per capita	.005	.0099	.0001
Crimes	1,400	700	700
Crimes per capita	.07	.07	.07
Lowest total crimes (efficiency)			
Total police	100	60	40
Police per capita	.005	.006	.004
Crimes	950	800	150
Crimes per capita	.00475	.08	.015

Table 13-6: Allocation of Police Patrol Resources on Equity and Efficiency Bases

The efficient allocation of police resources results in significantly different probabilities of becoming a crime victim in the two districts of Table 13-6. The lower-income resident faces five times the probability of being a crime victim than the high-income resident faces. Thus, the efficient allocation may not seem fair to society; however, as discussed throughout this book, equity and efficiency considerations can usually be separated, so that achieving equity does not require abandoning efficiency in the use of society's resources. In the example of Table 13-6, one possibility would be to compensate the victims of crime in the low-income area so that the net costs of crime were the same, on the average, for the low-income resident and the high-income resident. Suppose that the average costs to the victims of crimes committed in both districts is $1,000 per crime. In the high-income district, the average resident would incur private costs from crime of $15 per year ($1,000 times .015, the probability of being a victim); in the low-income district, the average resident would incur private costs from crime of $80 per year (.08 times $1,000). Thus, on grounds of equity, compensation could be paid to victims in the low-income district to achieve an average cost per resident of $15 rather than $80. This would require an average compensation per victim of $812.50 per crime (65/80 of the private cost to the victim), to partially compensate for the loss of $1,000.

Some states have implemented compensation programs for crime victims, although at this time they are relatively small in magnitude, and it is unknown what proportion of the total private costs of being a victim are covered. However, the total amount of compensation paid could not approach or exceed the actual private costs of the crime victim, or it would become profitable to "become a victim." For example, suppose that everyone who was a victim of a robbery automatically received $10,000 for the mental distress associated with the threat of physical harm (or actual physical harm). It is likely that there would be a rash of "robberies," since many people could maximize net private benefits by arranging to be robbed in order to collect the compensation.

In terms of achieving equity, there are many uses for various forms of compensation. For example, in the court system, if an individual incurs the opportunity cost of legal defense and foregone earnings from loss of work while involved in the trial process in order to prove himself innocent and is actually found innocent, the innocent party in this case incurs these private costs. On grounds of equity, compensation could be paid to accused parties who incur such private costs as part of the court system but are found innocent.

Types of Crime and Punishment by Income Group

As previously discussed, the estimated dollar amount of forced transfers resulting from white-collar crimes, such as embezzlement, income tax evasion, and fraud, is several times that associated with the FBI index crimes against property. It may be that white-collar crime "pays" in many instances, since the expected private benefits are high and the private costs are low, because many such offenses are never formally prosecuted but are handled privately by the parties involved—a person may lose his job but the police are not notified. The ability to commit many high-payoff white-collar crimes requires a large stock of human capital. For example, a highly skilled accountant is much more likely to be in a position and have the skills to pull off a major embezzlement than a low-income high-school dropout, and even if the accountant gets caught in a $250,000 embezzlement, the private costs of expected punishment are likely to be much lower than for the high-school dropout caught in a $100 stickup.

Since those with different jobs, incomes, and human capital have significantly different opportunities to commit crimes, some people have raised the question whether the criminal justice system is stacked against low-income, low-education (low socioeconomic class) groups, while lightly treating crime committed by those in higher socioeconomic classes. There is a definite relationship between socioeconomic class and the offenders run through the criminal justice system. Society has apparently assessed the social costs of low-class crimes (which usually involve the potential for violence) as much higher than white-collar crimes, which may not result in large social costs, although they result in large income transfers between individuals and groups.

REVIEW AND DISCUSSION QUESTIONS

1   Since central cities of large urban areas tend to have higher crime rates than suburban areas, any increases in resources for police patrols and investigation in urban areas should be allocated to central cities. Discuss.
2   Outline the costs and benefits involved in increasing the size of a city's police force.
3   Why do not all auto owners lock their cars to prevent theft? Why do not retail merchants spend more on preventing shoplifting and employee theft?
4   How does delaying conviction and sentencing in the courts decrease the private costs of a crime to the criminal?
5   Is a negative income tax program with a guaranteed income equal to the poverty cutoff level of income likely to have any effect on crime rates? Why?
6   Discuss the relationship between one's personal discount rate and one's likelihood of committing economically motivated crimes.
7   Explain why crime rates go up when economic conditions (unemployment) worsen.
8   "Outlawing the supply of a commodity does nothing to the demand for the commodity." What implications for the activities of organized crime does this statement have?
9   Discuss the benefits and costs of an illegal versus a legal supply of heroin.
10   What is the economic rationale for compensating crime victims for their losses?
11   Resources cannot be efficiently allocated within the criminal justice system, because the outcome would be an inequitable distribution of crime victims by income group. Evaluate.
12   From the point of view of this chapter, would we expect college graduates to commit fewer economically motivated crimes per capita than slum dwellers? Why? If so, then how do you explain the prevalence of white-collar crimes?

SUGGESTED READINGS

Fleisher, Belton. "The Effects of Income on Delinquency." *American Economic Review* (March 1966), 118 - 137.

Katzman, Martin. "The Economics of Defense Against Crime in the Streets." *Land Economics* (November 1968), 431 - 440.

President's Commission on Law Enforcement and Administration of Justice. "Crime in America." In *The Challenge of Crime in a Free Society*, pp. 17 - 53. Washington: Government Printing Office, 1967.

Rottenberg, Simon. "The Clandestine Distribution of Heroin, Its Discovery and Suppression." *Journal of Political Economy* (January - February 1968), 78 - 90.

Schelling, Thomas. "Economic Analysis and Organized Crime." In *Task Force Report: Organized Crime*, prepared for the President's Commission on Law Enforcement and Administration of Justice, pp. 114 - 126. Washington: Government Printing Office, 1967.

Shoup, Carl. "Standards for Distributing a Free Governmental Service: Crime Prevention." *Public Finance* (December 1964), 383 - 401.

Stigler, George. "The Optimum Enforcement of Laws." *Journal of Political Economy* (May 1970), 526 - 536.

14 / The Urban Public Sector: Part One

Preceding chapters have discussed major problems of inefficiency resulting from market failure and sources of inequity in urban areas. Some form of public intervention is usually required to correct such outcomes. The success of the public sector in correcting these problems of inefficiency and inequity depends, in large part, on the way in which it is organized and operated. The existence of a problem in an urban area does not necessarily mean that the urban government is most capable of solving it. This chapter develops a framework for examing the role of the urban public sector in the economy and develops criteria for achieving the efficient provision of public outputs. Chapter 15 applies these criteria to an examination of the efficiency and equity aspects of the provision of some specific public outputs, particularly education, and also covers the role of local taxation. Basic features of the framework developed in these chapters are compared with the urban public sector as it functions in the real world today. These comparisons indicate considerable room for improvement in urban government's attempts to realize its efficiency and equity objectives.

The Role of the Urban Public Sector in Achieving Equity and Efficiency Objectives

There are three general economic functions of government in a market economy: stabilization, income redistribution, and resource allocation. The stabilization goals of the government include maintaining full employment of resources and stable prices. The two major tools used to achieve these goals are monetary and fiscal policy, as discussed in Chapter 6. The federal (national) government is the only government unit which can and does execute such policies. There is no role for urban government in achieving stabilization goals, because an urban area is a very "open" economy, with many inflows and outflows of people and other resources across its borders that cannot be locally controlled. The role of local (subnational) governments versus the federal government in achieving income redistribution and resource allocation objectives is discussed below. The economic rationale for the appropriate role of urban government in these two functions differs significantly from what is found in the real world, and many difficult problems of urban governments are attributable to the inappropriate roles assumed by these governments.

Income Redistribution: A Role that Should Not Be Performed by Urban Government

The distribution of income among members of society as determined by the market system may not be considered acceptable by society.

Intervention by government into the economy is then required, for example, to realize short-run poverty programs designed to increase the incomes of those in poverty. Because local governments are very open economies (as mentioned above), income distribution objectives should be left to the national government, as the following example illustrates.

Consider a central city in a large urban area, which contains a much higher percentage of low-income households than the surrounding suburbs. Suppose the central city attempts to redistribute income locally to close some portion of the poverty gap of its low-income residents, perhaps through pricing services such as health care at less than their market price or through direct cash assistance. Low-income residents of the central city will receive an increase in net private benefits as a result of living there. Low-income residents of other jurisdictions outside the central city will come to realize that they could increase their net private benefits by moving to the central city, where the level of income redistribution is higher than where they presently reside. Thus, the attempt to redistribute income locally will create an incentive for the in-migration of low-income households. However, an inflow of lower-income households will mean that more income in total will have to be redistributed from high- to low-income families in order to maintain the same proportionate reduction in the poverty gap. In other words, if the total amount of income redistribution is not increased as the in-migration proceeds, the amount received by each low-income household will have to be reduced.

While the attempt to redistribute income to the poor provides an incentive for low-income households to migrate to the central city, it also provides an incentive for the out-migration of higher-income households. The local income redistribution program must be financed by higher taxes, or private costs, to higher-income households. But, since these higher-income households receive little or none of the benefits of such local income redistribution programs, they receive a decrease in net private benefits as a result of living in the jurisdiction. If such households were not mobile, this would present no problem; they would have to continue to reside in the central city. However, high-income households are in fact very mobile, and can easily move their place of residence to a suburban jurisdiction that has few low-income households and low levels of income redistribution activity. Within a major urban area, the decision to move to the suburbs may not be very costly to the household, since it does not usually involve changing jobs, as would be the case in moving to another part of the country, or moving so far from the place of employment that a change in jobs would be required. Thus, the higher-income household's move out of the central city results in an increase in net private benefits to that household whenever the increase in taxes in the central city is greater than the costs of relocation. A similar incentive is provided for the out-migration of business firms if such firms are heavily taxed to support redistribution activities.

In summary, a local jurisdiction such as a central city is a very open economy with a high degree of mobility across its borders. The attempt of such a local government to redistribute income increases mobility incentives and results in "dual-migration"; low-income households migrate in to increase their net private benefits and higher-income households migrate out for the same reason. There is no practical way for a local government to significantly redistribute income without stimulating dual-migration. If the central city continued to pursue a significant income redistribution program, the ultimate result would be a more equal distribution of income in the central city, but a much lower per capita income, since the city would be composed mostly of low-income people.

The dual-migration problem would be eliminated if the national government were completely responsible for tax and expenditure programs that redistribute income, because the nation is essentially a closed economy. Heavy in-migration into the United States is precluded by the immigration laws, which have resulted in only about 400,000 immigrants per year in recent years. Similarly, the taxation of high-income people does not result in significant out-migration from the country. The idea of renouncing one's citizenship and moving to another country to escape income taxes is a much stronger disincentive to mobility than moving from a central city to a suburb.

Ideally, income redistribution should be completely financed by the federal government. As a practical matter, the goal is to shift the financing of income redistribution programs to the highest level of government that is politically feasible. In general, the higher the level of government and the greater its geographic size, the less open the economy and the lower the dual-migration incentives. Thus, if central-city financing of income-redistributive activities were shifted to a government unit equal in size to the urban area, or better yet to the state government, some of the dual-migration incentives would be eliminated. However, a significant amount of income-redistributive activities are in fact financed by local governments today. The last three columns of Table 14-1 present estimates of various expenditures that are financed by local taxes, in the forty-eight largest central cities in the United States. The term "direct expenditures" in the first column refers to total expenditures actually made by local government, regardless of the source of the funds. The first three expenditure functions listed are the most explicitly income-redistributive: welfare, health and hospitals priced at less than cost, and housing programs, including public housing and urban renewal. While these data are relatively crude, it can be seen that perhaps $600 million of welfare expenditures are financed by local taxation and sizable amounts of the total expenditures on the other two kinds of income

EXPENDITURE FUNCTION	TOTAL DIRECT LOCAL GOVERNMENT EXPENDITURES	FORTY-EIGHT LARGEST CITIES AMOUNT FINANCED BY		
		TOTAL DIRECT EXPENDITURES	State Funds	Local Non-tax Sources
INCOME REDISTRIBUTIVE ACTIVITIES				
Public welfare	$ 7,707	$2,503	$1,905	—
Health and hospitals	5,805	1,674	174	$260
Housing programs	Not available	971	46	204
Public schools	43,612	3,167	1,253	139
RESOURCE ALLOCATION ACTIVITIES				
Streets and roads	5,792	877	325	109
Police	4,430	1,815	—	—
Fire	2,303	884	—	—
Sewerage	2,645	650	—	249
Sanitation other than sewerage	1,441	601	—	54
Parks and recreation	2,109	658	—	95
Libraries	Not available	215	—	—

Table 14-1: Selected Local Government Expenditures and Financing Sources for 1970-1971 ($ Million)

SOURCES: U.S. Bureau of the Census, *Governmental Finances in 1970 - 71*, Government Printing Office, Washington, 1972, pp. 34 - 35; U.S. Bureau of the Census, *City Government Finances in 1970 - 71*, Government Printing Office, Washington, 1972, pp. 87 - 88.

redistribution are financed by local taxes, although federal funds (not shown in the table) cover some share of these, particularly welfare and public housing. A significant portion of some of the other expenditures listed in the table may be considered income-redistributive in that they are higher than they would be if there were not a high percentage of low-income people in the central city. For example, the forty-eight central cities account for approximately 20 percent of the United States population, yet their police expenditures of $1,815 million are more than 40 percent of the United States total spent by local governments. A large part of this disproportionately high police expenditure in major cities is probably accounted for by higher crime rates associated with high concentrations of low-income households. In conclusion, the higher incidence of lower-income households in the central city of the urban area and the significant amount of income-redistributive expenditures financed by local taxation are major contributors to the "plight of the central cities." While the solution to the dual-migration problem is simple from the standpoint of economics, it is apparently very difficult politically, as the lack of appropriate legislation shows.

Resource Allocation: A Role
for the Urban Public Sector

Preceding chapters have discussed various cases of market failure in urban areas. When the market fails to achieve efficient outcomes, there is a role for government in improving the market-determined allocation of resources. In some cases, such as public goods, the resource allocation function may take the form of publicly providing the goods and services that are inefficiently provided by the market. In other cases, the preferable approach may be government regulation of market activities, such as safety inspection of steam boilers to reduce the potential of large negative externalities of injury and death through boiler explosions. If the national government is the only government that *can* perform the stabilization function and the only government that *should* perform the income distribution function, any role for urban government must lie in the resource allocation function. However, if the national government can perform all aspects of this function just as well as local governments, scarce resources will be wasted by local governments duplicating the bureaucracies and administrative costs of the federal government. The economic justification for the existence of local governments in urban areas rests on the superiority of a federal system of government as opposed to a single national government. A federal system is one with more than one level of government, with some units having superiority over others and different responsibilities, as established by a constitution.

There are several reasons why a federal system may be superior to a single central government system. One reason is the greater choice of governmental services (local public outputs) available to the consumer, who can choose to locate in the jurisdiction that comes closest to maximizing his net private benefits. Another possible advantage of a federal system is that an element of competition is more likely to exist. This should result in the production of public outputs at lower cost than in monopoly situations, where entrenched bureaucracies can become unresponsive because of the lack of competitive pressures. Assuming that a federal system is superior to other forms of government organization in performing the allocative function, the question becomes which level of government and which form of market intervention can best accomplish a specific resource allocation function. The economic answer to these questions is not simple, unlike the solution to the dual-migration problem.

Criteria for Efficient Provision of Local Public Outputs

The term "local public output" refers to outputs (goods or services) that local government has a role in providing; this term is used to avoid confusion with "public goods," which generally refers to commodities possessing collective consumption characteristics (as discussed in Chapter 4). There are three major elements in the efficient provision of a public output and the resource allocation function of the local government may include one or more of them. They are: (1) determining the demand for public outputs and (when possible) permitting each consumer to maximize net private benefits from consumption of the output; (2) achieving efficient production of the output; and (3) financing the costs of the output on the basis of benefits received (benefit-connected financing). Local government plays a large role in the resource allocation function, as indicated by the size of the expenditures in Table 14-1. Its role in the provision of local public outputs has to be examined on a case-by-case basis. In some cases, the extent of government involvement may be unwarranted on grounds of efficiency and more attributable to historical accident. In other cases, the methods of government provision may be inefficient compared with alternatives or, finally, lack of government involvement in provision may result in inefficiency.

Registering and Satisfying Effective Demands of Consumer-Voters

For goods and services allocated through the market system, each consumer can vary the quantity of each private output consumed, choosing that quantity at which the marginal private benefits of the last unit consumed equal the marginal private costs of that unit. The consumer of public outputs may not be able to maximize net private benefits, since there may be no mechanism that permits individuals to vary either the quantity consumed or the price paid per unit. Many decisions on the price to be charged consumers and the quantity of public outputs to be provided are made through the political process, by the consumer-voters going to the polls and voting on a majority-rule basis. The following examples illustrate the inefficient outcomes that may arise from the political process when all consumer-voters are faced with the same cost-quantity combination of a local public output, even though they have different preferences, and hence demands, for the output.

The median voter outcome   Consider a large urban area having only one local government unit (a metropolitan government), which has sole responsibility for the provision of parks (as well as other public outputs). Assuming there are no parks at present, suppose that the citizens are called to the polls to decide whether parks should be provided. To keep the example simple, assume that parks will be provided evenly over the whole urban area and that the costs will be shared equally by all consumer-voters. Figure 14-1 shows the marginal private benefit (MPB) curves for five consumer-voters in the community (alternatively, each MPB curve can be considered to represent the effective demands of five segments of the local population, each segment having the same number of people). Whether Figure 14-1 represents a five-person community or a large urban area, the equal-cost-sharing assumption is reflected by a constant marginal social cost curve divided by the number of consumer-voters in the community. In other words, MSC divided by the number of consumer-voters in the community equals the marginal private cost to each.

The five individuals (or groups) in Figure 14-1 are voting in a referendum on the amount of park space to be provided. At the present time there are no parks, and the referendum asks authorization to acquire fifty square feet of park space per capita (defeat of the referendum will, of course, leave the area with none). The figure indicates that such a referendum would pass by a 4 to 1 margin, since the marginal private benefits of individuals 2 through 5 equal or exceed the marginal private cost. (Technically, this is true only for the fiftieth square foot. However, individuals 2 through 5 receive greater net benefits from having fifty square feet of parks per capita than having none, while this is not true of individual 1.) After the passage of this first referendum, suppose that the metropolitan government decides to have another one, asking whether an additional fifty square feet of parks be provided, for a total of one hundred square feet. The

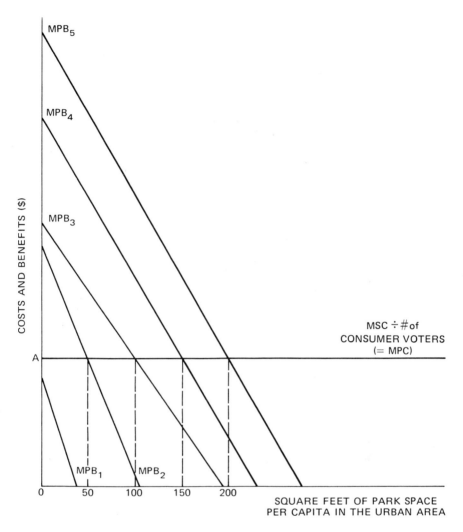

Figure 14-1 region labels:

MPB$_5$

MPB$_4$

MPB$_3$

COSTS AND BENEFITS ($)

MSC $\div$ # of
CONSUMER VOTERS
(= MPC)

A

MPB$_1$ MPB$_2$

0   50   100   150   200

SQUARE FEET OF PARK SPACE
PER CAPITA IN THE URBAN AREA

VOTING OUTCOMES

Square feet of park space	Voting outcome	
	Yes	No
50	4	1
100	3	2
150	2	3
200	1	4

Figure 14-1: Effective Demands cf Consumer-Voters and Voting Outcomes

result of this referendum, as shown in the figure, is a 3 to 2 passage, since individuals 3, 4, and 5 receive greater net benefits from having one-hundred square feet of parks as compared with only fifty. Similarly, if a referendum is held to expand parks further, to 150 square feet per capita, it would be voted down 3 to 2, since MPC exceeds MPB for three out of the five individuals.

In summary, the median voter's effective demand determines the quantity of public output provided in the community under the conditions stipulated above. All individuals having effective demands (MPBs) less than the median voter's will be dissatisfied, however, since too much of the public output will be provided. Further, while those voters having effective demands greater than the median voter will prefer the outcome of one-hundred square feet to having none, they too will be dissatisfied because they desire even greater amounts of the public output. In general, only those voters who have effective demands that coincide with those of the median voter will maximize their net private benefits; others will have to accept quantities that are either greater or less than those that maximize net private benefits, given the private cost per unit.

Voting outcomes and government size   The degree of dissatisfaction that a consumer-voter experiences from the voting outcome will depend on the extent to which his effective demand differs from that of the median voter. In terms of Figure 14-1, the majority voting outcome will be one-hundred square feet of park per capita. Individual 1 (MPB_1) receives total benefits from the provision of park space equal to the area under his MPB curve; however, the private costs he incurs are OA times 100 units. Thus, the total private costs are considerably greater than total private benefits, so that net private benefits are negative. As a result, individual 1 is worse off than if no parks were provided, which implies a rather high degree of dissatisfaction. If Figure 14-1 is representative of voters in a large urban area, then only a very small percentage will be satisfied with the amount of provision of the public output—those whose MPBs are close to the median. The rest (80 percent in this example) will be dissatisfied to a greater or lesser degree, and this dissatisfaction represents a major efficiency loss. Improving the situation will lead to greater net social benefits.

Many resource allocation decisions are made through the political process with cost-quantity outcomes that cannot be varied by individual consumer-voters, so that they cannot maximize their net private benefits. In such cases, a federal system of government has certain advantages over centralized government, namely, that consumers can be given some degree of choice regarding quantities. Similarly, metropolitan government tends to indicate that many consumer-voters may be dissatisfied with cost-quantity decisions regarding public outputs, yet have no recourse other than leaving the urban area.

In terms of consumer-voters achieving efficient registration of their demand for local public outputs, smaller governmental units within urban areas are advantageous in that voters can vote with their feet as well as at the ballot box. A person faced with overly high provision of public outputs can perhaps migrate to a jurisdiction where a smaller amount of public outputs is provided. With only a single government in an urban area, however, this is generally not possible unless the person leaves the area. With several packages of public outputs and prices available in the same urban area, individuals may be able to choose a package that comes quite close to maximizing their net private benefits by voting with their feet and moving to the jurisdiction providing the best package.

In Figure 14-1, all five individuals (or five groups of individuals with identical MPB curves) had to pay for the provision of one-hundred square feet of park space, but only the median voter was entirely satisfied with this outcome. Suppose that, instead of a single governmental unit for the entire urban area, the area were split into five areas and that all those with identical demands voted with their feet and moved into an area where the desired level of public output was provided. If each of the five groups of people was a majority in one of the jurisdictions originally and voted in the amount of public output it wanted, then that group could be joined by others of similar persuasion. Ultimately, as a result of changing from a single urban government to five jurisdictions in the urban area, each consumer-voter could maximize his net private benefits with respect to the provision of this public output. The implication is that diverse (heterogeneous) effective demands for local public outputs could be met by shifting people around through consumer-voter mobility. Those consumer-voters having the same effective demands would live in the same jurisdiction and dissatisfaction would be reduced. However, in order to achieve efficiency, this must obtain for all the public outputs; difficulties in attaining this outcome are discussed in the next section.

As another example of the potential efficiency gains from achieving more homogeneous groupings of consumer-voters by jurisdiction, suppose that there are 1 million consumer-voters in the entire urban area and 600,000 of these desire alternative A and 400,000 desire alternative B. With majority rule, the metropolitan government carries out alternative A, pleasing 60 percent while displeasing 40 percent. Now suppose the urban area is divided into two governmental units of one-half million each. In area X, 300,000 favor alternative B while 200,000 favor alternative A; in area Y, 400,000 favor A while only 100,000 favor B. Under majority rule, 700,000 (70 percent) now obtain what they want, compared with only 60 percent before. If the urban area were further subdivided, and there were consumer-voters who were unhappy with both alternatives A and B, they could vote with their feet and achieve a homogeneous grouping of people who would opt for alternative C. In summary, the greater the amount of choice and the more mobility possessed by consumer-voters, the greater the probability that all consumer-voters can find a jurisdiction that maximizes their net private benefits from the provision of local public outputs, given that such decisions are made through the voting process.

Conditions for achieving efficiency through consumer-voter mobility   Having a large number of government units in large urban areas that consumer-voters can choose among can lead to efficiency in the provision of public outputs only if certain conditions are met.[1] We have already mentioned the requirement of sufficient mobility so that households can in fact move to the desired jurisdiction. As was discussed in Chapters 7 and 8, the geographic housing choices of lower-income black households tend to be quite limited compared with those of high-income white households. While higher-income whites may be able to vote with their feet and choose to reside in any jurisdiction in the urban area, such choices may not exist for those of low income, or even higher-income blacks, who are often confined to the inner city. Also, consumer-voters must face the *real* costs and benefits of providing local public outputs in various jurisdictions; in other words, the financing of local public outputs must be benefit-connected, so that consumer-voters pay for benefits received, and neither receive benefits for which they do not pay nor pay for benefits not received. This condition of benefit-connected financing is also unlikely to be met in the real world. Considerable consumer-voter mobility is observed in the real world, but it appears that this is only partially related to achieving efficiency, and is also strongly related to two major causes of *inefficiency*, dual-migration and fiscal zoning.

The incentives towards dual-migration, previously discussed, appear to be one of the major reasons for consumer-voter mobility in the real world. Although local governments should not be engaged in redistributing income, they in fact are, since the federal government does not finance all the major redistributive activities (see Table 14-1). The proportion of low-income people in various jurisdictions of a typical urban area is usually quite variable, partly because of housing policies that exclude low-income households from certain jurisdictions. As a result, the local taxes for income redistribution and the level of local welfare benefits vary considerably among jurisdictions. Accordingly, strong incentives exist for migration of lower-and higher-income households among jurisdictions of urban areas. While this kind of consumer-voter mobility stems from a desire to maximize one's net private benefits, the process does not lead to a maximization

[1]For a complete discussion of the assumptions underlying efficient outcomes in a local government model with consumer-voter mobility, see Charles Tiebout, "A Pure Theory of Local Expenditures," *Journal of Political Economy* (October 1956), 416 - 424.

of net social benefits. The incentive for mobility provided by local income redistribution would be absent if the federal government properly assumed the total financial responsibility for all major income redistribution activities. In other words, such mobility is inefficient, because it implies that people and business firms move for reasons that are unrelated to the efficiency of production or consumption.

Fiscal zoning   Related to the inefficient mobility incentive provided by dual-migration is the incentive to engage in "fiscal zoning" that is encouraged by heavy use of ability-to-pay taxation to finance local public outputs. The property tax, discussed in Chapter 15, is the main source of such financing, and there is usually a poor correlation between the value of property (and corresponding property tax liabilities) and the benefits received from local public outputs financed by the property tax. Thus, an incentive is created for local public officials to encourage land use that results in higher property tax yields (high value of property per acre) and low demands on local public outputs. Table 14-2 is a numerical example illustrating fiscal zoning at work in two jurisdictions, A and B, with A being a winner from fiscal zoning and B being a loser.

	JURISDICTION	
	A	B
Land used for nonresidential purposes		
Market value	$100,000,000	$10,000,000
A. Property taxes (3% of market value)	$ 3,000,000	$ 300,000
Land used for residential purposes		
Number of housing units	1,000	10,000
Average market value per unit	$ 60,000	$ 12,000
B. Total residential property taxes (3% of market value)	$ 1,800,000	$ 3,600,000
C. Total property taxes collected by jurisdiction (A + B)	$ 4,800,000	$ 3,900,000
D. Cost of tax-financed local public outputs consumed by business	$ 1,000,000	$ 100,000
E. Revenue available to finance local public outputs benefiting residents (C − D)	$ 3,800,000	$ 3,800,000
F. Number of residents (assuming three per housing unit)	3,000	30,000
Revenue available per capita (E/F)	$ 1,267	$ 127

Table 14-2: An Example of Fiscal Zoning   For the reader who is unfamiliar with how property-tax liabilities are actually computed in the real world, an example of the steps involved in going from the estimated market value of a property to the property-tax liability is contained in Table 15-3.

Assume that both jurisdictions are of approximately equal geographic size, and all land uses are categorized as either residential or nonresidential. Suppose that the public officials of A have zoned half their land for business and commercial use and have attracted "clean" business activity, such as office parks and warehouses, which do not impose significant externalities on the residents of the community (like air, water, or noise pollution). However, for residential land uses the local zoning code specifies that minimum lot size is one acre and that minimum house size is 2,000 square feet. As a result of these and other zoning restrictions, which implicitly zone out low-income households, the average market value of houses built in jurisdiction A is $60,000. Thus, all land in jurisdiction A devoted to residential use is occupied by higher-income families.

While the business property pays taxes to jurisdiction A, much of the tax burden is not borne by citizens of A, since property taxes on business tend to be passed on to people outside the jurisdiction. (The incidence of property taxes on business will be discussed further in Chapter 15.) For jurisdiction A, the cost of local public outputs consumed by business is considerably less than taxes paid by business. This is usually the case in the real world because the largest proportion of local public outputs are consumed by residents and not by business firms. For example, as a national average, about half of the local public sector budget is devoted to elementary and secondary education. While business firms in jurisdiction A pay property taxes to finance schools, they do not consume such public outputs. As a result of business firms paying more in taxes than they receive in benefits, residents of A receive more benefits than they contribute in taxes. Thus, fiscal zoning provides an incentive to shift part of the costs of local public outputs onto others through taxing business for more than benefits received and exporting business taxes onto nonresidents.

While jurisdiction A is a winner from the fiscal zoning game, there have to be "losers," such as jurisdiction B, because fiscal zoning is a zero-sum game—the total of the gains must equal the total of the losses, as in a poker game. To state it differently, someone has to pay the real resource cost (the opportunity cost) of the local public outputs provided, whether it is consumer-voters of the jurisdiction or someone else. Jurisdiction B exemplifies a jurisdiction that has little business tax base to draw upon and a high incidence of lower-income families (as implied by the average market value per dwelling unit of $12,000), who impose large demands on local public outputs such as education and other people-related services (including health, hospitals, and welfare).

In summary, people do appear to vote with their feet; however, much of this incentive for consumer-voter mobility in the real world appears to be the result of dual-migration and fiscal zoning incentives. Such incentives to mobility promote inefficiency. If they were reduced, then mobility would better reflect the real resource costs of this decision, and it would improve efficiency. The removal of such incentives requires the elimination of non-benefit-connected financing of local public outputs via the elimination of local income-redistributive activities. In many cases, it appears that making local government resource allocation decisions through voting is not necessary; instead, many public outputs are of a nature where the costs and quantities can be varied by the consumer—they are "private goods" rather than the "public goods" discussed in Chapter 4—and, thus, problems inherent in voting can be eliminated. The benefit-connected financing of recreational outputs and elementary and secondary education is discussed in Chapter 15, as examples of methods of financing local public outputs on the basis of benefits received by individual consumer-voters.

Criteria for Efficient Production of Local Public Outputs

The preceding section on registering demand for local public outputs started with a single government unit (metropolitan government) providing all local public outputs in a large urban area. The disadvantages of such an arrangement were examined and some alternatives presented. This section will proceed in a similar fashion. Efficient production of local public outputs involves two basic aims: achieving least-cost production, and efficient handling of cost or benefit spillovers (externalities between government jurisdictions) that result from the production of local public outputs.

Economies of scale   The basic consideration here is achieving the scale of production at which the cost of producing a unit of output is minimized. For various reasons, the relationship between cost per unit and quantity of production (size or scale of plant) is usually assumed to be decreasing up to some scale of production. Beyond this scale of production, per unit costs are probably fairly constant, but they may increase after some further point. As shown in Figure 14-2, economies of scale are said to exist for increases in scale of production up to quantity OA because such increases in output result in a decrease in per unit costs of production. The efficient-sized production unit, defined solely on the basis of per unit costs, is one that produces a quantity between OA and the quantity where the cost curve begins to increase.

In practice, it is extremely difficult to determine the existence of economies of scale for local public output production. The difficulty is in defining and measuring the *unit* of output. For example, in the case of schools, defining the unit of output as an "educated student" is not sufficient, since this begs the question of what is an educated student. Since quality of output can vary considerably, it is not sufficient to measure output as number of student-years, either, since students can be run through the system at much lower cost (at a sacrifice in quality, of course). Because of the inherent difficulties involved in measuring outputs, it is common practice in the real world to make comparisons between producers, such as school systems, on the basis of expenditures made on inputs to the production process. However, measuring outputs in this way implicitly assumes that output is directly proportional to input expenditure and that no economies of scale exist. Since the type and amounts of inputs used in various production processes called "education" are different, there is no reason to believe that two school systems spending identical amounts per pupil are producing identical outputs. One school system may spend less on teachers (having high pupil-teacher ratios or fewer teachers with master's degrees) but more on books, materials, and physical plant. Without a measure of output stemming from these two different sets of inputs, except that per pupil expenditures are the same, we really have no way of knowing the relative "production" of the two schools. In other words, if school systems A and B spend $900 and $600 per pupil per year, respectively, it does not follow that the output (benefits) are 50 percent greater in A than in B.

Increasing relative costs of local public outputs   Because of the difficulties in defining and measuring public outputs, the present state of knowledge on what size of producing unit achieves economies of scale is essentially nonexistent. Yet the question of per unit costs of

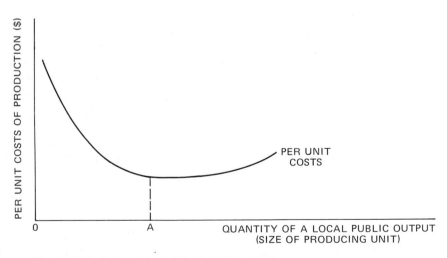

Figure 14-2: Economies of Scale in Production

production and methods of minimizing them is important for resource allocation, because there is reason to believe that such local
public outputs as police protection and elementary education will
require an increasing proportion of society's resources over time.
Labor costs account for a very large percentage of the total costs of
producing many local outputs, in some cases over 90 percent. If local
governments are to retain and attract personnel, salaries and fringe
benefits must rise along with those of private industry; otherwise,
government employees will see their standard of living falling relative to comparable employees in the private sector. If the producers of
local public outputs were able to increase labor productivity (output
per man-hour) in proportion to the increases in wage rates, there
would be no change in per unit costs of production. However, unlike
many producers in the private sector, local government appears to
have only a limited opportunity to utilize capital equipment (such as
automated machinery) to increase productivity, because of the heavy
dependence of the public sector on labor inputs. The implication is
that public sector outputs will become more and more costly, if
present quality levels are to be maintained.

Table 14-3 presents an example of the changing relative costs of
producing two outputs over time.[2] One output, the assembly of automobiles in the manufacturing sector, is technologically progressive
in the sense that there is considerable potential for substituting capital for labor inputs over time and achieving technological innova-
tions. The other output, the collection of trash in a residential area,
has changed little over time, since the primary input is the labor
involved in hauling the trash from trash cans to a truck. The table first
shows labor productivity, wages, and labor cost per unit of output
twenty years ago. The figures presented for today reflect a situation
where productivity has doubled in auto assembly operations but has
not increased at all in the collection of trash. Assume that wages in the
two sectors tend to increase in the same proportion; were this not true,
workers would tend to move to jobs in the sector where wages had
increased faster. Auto workers would not quit and become trash
collectors if their wages went up more slowly than the trash collectors, because present auto workers are of higher skill than trash
collectors. New workers would be more willing to collect trash at
higher relative wages, however, and this would tend to bring wages
back into the same relative positions as before. Thus, the existence of
some labor market mobility will tend to keep wages in general relationship with each other. The productivity of the auto worker (or the
output per man-hour) has doubled in our example, and we can as-

[2]The example and analysis presented here are based on a model developed by
William Baumol in "Macroeconomics of Unbalanced Growth: The Anatomy of Urban
Crisis," *American Economic Review* (June 1967), 415 - 426.

sume that his union has succeeded in gaining wage increases equal to this increase in productivity. This implies that the labor cost per unit of output has not changed and remains at $200. In the case of the trash collector, wages doubled (so that the relative standards of living of auto workers and trash collectors remained the same) while productivity remained constant (according to this example). As a result, the labor cost of collecting a ton of trash doubled (from $10 to $20) during this twenty-year period. These are changes in *real* costs and not merely the changes in money costs due to inflationary changes in the purchasing power of the dollar. The example assumes all figures are adjusted for inflation and are stated in constant dollars.

In summary, the relative cost of output produced by the technologically nonprogressive sector of the economy tends to increase over time. Most public outputs appear to fit into this category, so the relative prices of education, police protection, fire protection, and other local public outputs that use large labor inputs have increased over time and will probably continue to do so. When the unit of output is not as obvious as a ton of trash collected, the increase in relative costs is not so unequivocal. For example, labor costs per "student year" have certainly increased, but if the quality of education has significantly increased also, there may have been a much smaller increase in the cost of "education." As has been noted, however, there are no good measures of this output. To take another approach, if outputs are measured by cost of inputs, then one dollar's worth of input will always produce one dollar's worth of output, and output measured this way *must* go up at the same rate as expenditure. This is perhaps the clearest reason why cost of inputs is a poor measure of outputs. Were we better able to measure outputs, we should probably find that the relative cost of education and other public outputs has increased over time, but by an amount less than the per pupil expenditure implies. Since today's teachers are better educated on the average than those of twenty years ago, quality of education has probably risen, but it is quite unlikely that this quality increase has kept pace with the increase in productivity in the private sector.

Achieving least-cost production of local public outputs: Some implications and conclusions   There is a long tradition of advocating large governmental units (especially a single metropolitan government for an entire urban area) on the grounds of achieving economies of scale in the production of local public outputs. This contention lacks support for several reasons. First, as discussed above, empirical knowledge about economies of scale is essentially nonexistent. Second, large government producers tend to be "spatial monopolists"—the only producer of a public output in a large geographic area. As a result, there may be little incentive to minimize production costs

| | AUTO WORKER | | TRASH COLLECTOR | |
	Twenty years ago	Today	Twenty years ago	Today
A. Total full-time employees	4,000	4,000	50	50
B. Output (number of cars produced)	100,000	200,000		
Output (tons of trash collected)			12,500	12,500
C. Output per man-year (B/A)	25 cars	50 cars	250 tons	250 tons
D. Wages per full-time employee	$5,000	$10,000	$2,500	$5,000
E. Labor cost per unit of output (D/C)	$200	$200	$10	$20

Table 14-3: An Example of Changing Labor Productivity, Wages, and Labor Cost per Unit of Output

because such producers do not feel the pressures of a competitive environment. If it were possible to precisely measure public outputs, then the producers of, say, trash disposal in cities A and B could be compared. If A and B served approximately equal populations, the question of economies of scale would not enter as an explanation of cost differences. Under such conditions, the existence of higher production costs in city B than in city A would lead to public pressure in city B for the producer to either produce at lower cost or find a new job. This sort of information is rarely available in the real world, and, given this state of ignorance, it is very difficult to determine whether a spatial monopolist is a least-cost producer or not. Further, the larger the spatial monopolist is, the less opportunity there is for consumer-voters to vote with their feet, and the lower the pressure on the spatial monopolist to be a least-cost producer.

In addition to the above objections to large-scale governments with respect to production costs, the earlier section of this chapter on demand registration indicates that larger governments lead to smaller probabilities that consumer-voters can vote with their feet and obtain the package of public outputs and taxes that maximizes their net private benefits. However, even if large-scale governments were required to produce at lowest cost and were able to achieve the least cost through economies of scale, the objections above can be avoided by separating the government unit that determines the consumer-voter demands from the producer of these outputs. Separation of production and demand functions of local governments through the establishment of "contract cities" (such as the Lakewood Plan cities in Los Angeles County, California) permits small government units to determine the demand for local public outputs but to produce them either through the local government itself or through contractual arrangement with another governmental unit or through a private contractor.[3]

Separation of the government unit registering demand from that producing the local public output "institutionalizes competition" and provides an incentive for the producing unit to be a least-cost producer, which is absent in the case of spatial monopolies. The local government determines the type and quantity of local public outputs demanded, but has a choice of the method of producing these outputs: self-production, production by another government through contractual arrangement, or production through a private contractor. Thus,

---

[3]For a further discussion of the virtues of separating demand and production, and the Lakewood plan, see Robert Warren, "A Municipal Service Market Model of Metropolitan Organization," *Journal of the American Institute of Planners* (August 1964), 193 - 204 (reprinted in Arthur F. Schreiber, Paul K. Gatons, and Richard B. Clemmer, eds., *Economics of Urban Problems: Selected Readings*, Houghton Mifflin, Boston, 1971, pp. 261 - 278).

there exists an incentive for producers to be least-cost producers, since the only way they can maintain or expand their level of production is through winning contracts that are open to competitive bidding. Since the entire discussion of the question of economies of scale in this chapter has been thwarted by the extreme difficulties in measuring public outputs, institutionalization of competition seems to be a second-best answer to achieving least-cost production. Even if output units cannot be measured and compared among various producers, the incentive provided by such competition should lead to lower production costs than would exist in the absence of such competition (as in the case of the large spatial monopoly).

Viewing the separation of production and demand determination from the point of view of consumer-voters, the problem of inefficient demand registration and the degree of dissatisfaction associated with large spatial monopolies is greatly reduced. Given the efficient-sized government from the point of view of demand registration (which is probably quite small), any potential economies of scale that cannot be achieved by a government unit of this size can still be realized by having someone else supply it through contractual arrangement. At the same time, the large-scale producer faces competition from having to compete for bids with smaller governmental units. In addition, spatial monopolists would not be expected to have much incentive to generate better information on cost-output relationships. Institutionalizing competition through contractual arrangements may, in the long run, provide an incentive to generate such information and ultimately permit more satisfactory answers to the question of economies of scale in production of public outputs.

In conclusion, it appears that the economic necessity of having large local government units is mostly irrelevant for achieving either efficient registration of demand or least-cost production of public outputs. However, there is another major aspect to achieving efficient production of local public outputs—the question of efficient handling of spillovers of costs and benefits between local government jurisdictions. The next section of this chapter examines goverment organization and size in terms of potential for efficient handling of such spillovers.

Efficient handling of cost and benefit spillovers: General criterion   In place of producers or consumers imposing indirect costs or benefits on other producers or consumers, the term "spillover" refers to externalities between governmental jurisdictions, when a government engages in an act that generates externalities that spill outside its borders. In general, a necessary condition for achieving efficient resource allocation decisions is that such decisions be based on all the benefits and costs involved. Thus, the question becomes one of organizing local public sector decision-making so that all costs and benefits are considered, including those that spill over into other jurisdictions. There are two basic approaches to attaining this condition: (1) organizing the functions and geographic dimensions of local government units so that all benefits and costs fall within the jurisdiction established, thus eliminating intergovernmental spillovers; and (2) forming agreements between local governments so that benefit-cost spillovers are taken into account (voluntary agreements if between equal levels of government or involuntary if imposed by a higher level of government). Alternative methods of handling spillovers by both these means are presented below with emphasis on their advantages and disadvantages in light of the previously discussed criteria for efficient provision of local public outputs.

Designing government boundaries to eliminate spillovers: Metropolitan government and "problem-shed" special districts   While it is unlikely that unanimous agreement could be reached on the precise geographic area required to encompass the benefits and costs of local public outputs, Table 14-4 lists the assumed areas for some major local public outputs. If metropolitan government (equal in size to the urban area) is to determine the type and quantity of public outputs listed in the first column, the consumer-voters of the urban area (or their elected representatives) would be expected to base their decisions only on costs and benefits that affect them (local costs and benefits). If the political process works so that decisions are made on the basis of only local costs and benefits, any spillover costs and benefits will not be considered, and the chance that net social benefits would be maximized is very slim. Thus, metropolitan government would not efficiently handle the spillovers associated with the local public outputs listed in the first column of Table 14-4, since the geographic dimension of the costs and benefits of these activities is greater than the urban area. Similar reasoning would lead to the conclusion that metropolitan government would be effective in handling the spillovers associated with the local public outputs in the second column, since the potential spillovers are all within the urban area. Of course, the outputs in the third column would also be such that benefits and costs would be encompassed by a metropolitan government, since the geographic area there is much less than the urban area. In fact, metropolitan government is larger than is necessary to internalize these externalities.

In conclusion, it would appear that metropolitan government, as a method of handling spillovers of benefits and costs, is well suited to those activities whose costs and benefits coincide with the urban area. However, most local public outputs do not neatly fit the geographic dimensions of the urban area. Since there are other methods of handling spillovers, advocacy of metropolitan government on these grounds is weak compared with the disadvantages—the possibility of

SPILLING OVER THE BOUNDARIES OF THE URBAN AREA	APPROXIMATELY EQUAL TO URBAN AREA BOUNDARIES	PROBABLY MUCH LESS THAN URBAN AREA BOUNDARIES

Air quality
Water quality
Elementary education
Secondary education
Health
Solid-waste disposal
Expressway construction
  and maintenance
	Police protection
	Large parks and other
	  recreational facilities
	Secondary street con-
	  struction and
	  maintenance
	Commuter transit
		Fire protection
		Neighborhood parks
		  and recreational
		  facilities

Table 14-4: Assumed Geographic Dimensions of Costs and Benefits of Selected Local Public Outputs

production at other than minimum costs and lack of choice by consumer-voters.

An extension of the concept of internalizing spillovers is to specifically design the boundaries of local government units so that such boundaries coincide with the geographic dimensions of the costs and benefits associated with each public output. Problem-shed government of this sort would imply as many governmental units as there are different "problem sheds"—areas in which the costs and benefits fall. The creation of such special district governmental units would internalize the externalities and eliminate spillovers by definition.

Problem-shed government organization would mean that a consumer-voter in a given urban area would be a "member" of several, and possibly many, special district government units. For example, all consumer-voters of an urban area (plus many residents of surrounding areas) would be members of a special district designed to handle air-quality problems. This special district could easily encompass parts of several counties and parts of more than one state. However, a separate special district would have to be created to handle water-quality problems, since it is unlikely that the geographic dimensions of the water- and air-quality districts would coincide. Many special districts would have to be established, one for each public output, although some of these might have common geographic boundaries.

While the creation of problem-shed special districts would eliminate spillovers by definition, such government organization involves heavy costs with respect to the other criteria for efficient provision of public outputs. For example, consider the problem-shed associated with education. A person graduating from a local high school may eventually reside in any section of the country. This high degree of mobility would imply that the problem-shed for education must be at least equal in area to the entire United States. Obviously, a single school system for the entire United States would create a huge spatial monopoly lacking in incentives to minimize production costs and providing little choice to consumers with respect to variations in schooling outputs. Thus, while the problem-shed approach ranks very high in terms of eliminating spillovers, it ranks much lower in terms of the other criteria. Spillovers are eliminated but at a cost of the establishment of huge spatial monopolies and the resultant lack of responsiveness to cost and demand considerations.

Agreements between government units: Voluntary and involuntary   In some cases it may be possible for benefit and cost spillovers to be resolved by the affected parties getting together and reaching an agreement through negotiation. The potential for efficiently solving spillover problems via voluntary agreement will depend on the decision-making costs and the extent to which property rights are clearly established. If a spillover affects only two jurisdictions, decision-making costs (the time and effort involved in negotiations) should not be prohibitively high. Similarly, if one of the two jurisdictions has a clear legal right to engage in an activity that imposes indirect costs on the other, the question of property rights is easily answered and does not require costly legal recourse. Note that this does not imply that the indirect costs are necessarily continued. The "injured" jurisdiction might find it in its interest to "pay off" the other in some manner in order to reduce the indirect costs.

In the real world, spillovers may involve very large numbers of affected parties (for example, fifty jurisdictions in an urban area); the larger the number of parties involved, the greater the cost of reaching an agreement. Also, property rights may be ill-defined, as discussed in Chapter 11. As a result, there is a rather low expectation in the real world that bargaining, either directly with other governments or through an organization such as a metropolitan council of governments, will result in the successful resolution of spillover problems.

One of the difficulties with resolving spillovers between local governmental units is that none of these units has superior authority. In a federal system, such as the United States, the national government is superior to state governments, with its authority rights defined in a constitution. A similar relationship holds between state and local governments. Thus, under a federal system, a superior government might have the authority to impose outcomes on subordinate governments in cases of spillovers. As a result, many of the problems of decision-making costs and property rights are eliminated. Essentially, there are two means by which the superior government can handle spillover problems: establishment of minimum standards and conditional matching grants. Both methods affect the type and level of activity engaged in by subordinate government units. Conditional matching grants may be "negative grants" in the form of taxes, such as the effluent fees discussed in Chapter 12. The goal is to get the spillover-generating government to take the indirect costs and benefits of its activities into consideration when it makes resource allocation decisions. The reader is referred to the discussions in Chapters 11 and 12 on the efficient resolution of pollution externalities for some of the basic features and problems of designing grants or minimum standards to achieve efficient outcomes.

With respect to the criteria for efficient provision of local public outputs, the advantage of the use of grants (or minimum standards) to control externalities is that the size of the lower governmental unit is not critical. The use of grants for handling spillovers can be applied to lower governmental units regardless of their size. As a result, spillovers can be efficiently handled, while at the same time provision of public outputs by small local governments can be retained, along with the efficiency advantages of their arrangement.

REVIEW AND DISCUSSION QUESTIONS

1 If a central city of a large urban area wants to close some of the poverty gap of its low-income residents, it should implement its own local income redistribution programs. Discuss.
2 The smaller the size of local governments, the greater the likelihood that benefit and cost spillovers will remain unresolved; therefore, small local governments should be consolidated. Discuss.
3 Not all local government jurisdictions in an urban area can provide equal amounts of local public outputs per capita with an equal tax rate. Is this a problem? If so, what is the cause of the problem? Justify solutions in terms of efficiency.
4 The real cost (measured in dollars of constant purchasing power) per unit of education and other local public outputs, such as police and fire protection, has about doubled over the past twenty years. How do you account for this?
5 Economies of scale in the production of local public outputs require large governments to realize these economies. Discuss.
6 The central city resident pays more in taxes for financing welfare services for the poor than does the suburban resident. Thus, metropolitan government is needed, so that all people living in the urban area will be forced to pay their fair share of providing welfare services for the poor of the urban area. Evaluate.
7 Why are many individuals likely to be less satisfied by resource allocation decisions determined by the political process than by those determined by the market system?

SUGGESTED READINGS

Baumol, William. "Macroeconomics of Unbalanced Growth: The Anatomy of Urban Crises." *American Economic Review* (June 1967), 415 - 426.

Tiebout, Charles. "A Pure Theory of Local Expenditures." *Journal of Political Economy* (October 1956, 416 - 424.

Warren, Robert. "A Municipal Services Market Model of Metropolitan Organization." *Journal of the American Institute of Planners* (August 1964), 193 - 204. (Reprinted in Arthur F. Schreiber, Paul K. Gatons, and Richard B. Clemmer, eds., *Economics of Urban Problems: Selected Readings.* Boston: Houghton Mifflin, 1971.)

Advisory Commission on Intergovernmental Relations. *Urban America and the Federal System,* pp. 7 - 17. Washington: Government Printing Office, 1969. (Reprinted in Schreiber et al.)

15 / The Urban Public Sector: Part Two

Chapter 14 discussed some of the difficulties in voting and the political process of determining the quantities and cost-shares for local public outputs that will maximize the net private benefits of most consumer-voters of a jurisdiction. When consumer-voters are "stuck" with the politically determined outcome in a jurisdiction, the only effective choice mechanism is mobility: the consumer-voter can vote with his feet and move to another jurisdiction where the package of public outputs comes closer to maximizing his net private benefits. However, determination of local public output quantities and cost-shares via the political process may not always be an economic necessity. In many cases, it may be possible for people to make choices with respect to public outputs in the same way they make choices for private goods, by buying the quantity that maximizes net private benefits, given the price. This procedure is difficult to follow if the output has collective consumption characteristics, as with the public goods discussed in Chapter 4, since people are unwilling to reveal their preferences. However, many local public outputs do not possess the characteristics of public goods, and prices can be charged on the basis of benefits received.

Provision of Private-Benefit Outputs: The Role of User Charges

Many local public outputs appear to be provided through the local public sector because of historical accident or by means that have been politically determined without reference to economic criteria for their efficient provision. Many such outputs are "private-benefit outputs"; they are like private goods provided through the private market system, in that the benefits of consumption accrue mostly to the individual user, with no significant externalities in consumption involved. Further, unlike the case of pure public goods, individuals can be excluded from consumption of such outputs without incurring large administrative costs. While user charges (prices) are often imposed for local public outputs, in many cases prices are less than the marginal social cost (promoting inefficient use) and less than the price that would cover costs of operation. In such cases, public outputs have to be subsidized out of general revenues and are not totally paid for on the basis of benefits received. In other cases, private-benefit outputs are provided free of charge, so the entire cost of the operation must be covered from general tax revenues. These cases lead to high local taxes and incentives for those who do not receive the benefits of such outputs to migrate to other jurisdictions. This problem could be avoided if adequate user charges were imposed.

The failure to apply benefit-connected financing to private-benefit outputs provided by local governments is in part due to historical accident, but no doubt equity objectives have been important also. Given the lack of complete national government financing of income redistribution, there has been a tendency for local governments to assume this role and attempt to redistribute income in kind by underpricing such outputs as recreation. The justification for this has been that prices would exclude the poor from consumption of such outputs. However, the equity outcomes of such a policy can be rather perverse, as illustrated by the following example.

An Example: The City Zoo

Suppose that a city operates a zoo and charges no admission, financing operating costs by non-benefit-connected taxation levied on firms and households residing in the city. For the low-income city resident, the zero admission charge reduces the costs of attending the zoo, but there are other costs of attendance, such as transportation to and from the zoo. Some low-income residents will utilize the zoo, especially those living close to the facility who receive great benefits from attending the zoo. Most low-income residents will tend to prefer other leisure pursuits, however, and may live a great distance from the zoo. On the benefit side, horizontal equity is violated, because not all low-income city residents receive the same level of benefits. Similar reasoning would apply to higher-income city residents, indicating that horizontal equity would be violated for any income group. On the cost side, all city residents of the same income level would tend to pay the same taxes with respect to subsidizing the operation of the zoo. The attempt to redistribute income in kind to the poor might actually make most of them worse off, since nonattenders are subsidizing the operation. Further, if city taxes that pay for the zoo are regressive, the poor as a group may be made much worse off. Thus, for city residents, the provision of the zoo through general taxes is likely to be regressive.

When use by nonresidents is considered, the outcome becomes even more regressive. A large proportion of the users of a city zoo are likely to be nonresidents, not only suburbanites but also out-of-town visitors who are visiting the city as part of a vacation. Both groups are likely to be from higher income levels than the average city resident—those vacationing in a big city are usually not poverty-level households. Thus, a significant share of the users of a city zoo (and those receiving the benefits) may be higher-income nonresidents. This adds to the regressiveness, since the distribution of both costs and benefits is apparently regressive.

If most users of facilities providing private benefits can easily afford to pay a benefit-connected user charge, the inefficiencies and inequities discussed above can be avoided. With the existence of a nationally financed income redistribution program that closed most of the poverty gap, it could be presumed that low-income households having a strong preference for visiting the zoo would have effective demands high enough to enable them to pay the admission price, just as in the case of any private good. On the other hand, given the present state of income distribution, it is still possible to prevent the exclusion of low-income households while still applying user charges to everyone else. For example, passes could be issued to all households in the central city or the surrounding urban area whose incomes fell below some established limit. These passes could be used at the zoo and other public facilities in the area, with others paying an admission charge. Efficient financing would be achieved for all but the low-income households, and the adverse equity outcomes that stem from zero charges to everyone could be avoided.

Benefit financing of private-benefit outputs through user charges provides incentives to engage in efficient production and to produce only those outputs that are actually demanded by the consumer-voters of an area. In the case of the zoo, it may be found that there is no set of user charges that will cover the operating costs (even with annual admission fees discussed below). If users do not place a value on the benefits of attending the zoo (as reflected in user charge revenue) that exceed that costs of operation, the implication is that the zoo is inefficiently large (and perhaps the efficient size is zero). On the other hand, the number of people willing to pay the admission price may indicate that the zoo should be expanded and improved. In the absence of user charges, it is difficult to "get a handle on" the benefits received from the operation of the zoo so as to determine the efficient scale of operation. Also, if the zoo has to cover operating costs with admission fees, there may be a better incentive to produce at minimum operating costs, since the zoo manager cannot go to the city for ever larger subsidies to cover operating deficits.

While the example of a city zoo was used to illustrate some of the efficiency and equity features of financing the provision of private-benefit outputs with user charges, the same reasoning could be applied to many other private-benefit outputs provided by the public sector. User charges could finance a significant portion of the expenditures shown in Table 14-1, for libraries, parks and recreation, sanitation, sewerage, and many other activities of local government. In other words, since the private-benefit outputs of local government are relatively large, considerable efficiency gains could be achieved if local government financed such outputs on the basis of benefits received rather than relying heavily on general taxation.

Marginal Cost Pricing: A Dilemma

The above discussion centered on pricing of local public outputs so that financing would be on the basis of benefits received. Actually, consumers adjust to any price charged so that marginal private benefits are equal to that price—at a higher price, quantities will be less and marginal private benefits higher. Thus, it would seem that any price charged would equal marginal benefits, but remember that there is an efficient price, which will lead to the efficient quantity being purchased. If price is set equal to marginal social cost (marginal cost pricing), then efficiency will be attained if no externalities are involved. (The discussion of education below shows how this principle is modified in the presence of externalities.)

In the case of a park, a zoo, or an uncongested highway, the marginal social cost of an additional user may be very low or even zero. Once a zoo is built and filled with animals, an additional spectator may not add anything to the costs of provision; in such cases, MSC is zero and marginal cost pricing requires a zero price. A higher price will inefficiently restrict use (like a toll on an expressway at 3:00 A.M., as discussed in Chapter 9). On the other hand, if the zoo is congested, as on weekends and holidays, users impose costs on each other in the form of congestion, and an admission fee can be justified on the basis of efficiency, since marginal social cost, including the indirect costs, is no longer zero.

The problem is that the fees collected in these peak times may not be adequate to cover all the operating costs of the zoo, even though total social benefits exceed total social costs. Closing the zoo would be inefficient, as would be charging admission sufficient to cover costs. Ideally, the users of the zoo—those receiving the benefits—should pay for the operation, and this might be done by charging an annual admission fee plus additional fees on weekends and holidays. Once a person paid the annual fee, the marginal cost of attending would be zero in off-peak times, and thus the person would not be inefficiently excluded by a price at the margin that exceeded marginal social cost.

In the real world, the problem discussed here may be one reason why many public facilities are provided at zero price. Rather than finance such facilities out of general revenues, however, an alternative would be to have an annual admission charge. (This is a special case of a concept known in the economics literature as a two-part tariff.)

Provision of Mixed-Benefit Outputs: Elementary and Secondary Education

The single largest activity of the local public sector is the provision of elementary and secondary education (referred to simply as education hereafter). Table 14-1 shows that total expenditure on public schools, which includes state aid received by local school boards, by local governments (approximately $44 billion in 1970-1971) was greater than the *total* spent on all the other major activities listed in the table. As is the case with most other local public outputs, education is very labor-intensive; as a result, the relative cost of education has increased significantly over time. For example, expenditures per pupil in public schools, stated in 1969 dollars, increased from $233 to $936 between 1930 and 1970, a rise of 302 percent. Over this same period, the percentage of gross national product expended for public schools almost doubled, from 2.2 percent to 4.2 percent.[1] Given the magnitude and labor-intensive nature of education, achieving efficient use of resources in the provision of this output is an important concern with respect to overall economic well-being.

Mixed-Benefit Outputs and Benefit Financing

Education is a "mixed-benefit output," one whose consumption results in significant benefits both to the consumer (the student in this case) and to the rest of society in the form of indirect benefits. The major private benefit to the individual is the increase in one's stock of human capital, which translates into higher future income. An individual's investment in education also generates indirect benefits accruing to the rest of society, such as a better functioning political process because voters are literate and well-informed.

The benefit financing of mixed-benefit outputs such as education requires that the costs of the output be shared by the individual and society on the basis of the benefits received from the marginal unit of output. This concept is illustrated in Figure 15-1. Assume that the marginal social cost (MSC) of a "unit of education" is constant and equal to $15 per unit. (Of course, the example begs the question of adequately defining and measuring educational output.) The MPB curve represents the marginal private benefits accruing to the student (or his family, since minors are generally required to attend school up to a certain age). On the basis of private benefits received, the family would maximize net private benefits by purchasing 25 units of education for their child. This would be the private market result, if no public sector intervention were involved. This outcome would be inefficient, since there are significant externalities accruing to the rest of society that are not being taken into account. These indirect benefits are indicated by the MIB (marginal indirect benefit) curve in Figure 15-1. On the basis of indirect benefits received from the student's education, society would provide 50 units of education to the student as the minimum consumption requirement. However, the

---

[1]Roe L. Johns, "The Development of State Support for Public Schools," in Johns, Alexander, and Jordan, eds., *Financing Education: Fiscal and Legal Alternatives,* Merrill, Columbus, Ohio, 1972, p. 18.

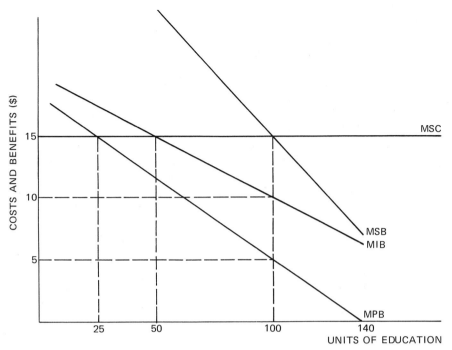

Figure 15-1: Efficient Quantity and Financing of Mixed-Benefit Outputs: A Student's Education

efficient quantity is that at which MSB equals MSC—100 units. The marginal social benefit curve is the *vertical* sum of MPB and MIB, since both the student's family and society receive benefits from education of the student. For example, for the hundredth unit, the student's family receives $5 in benefits (MPB) and society receives $10 in indirect benefits (MIB), for a total benefit of $15 (MSB). If the student's family pays $5 per unit for the 100 units of education ($500) and society pays $10 per unit ($1,000), efficiency is achieved. In such a case of mixed-benefit outputs, it is required that both the individual beneficiary and the rest of society pay part of the costs, on the basis of benefits received. For example, if the public sector decided to subsidize the entire marginal social cost by paying $15 per unit, then the family, perceiving the output as a "free good," would prefer to consume 140 units, the quantity at which marginal private costs (zero) are equal to marginal private benefits.

Evaluation of Present Methods of Providing Education

Present methods of providing elementary and secondary education in the United States are evaluated in this section with reference to the criteria for efficient provision of local public outputs developed in the preceding chapter. The financing of education is discussed with reference to the section above on financing of mixed-benefit outputs.

Demand registration Most production of education in the United States is public rather than private. With respect to the public schools, any household with children resides in a specific school system district. In most cases, residential location also determines the particular school in the system that the children will attend. As a result, the household is faced with a spatial monopoly—there is no choice of school to attend and the household is presented with a particular price-quantity package of education. Although there is nothing inherent in educational outputs that requires them to be the product of public monopoly, with limited choice available to families, public education is provided in such a manner. As a result, there are likely to be large numbers of dissatisfied consumer-voters, since they face a spatial monopoly and may have little or no effective choice.

The problem of lack of choice resulting from spatial monopolies in education is especially noticeable in large central cities (although there may be a choice between a vocational high school and college preparatory high school in such cities). The larger the spatial monopoly, the less likely that efficient demand registration will be achieved, and the consumer-voters of large central cities may face extremely large spatial monopolies. For example, the New York City school system has over 1 million students. The consumer-voter who is dissatisfied has little choice but to migrate to another jurisdiction if he wishes to receive another type or quantity of education. Were there significant differences within an urban area among schools in terms of outputs and methods, then effective demand registration could be achieved. This is unlikely to occur because of the large degree of control placed on public schools by the state government. State law may specify student-teacher ratios, the textbooks to be used (or a selection of approved texts), and similar restrictions on many other inputs. Further, mobility seems to be much more possible for upper-income whites than for lower-income blacks. Many of those with the least degree of mobility (low-income, black, central-city dwellers) tend to be faced with the largest and most intransigent spatial monopolies existing in public education, large central-city school systems. Also, in the real world much of the observed consumer-voter mobility is a result of dual-migration incentives and fiscal zoning, as discussed in Chapter 14. Since schooling is such a large expenditure and is not provided through benefit-connected financing, fiscal-zoning incentives created by the present methods of financing schools are quite strong. In brief, consumer-voter mobility may not achieve efficient demand registration and satisfaction with respect to educational outputs in the real world.

There is one other choice mechanism that is available to some consumer-voters and provides an opportunity to achieve a greater range of choice—the private-school option. However, private-school tuition is usually a sizable sum that precludes this option for all but those in high-income groups.

In summary, the likelihood of a household maximizing net private benefits from the consumption of education as presently provided is relatively high only for families with incomes large enough to overcome barriers of geographic mobility or to pay the costs of private schools. A majority of households have no such choice; they are faced with a spatial monopoly in which residential location determines the only school that can be attended and income or race precludes other options.

Production   The public monopolistic production of education places severe constraints on consumer-voter choice. The question arises whether some of this lack of choice may be justified on some economic grounds associated with the production of public outputs, such as economies of scale. In earlier times in the United States, the society was predominately rural, with low population densities, and the time and cost of transporting people were relatively high with the existing transportation technology. Under these conditions, cost considerations undoubtedly justified a public school monopoly in most geographic areas of the country. In many instances, the number of school-age children within reasonable commuting distance (i.e., walking distance) of a given place was so low that all that could be provided was the one-room schoolhouse. With such low levels of demand, imposing a monopoly made sense because production costs could be kept low that way. However, it is difficult to justify public monopolistic production of schooling in a modern urban context on these grounds. Population densities are such that, with modern transportation technology, students in urban areas are usually within commuting distance of several schools. Since public monopolies in the production of education can no longer be economically justified, it is difficult to explain them except as a historical hangover from an earlier time.

As discussed previously, public monopolistic production not only restricts consumer choice, but creates a lack of incentives to minimize production costs (even if inappropriate outputs are being produced that fail to satisfy consumer-voter demands). If educational outputs could be satisfactorily measured, it would be possible to bring pressure to bear on inefficient educational producers. However, since they are so hard to define and measure, little knowledge on this subject exists. Arranging production so as to "institutionalize competition" (see Chapter 14) can be expected to provide some incentive for least-cost production that would not exist otherwise.

Financing Public education is not financed on the basis of benefits. Instead, it is provided "free" at the schoolhouse door by financing the total public education costs through a combination of aid from higher levels of government and local taxation, usually the property tax. The amount of school taxes paid depends not on private benefits received from public schools (which are zero in the case of childless couples and businesses) but on the value of property, the value of his home to a resident. Thus, the relationship between private costs and private benefits is quite weak.

Secondly, the consumer-voters in a local school district may not pay property taxes for the public schools that in any way approximate the real resource cost (net of state aid) of producing education, because of fiscal-zoning incentives. Fiscal zoning can shift a large part of the tax burden to businesses, who in turn shift it outside the jurisdiction through higher output prices. In addition to zoning in business property, fiscal zoning can zone out low-value dwelling units so as to increase the assessed valuation per schoolchild in the district. Thus, the local costs of education (net of state aid) will be less than the real resource costs to those districts who win the fiscal-zoning game and much higher for districts who lose the game.

Table 15-1 illustrates the outcomes of the fiscal-zoning process with respect to school financing for the two jurisdictions in the example of Table 14-2. Of the total property tax revenue generated in the two jurisdictions, row A assumes that the amount available for financing schools is 50 percent, which approximates the national average. Row B assumes that the number of school students in each jurisdiction averages one per household; since jurisdiction B has ten times as many households, the resulting property tax per student is much less than that in jurisdiction A (as shown in row C). While the amount of aid from state and federal sources is usually inversely related to the amount of property value per student, it only partially compensates for such disparities (row D). Thus, the total revenue (and resulting expenditure) per student is more than four times greater in jurisdiction A than it is in B, even though the two areas have the same property tax rates (Table 14-2).

In summary, the present methods of financing public education tend to result in significant mismatches of benefits and costs, both between school districts and between households within a single district. The lack of benefit-connected financing leads to either more or less than the efficient quantity of education being provided in different school districts and also for households within districts.

Possible Methods for Improving the Provision of Education

To avoid the inefficiencies and inequities associated with present methods of providing education, as discussed above, three proposals

	JURISDICTION A	JURISDICTION B
A. Local revenue available to finance education costs (one-half of total property taxes collected, per Table 14-2)	$2,400,000	$1,950,000
B. Number of housing units (and number of school students, assuming one per housing unit)	1,000	10,000
C. Local property tax revenue per pupil (A/B)	2,400	$ 195
D. State and federal grants per pupil	$ 200	$ 400
E. Total revenues per student (C + D)	$ 2,600	$ 595

Table 15-1: An Example of Financing Disparities Between Two School Districts

for improving one or more aspects of providing education are evaluated below. The first two proposals are limited in scope, while the third, voucher financing of education, would result in a radical change from the present methods of provision.

Higher-level government financing   To avoid the horizontal inequities in the treatment of taxpayers and students that arise from large differences in the local tax base per student (as in the example of Table 15-1), a higher level of government (state or national) could finance a greater portion of the costs of education. As a result, there would be less incentive to engage in fiscal zoning, because of the reduced importance of school costs in the local budget. However, there are disadvantages of such a scheme, since the relation between benefits accruing in the local district and costs incurred locally for education might become even more distorted. Aid formulas would have to grapple with complex questions of determining the amount of dollars per pupil that will result in equal inputs into the educational process. For example, land for school buildings usually costs more in the central city than it does in rural areas. Also, equal inputs per pupil may not result in equal outputs, because of the influence of other factors such as home environment over which the school has no control. Thus, the equity question of deciding on the distribution of outputs must also be included in such deliberations.

Splitting up large school systems   One proposal, which has been tried, to increase the choice of schools available to the central-city consumer-voter, is to split up the large spatial monopolies into smaller ones, by creating several school districts out of a single large school system. However, as long as place of residence determines the particular school attended, the household is still faced with a spatial monopoly. More effective choice for the household might result from breaking the link between place of residence and school attended, by permitting open admissions, that is, permitting the household to choose any school in the school district. This choice mechanism is presently used at the high-school level in several large central-city school systems, and to a more limited extent at the elementary level. If households were provided with sufficient information to be able to evaluate differences between schools in a district, incentives would be provided for producing outputs more closely in accord with consumer-voter demands through the threat of losing "customers." Presumably, a school that was not meeting the demands of very many households would have low enrollments relative to its capacity and this could provide incentives for changing production methods, provided the individual school had the autonomy to make such decisions. If there were significant differences among the schools of a system and consumer-voters had knowledge of these differences, the expected outcome would be that some schools would have applicants far beyond their capacity and others would not have enough applicants to fill the school. If this occurred, then some form of rationing, probably on a random basis to avoid socioeconomic or racial discrimination, would be needed.

Education vouchers   As long as the consumer-voter is faced with a spatial monopoly, no significant element of competition is introduced. More competition could be introduced in an urban area by permitting a student to attend any school in any school system in the entire urban area and providing transportation to promote such mobility. If a student could choose from any public school in the urban area, considerably different methods of financing education would be required from the present system that relies heavily on the property tax. One device, which would provide sufficient flexibility and is also advocated on grounds of achieving benefit-connected financing, is the education voucher—a certificate to the household that can be applied toward a tuition payment to a public or private school. The idea of a voucher can be illustrated from the example of Figure 15-1. In this case, the efficient quantity of education for the household's children is 100 units, which cost $15 per unit for a total cost of $1,500. Based on the benefits received at the margin, the household would pay $500 and the government would finance $1,000. This could be achieved by selling the household a voucher with a face value of $1,500, for a price of $500, which could be used solely for the purchase of education.

The voucher method of financing education has several efficiency and equity features to recommend it. In terms of achieving efficient demand registration and providing an incentive to minimize production costs, the voucher would essentially eliminate the spatial monopoly aspects of present-day public education, provided it could be applied to any accredited school, public or private. Differences between income groups in the way they are treated by the public-school system could be corrected by inversely varying the percentage of the voucher paid by the government according to income. For example, in the case of an urban household with two children and $4,000 in annual income, the total cost of the children's education, up to some ceiling, could be paid by the government. On the other hand, households with incomes in excess of $25,000 would have to pay the entire education cost out of their own pockets. Voucher financing would reduce the amount of tax revenues at all levels of government that would have to be generated to finance education, since some households with children now in public schools would be paying some percentage of their children's education costs themselves. Since government would be financing only the indirect benefits of education, a higher level of government, preferably the national government, should finance the vouchers in order to achieve horizontal equity among all jurisdictions, even those in different states. Even if the state financed such vouchers, the incentives for fiscal zoning would be significantly reduced because of the elimination of local school taxes, which are large in magnitude and not related to benefits.

One of the major criticisms put forth with respect to voucher financing is that it would promote segregation on the basis of income and race. This would supposedly result from schools having the ability to select only those students of a preferred socioeconomic class. Compared with the present system, however, it is difficult to imagine that even this sort of policy on the part of schools would lead to greater segregation than now exists in urban areas in the United States. Many parents would be attracted to schools that maintained integration through a selective admission policy, as it is difficult to find stable integrated schools in the present situation. Many parents desire integrated schools, but not if their child is the sole evidence of integration. Racists would no doubt choose "segregation academies," but probably most parents are not in this group, so that vouchers might lead to a greater degree of integration than presently exists in cities that do not engage in citywide busing. The flexibility of vouchers might more easily achieve integrated school patterns with far greater efficiency than busing or forcing changes in residential patterns. For example, all parents could use their vouchers to apply to the three schools in the urban area that they rank the highest. If there were first-choice schools that were oversubscribed, admissions could be determined on a random basis, and these schools would probably be far more integrated than at present. Those not selected for admission to their first-choice school would go to their second or third choice.

Provision of Local Public Outputs: Conclusion

Analysis of two examples of present methods of providing public outputs in the local public sector and a comparison of some alternative means of provision lead to the conclusion that considerable improvements in efficiency and equity could be achieved. The present methods òf provision result in a lack of choice in the consumption of local public outputs, a lack of incentives to achieve efficient production, and a poor relationship between benefits received and costs paid for the outputs. However, the resulting inequities and inefficiencies, such as distorted land-use patterns, are not inherent in the nature of the activities undertaken by the local public sector. Instead, they appear to be the result of failure to change with the times, perhaps because of entrenched bureaucracies and because basic economic concepts are not applied in the operation of the local public sector.

Local Tax Revenue Sources

The role for local taxes based on some measure of ability to pay (consumption, income, or wealth) would be relatively small if the local public sector were to achieve benefit financing of as many local public outputs as possible. A larger role for user charges, vouchers for education financed by a higher level of government, and total federal-government financing of income redistribution activities would leave a relatively small role for local taxation. As a result, many of the inefficiencies associated with the heavy use of local government taxes, such as the dual-migration problem and fiscal zoning, would be greatly reduced. However, the local public sector in the real world does not achieve a very high degree of benefit-connected financing, as can be seen from Table 15-2. For all local governments and for the forty-eight largest cities, about three-fourths of total revenue generated at the local government level from general sources (which excludes primarily utility and liquor-store revenue) is from taxes. Charges for outputs (which are usually benefit-connected, and include charges for school lunches, hospitals, parks, trash collection and disposal, and sewerage) account for approximately one-sixth of total revenues, while all other revenue sources amount to less than 10 percent. Total tax revenues of all local governments in 1970 - 1971 amounted to more than $43 billion, a considerable sum. This section of the chapter applies three generally accepted criteria for evaluating alternative sources of non-benefit-connected tax revenues to an evaluation of the property tax (which accounts for 85 percent of all local tax revenues) and the major alternative tax sources, income and sales.

	AMOUNT ($ MILLIONS)		PERCENTAGE OF TOTAL OWN GENERAL REVENUE SOURCES		PERCENT OF TOTAL TAXES	
	All local governments	48 Largest cities	All local governments	48 Largest cities	All local governments	48 Largest cities
TAXES						
Property	$36,726	$ 4,776	64%	46%	85%	60%
Income	1,747	1,145	3	11	4	14
Sales	3,662	1,672	6	16	8	21
Other taxes	1,298	403	2	3	3	5
Total taxes	$43,433	$ 7,996	75%	76%	100%	100%
CHARGES	9,819	1,614	17	15		
OTHER SOURCES OF OWN REVENUE	4,239	879	8	9		
TOTAL OWN GENERAL REVENUE SOURCES	$57,491	$10,489	100%	100%		

Table 15-2: Local Government Tax Revenues and Other General Revenue Sources (1970-1971)

SOURCES: U.S. Bureau of the Census, *Governmental Finances in 1970 - 71*, Government Printing Office, Washington, 1972; U.S. Bureau of the Census, *City Government Finances in 1970 - 71*, Government Printing Office, Washington, 1972, pp. 87 - 88.

The Property Tax

The property tax is really a conglomeration of taxes on various forms of property ownership. The tax base may consist of a combination of real property (land and buildings, i.e., real estate), tangible personal property of households (furniture, autos, etc.), tangible business personal property (tools and equipment), and intangible personal property (legal rights to valuable things such as stocks, bonds, and bank deposits). Note that "personal" property means property other than real estate, so that businesses can own personal property as well as households.

Table 15-3 presents an example of the computation of the property-tax liability on a house. Ultimately, the property-tax liability is based on an estimate of the market value of the property ($25,000). This market value is multiplied by the assessment ratio (40 percent in the example) to obtain a measure of the assessed value ($10,000). The assessment ratio, or percentage of market value initially subject to taxation, may be set by law or may simply result from weak tax administration, which allows the assessed value to deviate from the market value over time. There is absolutely no economic rationale for the use of an assessment ratio other than 100 percent, since lesser ratios serve to confuse taxpayers and allow taxes to be increased without increasing tax rates (i.e., by increasing the assessment ratio). Doubling an assessment ratio from 50 to 100 percent and cutting tax rates in half would simplify tax computations while leaving revenues unchanged. After determining the assessed value of a property, property-tax exemptions are deducted from the assessed value to obtain the taxable value. The present example shows a $2,000 "homestead exemption," which applies in many states to owner-occupied housing; similar exemptions are granted for veterans and the aged in some states. Finally, a flat rate is applied to the taxable value to determine the tax liability. In many areas of the country, the tax rate is stated in "mills"—10 mills being equivalent to 1 percent of the taxable value of the property. Alternatively, a tax of x mills is equivalent to a tax of x dollars per thousand dollars of taxable value. Since assessment ratios, millage rates, and the other variables mentioned vary between jurisdictions, the only meaningful comparison of tax rates is on the basis of the "effective" tax rate—the property-tax liability divided by the market value of the property—which in Table 15-3 is 1.6 percent. In the fiscal-zoning example (Table 14-2), the effective property tax rate was 3 percent.

Equity As discussed in Chapter 4, a tax may be levied on an individual or business firm, but the burden of the tax may be shifted or transferred. Conclusions on the vertical equity, with respect to in-

A.	Estimated market value of property (owner-occupied house)	$25,000
B.	Assessment ratio	0.40
C.	Assessed value (A × B)	$10,000
D.	Homestead exemption	$2,000
E.	Taxable value (C − D)	$8,000
F.	Tax rate (50 mills = 5%)	0.05
G.	Tax liability (E × F)	$400
H.	Effective tax rate (G/A)	1.6%

Table 15-3: Example of Property-Tax Liability Computation

come, of the property tax or any other tax depend on the ultimate incidence of the tax rather than where it is initially levied. While the incidence of the property tax is somewhat controversial, a widely accepted statement of incidence is as follows:

> Property taxes on owner-occupied housing are borne by the occupants.
>
> Property taxes on rental housing are mostly borne by the renters; the tax is levied on the owner and paid by him initially, but he is able to shift most of it forward to tenants in the form of higher rents.
>
> Nonresidential property taxes are mainly shifted forward via higher prices to the buyers of the products of the business firms. To the extent that this occurs, the incidence is much like that of a sales tax. Since business firms do not themselves bear the incidence of any tax—all taxes are ultimately borne by people in their roles of consumers, owners, and laborers— the nonresidential property tax not shifted forward through higher prices is borne by owners of nonresidential property.

Given this incidence of various components of the property tax, the tax as a whole is regressive to some extent. With respect to residential property taxes, low-income people tend to spend a larger portion of their income on housing than upper-income people (although even this is disputed) and thus the property tax as a percentage of income declines as income increases, a regressive result. On nonresidential property taxes, the tax tends to be regressive to the extent that it is passed on to consumers, since similarly the proportion of income spent on the consumption of goods and services declines as income rises. However, any portion of the nonresidential property tax that is borne by owners of the property tends to be progressive, since such owners tend to be of higher income.

Figure 15-2 graphs an estimate of the overall incidence of the property tax for 1957. Regressiveness is indicated at the very lowest

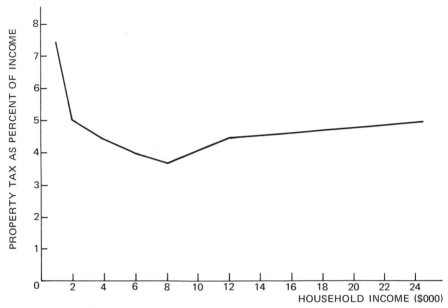

Figure 15-2: Estimated Vertical Equity of the Property Tax in the United States (1957)

SOURCE: Based on review and summary of property-tax incidence studies in Dick Netzer, *Economics of the Property Tax,* © 1966 by The Brookings Institution, Washington, D.C., pp. 40 - 59.

end of the income scale; however, the remainder of the curve (incomes of $2,000 up) approaches the horizontal. A completely horizontal curve for all incomes would indicate a proportional tax. Thus, from Figure 15-2, one might conclude that the property tax is roughly proportional except for regressiveness at the very lowest incomes.

With respect to horizontal equity on the basis of income, those who spend a greater portion of their income on housing pay more property taxes than those of the same income who spend less; thus, horizontal equity with respect to income (the ability-to-pay principle) is violated because of different preferences for housing consumption. A second source of horizontal inequity is poor property tax administration, which may result in two households with identical incomes, who occupy houses of identical market values, paying different property taxes because their properties were assessed at different ratios.

Economic effects   All taxes reduce the amount of income available to consumers to spend on private goods and services. In addition, some forms of taxation may force inefficient changes in the way consumers spend their after-tax income. These forced changes may lead to greater reductions in private benefits than the amount of income taken away would indicate. Chapter 12 indicated how a tax on a polluter might lead toward the efficient level of output, but suppose a tax were placed solely on an item that is already being produced in efficient amounts. This would result in inefficiently low production, and is an example of an adverse economic effect of a tax—an inefficient alteration in consumption patterns brought about by the tax. The discussion here refers to taxes not levied on the basis of the benefit principle, so the taxpayer perceives no benefit from the public outputs provided with the tax revenue. If the tax revenue is used to provide a public output from which the taxpayer receives benefits that are directly related to the taxes paid, then the tax is benefit-connected, whether intentionally or by accident. As discussed previously, benefit-connected financing, whether through user charges or taxes, is efficient; it has no adverse economic effects because the tax represents a payment for goods or services. It should be noted that, if a shift is made from nonbenefit financing of, say, tennis courts to a situation where user charges are employed, the quantity consumed may drop and consumption patterns will be altered. However, in such a case, the drop in quantity is an efficient move, since zero pricing had previously led to overuse of the facility. The economic effects considered here are of the type that move consumption and production away from efficiency.

To the extent that the residential property tax increases the price of housing relative to other goods and services, it reduces housing consumption to a level lower than would occur if it were replaced by a "neutral" tax, one that has no economic effects. However, since the property tax has many offsets, the economic effects may be smaller than indicated at first glance. Most new housing construction in recent years has been in the suburbs as opposed to central cities, and property taxes paid by suburban occupants tend to be relatively well benefit-connected. A large portion goes for education and the rest for services to property, such as sanitation, police, and fire. Thus, suburbanites having children in school pay property taxes for which they obtain perceivable benefits. To the extent that lower-income people are excluded from suburban areas, little or no property taxes go to finance income-redistributive services to low-income households. Also, as discussed in Chapter 8, the federal income tax subsidies to homeowners provide incentives to home ownership that are quite strong in comparison to any deterrent provided by non-benefit-connected property taxes. In the cities, however, the residential property tax is less connected to benefits. Incentives to improve older central-city properties may be weakened by relatively high property tax rates required to finance income-redistributive services and by increased assessments brought about by the improvements.

The nonresidential property tax on business firms and other nonresidential land uses may increase costs of production. Since the property tax is on capital inputs (business personal property tax), it may lead to some substitution of a tax-free input, such as labor for capital, in which case, the production cost (net of taxes) increases. However, these effects are not likely to be strong, since the advantages of substituting capital for labor may tend to overwhelm them. Also, there are taxes on labor, which may tend to neutralize this. However, the property tax on nonresidential property tends to be poorly related to benefits received from public outputs financed by the tax. Since about 50 percent of the property tax goes for education and another 20 percent for services to people (such as health, hospitals, and welfare), business benefits only from the services to property, which account for about 30 percent of property tax revenue. Thus, the relation between business property-tax liability and benefits received is weak. As a result, business firms have an incentive to choose the jurisdiction of the urban area that will minimize property-tax liabilities, since they tend to receive few benefits from the public outputs financed by such taxes.

Administration   The evaluation of alternative sources of tax revenue from an administrative point of view can be separated into the areas of tax collection and tax compliance. Even if tax laws were perfectly enforced (such that revenue collected just equalled the tax liability as legally stipulated), tax collection costs as a percentage of revenue collected would vary among types of taxes. From the taxpayer's side, the issue is one of tax compliance costs. These include the value of time and the monetary costs of record maintenance plus professional fees to lawyers and accountants. The sum of collection and compliance costs as a percentage of tax revenue collected can be compared with those for alternative sources of tax revenue in evaluating a tax from the administrative-cost standpoint.

No source of tax revenue will rank first on all three of the criteria for evaluating alternative sources of tax revenue (equity, economic effects, and administration). Thus, the decision on tax sources is ultimately a value judgment to be made through the political process. In the case of the property tax, even if it is acceptable on grounds of equity and economic effects, it ranks very low in terms of administration. The compliance costs on the taxpayer are quite low, but collection costs, including the costs of accurately determining the property-tax liability through assessment of properties, are very high and it may be impossible to achieve accurate property-tax assessment.

The most obvious problem with property-tax assessment is the difficulty of determining the market value of property. In the absence of a sales price, the determination of assessed value has to be guesswork to some extent. In the case of single-family detached dwelling units, this is not too severe a problem, because an extensive market in such property exists, and similar dwellings would have been recently sold. However, for apartment units and nonresidential property, the determination of market value is an extremely difficult task. Also, unless all properties are reassessed on a frequent basis (e.g., once a year), changing market values will result in underassessment. Thus, even if the assessment of property reflects the best of practices, violations of horizontal equity will be likely—owners of property of equal market value will be assessed differently and will thus pay different taxes. However, it appears that many discrepancies in assessment ratios among different classes of property are intentional, with businesses often being assessed at higher ratios. In response to dual-migration and fiscal-zoning pressures, local governments may tend to assess "captive" properties, such as downtown offices of banks and other establishments that require a CBD location, at higher ratios, while assessing middle-income dwelling units at lower rates to help curb out-migration to the suburbs. Similarly, the effective assessment ratios for apartment buildings may be higher than for single-family houses, because it is felt that apartment dwellers are a burden to the community in that they receive benefits from local government in excess of taxes paid. Thus, extralegal raising of the assessment ratios may be done to counter this problem. (Whether apartments are actually a burden is debatable, but the widely held belief that they are may evoke the above response.) Another source of property-tax assessment ratio differences occurs between new arrivals to an area and older residents. The new arrivals may be met with a new assessment, while long-term residents may not have been reassessed for several years, so that their assessment ratios are depressed. Whether the inequalities in assessment ratios are inherent or intentional, they cause the property tax to rank low in terms of the administrative criterion.

Alternatives to the Property Tax

In this section, local tax sources based on consumption and income are briefly discussed and evaluated with respect to the three criteria of equity, economic effects, and administration.

Sales taxation   Taxes based on consumption may have narrow or broad bases. So-called excise taxes have as their base narrow forms of consumption, such as liquor, cigarettes, and hotel-motel occupancy. General sales taxes, such as most state sales taxes, have a much broader base, since sales of most commodities (other than housing and some services) are taxed.

In terms of vertical equity with respect to income, most sales taxes are regressive to some extent, since it is generally held that the consumer bears the burden of the tax, and, further, sales taxes are flat-rate taxes, and the purchase of goods and services subject to the tax become a smaller proportion of income as income increases. However, this regressiveness can be reduced by several means. For example, consumption items that account for a large proportion of the expenditures of lower-income families (such as food) can be exempted from the sales tax base. Also, a credit against other taxes (such as state income taxes) may be implemented, which amounts to a refund for a certain amount of sales tax paid. Thus, although sales taxes have been traditionally criticized by many people for their regressiveness, there are fairly easy means of eliminating this, if society wishes to do so through the political process. Horizontal equity with respect to income is violated to some extent, in that not all individuals with the same income spend the same amount on goods and services subject to the tax, and thus they pay different amounts of sales taxes.

The economic effects of local sales taxes are most obvious in their impact on the location of sales. For example, if the central city has a local sales tax, it is much easier for the central-city resident to avoid the sales tax by making certain purchases outside the city limits than it is to avoid property taxes (which would require changing the place of one's residence). Thus, there is an incentive for buying outside the central city whenever the private costs are less than the private costs of buying in the city. Generally, the total costs of buying small miscellaneous items will be lower in the city, since transportation cost must be added to the purchase price including the sales tax. However, for "big-ticket" items like color television sets and automobiles, the saving in sales taxes may more than offset the additional travel costs. Such outside buying can be eliminated to the extent that the taxing jurisdiction can levy and enforce a use tax (a levy on outside purchases by residents). However, the use tax tends to be unenforceable even for states, except for items that are registered, such as automobiles. When a person buys an auto outside the taxing jurisdiction, it is registered with the state motor vehicle department as a part of the title process. The state can report to the taxing jurisdiction that an auto has been purchased, so that the tax can be collected, or perhaps the state will collect the tax for the local government when it collects the state use tax. In the case of nonregistered items, the use tax is unenforceable, since the taxing jurisdiction has no way of keeping a record of outside purchases by residents.

In terms of the administrative criterion, the compliance costs are on the retailer, who has to collect the tax and remit the payments. The administration of a local sales tax by a local government may result in high collection costs as a percentage of revenues collected, since the collection costs would include auditing retail merchants. However, the local sales tax can rank relatively high on the administrative cost criterion by "piggybacking" the local tax onto an existing state sales tax. For example, if a state has a 3 percent general sales tax and a city in the state wishes to adopt a 1 percent local sales tax, with an identical tax base, the local government can make an agreement with the state whereby merchants collect a 4 percent tax and the state remits 1 percent to the city (perhaps after subtracting a certain fee for the service). Thus, a piggyback tax eliminates duplicate tax administration and reduces collection, as well as compliance, costs, since retailers are collecting only one tax instead of two.

Local income taxation   The ranking of a local income tax on the criteria for evaluating revenue sources depends on the definition of income that is used in defining the tax base. The spectrum of income-base possibilities ranges all the way from an earnings tax (a tax levied on salaries and wages only) to a base that is more comprehensive than the existing federal income tax (which includes rents, dividends, capital gains, and interest in the tax base but gives preferential treatment to some sources of income and allows many deductions).

In terms of horizontal and vertical equity with respect to income, a local income tax can be designed to achieve any outcome desired. The obvious reason for the superiority of income taxes on grounds of equity is that equity is measured in income, and income is the tax base, while for other types of tax, payments are not so closely related to income. It is not difficult to design an income tax system in which those of equal incomes pay equal taxes and horizontal equity is achieved. In terms of vertical equity, combinations of tax-base definition and rate structure can achieve any desired degree of regressiveness or progressiveness. Many local income taxes in the real world are earnings taxes levied at a flat rate, often 1 percent. Such taxes are regressive, because upper-income households receive a large portion of their incomes from sources other than salaries and wages (such as dividends and interest).

A case can be made that local income taxes (or any form of local non-benefit-connected tax) should be proportional, taking away the same percentage of income from all income groups. This relates back to the discussion in the first part of Chapter 14 regarding the role of local government in redistributing income. Since local income redistribution creates dual-migration incentives, the implication is that local taxes should not redistribute income. To the extent that a tax is proportional with respect to income, no income redistribution occurs through local taxation.

In terms of economic effects, income taxes may be considered superior to consumption or property taxes because they do not affect the relative prices of goods and services. However, they do tax work effort and provide incentives to reduce the number of hours worked, although the effect of a 1 percent tax is likely to be slight. The effects on location of economic activity in an urban area where only the central city has an income tax will be less than from a sales tax, which can be avoided easily by purchases being shifted out of the city. As in the case of the property tax, the individual taxpayer must generally move his residence to escape the tax. Since local income taxes are sometimes levied on all city employees regardless of residence, even a move to the suburbs may not allow the income tax to be avoided.

A key consideration in the case of a local income tax is the "situs" of the tax, alluded to above. For example, if a central city is to levy a tax, the situs question is whether the tax will be levied on all *residents* of the city or on all *employees* in the city. If the tax situs is place of employment, the central-city public sector wins, relative to resident tax situs. If both the central-city and suburban jurisdictions are permitted by state legislation to levy local income taxes, the situs question becomes a major political controversy, involving equity issues. Naturally, suburban legislators would prefer local income taxes with a residence situs while central-city legislators would prefer an employment situs, because more suburban residents are employed in the central city than vice versa. In the real world, where both central-city and suburban jurisdictions are permitted taxes on income, the situs problem is how to develop a formula in which individuals working in one jurisdiction and living in another pay taxes that are shared by the two jurisdictions.

Arguments over whether the central city or the suburbs of the urban area should be the situs for local income taxes are usually couched in terms of the exploitation hypothesis. The question is whether the suburbs "exploit" the central city by receiving services (or imposing costs) for which they do not pay. Do commuting workers and shoppers necessitate the central city's provision of greater amounts of streets, traffic control, and police protection for the large daytime population without compensation? Do commuters impose costs on the central city in the form of congestion and pollution? If the answers are positive, then the central city's taxes may be higher as a result. However, this is only looking at the benefit side of the coin. An accurate answer to the question of exploitation also requires that the incidence of central-city taxes be considered. The local taxes paid by business firms in the central city may pay for the services consumed by the firms' employees and customers. Also, to the extent that central-city taxes are exported outside its boundaries in the form of higher product prices or reduced business profits to owners of central-city business firms who do not reside in the central city, the tax burdens are not imposed on residents of the city. Thus, government services may be paid for indirectly on the basis of benefits received and no exploitation may exist. The incidence of both benefits and costs from central-city government must be considered to answer the question.

If the local jurisdiction is to administer a local income tax itself, the form of the tax will have to be restricted to an earnings tax based on place of employment, in which all employers in the jurisdiction are required to withhold the income tax from payrolls. Otherwise, either the collection and compliance costs will be excessively high or the tax will be only weakly enforceable. Thus, the nature of the local income tax presents strong arguments for adopting it as a piggyback to a state tax on income. The tax could be collected by the state along with its income tax (provided the state has one) and the portion assessed by the local government could be returned to that government on the basis of tax situs. Administrative costs are minimized as a result and the difficulties involved are relatively small in an era of sophisticated data processing.

The "Plight of the Central City": Equity Versus Efficiency

For reasons discussed in other chapters of this book, the incidence of low-income households is higher in central cities than it is in the suburban parts of major urban areas. With present methods of financing local public outputs, many of the expenditures in the budget of the central city are much higher than they would be if there were fewer low-income households in the city. These poverty-related expenditures include not only obvious items such as welfare and hospitals but also many other activities such as police protection (given the relationship between crime and poverty).

Since non-central-city land becomes increasingly accessibile as transportation improves, many business firms and households presently located in the central city have a strong incentive to migrate out. This tendency is accentuated when taxes are incurred for which no apparent benefits are received. As long as local taxation is heavily tied to non-benefit-connected financing, the "plight of the central city" will continue. Individual consumers and producers will continue to vote with their feet for equity rather than efficiency reasons. Thus, the plight of the central city is largely attributable to a failure to distinguish between equity and efficiency considerations as causes of urban problems and to propose solutions accordingly—a recurring theme of this book.

REVIEW AND DISCUSSION QUESTIONS

1 Elementary and secondary education is provided by the local public sector because it is a public good. Evaluate.
2 Pricing government services by placing user charges on beneficiaries may be efficient, but poor people would be excluded from consumption of these services. Discuss.

3 The most serious drawback to the property tax as a source of local tax revenue is that it is regressive. Evaluate.

4 On what economic grounds, if any, can public subsidization of elementary and secondary education be justified, as opposed to a completely private system in which each student pays the market price of providing education?

5 If all local public outputs were financed on the basis of benefits received, there would be a very minor role for local taxation. Evaluate.

6 Do the suburbs "exploit" the central cities of urban areas?

7 Why is public education a spatial monopoly? Why are households less likely to be satisfied with this method of providing education than one in which they had some choice?

8 Discuss the efficiency and equity rationale for financing education with vouchers.

SUGGESTED READINGS

Downs, Anthony. "Competition and Community Schools." In *Urban Problems and Prospects*, pp. 264 - 293. Chicago: Markham, 1970.

Katzman, Martin. "Pricing Primary and Secondary Education." In *Public Prices for Public Products*, edited by Selma Mushkin, pp. 371 - 393. Washington: The Urban Institute, 1972.

Maxwell, James. *Financing State and Local Governments*, pp. 80 - 103. Washington: The Brookings Institution, 1969.

Neenan, William. "The Muncipal Income Tax." In *Political Economy of Urban Areas*, pp. 279 - 330. Chicago: Markham, 1972.

Netzer, Dick. "Federal, State, and Local Finance in a Metropolitan Context." In *Issues in Urban Economics*, edited by H. S. Perloff and L. Wingo, Jr., pp. 435 - 476. Baltimore: The Johns Hopkins Press, 1968.

Netzer, Dick. "Financing Urban Government." In *The Metropolitan Enigma*, edited by J. Q. Wilson, pp. 76 - 95. Garden City, N.Y.: Anchor Books, Doubleday, 1970.

Netzer, Dick. "Impact of the Property Tax: Its Economic Implications for Urban Problems." Supplied by the National Commission on Urban Problems to the Joint Economic Committee, pp. 29 - 47. Washington: Government Printing Office, May 1968. (Reprinted in Arthur F. Schreiber, Paul K. Gatons, and Richard Clemmer, eds. *Economics of Urban Problems: Selected Readings*, Boston: Houghton Mifflin, 1971.)

Schultze, Charles, et al. *Setting National Priorities: The 1973 Budget*, pp. 291 - 317, 318 - 366. Washington: The Brookings Institution, 1972.

Stockfish, J. A. "Fees and Service Charges as a Source of City Revenues: A Case Study of Los Angeles." *National Tax Journal* (June 1960), 97 - 121.

16 / Benefits and Costs of Urbanization

As discussed in Chapter 2, the general pattern in the United States has been the gradual urbanization of the population, with recent urbanization at a lower density than in the past. Urbanization has resulted from technological change that produced large benefits from locating in proximity to other economic units. This chapter will examine some of these benefits (the reasons for urbanization itself). However, urbanization also has costs associated with it and this book has examined some of the more important of them. These costs tend to offset the advantages and will be briefly reviewed here for purposes of considering the benefits and costs of urbanization in the past and in the future, and public policy directions for dealing with urban problems.

The Benefits of Urban Economic Growth

The historical location of most large urban areas in the United States was determined primarily by a need to minimize the costs of transporting goods and raw materials. The early dependence on trade with the Old World and other colonies necessitated location on excellent natural harbors (Boston and New York). Since waterways were the cheapest mode of inland transportation, many of the present large urban areas were founded on waterways (St. Louis and New Orleans). Some urban areas grew near the site of raw material deposits (Pittsburgh, with two of the major ingredients of steel production), while the births of other cities may be due to historical accident (Salt Lake City and Washington, D.C.). Other cities grew up around locations where railroads intersected (Atlanta) and currently some of the fastest growing cities in the United States are those in locations desirable for airline stopping points (Dallas-Fort Worth). Overall, initial settlement tended to be based on benefits accruing to certain locations. The urban areas grew not only as a result of these benefits, but also as a result of the benefits of accessibility that firms and households received from urban locations. Two interrelated factors, referred to here as demand and supply economies, help explain some of the benefits of urbanization.

Demand Economies

In Chapter 14, the concept of economies of scale was discussed; the main idea is that, at least over a range, an increase in output will lead to a decrease in per unit costs of production. This does not imply that a very large scale is always the most efficient. In order to determine the lowest-cost means of producing a commodity, demand for that commodity must be considered. A highly automated automobile production line is certainly not the lowest-cost way of producing a single auto in a year, since the production line would be operated for only a few minutes during the year and high capital costs would be involved. An obviously cheaper way to build the single auto would be in a machine shop, where costs would be perhaps $200,000 compared with several million for the production line. While lower costs of production can be realized with larger scales of operation, these larger scales of operation can be achieved only if the output can be sold (that is, if demand is high enough). Therefore, this concept is referred to as *demand economies*—lower per unit costs of production are achievable because of higher demand.

Figure 16-1 illustrates the concept of demand economies and the related concept of threshold level of demand. The idea behind this is quite simple. Production of a commodity is profitable only if, for some quantity, per unit price (shown by the demand curve) is at least equal to per unit cost. Were this not true, then a business would lose on every unit sold and would go out of business after a certain amount of time (when it no longer had any net worth). Three demand curves are shown: D_1 illustrating demand below the threshold, D_2 illustrating demand just at the threshold, and D_3 showing demand sufficiently beyond the threshold that production can take place at lower per unit

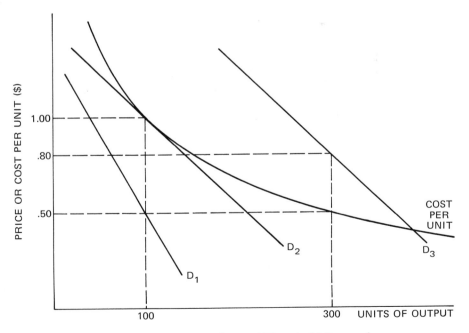

Figure 16-1: Demand Economies and Threshold Demand

cost than at D_2. Thus, the movement from D_2 to D_3 illustrates the concept of demand economies: lower per unit costs brought about by greater demand. It should be noted that threshold demand does not imply the production of some unique quantity, since demand curves may be of different slopes. The important thing is whether the demand curve touches the per unit cost curve. If it is entirely below the per unit cost curve, then demand is below the threshold, and the commodity will not be produced at all (at least not for very long).

The unit of output on the quantity axis in Figure 16-1 can be anything from buckets of balls at a golf driving range to medical services to ice-cream cones. As indicated by the figure, with demand at D_2, 100 units can be sold at \$1 each, but any other price and quantity combination will not allow the firm to stay in business. If demand rises to D_3, for example, because this represents the sum of individual demands of a larger population in a larger urban area, then 300 units can be sold for 80¢ each and produced at a per unit cost of 50¢. This movement down the per unit cost curve from \$1 to 50¢ because of greater demand is an example of a demand economy.

To this point, we have shown only one producer in a market, which is monopoly by definition. As demand grows further, competitors will be enabled to come in and produce the same commodity. As this happens, price tends to approach per unit cost, since the existence of profits is a magnet that draws in new firms. In the case of D_2, however, only one firm can exist, since splitting up the market will mean that neither can cover per unit costs.

Economies of scale are so substantial for some commodities that they are only produced for national markets, even though they must be transported great distances in some cases. Although auto assembly plants are becoming increasingly dispersed, key manufacturing operations involving such things as engine blocks are carried out in centralized locations. Thus, we do not see regional brands of autos, and regional brands of beer are disappearing rapidly (even though there may still be beer production in these regions). No doubt, an important factor is economies of scale in advertising. An ad that hits everyone in a region will also hit nonresidents, while, if the article is sold nationally, the ads will nearly always reach potential customers. Further, media such as television and national magazines are more amenable to advertising by national companies. However, the concern here is mainly with goods and services that are produced and sold within urban areas. If an area is large enough, it can support more kinds of activity. Small urban areas do not usually have major professional sports (unless the urban area is Green Bay), but, as an urban area grows, it can support several teams. Fine restaurants tend to be located in large cities, and usually only in large cities would one find Serbian and Korean restaurants. For some activities, the population of the urban area by itself is not sufficient to generate demand above the threshold; however, the demand of the total population of the region in which the urban area is located may be adequate. If regional demand is above threshold, the activity will usually be located in a population center of the region, as opposed to a rural location, in order to minimize the transportation costs (or, to say the same thing, maximize accessibility) of *all* users, both urban and rural.

Perhaps the best example of a change through time in economies of scale in the provision of a service would be medical practice. At one time, the general practitioner could carry the most advanced medical tools and skills around in his buggy, providing services to a local population. Nearly every family had need of these services from time to time, and specialization had not become widespread. Thus, when one wanted medical services, one would contact the local doctor, and a doctor could maintain a practice with a relatively small population. Technological changes in medical practice have resulted in greater investment in both physical equipment and additional years of medical education. Since a relatively small proportion of the population would require the services of, say, a urologist, a person with such training will locate in a large population center to maximize his accessibility to potential patients. However, transportation allows people who live in rural areas to avail themselves of his services. The greater geographic market size thus allows further demand economies for specialized medical services, resulting in the establishment of regional medical centers in major population centers.

The concepts of demand economies and threshold size imply that large urban areas tend to produce a greater variety of goods and services than small areas. This can be determined empirically by examining the array of goods and services in the *Yellow Pages* of the telephone directory of various urban areas. The larger the urban area, the more goods and services that will be above the threshold level of demand. Some functions may be so specialized that they are provided in only one urban area in the country. These considerations suggest that there may be a hierarchy of urban areas, based on the relationship of population to the number of functions performed.[1]

The availability of a larger variety of goods and services is one of the main reasons why people live in urban areas, and this has become more important as standards of living have risen. A higher income needs to be translated into consumption if it is to mean a higher standard of living. Thus, urban areas have grown because of the consumption opportunities that exist there as opposed to areas of smaller population; and the demand economies inherent in larger urban areas have been among the benefits associated with location in an urban area.

[1]For an example of city classification by size and number of functions, see Hugh Nourse, *Regional Economics*, McGraw Hill, New York, 1968, pp. 57 - 62.

Supply Economies

The concept of demand economies is best illustrated as a movement down a per unit cost curve because of higher demand. Supply economies, on the other hand, are the result of factors that lead to lower per unit costs without expanding output; that is, the per unit cost curve itself is lower in one geographic area than another. Figure 16-2 illustrates this concept, where C_1 represents the per unit cost curve in one area and C_2 represents a lower per unit cost curve (brought about by supply economies) in another area. There are many possible reasons for this lower per unit cost curve, most of which can be considered as lower input costs. Basic steel production requires huge amounts of water, for example, and a location near one of the Great Lakes assures an ample supply of this crucial input (the Chicago-Northern Indiana area is the largest concentration of steel production in the United States). The production of aluminum requires a great deal of electricity, so aluminum plants are located near sources of cheap electric power.

An urban area with a large population may offer an incoming firm a potential cost advantage over a smaller area. The larger area may be the only place that offers a readily available labor supply with a particular kind of skill. Although wages may be high, the total costs of employing this kind of labor may be lower, since there is less need for training the labor force. Output per man-hour may be greater with this skilled labor force and result in lower per unit costs of production than in other areas. In addition, a large labor pool increases the probability that a firm can obtain workers with a skill required by that firm, avoiding costly training or importing of workers. Finally, a large population center may offer amenities that tend to attract workers at lower wages than they would otherwise demand. Examples of such amenities would be cultural activities such as symphony orchestras and museums, athletic events including professional sports, fine restaurants, and theaters. To attract workers with high education and income levels to live and work in rural areas lacking such cultural amenities may require higher wages in the form of "boredom pay." The lack of such amenities in rural areas is usually considered to be a prime factor underlying the out-migration of the younger and better-educated population from such areas.

Cost reductions may accrue to the business firm that locates in close proximity to other firms having a demand for similar services. If a sufficient number of firms have a demand for certain services, such as banking or transportation, these services can be profitably provided and increase in demand can lead to reductions in per unit cost.[2] For a

---

[2]Note that this means nothing more than that firms providing the service inputs must have a market above threshold size and may experience demand economies.

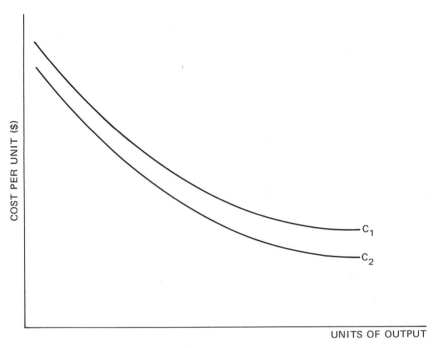

Figure 16-2: Supply Economies

firm having a demand for these services, self-provision or importation may be either impossible or too costly. For example, businesses often require the expertise of specialists such as the consulting engineer, the management consultant, or the data processing expert, who generally locate in large urban areas. The cost to the firm of employing a full-time specialist is often prohibitive, and waiting for one to arrive from out of town may be costly. Therefore, locating in a large urban area is often critical to business operations and will result in lower per unit costs of operation.

A business firm may be able to achieve per unit cost reductions by hiring subcontractors to do parts of an order or a production process, thus avoiding investment in specialized equipment. This option is especially important to firms that are sensitive to changes in style and technology and whose outputs cannot be efficiently mass-produced. The necessary supply of subcontractors may, again, be found only in the large urban areas where there are a sufficient number of potential customers. Whatever the reason for initial location of subcontractors, their availability will attract other businesses who use these services.

Advances in communications and transportation technology tend to lead to concentration of business activity in fewer and larger urban areas. Potential supply economies are realized through utilization of electronic data processing, more sophisticated forms of audio and visual communications devices, and jet transportation. A large firm may now profitably administer its operations from just a few locations (maybe only one) rather than from a large number of locations. For example, it was often necessary in the past for a large company to maintain district offices in almost every state in which it did business. These offices served as headquarters for salesmen, who needed to be close to customers, and also housed clerical personnel, who kept customer accounts. Now, because of transportation and communication advances, salesmen may be stationed at fewer offices and still adequately service their customers; therefore, the cost of maintaining many offices for this function can be eliminated.

Computers also reduce the need for district offices and clerical personnel to perform accounting and other administrative functions. They provide substantial incentives to concentrate these functions into more centralized facilities. In addition, improvements in communications technology provide the means to get information required for timely decision-making to a more centralized location, thereby reducing the need for district managers. Thus, technological advances have contributed to the rise in regional or national offices in a few urban areas at the expense of other urban areas that were previously used as district offices.

Interrelation of Demand and Supply Economies

Demand economies and supply economies are obviously interrelated and, in fact, are often lumped together and called agglomeration economies. The approach here is that explanation is better served by first presenting the concepts as if they were independent and then indicating how they are interrelated. Demand economies and supply economies together give a simplified picture of urban growth and urban growth differentials. Whatever the reason for location of an urban area, once an area gets going, it develops a certain momentum that can be viewed from the perspective of a certain number of local industries being above threshold demand levels. The attraction of more people to the area leads further goods and services to be provided, as more and more commodities have a demand above the threshold level, resulting in further demand economies being created.

A demand economy for one firm may be a supply economy for another. For example, producing electric power can be done more cheaply in a large facility than in a small one, through economies of scale. Because a demand economy enables a large plant to be built, electricity will be cheaper, and firms may be attracted to the area because of cheaper power. This is a demand economy from the point of view of the power company but a supply economy from the point of view of the power company's customers. Further, the existence of a supply economy in a particular area (hydroelectric power, for example) may lead firms to locate there, and people to move in, thus creating demand economies for locally produced goods. As more and more firms move in, further supply economies may likewise be created, since firms that provide supportive services to other businesses may then tend to locate there.

Costs of Urbanization

While there are substantial benefits from urbanization, as explained by the concepts of demand and supply economies, significant costs are also incurred when people and businesses cluster in urban areas. Particular varieties of these costs have been examined in previous chapters, and suggestions have been made for dealing with these problems of urbanization. In this chapter, the focus is on urbanization and size of urban areas per se. From this point of view, it is obvious that certain problems are much worse in urban areas, and negative externalities per capita may be higher, the larger the urban area. Thus, supply and demand economies may be offset by *diseconomies*. In fact, were this not true, we should expect far more centralization than exists.

Chapter 2 examined the pattern of land rents that has evolved in urban areas. If an area (say the CBD) has certain cost advantages for a certain class of firms, they will be willing to pay higher rents, but these higher rents tend to partially offset the advantage of location in that area. Thus, higher land rents tend to check the growth of the more desirable parts of the urban area. Other kinds of cost likewise tend to offset the advantages of certain parts of urban areas, and may even offset the advantages of urban areas per se. For examples, consider the topics of the previous chapters. Pollution and traffic congestion tend to be worse the larger the urban area. While substandard housing tends to be more prevalent in rural areas (as a percentage of the total), substandard housing in urban areas affects more people, thereby usually generating larger negative externalities. Even after adjusting for data inaccuracies, crime rates in urban areas are higher than in nonurban areas and are related to the size of the urban area.

If costs of housing, traffic congestion, and pollution are higher for the resident of a large urban area than the resident of a smaller one, wages and salaries will have to be higher to compensate for these costs. Other costs of business firms may be higher also, such as costs of land (previously discussed), taxes, and more stringent business regulations that may be set in an urban area. All these items make the large urban area less desirable and tend to offset the advantages of location there. The reasons that taxes tend to be higher were discussed in Chapters 14 and 15; essentially, services that redistribute income are in part financed locally and the costs of providing a given level of services may be higher in an urban area.

Another category of costs of urbanization is concerned with the historical development of the urban area, discussed in Chapter 2. Because the typical United States city grew up being heavily dependent on the core, and of necessity clustered around the core, much of the housing stock in our central cities exists in a ring surrounding the CBD. This would not be a problem, except that this housing tends to be obsolete, and those who can afford better housing do not generally choose to live there. Thus, this central-city housing turns out to be the lowest-cost housing in the urban area and, therefore, the people with the lowest incomes tend to live there. Since job opportunities have migrated outward, the poor are increasingly spatially separated from new employment opportunities. The downtown-commuting pattern of high-income people has greatly added to the problems of traffic congestion and pollution, since these high-income people tend to live at greater and greater distances from the CBD.

Overall, urbanization stemmed from the benefits derived from locating in urban areas, but, as urbanization has proceeded, the costs of this process have surfaced. From the patterns of urbanization and decentralization within urban areas, we can deduce that the costs of intense centralization (as in the nineteenth century) are greater than the benefits, while the benefits of location somewhere in an urban area do exceed the costs for many business firms and households. Of course, this conclusion rests on the assumption that decisions to urbanize made through the private market system are not totally counteracted by market failure—a topic that will be discussed further at a subsequent point in the chapter.

The Future of the Central City

When world population was smaller, and countries were predominately rural and agricultural, cities were relatively small entities that housed only a small fraction of the population. As the industrial age spurred the growth of cities, concerns over urbanization and the costs involved in this process grew (although concern over urbanization itself is ancient, e.g., the Biblical story of the tower of Babel). While previous concern seemed to be related to the rise of the cities, recent concern is over the decline of cities (more correctly, the decline in the central-city portion of the urban area). This decline is seen by many as a problem per se, the implied solution being a reversal of the decentralization process. Some of the preference for large central cities seems to be based on incompletely developed concepts of social costs and benefits. The resources required to house a city in a gigantic cube are easily several times those required to house a conventional city; yet, such proposals have been made on the basis of their resource cost savings. Further, such plans often ignore either individual preferences (the *basis* of social benefits) or those preferences that conflict with preconceived value judgments (e.g., anyone who prefers to drive a car rather than ride a train is held to be not worthy of consideration in a social calculus).

On the other hand, many have taken extreme positions that cities are inherently evil places that corrupt and debase their residents. Frank Lloyd Wright, for example, considered big cities to be "vampires" that presumably need stakes driven into their hearts (the CBDs?).[3] Were one to take his first trip to a city by going to Chicago and then taking a ride on the "El," his impression would no doubt be one of extreme revulsion. A similar experience could be had in almost any other city of appreciable size. While the large downtown buildings may be impressive, the inhabitants may seem less so, as they rush about, and the housing surrounding the CBD may seem beyond hope.

Prognosis about the future of the city or even the most desired future of the city should not be based on an extreme position at either end of the spectrum. What is happening is that the central city and the CBD are declining relative to the rest of the urban area, and perhaps even in absolute terms in some urban areas. By itself, this fact is neutral, since it is the implications of the fact that involve costs and benefits. Perhaps the most useful way to look at the situation is to speculate on what an urban area of 1 million would look like if it were built from scratch and followed the forces that are at work today without trying to counteract them.

A new urban area would not be built around a certain point, except that some location would happen to be the center of the area. There would be several nodes around which economic activity would revolve. Each of these would no doubt have rent gradients emanating from it, and these would mingle with the others, to give, as discussed in Chapter 2, a rather mountainous appearance to the urban area's rent gradient when viewed in three dimensions. The outlying parts of the urban area would probably be much like the outlying parts of present urban areas that have grown rapidly. Rather than build a circumferential highway to enable people to by-pass the downtown area, this same highway should probably be built to serve as the "main street" of the urban area. Other highways would be built with a view toward serving this circular highway. What would be the form of the area inside the circular highway? Probably it would be similar in some respects to the present situation, in that there would be advantages to

[3]Cited in Wilfred Owen, *The Accessible City*, The Brookings Institution, Washington, 1972, p. 10.

be gained from having major highways emanating from a point and crossing the circumferential highway. For some businesses, location near the point where these highways originate would be advantageous, since this would be the point of maximum accessibility for the whole urban area. These would not necessarily be the same businesses presently located in the CBD, however. Banking and financial institutions might tend to cluster somewhere else, for example, near the airport, so they could have greater accessibility to that facility as well as each other.

The main difference between the urban area described here and present urban areas would be that there would not be the inner-city ring of low-income housing that is the present land-use pattern. This pattern exists because of previous history, and because the most profitable use of this existing heritage is for low-income housing. This does not imply that identical structures would be built to house the poor in a future urban area. Other things being the same, the poor would probably tend to live further out from the center of the urban area. There would still be areas of high and low incomes, but these would not necessarily follow the pattern of present urban areas. In smaller towns, the typical pattern is that the rich live close to the center, while the poor live on the outskirts. To some extent, this pattern would probably be more typical of the urban area of the future; but, since the poor tend to have a lower demand for land area and a greater demand for public transportation facilities, it might be expected that they would live near such facilities. At present this means near the CBD, but in the urban area of the future, this would mean near accessible points on the transportation system, including the center of the urban area but also including places in the outlying areas. Probably a major reason why the poor do not now live in outlying areas (aside from discrimination) is that to live, say, near a shopping center would require residing in a new building. Even a tiny apartment would cost more to construct (and hence to rent) than an apartment in an older building in the center of a present city. In the urban area of the future, however, such a stock of decaying building would not exist. New buildings would be required to house the poor, and these would be built in more dispersed locations. (Obviously this would cost them more than presently, unless they were to receive a housing subsidy.)

The preceding speculation on some basic features of an urban area of the future presents a picture that is quite similar to what exists today. Our feeling is that it is all too easy to ignore individual benefits and costs when trying to plan for cities of the future. When these individual benefits and costs are not considered, planning can serve primarily to impose the values of the few on the many. However, it is obvious that some kind of planning is necessary because of the complex interactions in a modern society. And the main role of such planning should be directed at designing and implementing policies for solving the problems of externalities inherent in an unregulated private market system.

Future Public Policies and the Urban Area

Certain government policies have strongly affected the way cities and suburbs have grown. The financing of welfare-related services by the central city has encouraged migration of higher-income people to suburbs. Heavy government subsidies to expressways have also led to greater outward movement than would have been the case without such subsidies. Thus, it is obvious that government policy can and does strongly influence the pattern of growth of urban areas. This book has attempted to indicate how present governmental policy might be improved with respect to equity and efficiency, and the same considerations apply to the development of policies to deal with future urban problems.

In terms of the benefits and costs of urbanization, one might be able to make an argument that most of the benefits have accrued as private benefits and thus have been taken into consideration by business firms and people in their decisions to locate in large urban areas. On the other hand, if many of the costs of urbanization accrue as negative externalities (indirect costs), which are not taken into consideration by individual decision-makers, this market failure has led to a greater than efficient amount of urbanization. If some amount of urbanization is in fact attributable to such market failure, then the appropriate public policy approach is to correct for such cases of market failure by means such as those discussed in this book; thus, individuals would have to consider all the costs of their location decisions.

In contrast to this approach, current awareness of some of the symptoms that have resulted from the concentration of jobs and people in urban areas has led to discussion of public policy measures designed to make rural life more attractive and to encourage locations in smaller towns and cities. Such inducements might take the form of tax breaks or subsidies to business firms that choose such locations, or perhaps investments in transportation facilities that make these areas more accessible to major urban areas. However, such policies that provide subsidies to reduce the costs of alternatives to urbanization are not likely to be an efficient use of resources. As has been illustrated at numerous junctures in this book, programs that subsidize one alternative in order to increase its net private benefits relative to other alternatives may be relatively ineffective and also involve large resource waste. On the other hand, policies that get the individual producer or consumer to take into consideration *all* the costs of his decisions provide the incentives to achieve efficiency; the use of congestion tolls and effluent fees in the cases of transportation and pollution are prime examples of this approach. If location away from our major urban areas can be justified on grounds of reduction of externalities, then policies could be designed to efficiently accomplish this end. All too often, however, policies are implemented because of some vague feeling that it would be "nice" if rural areas and small towns were revitalized. Future technological changes will probably make rural locations more attractive; however, until such changes actually occur, subsidizing relocation may involve serious waste of limited resources.

Democracy and the Private Market System

A growing number of people are dismayed with our current economic system. It seems impossible to them that a system built on self-interest could even remotely work to the benefit of society as a whole. Thus, they have concluded that the private market system is inherently defective. While decentralized decision-making has led the United States and other nations to very high standards of living, this seems irrelevant to many today because of the indirect costs incurred in production and consumption activities. "Growth for the sake of growth" is a label pinned by many on the business community today. Gross National Product has been attacked as being an indicator of how badly the country is doing rather than as a measure of well-being. Economists are more aware of the deficiencies in the concept of GNP than anyone, and probably in the future the concept will be changed to more closely reflect well-being. Presently, an increase in GNP that entails an increase in pollution levels is not necessarily a social improvement (or setback either), but labeling all increases in GNP as setbacks for the society is absurd. The resources of society can be used to curtail pollution and beautify the nation as well as degrade it. Hopefully this book has provided some insight into how this can be done, and how it can be decided whether it should be done.

Since no other kind of society has led to so high a level of material wealth, it seems more reasonable to attempt to correct the failings of the system than to scrap it and start over. The system requires intervention, however, because of market failure. An attempt has been made to indicate the form such intervention should take. In contrast, many "proposals" for dealing with society's problems seem to be essentially punitive and vindictive. While this sort of approach lends itself particularly well to polemics, it does not stand up as well when one resorts to rationality (if one does). The approach in this book has been to identify specific cases of market failure and propose ways of patching up the private market system so it will work even though such problems exist.

A problem with government intervention must be mentioned. If it is not carefully thought out, it can lead to unexpected and undesirable results. For example, urban renewal (discussed in Chapter 8), as the name implies, was supposed to improve housing conditions of the poor, but seems to have had the effect of relocating slums and destroying housing without replacing it fully. It is not within the scope of this book to examine all the reasons why the political system has not done well at correcting the causes of market failure. Perhaps some of this can be attributed to the lack of understanding on the part of legislators of basic economic facts (or ignoring them because they are politically embarrassing). In some cases, the political lobbying efforts of certain groups on equity matters (such as the ownership of property rights to use the environment for waste-disposal purposes) have led to legislation of policies that neglect the attainment of efficiency. Also, the lack of the ability of the political system to foresee potential problems has been at fault. The allocation of a small amount of resources to experimentation in various solutions to cases of market failure may avoid wasting a much greater amount of our resources on poorly conceived programs. While the historical political power of rural interests has resulted in the allocation of many dollars to agricultural research, it was not until quite recently that virtually any resources have been allocated to research on socioeconomic problems in the urban environment. Experiments are presently being conducted to explore the effects of various tax rates in negative income tax programs designed to provide income and work incentives to the urban poor. Similarly, experiments are being conducted with respect to the outcomes of various housing subsidies and education vouchers. A few million dollars spent in attempting to answer such questions can prevent serious misallocation of resources to long-term projects.

Economists can identify causes of market failure and potential solutions, but the ultimate implementation of these solutions requires endorsement of the political system. The pessimist who has read this book will conclude that the resolution of major urban problems borders on the impossible because of the lack of responsiveness, knowledge, and foresight of the citizens and political leaders alike; in other words, market failure cannot be corrected because of "political failure." The optimist will hopefully have found an analytical framework that he will endeavor to apply to present and future urban problems.

REVIEW AND DISCUSSION QUESTIONS

1 Current urban problems can perhaps be better understood by reference to the changes in *location* of jobs and people within

urban areas than by reference to the *growth* of urban areas. Discuss.

2   Many of the most critical urban problems, including poverty, poor housing, congestion, and pollution, have a common underlying cause: the suburbanization of jobs and people in urban areas. Evaluate.

3   If the degree of urbanization we have today is attributable to business firms and households making their location decisions on the basis of their net private benefits, we have more than the efficient amount of urbanization. Evaluate.

4   If poverty were eliminated, so would be most urban problems. Evaluate.

5   Demand and supply economies, changes in production, communications, and transportation technology, and other causes of urban growth lead to the conclusion that practically all jobs and people (except farmers) will be located in major urban areas in the future. Evaluate.

6   Why would you find a larger variety of goods and services in New York City than in Baltimore?

7   Once you are out of school, do you plan to live where you were raised? Why or why not?

SUGGESTED READINGS

Chinitz, Benjamin, "Contrasts in Agglomeration." *American Economic Review* (May 1961), 279 - 289.

Nourse, Hugh. "The Impact of Growth on Regional Structure." In *Regional Economics,* pp. 209 - 224, New York: McGraw-Hill, 1968.

Thompson, Wilbur. "Internal and External Factors in the Development of Urban Economics." In *Issues in Urban Economics,* edited by H. S. Perloff and L. Wingo, Jr., pp. 43 - 62. Baltimore: The Johns Hopkins Press, 1968.

Vernon, Raymond. *Metropolis 1985.* Cambridge, Mass.: Harvard University Press, 1960.

ART CREDITS

Chapter 1   Cecil Braithwaite/HUD
Chapter 2   Ken Kobre
Chapter 3   Edward C. Topple
Chapter 4   Elizabeth Adams
Chapter 5   Ken Kobre
Chapter 6   Ken Kobre
Chapter 7   Ken Kobre
Chapter 8   Ken Kobre
Chapter 9   Ken Kobre
Chapter 10   American Public Transit Association
Chapter 11   Federal Water Pollution Control Administration
Chapter 12   Bill Shrout/EPA DOCUMERICA
Chapter 13   David A. Krathwohl
Chapter 14   Kathleen Foster
Chapter 15   Lucille M. Lavallee
Chapter 16   Mayor's Office of Public Service, Boston

Cover photo Jim Scherer

INDEX

Aaron, Henry, 120n, 122n, 138n, 169n, 173n, 184n, 185n
Ability-to-pay principle, 73, 74-77, 74 table
Aid to families with dependent children (AFDC), 122-126
Air pollution, 248-253, 251 table, 256-258
  existing programs, 285-290
Allocation, resource, see Resource allocation
Alonzo, William, 21n
Atlanta, Georgia, 9, 10 map, 18, 225, 382
Attendance, 45
Automobiles, and pollution, 287-290

Banfield, Edward, 104n, 111
Banks, 15, 17
Baumol, William, 85n, 345n
Benefit
  grand total social, 34-36, 36 table
  marginal social, 37-42, 38 table, 40 diag., 41 diag.
    defined, 37
  net, 77, 79-83
  net private, 46
    apparent, 66-68, 68 diag.
  net social, 36-38, 40-41, 38 table, 40 diag., 41 diag., 64
    defined, 37
  pecuniary, 85
  private, 45
  social, 33, 58
  total social, 34-42, 38 table, 40 diag., 41 diag.
Benefit-cost analysis, 4, 78-86
  abuses, 86
Benefit-cost ratio, 86
Benefit principle, 73-74, 74 table
Bid-rent curves, 22-28
Biochemical oxygen demand (BOD), 253-254
Blockbusting, 163-164
Bookkeeping industries, 15-16
Boston, Mass., 382
Bronfenbrenner, Martin, 95n
Building codes, 155-158
Bus, rapid, 228-229

Capital, human, see Human capital
Car pools, 207-208

Central business district (CBD), 3, 16-18, 390-393
  defined, 9
Central city
  defined, 8
  employment, 19
  future of, 390-393
  plight of, 379
Centralization, see Urbanization
Chicago, Illinois, 252, 257, 391
Child care, 108
City, 8
  core, 8, 12
  core-dominated, 11-18, 13 diag., 22
Clark, Ramsey, 315n, 323n
Clayton Act, 66
Clemmer, Richard, 16n, 348n
Clerks, 15
Coase, Ronald, 59n
Collective farm, 53
Common property resource (common pool), 203, 245-247
Communications, face-to-face, 16-17
Community development block grants, 186-187
Commuting, see Journey-to-work
Congestion, Traffic, 3, 5, 197-202
  efficient level, 201-202
Consumption, collective, 61
Core (of city), 8, 12
Core-dominated city, 11-18, 13 diag., 22
Corrections (in criminal justice system), 314-316
Cost, marginal social, 37-42, 38 table, 40 diag., 41 diag.
  defined, 37
  opportunity, 33
  private, 45
  social, 33, 58
  sunk, 44-45
  total social, 34-42, 38 table, 40 diag., 41 diag.
Courts, 312-314
Crime, 5, 295-328
  amount-and types, 296-302
  drug-related, 320-323
  economic conditions, 316-317
  efficient level of, 298-302
  equity aspects, 323-327
  organized, 317-320

of passion, 310
 as urban problem, 302-303
 victimless, 317-320
Crime prevention, 307-317
Criminal justice system, 309-310
 corrections in, 314-316
Criminals, costs and benefits of, 303-307, 306 table
Cross-commuting, 219

Dallas-Fort Worth area, Texas, 382
Data processing, 16
DDT, 254
Decentralization, 3, 11-19
 barriers to, 14
Demand, 49-54, 50 diag., 51 diag., 53 diag., 54 diag.
 defined, 49
 effective, 335-343, 362-363
 threshold, 383-385
Demand economies, 382-385, 383 diag., 388-389
Department stores, 15
Depreciation, 175-176
Discount rate, 43, 79, 105
Discrimination, 26, 100-101, 109-111
 housing, 160-164
Domencich, Tom, 233n
Donora, Pennsylvania, 247
Downs, Anthony, 169n, 208n, 236n
Dual migration, 331 - 334

Eckert, Ross, 238, 238n
Economies, demand, see Demand economies
Economies, supply, see Supply economies
Economies of scale, 343-344, 344 diag.
Economy, "open," 330
Education
 financing, 364
 investment, 82-84, 83 table, 103-105
 public provision of, 359-368, 361 diag.
 vocational training, 105-107
Efficiency, 4, 31-88
 criteria, 33-39
 incorrect, 43-45
 private market system and, 48
 transportation, 198-199, 203-208
Effluent fees, 270-277, 272 diag., 289
 real world, 276-277
Effluents, 244-245
 ambient levels of, 267
 reduction, costs of, 268 table
Eminent domain, 148-149

Environment
 efficiency, 258-263, 259 diag.
 equity aspects, 277-280, 280 table
 rationing use of, 266-277
 long run implications, 290-291
Equilibrium, 50
Equity, 4, 32, 67-78
 horizontal, 73-77, 74 table
 defined, 74
 transportation investments, 234-236
 vertical, 73-77, 74 table
 defined, 73
Exemption, homestead, 369
Externality, 57-65
 defined, 57
 housing, 145-149, 146 table
 internalization, 147
 negative, 58, 63-65, 64 diag.
 efficient amount of, 65
 public policy, 65
 positive, 58, 59-63, 60 diag.
 public policy, 59-60
 spillovers, 59, 349-353, 352 table

Family planning, 108-109
FBI index, 296-300, 297 table
Fiscal policy, 132-134
Food stamps, 124-130
Freight terminal, 12, 14
Fried, Edward, 119n

Game, zero sum, 342
Gasoline prices, 32, 51, 222
Gatons, Paul, 16n, 348n
Goetschius, Gary, 115n
Golden Gate Bridge, 206
Gomery, Douglas, 184n
Goods, public, see Public goods
Gouging, 51
Green Bay, Wisconsin, 384
Gwartney, James, 110n

Health and rehabilitation, 107, 130-131
Heroin, 320-323
Highways, 15, 197-215, 226-228
Hilton, George, 238, 238n
Holdout problem, 148-149
Horse and wagon, 12, 14
Household, defined, 90
Housing, 5, 137-191
 codes, 158-160
 consumption, measurement of, 137-141
 filtering, 170-171
 finance costs, 149-154
 low income, 12

programs, 167-191
  public, 181-185
  service units, 140-141
  substandard, 138-140, 139 table
  turnover, 169-171, 173 - 174
  vouchers, 187-189
Housing market, 21, 141-143
  inefficiencies, 144-166
Houston, Texas, 19
Human capital, 99-100, 102-107
Hydrocarbons, 249

Incidence, tax, 76-77
Income
  in-kind, 91-92
  money, 90-95
  redistribution of, 71-72, 124 table,
    330-334
Income distribution, 4, 68-77, 69 table
  relation to efficiency, 69-71
Inefficiency, 4, 57-67
Information, imperfect, 66-67
In-kind income, 91-92
In-kind transfers, 71-72, 114-115, 129-131
Intergovernmental agreements, 252-253

Jitneys, 238-240
Jobs and people, 3. See also Land use
JOBS program, 106
Johns, Roe L., 360n
Journey-to-work (commuting), 24, 26,
    199, 218-223
  bus versus auto, 222 table

Kain, John, 16n, 17, 18n, 161n, 162n,
    174n, 230n
Kansas City, Missouri, 280
Kraft, Gerald, 233n

Labor
  market, 132-134
  productivity, 344-347, 347 table
  unions, 157-158
Lakewood plan, 348
Land, price, 15
Landsberg, Hans, 291n
Land use, 2-30
  relation to urban problems, 26-29
London, England, 247
Los Angeles, California, 19, 252, 257

McKay, Roberta, 237n
Manufacturing
  employment, 20
  technology, 15, 16, 26

Market failure, 57-65, 77
Market system, see Private market sys-
    tem
Meat, shortage of, 52
Median voter outcome, 336-340, 337
    diag.
Metropolitan government, 350-353
Meyer, John, 16n, 17, 18n, 230n
Migration, dual, 331-334
Minimum wage, 127-128, 127 diag.
Mixed-benefit output, 360-368
Monetary policy, 132-134
Monopoly, 65-66
Monorail, 228
Mooney, Joseph, 174n
Moore, Mark, 322n
Moses, Leon, 11n, 14, 14n, 233n
Muth, Richard, 21n

Negative income tax, 116-122, 118 table
  hours-wage form, 120-122, 123 table
New Orleans, Louisiana, 382
New York City, 247, 382
Nitrogen oxides, 249
Nourse, Hugh, 385n

Olsen, Edgar, 140n
Output, mixed-benefit, 360-368
Owen, Wilfred, 391n

Particulates, 249
Philadelphia, Pennsylvania, 17
Pittsburgh, Pennsylvania, 382
Plea bargaining, 312
Police, 310-312
Police patrol, allocation, 325, 325 table
Pollution, 5, 44, 244-293
  air, 248-253, 251 table, 256-258
    existing programs, 285-290
  autos, existing programs, 287-290
  defined, 244-245
  determinants of, 248
  efficient level of, 245-247, 246 diag.
  reduction, alternatives, 260-264
  rights, market for, 275-276
  subsidies, 283-284
  types, 248-251
  urban areas, 155-158, 258 table
  water, 63-65, 64 diag., 253-255
    existing programs, 281-285
Pollution tax, see Effluent fees
Poverty, 89-135
  and age, 97
  causes, 99-101
  cutoff, 90-95, 95 table

and education, 97-98, 98 table
gap, 93, 98
long-run approaches, 101-111
population, 95-96, 96 table
and race, 95-97, 97 table
by residence, 97 table
short-run, 113-135
statistics, 94-99
symptoms, 101-102
temporary, 99
war on, 90, 94
Poverty threshold, see Poverty cutoff
Present value, 43, 79, 80-86
calculation of, 80-81
Price rationing, highways, 203-211
Private market system, 45-54, 394-395 see also Market failure
Problem shed governments, 350-353
Production possibilities schedule, 34-35, 34 table
Productivity (labor), 344-347, 347 table
Progressivity, 75-76, 76 table
Project analysis, see Benefit-cost analysis
Property tax, see Tax, Property
Proportional (tax), 75-76, 76 table
Psychic costs, 307
Public goods, 61-63
Public output, 335
increasing relative costs of, 344-347, 347 table
Public sector, see Urban public sector
Public services, local, 5

Quigley, John, 161n, 162n

Radio station, 62-63
Railroads, 11-18
Rail transit, 225-226, 229
Rationing
environment, 258-263
highways, 199-215
Recycling, 261-263
Redlining, 150
Rees, Albert, 121n
Regressivity, 75-76, 76 table
Rent
gradients, 22-27, 23 diag.
supplements, 185
Resource allocation, 4, 32-45
misallocation, see Inefficiency
optimal, see Efficiency
urban public sector, 334-353
Reverse commuting, 220. See also Journey-to-work
Rothenberg, Jerome, 178n

St. Louis, Missouri, 280, 382
Salt Lake City, Utah, 382
Scarcity, 4, 32
Schiller, Bradley, 93n
Schreiber, Arthur, 16n, 348n
Schultze, Charles, 108n
Section 8 housing, 186-187
Segregation
academies, 367
tax, 163
Sherman Anti-trust Act, 66
Shopping centers, 16
Situs, tax, 378
Slum, 141
Smolensky, Eugene, 184n
SMSA, see Standard metropolitan statistical area
Social Security, 126-129, 128 diag.
Spillovers (of externalities), 59, 349-353, 352 table
Standard metropolitan statistical area (SMSA), 9
employment, 20 table
population, 9, 11
Storey, James, 124
Suburbanization, 27
Suburbs
population, 18
suburban sprawl, 27
Sulfur oxides 249
Supply, 49-54, 51 diag., 53 diag., 54 diag.
defined, 49
Supply economies, 386-389, 387 diag.

Tax
administration, 374-375
collection and compliance, 374-375
equity, 72-77
gasoline, 213
incidence, 76-77
income, as housing subsidy, 171-173, 175-176
local, 377-379
neutral, 373
property, 6, 152-153, 370-375, 369 table, 371 table, 372 diag.
proportional, 75-76, 76 table
sales, 375-377
segregation, 163
situs, 378
Technology, see Manufacturing technology; Transportation technology
Tiebout, Charles, 340n
Time
relation to costs and benefits, 42-43

value of, 221-227

Tipping point, 162

Tolls, peak hour, 203-205, 205 table

Transfers, in-kind, 71-72, 114-115, 129-131

Transit, *see* Transportation, Public; Rail transit

Transportation
  auto, 195-196, 195 table
  costs, 12-16, 199-201, 221-236
    comparative, 229, 230, 229 diag.
    indirect, 225-230
    operating, 225-230
  efficiency, short run, 196-216
  investment, benefits, 218-221
    costs, 221-230
  long run, 218-242
  long run effects of short run policy, 214
  low income, 236-239
  public, 25, 28, 193-195, 194 table
    a proposal, 239-240
    rail, *see* Rail transit
  short run, 192-216
  subsidies, 230-236
  technology, 11-16, 26

Tree rustlers, 316

Trolleys, 12-15

Trucks, 14-16, 193

Tye, W., 233n

Uniform Crime Reports (UCR), 296-298

Urban area
  defined, 8
  future public policy, 393-394

Urbanization, 3, 4, 382-396
  benefits and costs, 6, 381-396

Urbanized area, 9
  defined, 8

Urban Mass Transportation Administration (UMTA), 232-234

Urban place, 10
  defined, 8

Urban public sector, role of, 330-335

Urban renewal, 177-181

User charges, 74, 356-359

Vaccinations, efficient quantity of, 59-60, 60 diag.

Vampires, 391

Vickrey, William, 205n, 211n

Victimization, 323-324, 324 table

Victimless crime, 317-320

Vocational training, 105-107

Voting, 335-343

Vouchers, 71
  education, 366-367
  housing, 187-189
  See also Food stamps

Warren, Robert, 348n

Washington, D.C., 280

Water pollution, 63-65, 64 diag., 253-255
  existing programs, 281-285

Welfare, *see* Aid to families with dependent children

Wicks, John H., 115n

Williamson, Harold J., 11n, 14, 14n, 233n

WIN program, 106

Wohl, Martin, 16n, 17, 18n, 230n

Wolf point, 95

Wombats, attacks of, 381

Work incentive experiment, 121

Wright, Frank Lloyd, 391

Zoning, 26, 153-155
  fiscal, 341-343, 341 diag.

Zoo, 357-359